dazzling stranger

dazzling stranger

bert jansch and the british
folk and blues revival

colin harper

BLOOMSBURY

First published in Great Britain in 2000

Copyright © 2000 by Colin Harper

The moral right of the author has been asserted

Bloomsbury Publishing Plc, 38 Soho Square, London, W1V 5DF

A CIP catalogue record for this book
is available from the British Library

ISBN 0 7475 4810 2

10 9 8 7 6 5 4 3 2 1

Typeset by Hewer Text Ltd, Edinburgh
Printed in Great Britain by Clays Ltd, St Ives plc

For Karl Dallas

Contents

Author's Note

This book is the product of two distinct periods of work: 1991–92 and 1998–99. Very little of the writing that was completed during the former period, which focused exclusively on the Pentangle era, was used directly in this book although the interviews, accumulation of print sources and other researches conducted during that time have proved invaluable. This book does not purport to be a definitive biography of the Pentangle. Firstly, that group was a product of five individual talents, and it would consequently require the co-operation of all five as a minimum requirement to the delivery of such a work. Secondly, while the group represents an important part of the Bert Jansch story – the apogee, albeit within a collective, of his commercial popularity – it is secondary and supplementary to his rise as a solo artist without precedent during the earlier years of the sixties. The question of how someone of Bert Jansch's unlikely if revolutionary qualities could reach the point of making a record at all during that era has been at the heart of my approach.

While a wide variety of print sources have been consulted, and acknowledged in the bibliography and endnotes herein, the diligent reader may notice occasional (and mostly minor) differences in detail. Similarly, those familiar with my own previous writings on Bert Jansch and his peers in a variety of newspapers, magazines and sleeve notes may also spot the odd deviance. If at all possible, particularly with regard to chapters two to six, I have gone to inordinate lengths to try to verify conclusively every point of detail used. Where this has not been possible – for example, the dating of Brownie McGhee's visit to the Howff which so influenced Bert in the early weeks of his guitar playing – I have provided endnote discussions on the matters in question. As a rule, however, if something is presented as fact, particularly in those early chapters which have benefited from the most rigorous draft refereeing from both interviewees and independent experts on the period, it overrides anything to the contrary published previously by either myself or others. This is not to say that my work is infallible but rather to assert that everything reasonable and viable has been done to attain the goal of maximum accuracy.

Ironically perhaps, the final chapter proper is the most sketchy in its detail: in defence, this is partly to avoid situations which may yet have repercussions for Bert Jansch and/or for others. There is, for example, one pseudonym employed in this chapter which, while obvious and no doubt amusing to those in the know, is there by that individual's request. Save for that one, I welcome of course any correspondence on the matter of corrections.

Prologue

Being in America for the first time was proving an awesome experience, very different from London or Glasgow or Edinburgh. There had been the trips to France in 1961 and '62; Morocco in '63 – getting married on the way, splitting up on the way back; Denmark in '65 – for the first time, a recording artist on tour. The world had opened up to Bert Jansch by virtue of the songs which that same world, in its wonder, had inspired in him. But there had been nothing to forewarn him of the nature of America. The world was indeed a bigger place in 1969.

From a post-war slum kid who had marvelled at the primitive sounds of black America – the records that Big Bill Broonzy had made in Europe, hearing Brownie McGhee at close range in an Edinburgh folk club – Bert had finally arrived in the place where his path had begun. Yet all he was finding were the soul-less sheds of the new 'underground', other Britons on the road and the endless interiors of hotels. In New York his band, the Pentangle, had played the Fillmore East, tuning up backstage from memory alone as the building shook to the volume of Canned Heat. Snowed-in at the Algonquin for a week, already the drinking had started: running a hotel bar dry of champagne – what else was a whole tour's promotional budget for? Those five individuals who had drifted together in the 'summer of love' for Sunday night sessions in a Soho pub were now locked together on some insane treadmill that had apparently nothing to do with real life. But what was real life anyway for a twenty-six-year-old who had already spent the previous ten years on the edge of conventional society with only music as a goal?

At least now he had a band, a band with a startlingly fresh, delicate sound and a very real chance of 'making it'. Was that not what musicians and songwriters were meant to do? John, the esoteric medievalist, was a brilliant technician on guitar; Jacqui's crystalline voice and serene demeanour embodied, for wide-eyed Americans, a wholly English mystique; Danny, on double bass, was larger than life, a raver to match anyone the rock underground would care to put up; Terry, on drums and glockenspiel and things to be tapped, was the solid pro, calm and reliable and clearly enjoying the trappings of pop after a decade in jazz clubs and polo-necks; and then there was Bert. Bert was the loner, inscrutable and otherworldly at times but quite clearly a man with a gift – a man with very little to say in conversation but whose job it was, by default, to make the introductions onstage, to do the interviews, to write the songs. And in songs he could always find something to say and a way of doing so that would help to explain some universal truth or simple emotion to a generation. And his music was almost completely without precedent.

In Boston they played five nights at the Unicorn and met up with Jethro Tull. Tull mainman Ian Anderson, who had grown up with Bert's records as a totem of discernment and a doorway to musical adventure beyond the confines of conventional chording and a backbeat in 4/4, was under instructions to write a hit single. Later that day, he would deliver a mischievous little melody in 5/8 called 'Living In The Past'. It would find its way into the British Top 5 – and so too, brimming as it was with unlikely rhythms, plainsong and traditional themes, would the next Pentangle album. It was no longer possible to judge what musical convention was. Everything was changing – pop words had become poetry, pop music was rubbing shoulders with jazz in its complexity, and the folk revival had now bled into rock. Produced by Shel Talmy, the man responsible for The Who's explosive beginnings back in '65, a Pentangle single had come out on US Reprise in time for the tour. It was an old English folk song, 'Let No Man Steal Your Thyme'. The issue of 'stealing' had often reared its head on the folk scene back home – from the curious case of the Chas McDevitt Skiffle Group and Elizabeth Cotten's 'Freight Train' in 1958 to the can of worms opened up in the wake of Bob Dylan, traditional melodies a-plenty and the chancers who claimed them as their own. Paul Simon had had the foresight or the gall to copyright Martin Carthy's arrangement of 'Scarborough Fair' in 1965: one of them had since enjoyed a great deal of success with it.

Then to Los Angeles, for a week at the Troubadour. Paul Simon came along to see his old friend's new band. Bert, in truth, had never really cared for the man, but they had been fellow-travellers for a time – stars in the making on the weird, bohemian folk scene that had blossomed in Soho during 1965 and had ever since been a magnet for every non-electric guitar hero and bedsit philosopher-in-waiting. For Bert, the days of being king in that particular castle were over: the new band meant playing your songs on TV, radio sessions on the BBC, open-air stages with the Jimi Hendrix Experience, the Royal Albert Hall, the Festival Hall, Coventry Cathedral for goodness' sake. The onset of fame was a whole new ball game.

Finally it was San Francisco: four nights with the Grateful Dead at the

Fillmore West, doing your best to avoid the water spiked with acid. Failing to do so. Somewhere in the middle of it all somebody plays you a record of a hot new band from England. It's just come out and, listen to this, they say, isn't there something familiar about that tune?

Led Zeppelin was the name of the album, and of the band. They were loud and exciting and destined for great things – that album alone would spend seventy-five weeks in the British charts. The tune that was causing eyebrows to rise among the cognoscenti, here credited to guitarist Jimmy Page, was a guitar instrumental of exotic, modal flavour entitled 'Black Mountain Side'. Three years earlier, on an album called *Jack Orion* that had all but defined a new strand of music – British fingerstyle, folk-baroque, or whatever it may be called – Bert had taken a series of traditional tunes and had woven around them sensual, dextrous and vaguely eastern-ised guitar backings – some delicate, others fiery – using altered tunings and ideas adapted from the folk scene's guitar godfather, Davy Graham. What Bert had played on that album was singularly and identifiably *his* playing. For 'Blackwater Side' he had only detuned the low E string to D: any magic was still mostly in the fingers.

Page had probably bought *Jack Orion* as soon as it appeared in September 1966 and marvelled, as he had with Bert's two other albums before it. This was a period, he later recalled, of being 'obsessed' with Bert Jansch. At that time one of the London record industry's top session players, Page could certainly have worked out the rudiments of any Jansch song or instrumental – nothing that Bert did was ever intended to be complex for the sake of it – but as luck would have it, with one of *Jack Orion*'s most beautiful arrangements he did not need to do so. He already knew it.

Earlier that year another devotee, Al Stewart, who had been struck by Bert's playing of 'Blackwater Side' around the folk clubs, was making his own recording debut with a single entitled 'The Elf'. 'The B-side was called 'Turn Into Earth',' says Al, 'and Jimmy turned up to play a rhythmic "chunk" on it. While we were doodling around between takes I showed him what I thought was Bert Jansch's version of "Blackwater Side". He seemed to like it. But not being a particularly good guitar player, I hadn't really taught Jimmy Bert's rendition of the tune anyway – I'd taught him what I thought it was. Maybe some Zeppelin royalties should be owed to me!'

Al had presumed Bert's guitar tuning to have been DADGAD, an invention of Davy Graham's, designed for the playing of Moroccan music but serendipitously convenient for the accompaniment of modal Irish tunes. One of these, an extemporisation on 'She Moved Through The Fair', had been Graham's first recorded foray with the new tuning back in 1963. A year after learning the tuning from Al, Page would revamp Graham's old chestnut as 'White Summer' on a US-only LP that marked his temporary involvement with the Yardbirds, a once popular British R&B group in the process of dissolving. By the end of 1968 Page had remodelled the remnants of that group into something wholly new: Led Zeppelin, the loudest folk group in the world.

The Pentangle returned to England in March '69. Strangely, the group's manager, Jo Lustig, a brash New Yorker with a hard-hitting reputation, did not get involved. Instead, the matter was deferred to Bert's publishers, Heathside Music, effectively a branch of his record label, Transatlantic. Bert Jansch as a solo artist and the Pentangle as a group were the biggest acts on the label, one of Britain's pioneer independents but still a small-beer operation next to the colossus of Led Zeppelin's Atlantic Records. Nat Joseph, the founder of the company, was nonetheless a tenacious individual. After taking legal advice, consulting two eminent musicologists and in-structing John Mummery QC – one of the most prominent copyright barristers in England at that time – a letter was sent to the Led Zeppelin management stating the cause for concern. Any conscious plagiarism was denied, and Nat was faced with a difficult choice: 'It had been reasonably established that there was every chance that Jimmy Page had heard Bert play the piece at a club or a concert or on a personal basis, or that he'd heard Bert's recording. However, what could not be proved was that Bert's recording in itself constituted Bert's own copyright, because the basic melody, of course, was traditional.'

Bert had learned the tune, and adapted his own peculiar settings to it, from Anne Briggs, a young woman who had herself learned that song and many others from a characterful old folklorist by the name of Bert Lloyd. There weren't many folklorists around in the sixties. Bert Lloyd, as a pre-eminent source for the young revivalists, was in a position of great influence. What was not widely appreciated at the time was that Lloyd's fascination with the modes and rhythms of Eastern Europe was feeding into his 'reconstructions' of fragmentary traditional songs from the British Isles. As Oscar Brand, Lloyd's counterpart in America, was wont to say, 're-composition is better than decomposition'. It was becoming hard to see the joins. Back in 1952 Peter Kennedy, a similarly controversial collector, had made two field-recordings of 'Blackwater Side' for the BBC, from women in rural Ireland. They were available for consultation on 78 rpm discs at the BBC and at Cecil Sharp House, the headquarters of the English Folk Dance & Song Society. But woe betide anyone who dared to record their own versions.

'It was like a bad joke on the folk scene,' says Dave Arthur, subsequently a luminary of the Society himself. 'Every time one of us did an album, Peter

Kennedy would jump in and say, "I collected that song!" And "Blackwater Side" was obviously one of them. As soon as you brought a record out, Peter Kennedy would be suing the company or writing you letters demanding his copyright.'

Hot air amongst the big and small fish of a tiny pond was all very well, but trying to take a corporate giant to the cleaners on an untried principle of law was another matter entirely. Al Stewart, aware of the bully-boy reputation of Zeppelin's manager Peter Grant, was becoming a little hot under the collar: 'I was getting messages from various people umming and ahhing,' he says, 'thinking about the possibility of going to court, but it never really reached that point.'

'For some reason Transatlantic ran out of steam,' says Bert, who was certainly annoyed but not obsessive on the matter. 'You've got to keep these things up or they just fizzle out. It didn't bother me. It still doesn't *really* bother me. There's the effort of doing these things – you'd get diverted from your normal course of events. You'd be as well to give up music and start suing people! If you want to make your living that way, it's what beckons you. It's okay if you've got a million pounds in the first place – you can go and sue somebody. If you haven't, it's a very difficult process.'

It was, indeed, all down to money: 'What Mr Mummery advised,' says Nat, 'was that whereas there was a distinct possibility that Bert might win an action against Page, there was also the possibility that all sorts of other people might then say, "Ah, but Bert heard it from me." Given the enormous costs involved in pursuing an action, and the thought that one could be litigating, or being litigated against, for the next twenty years on the basis that everybody and his dog would claim "Blackwater Side" or "Mountain Side" or any other kind of side, we left it at that. As the "writer", Bert would have had to share the costs with us fifty/fifty – and they were not the sort of costs that *we* could afford, let alone Bert. But in many ways it was a very interesting case. If you think about it, almost any "traditional" song that somebody does an arrangement of, somebody will have done something vaguely similar before. The difficulty appears to be one of really establishing, amongst hundreds of arrangers, who it was that made the arrangement "original".'

'When people sang for pleasure and nobody got any money there were none of these problems,' says Anne Briggs, a beacon of non-materialist wisdom. 'All this borrowing and influencing: it's been done throughout history. It's how music develops. It only becomes a very large philosophical question when money enters into it – which is why this bloody old chestnut is still clonking around the universe.'

Bert and Jimmy and the case of the un-called bluff at the end of the

'Swinging Sixties' has become a well-worn tale. The Pentangle era was a short, self-contained part of Bert's life – five years of international touring and some level of fame. Once the band had reached its natural conclusion, he simply resumed the role of solo artist, returning to the semi-obscurity / semi-celebrity of cultdom that he had previously enjoyed. Led Zeppelin became the biggest band of the seventies, and it was an open secret that one of their signature tunes had perhaps come from a little guy still playing in folk clubs and bars.

In 1987, one of the last of the great bluesmen, Willie Dixon, settled out of court with Led Zeppelin his own claim to the copyright of 'Whole Lotta Love'. Page's colleague Robert Plant was reported to have said at the time: 'You only get caught when you're successful. That's the game.' Almost at the very start of his recording career, on the sleeve of his second album, the presciently titled *It Don't Bother Me*, Bert Jansch had explained his philosophy in its essence: 'To sell your music is to sell your soul. To give your music is to buy your freedom.' His song, to this day, remains the same.

CHAPTER ONE

Birthday Blues

A t some point in the Victorian era, Carl William Henry Jansch and his parents Johann-Christian Wilhelm and Wilhelmina arrived in Britain from Hamburg, where Carl had been born circa 1863. Berwick-upon-Tweed, near the border between England and Scotland, is believed to have been their new home for a period, although there is no trace of anyone named Jansch in the 1881 census of Scotland. In 1888 Carl, by now calling himself Charles, married Jane Ann Trott, known as Jeannie, in Edinburgh 'after Banns according to the forms of the Church of Scotland'. Charles's address is given as the Red Lion Hotel in Berwick, where he worked as a waiter. His father is described on the marriage certificate as a sea captain and on a subsequent certificate as a 'master mariner'. Jeannie lived and worked as a domestic servant at 22 Princes Street in Edinburgh.

Ten months later, in 1889, and at lodgings in Braemar, Jeannie Dorothea Jansch, thereafter known as Daisy, was born. Six further children followed at fairly regular intervals up to the end of the century. The first of these was born in 1891 in Aberdeen, but by the end of that year the family were firmly settled in Edinburgh. Jeannie died in 1901; in 1921, with no record of a remarriage, a further son named William Henry was born to Charles and Mary Fell. Charles, who was variously described as a hotel waiter or billiard salon attendant in the birth certificates, died eleven years later in 1932.

Pronounced 'Janch' by Bert and his immediate family and generally 'Yanch' by media folk and those familiar with the workings of European languages, it would be hard to imagine more than one family of that name settling in Edinburgh at the turn of the century. One may speculate that even in the Germanic nations it is less than common.[1] Nevertheless, in the quiet Liberton area of Edinburgh where Bert's sister Mary and her husband Bob currently reside there is at least one other Jansch family, personally unknown to Mary, with several others around Scotland and, most curiously, in Newcastle-upon-Tyne in the North East of England. It would appear that the siblings of Daisy Jansch were not idle in their furtherance of the line. Neither, it is believed, was/is her son.

Herbert Jansch was born out of wedlock in 1911 when Daisy was twenty-two. There is no father listed on the birth certificate and, as was the norm in those days, the child was put up for adoption. 'As far as I understand it, and I don't have any proof of this, he was adopted by people called Luff,' says Mary. 'He came from a place called Tillycoutry, not far from Stirling. That's where my mother met him, at a dance. I never met the Luff family and neither did my mum. I don't know if they came to the wedding – all I know is that my mother met Daisy, his real mother, once. Daisy eventually married a Mr Walter Robb. My mother's story is that my father looked like this Mr Robb, but I don't know. This is all just stories.' Daisy Jansch and Walter Robb were indeed married, in Edinburgh in 1914 'according to the forms of the Scottish Episcopal Church'. Another vestige of a story tells of Herbert's grandparents, Carl/Charles and Jane, being interned during the Great War, but Herbert himself disappeared from view in 1949 and little else of the Jansch family history is known. It is painful for the family, but it is believed that Herbert Jansch may well be living and very possibly in Newcastle-upon-Tyne.

Margaret Henderson Robertson Winton was born in Leith, a docklands area just outside Edinburgh, in 1912 – the fourth youngest of nine. Her father Thomas was a boxmaker, from a long line of working-class craftsmen who can be traced back as resident in the Edinburgh area to the early years of the 1700s. Margaret Winton and Herbert Jansch were married, aged twenty-two and twenty-three respectively, at a registry office in Edinburgh on New Year's Eve 1934. Herbert was described as 'the son of Daisy Jansch, waitress, subsequently married to Walter Robb, waiter'. The address given for both bride and groom was the same: 45 Sandport Street, Leith. A couple of neighbours witnessed the proceedings and within nine months the first of their three children was born.

The recurrence of forenames within Scottish families is well established. By tradition, the eldest son is named after the paternal grandparent, while the eldest daughter and second son are named after the maternal grandparents. Curiously, this is true for the first two but not the last of Margaret Winton and Herbert Jansch's three children: Charlie (born 1935, after his late grandfather (Carl/Charles/Jansch); Mary (born 1937, after her late grandmother Mary Winton). By the same tradition Bert, born in 1943, should have been Thomas, after his grandfather Thomas Winton. Instead, he was registered as Herbert Jansch, after his father, and known thereafter as Bert.

Bert Jansch was born on 3 November 1943 at a place now known as Stobhill Hospital in Glasgow. At the time the family were living in Glasgow, at 247 Bernard Street. Herbert senior's occupation is given dually as 'contractor's labourer' and 'Private (Royal Army Service Corps)'. The Second World War was still in progress. This was a difficult time for the family. Margaret was ill both before and after Bert was born, and neighbours looked after the three children for a period. As for their father, 'he was mainly a coal miner,' says Mary, 'but he did change his job quite a lot'. Three months after Bert was born the family moved into a house owned by Bert's grandfather in West Pilton, one of the poorest areas of Edinburgh, on the city's north side. 'Tenement buildings, six on a stair,' says Mary. 'We were on the first floor. Apart from it being a poor area, you really lived a lot differently than you do now.' With his father's employment situation at best changeable, Bert's mum took various cleaning jobs at private houses and at the city's telephone exchange, and later worked at a litho printer's.

If money was always a problem for the family, it was not the worst. 'My dad walked out on us several times,' says Mary. 'And when he did leave it was usually in circumstances that were very difficult to get out of financially. It's commonplace today, but although it was a poor area we were living in it was very family oriented. We had a pretty hard time – we lurched from one financial crisis to another, really. Our mother did her best but she was just an ordinary person. I honestly don't know why my dad kept walking out but they couldn't have been compatible.'

The last time Herbert Jansch abandoned his family, never to be seen or heard of again,[2] it was 1949. Mary was twelve and Bert five or six. It was major, formative incident in his life and perhaps the root of the 'angst' that many would later identify in his early musical work and in his personality. 'I've got a very bad memory for things I don't want to remember,' he said later, in his mid-twenties and in the supposed comfort of his relative fame.[3] Being a close-knit community and desertion a then rare domestic circumstance, the neighbours rallied round Mrs Jansch and her family. Mary recalls one neighbour, a Mrs Mercer, as being especially good to the family. Years later, in 1967, Bert recalled the same woman vividly in 'A Child's Hang Up' – one of two short poems contained in a generally curious sleevenote he wrote to accompany Roy Harper's album *Come Out Fighting Genghis Smith*:

'Bertie, what have you been doing
up the backstairs?'
'Nothin' Maw.' 'Ask Mrs.
Mercer fir some sugar.'
Spotless linoleum, shining
and slippery. Roaring fire,
apples and oranges, a long
flowered apron,
white hair. 'Tell yer
Mum she can give it
back tomorrow.'

As far as can be gleaned, the Jansch family had had no great history in music. Within genealogical documents the closest they come is the marriage of Bert's great-aunt Charlotte to a Mr Galbraith whose father was intriguingly described as a 'music seller'. There is, nevertheless, some family lore on the Winton side concerning a substantial, if not professional, involvement with a musical variety theatre in Leith and Mary Jansch, though not Bert, remembers their mum being able to play piano by ear. Within months of Herbert walking out Margaret Jansch invested what little spare money she had in giving her children a taste of music-making. She bought a second-hand piano.

'This was just a battered old thing with cigarette burns on it,' says Mary. 'It must have been one that somebody was throwing out, but she decided we should go for music lessons. Mum didn't really have the money so in the end we were both sort of giving it up – we only went for about three months. I fell away but the teacher came after Bert, said he showed ability at music and she would come to the house to teach him. But he wouldn't stay in for her!'

At the time, in concurrence with so many other restless children then and now, gifted or otherwise, Bert was simply bored with the idea of taking lessons in piano. But he was still fascinated with music. He would regularly accompany his older sister, now earning and spending her own money, on record-buying trips to the city centre on Saturdays. For Mary and her friends in the mid-fifties, music was a big social emollient: 'In my generation we went to the dancing and that was our interest – dancing and buying records. My elder brother liked traditional jazz and country and western. There was a lot of that at the time, Hank Williams and that sort of thing. I mainly bought big band jazz – Ted Heath, Chris Barber, Stan Kenton . . . So Bert would be listening to all the records we bought. Actually, it wasn't a record player we had at home, it was an old-fashioned cabinet, my grandmother's originally, with a handle. It was 78s that we bought, and when we played them you had to run and wind it up before the end of the record!'

Bert was intrigued by the records his sister played. Aside from the British jazz bands 'she was listening to Frank Sinatra and Johnny Ray, but she was also into Elvis Presley and Little Richard so I kind of picked up on that'.[4] Saturday morning picture shows were another part of growing up in those days, recalled many years later with clear affection in 'The Saturday Movie'[5] – the rush of imagination from seeing cowboys, indians, pirates and dragons. The new wave of rock'n'roll movies was also coming to the local cinema. Asked once about who or what had set him on the road to folk, Bert offered Presley as the unlikely inspiration: 'He was folk as well,' he explained. 'All his early songs were from the old blues singers. I rejected Bill Haley and stuck to Elvis. Then I left school and started going to folk clubs and it was there that I slowly became aware there was a lot more music than was being pumped out on the radio.'[6] Jimmy Shand, the unsmiling king of Scottish strict-tempo accordion bands, made the first record Bert ever bought. It was a present for his mum. Bert was never a record buyer himself – they were unaffordable luxuries. The first record he would own, and the only one ever recalled, was a 45 rpm EP by American blues singer Big Bill Broonzy. It was purely by chance – a school friend had found it in a shop, and something about the name must have appealed to Bert's imagination. As the discovery occurred during his brief time as an apprentice nurseryman, he had the money to investigate. It would prove to be a most illuminating investment.

Bert's obsession with the guitar as an object and as a device to make music began at school. The second *Genghis Smith* poem, 'The Writing's On The Wall', was a recollection of school days – 'sports day rave ups', hearts and arrows on the walls, playground fights, the fascination with girls and 'the morning parade in the open square, where the smokers are weeded out'. In some contrast to the solitary nature he developed in his later teens, Bert was by no means a misfit during the greater part of his formal education. In Mary's time, secondary schooling in the area was split: girls would go to Flora Stephenson secondary, boys to Ainslie Park; by the time Bert was a pupil, Ainslie Park was mixed. His primary education had been at Pennywell School. Bert was popular with his classmates, played football and had a number of friends he would hang around with outside school hours. He had, in his own words, 'all the usual childhood friendships and did all the usual childhood things'.[7] He was particularly good at woodwork and was considerably more gifted academically than anyone in the family had expected. 'We didn't know that Bert was really quite intelligent until he got his last report,' says Mary, 'and the headmaster told us he wanted Bert to go further in education. He was actually "dux" of the school – top of the whole school. He got a medal which my mother kept for years.'

'The first time I actually saw a guitar,' said Bert, 'was when my music teacher brought one into the classroom for everyone to have a look. I suppose my interest in the instrument could be traced back to that, because I think it was there and then that I decided I wanted to be a guitarist rather than a pianist. I couldn't afford to buy a real guitar so I used to try and make them. I'd been trying since I was five years old. I used to get sheets of hardboard, bits of wood, and cut it all out. When I was about twelve or something, really for real, I honestly managed to get one that was reasonably playable. That was from a guitar kit that I'd got for Christmas. At that time skiffle and Lonnie Donegan especially were going full tilt but I didn't know the first thing about the way to play the guitar, though my six months or so at the piano had given me a rudimentary knowledge of things like keys and scales. I learned to play D on it. The strings were so far off the fretboard it was almost impossible to play – the D was the only chord I could hold down, where the strings were nearer to the frets. I think from then on it was ordained that I should play guitar! It fell apart eventually and I didn't really play a guitar – a real guitar – till I left school at sixteen.'[8]

In September 1959 Bert complied with his old headmaster's advice and went on to Leith Academy. 'At [Ainslie Park] I had several choices as to what I should do,' says Bert. 'One of them was to go to the art college. The art teacher desperately wanted me to go to art college, and I rejected all of it. After that I went to Leith Academy for further education for about three months, but I gave it up. I just couldn't stand it because it was academic, the emphasis wasn't enough on the arts. It was purely written stuff, which I just couldn't handle at all. I remember packing all the books up and saying there you are, thank you and goodbye.'[9]

In addition to the emphasis of its curriculum, school uniform was compulsory at Leith Academy and Mrs Jansch simply couldn't afford it. Bert would attend wearing jeans and a blazer, which was not helpful in terms of fitting in with his peers. By the first term of the new year he had left. 'That,' says Mary, 'was when my elder brother got him a job in market gardening.' Mary had already left home for a job in the civil service in 1953. Her elder brother Charlie's comings and goings were more complex. Before his statutory period of national service in the early fifties, Charlie had worked in a market garden in Edinburgh's Comely Bank area, near Queensferry Road. There had been the suggestion of a partnership with the owner or some other enhancement of his position in the business upon his return, but this failed to materialise. Charlie got married, left the gardening and signed up again with the Royal Air Force. But not before introducing the prospect of life as a market gardener to his younger brother.

The family had never had a garden of their own but one green-fingered relative, Bert's Uncle Adam (on his mother's side), lived with them. 'Dear old Uncle Adam' made quite an impression, turning up much later on as the subject of world-weary envy in a song, 'When I Get Home'. Never marrying, never owning a home, working hard, getting drunk – Uncle Adam personified a life of honest toil, no responsibilities whatsoever and every weekend an escape route to oblivion.[10] 'Uncle Adam had an allotment,' says Mary, 'like a lot of people during the war, down near the railway in the area we lived in. There was a lot of hardship for everybody, with rationing and so on, and he supplied us all with fresh vegetables – the whole stair. Maybe that's where Bert got his original interest in gardening.' It may have had an effect, but certainly, from the age of five until he left school at sixteen, Bert spent a great deal of time visiting his brother at the nursery. On Charlie's recommendation, his little brother was taken on as an apprentice nurseryman, 'earning three quid a week or whatever',[11] and although his employment there may have been as little as three months, certainly no more than eight, it was a profound time. 'My first period of real isolation,' he recalled. 'I was completely cut off from the world there – just me and five thousand plants.'[12]

With his new-found wealth Bert bought himself a guitar on hire purchase. His boss, a man whose name is no longer recalled, signed the agreement as guarantor. Not knowing the first thing about the variety of instruments available or the suitability of the different models to particular styles of music, Bert bought a Hofner cello guitar: a bulky jazz model. In the early weeks of 1960, insofar as can be determined, Bert and one of his pals from school, Harry Steele, discovered a strange and exotic establishment up some winding stone steps, a few feet above the steady incline of the street on the city's 'Royal Mile'. It was something called the Howff – a folk club, whatever that was – and most importantly it offered guitar lessons. Bert wanted to sound just like Big Bill Broonzy, the guy on his EP who sounded a million miles away from his sister's jazz bands, from Elvis Presley, Lonnie Donegan and all those other people on the radio. He would have doubtless been astounded to have known that over the previous few years Big Bill had played concerts in Edinburgh and had maybe once stood on that very spot. It may well have happened in the recent past, but it wasn't going to happen again. Bill Broonzy was six months dead.

CHAPTER TWO

London: The First Days

Born in the 1890s in Mississippi, Bill Broonzy had an extraordinarily rich life and in the process, through the rare articulacy of his music, became a bridge between numerous styles and traditions – and not only in America. It has been said that Broonzy's music 'exemplifies the movement made by the blues from locally made folk music to nationally distributed, mass media entertainment'.[1] Even within the black blues context in America he is widely credited with combining a flavour of the Mississippi Delta blues with the more sophisticated urban sounds of Chicago, where he later made his home. Working first as a field hand then as a preacher and then serving as a soldier in the Great War, Broonzy took up the guitar relatively late in life, in his twenties, learning from one Papa Charlie Jackson in Chicago. In what may fancifully be deemed a correlation with Bert's life, he had already made himself a violin as a kid. Accomplished as a songwriter, vocalist and instrumentalist, he was a mainstay of the 'race' record industry right up to its enforced sabbatical during the Second World War. Famously, he replaced the then recently deceased Robert Johnson on John Hammond's now legendary 'From Spirituals to Swing' revue in 1938 at the Carnegie Hall, where he doubtless played up to his onstage introduction as 'a sharecropper from Arkansas'. While the evolution of British rock in the sixties – the Rolling Stones, Cream, Led Zeppelin et al. – paid homage to the dark myth of Robert Johnson as its spiritual source, the folk movement seemed content to preserve and aspire to the folksy accessibility of Big Bill Broonzy's brand of blues.

The folksiness that British audiences saw and loved was something of an affectation, but a harmless one. Broonzy's style and material adapted regularly to changes in black tastes and, after the war, to the white audiences drawn in from jazz and the gathering folksong revival. In essence 'his immense talent was always at the service of his audience and their expectations'.[2] In 1951, as one of the earliest ambassadors for the blues, Broonzy embarked on a trip to Europe and it was in Germany that he ran into Bert Wilcox, a British jazz promoter who brought him to a Methodist Hall in London to perform 'a recital of blues, folksongs and ballads'. From blues scholar Paul Oliver's own recollection, about forty people turned up. That same year Broonzy's recordings also made their debut in Britain, when Vogue issued no fewer than six 78s, including his civil rights anthem 'Black, Brown and White'. Between 1955 and the mid-sixties Vogue, Pye, Columbia, Mercury and other labels serviced Broonzy's rapidly expanding UK market with fourteen EPs and several albums. Few of those who made their names in the British folk/blues boom of that decade had ever seen Big Bill in concert, but he cast one hell of a long shadow. Everyone, not least Bert Jansch, had heard his records.

The very first solo black American bluesman to visit Britain, a year prior to Broonzy, was Josh White. A commitment to eulogising the plight of the black man in modern America notwithstanding, White's style was based more on English and Irish folk and gospel, and he was experienced in mainstream cabaret – all of which made him broadly accessible. Broonzy shared enough of White's populist sensibilities to appeal to a similarly wide audience. He was always well dressed and impeccably courteous. Even on his electric jazz-flavoured recordings from the 1940s, the big man still brought an aura of gritty authenticity to sophisticated arrangements, clean sounds and the clear diction of an effortlessly smooth vocal. Casually convincing the wide-eyed, embryonic English blues fraternity that he was indeed, as he was often billed, 'the last of the Mississippi blues singers', and playing for British audiences what was generally regarded back home as old-fashioned country blues, he was only doing so – on both counts – because it seemed precisely what his new friends wanted to hear. But Broonzy was no phoney and no fool either. 'He knew that once he had come, others would follow, especially those singers who were now re-garded, in his words, as "old fogies" but who could find a new audience in Britain.'[3] Where White, under increasing pressure from the FBI, was sometimes afraid to air his civil rights views on public stages, Broonzy was brazen, though not without emotion: 'For him, singing to white people songs like "Black, Brown and White" and "When Will I Get To Be A Man?" was the most moving thing,' says Norma Waterson, of pioneering folk revivalists the Watersons. 'The first time he sang at Hull City Hall we went backstage and met him and became friends. He came and stayed in our house the next time he was over [in 1957]. The Watersons were singing together informally at that point but we never sang for him, we just talked about music. He was very appreciative of us. Just such a nice man.'

Broonzy's decency was, at least on his first visit, hardly returned by his host: Wilcox charged him for rent, food, taxis and much else. A famous memoir from a man who was otherwise the very essence of humility contains the memorable conclusion that 'I never did meet a meaner man'.

On later trips he would find Chris Barber a much more affable benefactor. The leader of a popular 'trad jazz' band, Barber was also heavily involved in the birth of skiffle and, like his friend, sometime colleague and contemporary Alexis Korner, had been an avid collector of blues recordings. Between 1954 and 1964 Barber effectively sponsored a series of what would prove to be hugely influential tours of Britain, often including Bert's home town of Edinburgh, by black American artists from the blues and gospel traditions: Big Bill Broonzy, Sonny Terry & Brownie McGhee, Muddy Waters, Sister Rosetta Tharpe and Memphis Slim.

'From '54 onwards most people who were musical probably came to concerts like mine anyway,' says Barber. 'We were the thing that was happening, the liveliest thing you could find in those days. And when we brought Big Bill with us to Edinburgh two or three times, and Sonny & Brownie were there with us once at least, and Sister Rosetta Tharpe, that exposed people to them who were not preconceived blues or folk fans, just people who liked music. We did it for the love of music. Particularly with Rosetta Tharpe, Sonny & Brownie and Muddy Waters every promoter said to me, "What do you want to bring these people along for? You'd fill that hall by yourself. We can't put any more on the ticket for someone people have never heard of – if you want to bring them along you'll have to pay them." So it was our gift to the British electorate! If we hadn't paid for them, they wouldn't have been here. Now I don't expect a medal for that, but what I would like is not to get knocked for it, because people have said that we cashed in on the blues. We didn't. We cashed out on it!'

The gesture was not unappreciated. 'I used to love listening to Brownie McGhee,' says Bert, 'particularly when you could see him in the flesh, at the Howff. I missed out on Big Bill Broonzy. I know people who have actually met him in real life, and I'm always envious of that.'[4] Bill Broonzy fell ill with cancer on the European leg of his 1957 tour and returned to Chicago. 'While he [had] prophesied the impending demise of the blues in his conversation, he mentioned enough singers to indicate that at the time, many blues singers were still actively working.'[5] Broonzy had been canny enough to corner the nascent British blues market while he could, allowing willing recipients of his wisdom to believe in the romance that here was, indeed, the last of the Mississippi blues singers. But on his own recommendation Sonny Terry & Brownie McGhee came to Britain the following year. Bill had already fulfilled his British engagements for 1957. 'On his last appearance you could tell the voice was going,' says Norma Waterson, 'but he was still a great performer and an incredible guitar player. His sense of rhythm was just majestic.' A number of the UK jazz and skiffle musicians who had become his friends organised benefit shows to pay his hospital bills.

Bill passed away in August 1958. His friend and protégé Muddy Waters, a symbol of the next generation of the blues, was among those carrying the coffin.

'Noisy, unsubtle, depending heavily on the repertoire of Leadbelly and Broonzy, "skiffle" was a rough out-crop from the New Orleans jazz revival of the early fifties,' wrote one commentator.[6] Some may state the case with names like Billy Fury, Johnny Kidd or Cliff Richard but Britain never did move far enough out of its grand tradition of variety to come up with anything that could seriously be said to equal the compelling power and spontaneity of rock'n'roll in America on anything like a consistent basis. Skiffle was the English equivalent: 'folk song with a jazz beat' as the movement's first chronicler, Brian Bird, termed it[7] – a rhythmically driving, anglicised combination of American blues, country and folk with exotic imagery and chord sequences reduced to a minimum. It was a lively alternative to jazz and the smooth balladry of the day, and it was Britain's first post-war youth craze. Anybody could play it, and on the back of Lonnie Donegan's infectious personality and his three million-selling debut single 'Rock Island Line' thousands were inspired to do just that. It is no exaggeration to say that guitar playing in Britain, as a mass popular activity, can be traced back to Donegan – 'the first king of Britpop'[8] – and the skiffle craze he inspired.

The word 'skiffle' itself can be traced back to 1926, when it was a term associated with the 'rent parties' run by poor black people in the northern United States, where music was played using low-cost or makeshift instruments.[9] In 1948 a Harlem newspaper editor named Dan Burley formed a group to record some of the rent party music he recalled from his youth in the twenties and thirties. Calling themselves the Dan Burley Skiffle Group, their number included one Walter 'Brownie' McGhee on guitar.

Born in Tennessee in 1915, McGhee had grown up in a family where music was at least a part-time occupation. By the time he was eight, he had mastered guitar, piano and foot-treadle organ and was singing regularly in a Baptist quartet at church. Having left school in his teens he hitch-hiked around the Smokey Mountains with guitar and kazoo and took casual work as an entertainer, travelling with medicine shows and eventually winding up, in 1940, at the home of guitarist Blind Boy Fuller in North Carolina. Staying with Fuller at the time was his similarly impaired protégé – a young man from Georgia named Saunders Terrell, otherwise known as Sonny Terry. Sonny played harmonica well, sang with an intriguing waywardness and, like Broonzy, had appeared at John Hammond's 'Spirituals to Swing' bash at the Carnegie Hall in 1938. Whether he was totally blind is a matter of some conjecture, but he hit it off in a workable fashion with McGhee – whose eyesight was fine, but who had limped since childhood – and that year the pair travelled to New York to cut some records. Following Blind Boy Fuller's death in 1941 they settled there permanently.

From the streets of Harlem they moved quickly on to concerts and Broadway musicals and began a loose, often fractious but remarkably enduring partnership that lasted almost up to Sonny's death in 1986. During the forties, Brownie would record prolifically under his own name, as a duo with Sonny and as an accompanist for many others. 'At first, McGhee was a country blues performer in the tradition of Big Bill Broonzy, but as the years went by he smoothed-out his voice – deleting the harshness of Big Bill's delivery – and sang with a tenderness and whimsical humour that contrasted beautifully with Terry's more primitive work.'[10] The Dan Burley session was par for the course and none of those involved could possibly have expected such a harmless exercise in ghetto nostalgia to trigger a mainstream phenomenon thousands of miles and half a world away. Indirectly as may be, it did just that.

Chris Barber's recording career, like Lonnie Donegan's, began in earnest in 1954. But three years earlier, and three years after the Dan Burley session, in 1951, he had cut a brace of 78s for the Esquire label. One disc was shared with the Crane River Jazz Band, with his side credited to Chris Barber's Jazz Band. The other disc (which apparently also featured Lonnie Donegan) was credited to Chris Barber's Washboard Wonders. These performances were, as one authority notes, 'not skiffle, but steps in that direction'.[11] The Crane River boys had formed in 1949 around brothers Ken and Bill Colyer and were dedicated to the resolutely purist New Orleans jazz sound of Bunk Johnson, although it is believed they also featured a 'skiffle' segment in their shows. Indeed, even Donegan credits Bill Colyer with making the connection to the Burley sound and thus giving a name to the novelty section of their show. In 1949 the Colyers had also met Barber's friend Alexis Korner, now widely regarded as a founding father of British blues. Along with some others they would meet regularly at Korner's house during this period and, with Alexis putting off the inconvenience of actually learning his instrument by bluffing away on a guitar openly tuned to B flat, which required little more than one finger at a time, would jam around on the theme of a Leadbelly song called 'Midnight Special'.[12] In a few years it would be the proud property of every gang of kids with washboard, tea-chest bass and cheap guitar between them, the length and breadth of the country.

But who was this Leadbelly anyway? With no little irony, in the very year, 1949, that had seen Colyer and Korner fool around with his songs while the then Tony Donegan (he changed his forename after seeing bluesman Lonnie Johnson in 1952) got together for the first time in a band with Chris Barber, the man who would effectively bankroll the next decade for the lot of them passed away. That same year he had played the jazz clubs of Paris – his first and only visit to Europe. Had he lived longer he would undoubtedly have travelled to Britain and enjoyed the same respect given to Broonzy, Sonny & Brownie and all those who followed and, perhaps also, a little of the massive success that his songs would generate for the Brit-skifflers.

Hudson Ledbetter, known universally as Leadbelly, was born on the Texas – Louisiana border in 1889. He was 'discovered' during the second of two prison sentences – the first for murder, the second for attempted murder – by folklorist John Lomax and his son Alan, who were searching the jailhouses of the deep south for material of interest to record for the Library of Congress. With a pardon purportedly won at least partly through the power of song, he was employed by the pair and taken to New York. As a musical find, the Lomaxes had struck gold. Leadbelly could play any number of instruments, but principally twelve-string guitar. Defining what blues scholars now regard as a 'songster' as opposed to a performer of some strict discipline of the blues, he had amassed a vast repertoire of songs from the rural south of his youth to which he was constantly adding refinements of his own, together with writing new songs and picking up material from whatever fresh sources presented themselves. 'It was his apparently inexhaustible collection of older songs and tunes that most fascinated the northern audience, embracing as it did everything from versions of old European ballads through Cajun-influenced dance tunes and sentimental pop to dozens of black work songs and field hollers, southern ballads, gospel, prison songs, many tough blues and even cowboy songs.' By turns spine-chilling, barn-storming, nostalgic and socially aware, Leadbelly was the real thing: a walking, talking microcosm of America's folklore tradition.

In the 1920s he had, like Josh White, spent time with Blind Lemon Jefferson and later plied his songs in the red light districts of towns around Louisiana and Texas. In New York he mixed and recorded with both Josh White and with Sonny Terry & Brownie McGhee and, like them, he was recording simultaneously and quite separately both for the growing white 'folk' audience and for the 'race' market. He would also rub shoulders with Woody Guthrie, godfather of the white troubadours and protest singers of the 1960s, whose songs on the grand and nebulous themes of freedom, rambling and such like were a further conduit into first skiffle and subsequently the British and American folk revivals. Like Bill Broonzy, Leadbelly was unafraid of writing songs that dealt with racial prejudice. And, as with Broonzy, his recordings started appearing on British labels from 1950. If

Broonzy's music was, even in its most down-home form, considerably more polished in its presentation than Leadbelly's, between them they had pretty much all the repertoire and truth that a nation of British youngsters with three chords would require.

Leadbelly may have been an interesting curio for Ken Colyer at the start of the fifties, but Ken was obsessed with the sound of New Orleans, and rejoined the Merchant Navy (with whom he had earlier served national service) with the sole object of getting there. He returned in early 1953 and worked briefly with Chris Barber (who had meanwhile turned professional) in a line-up which included Alexis Korner and Lonnie Donegan and with a repertoire that featured skiffle as an interval item within the dominant jazz set. It was too many egos for one band.

In July 1954, two months after Colyer and Barber had inevitably split, the Chris Barber ensemble recorded their first 33rpm LP, a ten-inch entitled *New Orleans Joys*. They wanted to include a couple of 'different' numbers that had been going down well in their live act. As Lonnie Donegan's own 1998 press material put it: 'The A&R man thought it was a waste of time and wanted them to stick to recording the jazz album they were being paid to make. After a little cajoling he relented and left the excited band together with a "live" mike (always a dangerous combination). Skiffle was born.'

Frenetic takes of the traditional 'John Henry' and the Leadbelly train song 'Rock Island Line' were recorded that day. The album was issued in 1954, while a 78rpm single release of the coupling (credited to the Lonnie Donegan Skiffle Group) sneaked out around Christmas the following year. Peaking at number eight in January 1956, it spent twenty-two weeks in the UK charts, single-handedly ushered in the nationwide craze and also made the US Top 20 – a feat unheard of at the time for a British artist. As one commentator has pointed out, 'George Melly had recorded the song a couple of years earlier and had provoked no such interest.'[13] Having honed his routine in the intimate coffee bars of London's Soho district, Donegan found himself playing to huge audiences (and for correspondingly huge fees) in the States, sharing bills with the likes of Chuck Berry, Bill Haley and the Harlem Globe Trotters: 'I was offered a gig in New York for $2000 – a massive sum then. Twenty quid would have done!' As had happened previously to Ken Colyer in New Orleans, Donegan would also find himself vilified and on one occasion run out of town by his own promoter for hanging around with black musicians and buying blues records. Such a heinous crime in deep south America was still a rare luxury back home: 'We had to scrabble for everything in Britain. I used to go to the American

Embassy in Grosvenor Square, which had a Library of Congress section with thousands of "ethnic" records.[14]

Between 1956 and 1962 Donegan went on to rack up no fewer than thirty-four UK singles chart placings, including seventeen Top 10s, wisely broadening his repertoire when the initial craze for skiffle subsided. In 1957 BBC radio, responding to an obvious demand, launched *Saturday Skiffle Club*, which enjoyed a weekly audience of two and a half million. Its producer Jimmy Grant was quoted in the *Melody Maker* at the time as concerned that 'the trouble with most amateur skiffle groups is that they lack basic musicianship'. But then that was the whole appeal of the thing. By October 1958 the show had quietly dropped the word 'Skiffle' from its title but remained an oasis for live, British pop music in an otherwise dusty broadcasting schedule and in an era long before commercial radio, pirate radio or even BBC regional stations. A snowball was rolling slowly but surely down a hill.

Made by an awe-struck schoolboy named Frank Coia, unique reel-to-reel recordings of a series of folk club performances in Glasgow spanning 1962 to 1965 document the presence in Bert Jansch's early professional repertoire of many songs written by or associated with Broonzy, Leadbelly and Brownie McGhee. But, unusual amongst his peers who made their names in the folk clubs, the jazz scene or the embryonic British blues movement of the early sixties, Bert had no significant involvement in the skiffle craze. He did once comment that, as a kid trying to make guitars, he was inspired not so much by a fascination with the instrument as by the very sound of skiffle: 'Lonnie Donegan was about my first influence into the whole world of music,' he concluded.[15] But although practically everyone else of similar age and musical disposition, from future members of The Beatles to fusion virtuoso John McLaughlin, were members of a skiffle group, Bert Jansch never was. In his hands, the songs of Broonzy and Leadbelly could be played in darker and more intriguing ways than a three-chord thrum, a 4/4 backbeat and a singalong refrain. More by virtue of chance than veneration, having quickly found his Hofner unsuitable to folk music, Bert had exchanged it for a Zenith, a model of guitar once marketed as a 'Josh White' but, by 1959/60, inevitably repromoted as a 'Lonnie Donegan'. Within three months it was stolen. Bert continued to pay the h.p. instalments but it was years before he would own a guitar again.

Donegan's hit parade swansong 'Pick A Bale Of Cotton' peaked just two months prior to The Beatles' first. Appropriately enough, it was another Leadbelly song. The worlds of pantomime and cabaret were beckoning: 'I was bitter,' he says. 'I was the king! All of a sudden The Beatles were king. I spat, fought and cursed, but a new generation had come along. At the same time, the variety theatres were in decline, so we had to learn to play the cabaret clubs which were taking off. In fact, cabaret paid much better – £1000 a night. You wouldn't get that for a week in theatre.'[16]

Indeed not. And you would certainly not have got it for a month's work at even the swishest of the coffee bars in Soho. For the Jansch generation of singer-songwriter guitar heroes that would come to prominence in the mid-sixties, the compact bohemia of Soho would be the epicentre of their world as it had been a decade earlier for the skifflers. By 1965 it would be buzzing with pub and cellar folk clubs, some of them all-nighters; by the end of that year Bert Jansch would be the king of the castle and a tiny little club called 'Les Cousins', in an airless cellar beneath a restaurant at 49 Greek Street, the castle of his kingdom. It was, by all accounts, a crazy scene.

Why, for two generations of post-war British music pioneers who worshipped at the same shrines of two recently deceased black Americans, and their dutiful re-creations of pre-war hokum, did Soho become the playground of tomorrow's stars? John Platt, fascinated with the literary and musical heritage of the area, wrote a definitive magazine sketch on the subject in the late seventies, surveying its pubs, coffee bars and other music venues in the context of the area's rich history. He defined Soho as being geographically 'a square mile dropped into London's West End, bordered by Oxford Street in the north, Regent Street in the west, Coventry Street in the south and Charing Cross Road in the east' although certain outlying areas could be said to have honorary inclusion. 'Modern Soho,' he argued, 'came into being towards the end of the nineteenth century when it began to be settled by various immigrant groups, especially Italians. The immigrants, simply by bringing some of the flavour of their native countries to London – particularly as so many opened restaurants and bars – gave Soho a reputation amongst those who cared for such things for the exotic and the unusual. Soho was that oddity – a village in the city, where you could feel part of a genuinely urban life but live on an essentially human scale. This fact, coupled with its cosmopolitan quality, is what has given it its continuing appeal.'

In the 1920s and particularly the 1930s, Soho and the adjoining Fitzrovia quarter were becoming popular with artists and writers, most famously perhaps with Dylan Thomas. Those on leave in London during the war were attracted to the area as a refuge from nine-to-five drudgery. Platt goes on to explain that 'after the war a new bohemian type was emerging, especially from the art schools of the area. Whereas previously the bohemian types had been fairly respectable – at least outwardly – the new generation opted for a good deal less conformity and were altogether more outrageous in their behaviour. There was a split from a literary based community to a musically based one. The new denizens of Soho were jazz fanatics for whom literature, though important, took second place to music. There had been coffee bars (or at least cafés) before the war, but after the first new-style place with an Espresso opened in 1953 (the Moka in Frith Street) the whole area became overrun with them. Most of the coffee bars were just that – a place to go and drink coffee – but many acquired a mystique of their own. Often open practically all night, they became a quasi-secret network of meeting places for young people, generally run by like-minded individuals, where for the price of a coffee one could indulge in apocalyptic conversation till dawn. Many provided music too – jazz initially, then skiffle and later folk.'[17]

Acts like the Vipers Skiffle Group and the Chas McDevitt Skiffle Group, featuring the implausibly named Nancy Whiskey, jumped very successfully aboard Donegan's bandwagon during the brief heyday of the new sound in 1957, even charting with some of the same material. The whole thing was quite clearly outrageous and at the very height of the craze one national newspaper had this to say:

'Soho is no longer London's naughty square mile. It has become Espresso Land, bright with the coloured neon lights of oddly-named coffee bars – Heaven & Hell, Prego, the Macabre and the 2 i's – and noisy with the yowling screams of skifflers. Now, instead of razor-armed mobsters and cosh boys, you meet bearded young men in duffle coats carrying double basses and washboards, and pimply faced rock'n'roll fans in their tapered pants. And in the cellars where the spielers once ran their all-night dice and poker games, the skiffle bands have taken over and the youngsters are jiving.'[18]

Most of these exotic new venues, including others in the area like the Nucleus, the Partisan, the Gyre & Gimble and Bunjies, were catering for the beatnik crowd, those bearded fellows with the duffle coats that the Sunday papers were so concerned about. Jack Kerouac's *On The Road* and other such products of the American 'beat' school of writing became the manuals of this tried and tested alternative lifestyle, and as much so in the Edinburgh that Bert Jansch was on the cusp of discovering as in the London that Lonnie Donegan's success had served to shine a spotlight on. The 2 i's itself, so closely identified with the vagaries of a certain era as the birthplace of British rock'n'roll, was an anachronism by the end of the fifties although the majority of the coffee bars survived well into the sixties.[19] Alongside the platforms provided by Ewan MacColl and by Alexis Korner and Cyril Davies, in the upper rooms of various public houses, they were the earliest stomping grounds for many of that decade's key figures in British folk: Robin Hall and Jimmie Macgregor, Davy Graham, Steve Benbow, Martin Carthy, Wizz Jones and Clive Palmer among them.

Situated beneath a restaurant at 49 Greek Street, though not a coffee bar as such, was a club called the Skiffle Cellar. It did not not take long to abandon the S-word, and from May 1958 to the close of 1960 it would be known as the Cellar, running two folk sessions on a Saturday and featuring the Steve Benbow Folk Four in a Tuesday night residency. After a short period as a strip club it would reopen in 1965 as 'Les Cousins', the most legendary of the 'Swinging London' folk joints. But in its original mid-fifties incarnation it was owned by one Russell Quaye, whose City Ramblers were thus effectively the house band.[20] A staggering amount of people would seem not only to have dropped by of an evening but to have passed through the ranks of Quaye's band. One individual of greatly underestimated importance who did not do so but who had established early on his own Sunday night residency there as a soloist, performing not skiffle but bona fide British folk music with arrangements for guitar, was Steve Benbow.

In the same way that Davy Graham has long been viewed as the more shadowy precedent to the revolutionary guitar of Bert Jansch – however much Bert's initial development was in truth very largely independent of Graham's influence – there will always be someone or something lurking in the pre-dawn of every great happening in music just waiting for the analysts of history to stumble in. For the very concept of British folk songs played to the accompaniment of a guitar, Steve Benbow is where it all begins.[21]

Born in London in 1931, Benbow recalls his mother singing a lot of folk songs when he was a kid, but his own involvement in music began relatively late in life, at twenty-three. Exceptionally good at languages, learning French and German at school and Arabic from his father, Benbow joined the army in 1950. He was posted to Egypt and within six months was working out his tour of duty as an interpreter. Within a couple of years he had taken up guitar and was singing material from the repertoires of Jimmie Rodgers, Frank Crummit and Burl Ives. After national service he got a job touring in a concert party, singing songs like 'The Foggy Dew', 'The Fox' and 'Unchained Melody'.' That microcosm of repertoire illustrates fairly well the benchmarks of Benbow's subsequent career – simple traditional ballads and easy-listening standards with a hint of jazz. Steve was a pragmatist. Life was not easy in those days and you did what you could: he happened to like music, he was a good player and in 1957, with a little serendipity, he lucked into the unadvertised vacancy of Britain's First Folk Guitarist.

Steve had been playing trad jazz in a band led by trombonist Dave Kier. Dave knew Ewan MacColl, a fellow Communist who had recently turned his attention from propagandist theatre to the untrodden paths of harnessing his country's musical past to the furtherance of its socio-political future.

MacColl was on the lookout for someone with an interest in folk music to play guitar for him on a record[22] and at that year's International Youth Festival in Moscow. Steve very probably raised an eyebrow. But not so you'd notice: 'We were all a bit left-wing in those days,' he says. 'But I was a professional musician. I'd charge as much to sing "God Save The Queen" as I would "The Red Flag".' Steve went to Russia and while there, from a position of not really knowing anyone on the British music scene, became acquainted with the City Ramblers, Jimmie Macgregor, Ewan MacColl and somebody called 'Banjo' George with whom, on returning to London, he secured a regular gig at the Tatty Bogle in Beak Street. 'I used to get thirty bob a night, every night,' say Steve, 'which was a bloody sight better than milking cows! I'd been doing that from four-thirty in the morning till six at night for £9 a week. So I couldn't believe my luck when I got this gig.'

'Banjo' George does not loom large in this nor perhaps in any other story, but the security of his trad jazz pub residency and the prospect of working on folk music with MacColl was enough for Benbow to make the transition to full-time guitar slinging in the West End. It is not certain whether MacColl himself was to be found at all or with any regularity in the environs of a skiffle club, but one of his cohorts and fellow architects of the British folk revival certainly was. In a scene where jeans and pullovers were the norm, A. L. 'Bert' Lloyd – never seen out in anything less than a three-piece suit and wide grin – was a distinctive fellow. The archetype of a jolly fat man, with bookish enthusiasm, Ewan MacColl once described him with no small affection as 'a walking toby jug', not unlike something out of Trollope. Generous with knowledge and encouragement, Bert Lloyd enjoyed his odd recreational forays to the cellars, regaling the young skifflers with feisty curios from the backwaters of British folksong and, according to Karl Dallas, going 'out of his way many times to remark on Steve's quality and the influence of Greek music on his playing'.

Aside from a whaling expedition to South Georgia in the 1930s, Lloyd, born in 1908, had already made several field-recording trips to Eastern Europe and had, even by the late fifties, the double distinction of being a professional English folklorist in a field of one and of being only the second author that century to have published a book on the subject. It was all a matter of self-belief: 'Tell a person that you are a folklorist,' wrote MacColl many years later, 'and that person will almost certainly respect you, in spite of the fact that he or she hasn't the foggiest notion of what a folklorist is or does. Tell them you are a folk-singer and they will look embarrassed and hastily change the subject.'[23] Karl Dallas for one – the Melody Maker's great champion of folk music – would always harbour the suspicion that Lloyd's oft-told stories of Australian sheep-herding, Antarctic whaling and the like were straight out of the realms of fantasy, but as a practising authority on folk music Bert Lloyd was not only a colourful character. He knew what he was talking about.

The relationship between British folksong and the rhythms and drones of the Balkans held a particular fascination for Lloyd. Steve Benbow wrote little in the way of original material but one number strongly identified with him is the Greek song 'Miserlou'. He had picked it up on national service in the Middle East and it was later recorded as an exercise in instrumental exoticism by Davy Graham, among others. By the time the heyday of guitar-toting folkist virtuosos came around, Lloyd's influence had quietly taken root. It is a moot point that the tangible suspicion of Balkan modes and time signatures that pervaded many interpretations of the supposedly English and Irish songs recorded by Bert Jansch, Martin Carthy and others during the 1960s had a common source in the cross-cultural surgery of Bert Lloyd's imagination. Benbow accompanied Lloyd on some of his Soho recitals and shortly afterwards did so on record. It was convenient that, for reasons no one can quite explain, Bert Lloyd was more or less the man in control of who and what was recorded for Topic Records during the fifties and sixties.

Founded in 1939 and believed to be the oldest independent record label in the world, Topic had originally been the plaything of the Workers' Music Association. Although viewed as a cultural wing of the Trades Union Congress, the WMA in fact never received official TUC support, although prominent members Alan Lomax and Ewan MacColl performed extensively for individual unions and TUC branches. 'Though denounced by some as a Communist front,' says Karl Dallas, himself both a Communist and active on the fifties folk scene, 'the WMA and indeed all of us folkies were distrusted by the apparatchiki of the Party's King Street HQ.' It can nevertheless be generalised with confidence that the various left-wing organisations and the individuals prominent in folk music during the 1950s formed a complex, incestuous web. Topic parted company from the WMA in 1958, although it retained informal links. It was still, at that time, the only significant label in Britain dealing in genuine folk and traditional music.

The Benbow/Lloyd recording of the English racehorse ballad 'Skewball' for Topic on a 1957 EP entitled *Bold Sportsmen All* was a landmark, but Steve was already in his own act performing a number of English traditional songs such as 'Turpin Hero', 'Whaling In Greenland' and 'Musgrave And Lady Barnett'.[24] His earliest and rarest solo recordings, from 1957, are a pair of EPs for the 77 label – one of English songs, the other of American. The label was a short-lived operation run by Dobell's, London's leading specialist record shop of the period. Their patronage was not matched by competence: when the records were issued Steve was horrified to find the tapes had been unintentionally speeded up by a semi-tone. Steve Benbow would find himself in great demand for quite some years to come as an artist suitable for what in today's terms would be unimaginable radio and television exposure, but notwithstanding a fair few opportunities – and almost comical strokes of ill-luck to match – the selling of records in appreciable quantities was not to be. Given Steve's unashamedly broad tastes in music, tasteful style in playing and a tendency, now regretted, to follow an easy-listening path, with all manner of choirs, bands and orchestras peppering his recorded work of the sixties, a critical renaissance seems unlikely. But in terms of folk music, in London in the late fifties, before anyone had heard of Davy Graham let alone Bert Jansch, Steve Benbow was almost certainly the best guitar player on the scene. He was all over the radio and, outside of the visiting black Americans, if you played guitar and sang folk songs he was the guy you aspired to.

Clive Palmer, a young man with a banjo, intrigued by the sound of Russell Quaye and his subterranean dance band, was one of the regulars down at the Skiffle Cellar and at many other haunts around Soho. Equally intoxicated by the same scene was a young man known as Wizz Jones. Within a few years both would find themselves firmly established as enduring touchstones in the story of Bert Jansch. Both were Londoners, Clive born in 1943 in Edmonton in north of the city, and Raymond 'Wizz' Jones born in 1939 in Croydon in the south. From the age of eight Clive had been performing on stage as a vocalist with the Foster-Miller Dance Troupe – a tap-dance act – and in the various minstrel shows and music-hall evenings his local church organised. A little later he found a guitar which his brother, a French polisher, had renovated, swapped it for a banjo and started a little skiffle group – getting as far as the *Carroll Levis Junior Discoveries* show on TV. Subsequently at art school, Clive gravitated simultaneously towards the Soho coffee bars and the weekly meetings of something truly bizarre: 'They used to be called BMG bands,' he says, 'banjo, mandolin and guitar players who would play in something like an orchestra. They introduced me to Alfred Lloyd, a Welshman, who was the best teacher of his day. He'd more or less retired from playing, but anyway I got an introduction and had these banjo lessons – all old Victorian stuff.'

Wizz and Clive did not actually know each other in the fifties. 'I came across him in Paris [in 1960],' says Wizz, 'sleeping under a bush in the Bois de Bologne. He told me always to carry a wet flannel.'[25] They had frequented the same places in Soho and Wizz does recall seeing Clive around, this odd fellow with 'a mysterious aura of aloofness', but Wizz's family background and post-war gloom in general had set him well on the way to developing his own reactionary lifestyle. 'We were paupers but there was this middle-class attitude. I reacted against it. It was really juvenile, but I know why I did it. I was trying to break away from these chains, and it worked.'[26] Wizz, with his outrageously long hair, patched Levis and a battered guitar purportedly held together with bits of leather, turned up in 1960 on an Alan Whicker report for BBC television's *Tonight* on the phenomenon of beatniks in Cornwall. Sitting on a beach in Newquay, quite clearly a candidate for Britain's first hippy, Wizz told the nation that all he wanted to do was play his guitar and travel. And that is exactly what he did.

'Roy Hudd originally put me on a stage, gave me my first build-up: *"Wizz Jones and the Wranglers!"* I was eighteen years old, at this boys' club that the police had started. It was a wonderful gig! That was directly out of the Bentley and Craig thing, because it caused such a terrible stir in Croydon: "What are we going to do with kids like this?" '[27] East Croydon, his local station, was on the London to Brighton line, convenient for skipping off on a rave to the south coast. There were several theatres, music halls and cinemas in the town. One cinema, the Davis, was reckoned the biggest in Europe at the time and was on the touring circuit for top-drawer pop artists. As a teenager Wizz was able to see Bill Haley and Buddy Holly in the flesh, although whatever magical sheen the first names of rock'n'roll had it didn't translate a few stops up the line to Tommy Steele and the 2 i's contingent: 'We were pretty disdainful about all that,' said Wizz. 'We didn't mix with them – we were alternative!'[28]

It had all started for Wizz in the days before even skiffle: 'All us kids used to hang around on the jazz scene, but we didn't really understand jazz, it was just fashionable. And then when skiffle came along that was easier to understand, and we discovered the blues through that.' As early as 1955 Cyril Davies had been running the London Skiffle Centre upstairs at the Roundhouse, a pub on the corner of Soho's Wardour and Brewer Streets. Born in Wales in 1932, brought up in Buckinghamshire and by this point running his own panel-beating yard in South Harrow, Davies had a ferocious reputation as a man not to cross, a man whom Alexis Korner's biographer Harry Shapiro believes to have been 'caught in a strange fantasy world of violence and paranoia'. But Davies also had a passion for the blues, was courteous to women and good pals with Steve Benbow: 'He was a hard case,' says Benbow, 'always got money out of people who owed him, throwing typewriters out into the street and all that. But he was a nice man, actually. I always found him so anyway. We had great fun together.'

Primarily an accomplished twelve-string acoustic player, though latterly – through turning on to Muddy Waters's Chicago sound – a pioneer of amplified harmonica, Davies made only a few recordings before his untimely death in 1964, and these can only hint at the extent of his influence. But it is as much for the platforms he provided for others as for his own musical work that he remains an icon of British blues and folk. As soon as the craze caught fire, the London Skiffle Centre, running more or less weekly, became a successful enterprise. Then, as Alexis Korner recalled, 'One day Cyril said to me, "I'm fed up with all this skiffle rubbish, I want to open a blues club, will you run it with me?" I said yes. One week we shut down with a full house – the next we opened the Barrelhouse Blues club and three people turned up.'[29]

The chronology may be a little squeezed for effect (the new club took several weeks to open) but the end result rings true enough. And very probably all three punters that night went away with a truckload of inspiration and returned at some point as performers themselves. 'Alexis was a great opportunist,' says Chris Barber. 'I was at school with Alexis, knew him a long time. He sometimes did certain things which were ethically, business-wise, a bit questionable in order to further his objective. His objective was stated to be the furtherance of the blues but that was never going to happen without the furtherance of Alexis Korner as well. Which is fair enough. Without enlightened self-interest we wouldn't have millions of jobs in the car industry because Henry Ford wouldn't have bothered.'

The Blues & Barrelhouse club, convened in a long room holding just over a hundred people, would run on into 1961 and towards the end would play host to the earliest stirrings of Davies and Korner's seminal electric band Blues Incorporated. Noise-wise, the landlord of the Roundhouse was having none of it and pulled the plug. By January 1962, Chris Barber was assisting Cyril and Alexis in an electric R&B interval set during his own band's weekly residency at the Marquee club, at this time located in the basement of the Academy Cinema in Oxford Street. Two months later Cyril and Alexis had grasped the nettle and taken a risk on starting their own club in Ealing in West London. It was Britain's first bona fide R&B venue, and a story in itself. But the importance of the Blues & Barrelhouse club had been the breadth of its musical policy. Advertised as a 'folksong' club, and featuring regular spots from the likes of Alex Campbell – a melancholic, hard-travelling Glaswegian and almost certainly Britain's first folk-singing troubadour of modern times – it ran in parallel with the decidedly stricter regime operated by Ewan MacColl at his own club, the Ballads & Blues. Some of the impressionable youngsters, eager to grasp whatever musical exotica was available, went to Davies and Korner's club at the Roundhouse, while others kept themselves abreast of the pub-crawling movements of MacColl's venture. Some, like Wizz Jones, managed both.

'I was taken to Alexis' club by a friend,' he says. 'I didn't play guitar then but we just walked through the door and there was Big Bill Broonzy. And the following week I saw Jack Elliott and Derroll Adams, then Muddy Waters and Otis Span. I used to go there every week. Cyril Davies would be playing twelve-string guitar, Alexis would be sitting on a stool playing the mandolin – and he introduced me to the music, really, along with Ewan MacColl. Ewan was very heavy about the tradition. I admired him, I thought he was a brilliantly talented guy, but he couldn't resist being phoney at times. I heard him on the radio years later saying, "Oh, what was that song I wrote? Oh yes, 'Dirty Old Town' . . ." I had to laugh! The guy was a genius, but he couldn't resist putting on that show.'

'The artist,' wrote Ewan MacColl in one of his many published polemics on folksong, 'is concerned with constantly extending his own awareness of reality and communicating his vision to those around him.'[30] Of all the architects, builders and foremen of the British folk revival, the figure of MacColl looms largest. 'I knew his singing and met him a few times,' says Chris Barber, 'but I never knew what his vision was.' MacColl's contribution is still difficult to analyse. He imposed strict rules in his clubs but clearly bent them for his own performances; he championed the tradition with an iron grip but wrote some extraordinarily beautiful and enduring pop songs; and he had an opinion on everything and regularly gave the press controversy on a plate. He also knew exactly what he was doing. From the early days of the folk revival right through to the late sixties, when his views had little relevance to the Soho scene that Bert Jansch represented but still held currency in the regions through the sheer stature of his reputation, it was impossible to ignore Ewan MacColl and always compelling to hear what he had to say.

'He made himself visible,' says Martin Carthy. 'His perception was that if the movement was to get off the ground, somebody had to stand up and be a target. He made himself the target and people discussed it – people got furious with him because he insisted in his club if you were English you sang English songs, if you were Scottish it was Scottish songs. Ewan had absolutely nothing against having musicians from other cultures. All he said was, "This is my club. In my club you will play by my rules. I don't want to hear you sing an American song when there are a load of Americans sitting over there who could do it better. If you want to sing an American song, go and start your own club." His influence was both positive and negative. Regarding the presentation of traditional music, there were perhaps a handful of people who were unaffected by Ewan. But he and Bert Lloyd are basically responsible for the way the English revival sounds.'

For the revival to sound like anything at all, it would need to disseminate more than a handful of records. While the buying of unadulterated folk music on record was never a thing of epidemic proportions in Britain, it did become a minority occupation of some widespread virtue at its peak in the 1960s. But during the fifties the industry was so minuscule that MacColl himself made more records for labels in America (Prestige, Tradition and Riverside) than in his home country. And what was his home country? MacColl let it be known during his lifetime that it was Scotland, suggesting that he had been christened Jimmie Miller at Auchterarder in 1915 and later, as a nationalist statement of sorts, adopted the name of an obscure figure from Scottish literary history. It is now believed that he was born and raised in Salford, near Manchester. When he left school at fourteen he went immediately into political theatre, strengthening his resolve to make a difference through the bleak experience of life during the Depression of the 1930s. In 1946, as playwright, actor, director and singer, he co-founded the Theatre Workshop company at Kendal with Joan Littlewood, who became his first wife. For eight arduous years Theatre Workshop, most of that time without a base, pursued a vision of 'revolutionary theatre', offering Marxist messages on bare stages to the working-class masses in the nether-world beyond London. It was during a run of one of his plays as a peripheral event to the Edinburgh Festival in 1948 that MacColl met Irish songwriter, wit and raconteur Dominic Behan. Brother of the more celebrated Brendan, Dominic had been invited up by folklorist Hamish Henderson.[31] Along with Ewan, Hamish and Dominic, the great 'source singers' Jeannie Robertson and Jimmy MacBeath were there and a singing session ensued. Some time later Behan was invited to a musical evening in London:

'The evening,' wrote Behan, 'consisted of Ewan MacColl singing some of the songs he had published and I capped it for him by tapping him for a "dollar" – maybe that was the first money I had ever gotten for singing a folk song and, in the tradition of the song, was the payment for begging. Not long after this Ewan got a loan off the Theatre Royal, Stratford-atte-Bow, from Joan Littlewood, and proceeded to hold folk evenings there on each Sabbath. He invited, among others, me and Rory McEwan and a chap from Botany Bay called Bert Lloyd who had possibly the worst voice and the most inane repertoire that all but gave reassurance to the public that transportation had its good points too. We left the Theatre Royal to try our hand in London and took up residence at the Princess Louise pub of High Holborn where we proceeded to entertain the masses and, by God, do I mean masses.'[32]

Inspired in 1950 by an encounter with Alan Lomax, the American folklorist whose father had discovered Leadbelly, MacColl had determined to devote his considerable energies to exploring and reviving the indigenous folk music of the British Isles, with a notion to mustering its venerable authenticity to the furtherance of his socialist views. Theatre Workshop's entire existence had been fraught with crises and in 1954, when the company made Stratford in East London its base, MacColl's interest in the medium waned. Songs that Ewan had composed – in his head rather than on paper – had always been a strong part of Theatre Workshop's productions, but were ephemeral in nature. 'Dirty Old Town', inspired by his upbringing and originally a set-change interlude in his 1950 play *Landscape With Chimneys*, was the unique survivor from those days. Now there was a new cause with songs at its very heart – old songs, new songs and a great hope beyond hope 'to arrest the plasticisation of the popular culture'.

Over the next few years MacColl gathered around him like-minded or suitably impressionable individuals including Bert Lloyd and Dominic Behan; American banjo/guitarist Peggy Seeger; Geordie singer Isla Cameron; Scottish traditional singers Isobel Sutherland and Rory McEwan; Sussex traditional singer Shirley Collins, who would also travel with Lomax in America; Londoners Sandra Kerr and John Faulkner (subsequently renowned among the cognoscenti as Madeleine the Rag Doll and Gabriel the Toad in *Bagpuss*); Liverpool songwriter, humorist and mathematician Stan Kelly; organiser of the ensuing Ballads & Blues club Malcolm Nixon; budding journalists Karl Dallas and Eric Winter, and others whose names concern us less. They were mostly, if not entirely, members of the Communist Party and they were not afraid to say so. What these people generally were afraid to say was anything in contradiction of MacColl.

'He was a very moody man,' says Steve Benbow. 'One minute he was fine, the next he was very bad-tempered.' While Steve had accompanied MacColl on a couple of records, his easy-going pragmatism in music and political soft-focus were hardly conducive to membership of MacColl's inner circle. In any case, Steve was a stopgap for MacColl until such times as Peggy Seeger – whom MacColl had met early in 1956 and fallen deeply in love with – could surmount the problem of acquiring a UK work permit. By 1959 a solution had been realised with daring ingenuity and Ewan and Peggy would become partners in both music and life. By that stage Eric Winter and Karl Dallas, both day-job reporters, were contributing occasional items on folk music to the most substantial music paper of the day, the *Melody Maker*.

Winter became the initial champion of the folk revival with what was by the turn of the sixties a more or less weekly column in that publication. He was also the editor of *Sing*.[33] But by the time Bert Jansch had established himself in London, during 1965, Dallas was the *Melody Maker*'s chief chronicler of the genre. He would remain for many years the most vigorous, influential and informed folk music journalist in Britain.[34] As with MacColl, the mantle of a big fish in a small pool meant Dallas and his published views, throughout the sixties and beyond, were a regular source of debate and controversy amongst the growing numbers of those who cared. Many musicians suspected his very name to be an affectation, and those who felt in some way ignored, misrepresented or badly reviewed would refer to him derisively as 'Fred Dallas'. In fact, both names were genuine and the man's left-wing credentials consequently impeccable.

'I was named Karl Frederick Dallas, after Karl Marx and Friederich Engels,' he explains, once and for all, 'and was enrolled in the Independent Labour Party on the day I was born. I was always meant to be called Karl. My mother left my father, who was a wandering political agitator, because of his drinking and went back to her mother, who said she wouldn't have a child with a German name about the house, so I became Fred for the next twenty-five years or so. When I began in journalism, I was already known in political and musical circles as Fred Dallas, and to try to keep the two worlds separate I worked under the name Karl as a reporter. However, I first met Ewan at a social at my branch of the National Union of Journalists, so when he recorded my "Derek Bentley" song [on *Chorus From The Gallows*, 1960] he credited it to "Karl" since that's how I was introduced to him.'

Dallas eventually tired of the confusion and became simply Karl, 'which brought me to the attention of a witch-hunting MP who wrote about me in the *Daily Telegraph* and I got fired from my day job'. The loss to mainstream reportage was, in retrospect, to the gain of folk music. Initially joining Billy Smart's Circus as advance man, in which position he toured Britain – seeking out its hotbeds of folk music and reporting back to the *MM* along the way. Dallas later secured and expanded his niche at the paper. The growing quantity of his input, from odd reviews and a weekly column tucked away in a corner to more substantial features, would reflect the growth of the folk boom itself.

The origins of the Ballads & Blues club were in a BBC radio series of the same name. One of numerous commissions offered to MacColl in the wake of the modest international success of his play *Uranium 235*, the series consisted of six half-hour programmes. Each dealt with a different theme such as war and peace, love, and the sea. In that respect alone, the *Ballads & Blues* series was a forerunner to MacColl's more celebrated and ground-breaking *Radio Ballads* series, which began in 1958 with the broadcast of *The Ballad Of John Axon*, using the recent heroic death of a railwayman to explore the life and heritage of the British railway system and its workers. A further seven hour-long programmes on a given theme were commissioned.

By including the reminiscences, hopes and fears of real people expressed in real regional accents, alongside specially composed songs with often unusual and exciting accompaniments, the *Radio Ballads* not only became corner-stones of the folk revival in Britain but revolutionised the whole concept of radio documentaries.[35]

Ewan had already done a fair amount of work for the various strands of the BBC as actor, singer and apologist for experimental theatre. But in 1954 something as daring as the *Radio Ballads* would have been unimaginable. It was enough to be gathering in a BBC studio with a group of like-minded souls, choosing a theme and simply singing 'ballads and blues' on that theme to whoever was out there listening: 'Each of the [*Ballads & Blues*] pro-grammes featured seven or eight British and American songs about their subjects,' wrote MacColl, 'sung by American singers Big Bill Broonzy, Jean Ritchie, Ma Rainey and Alan Lomax. Bert Lloyd, Isla Cameron and Ewan MacColl sang the British songs. Humphrey Lyttleton's band were there to provide instrumental colour. The main objective of the series was to demonstrate that Britain possessed a body of songs that were just as vigorous, as tough and as down-to-earth as anything that could be found in the United States.'

The ethos of the later Ballads & Blues club would be similar. MacColl stated many years later that the club began in 1954. Certainly, it was inspired directly by the radio series and by the success of a trio of musical benefits at Stratford for the perennially penurious Theatre Workshop.[36] By 1957 the name was appearing in adverts tucked away in the *Melody Maker*'s jazz listings, with the club firmly established as a regular entity at the Princess Louise pub in High Holborn. It had the sheen, even then, of a forum for folksong as a puritanically intellectual activity. MacColl himself despised accusations – which dogged him long after he had severed his ties, acrimoniously, with the Ballads & Blues – that he was catering for middle-class leftist intellectuals. The plain fact that he had, by 1964, formalised the loose coterie of his acolytes under an almost self-evidently notorious banner as the 'Critics Group', with a mission to analyse the content and presentation of traditional song, did not seem in his view to constitute evidence for the prosecution. Taunting his detractors with vitriol about 'the intellectual brick-layers and existentialist Irish navvies' who were to be found when his clubs were in session, and accusing the weak-willed of shying away in fear from the idea of 'a popular movement in music based on something other than mere entertainment', MacColl nevertheless ensured that his published tirades were not so dogmatic as to pin him inextricably against a wall of expectations concerning the imminent rise of a genuinely populist folk movement without some kind of get-out clause: "Can it compare in numbers with the twist or rock public?' asks the critic with a superior smile. But can Shakespeare or Beethoven or Brecht compete with the bingo emporiums? And does the fact that they cannot compete make their work invalid?'[37] And so he went on.

Nobody did more for the cause of the folk song than MacColl, and even years later, out in the regions where folk clubs were flourishing by the late sixties, his influence could be felt and his every murmuring was like something writ large upon a tablet of stone. By that stage MacColl was firmly ensconced in London at the helm of his even more rigorous post-Ballads & Blues vehicle the Singers Club, while Christy Moore, a young bank clerk from Ireland, was carving out a niche for himself on the thriving club scene around Manchester: 'He had a huge reputation in those days,' says Moore, 'because he was the godfather of the whole scene really. There were a few other people – Bert Lloyd, a lovely man, and Dominic Behan – who would have been mentioned not quite in the same breath but perhaps in the same sentence! But by then there was an aspect to the man, a lot of which was based on rumour. You'd have all these stories emanating from London of "MacColl said this, and MacColl did that," and so on. It wasn't really my experience of the man but then again, had I gone to the Singers Club and done the kind of set that I did on a Saturday night I'd probably have got fucked out of the place!'[38]

MacColl was never one to shirk from confrontation or compromise his principles. At some point in 1959, seemingly over the summer, he had a row with Malcolm Nixon, the organiser (hire of premises, advertising, and so on) of his club. The reasons are unclear. Some believe it was simply that Nixon wanted to commercialise the operation and/or become a professional agent for folk musicians and/or become MacColl's manager – doubtless hoping to capitalise on the pulling power of an individual now established as the leader of a movement. In the event, Nixon took the name Ballads & Blues while MacColl retreated from view for a while and licked his wounds.[39] He soon re-emerged with a new loyal organiser in fellow Communist Bruce Dunnet.

'I'd started going to the theatre round Stratford when the first Ballads & Blues nights were run,' says Dunnet, 'with Ewan MacColl and Tom Driberg, the Labour MP who later became chairman of the Labour Party. He was MC. I was going because it was advertised in the *Daily Worker*. People got fed up going out to Stratford so they moved it to the Princess Louise. Malcolm Nixon, who was also a Communist, had been British First Secretary of the World Federation of Democratic Youth. He left that and became an organiser of folksong clubs with Ewan MacColl, and according to Ewan he fiddled them, stole the name Ballads & Blues and went off with Long John Baldry.'

The six foot seven Baldry, born in London in 1940, had the added distinction of being a young, white blues singer of unassailable stature. In the days when very few blues recordings were available and everyone was doing Broonzy, Baldry sought out and mastered the most obscure and extra-ordinary material – the likes of work songs and field-hollers recorded at Parchman Farm prison by Alan Lomax and available then on album as *Murderers' Home*. He performed with breathtaking authenticity and tanta-lised audiences with a melange of natural charisma and whimsical affectation. 'He'd come down to the Gyre & Gimble,' says Wizz Jones, 'where Davy Graham would be playing through the night, being totally ignored by more or less all the punters, and start singing in a really loud voice. He'd sing half a song and stop – "Oh, to hell with it," he'd say – and then start into something else. It was years before I saw him finish a complete song onstage.' Skiffle, jazz, folk or blues: if there was a platform to perform on in London during the late fifties and early sixties Baldry was on it. He was also, like Malcolm Nixon, a homosexual, and would become more flamboyantly so as the sixties progressed.

By September 1959, after the club's usual summer break, Malcolm Nixon had established his breakaway Ballads & Blues at 2 Soho Square, head-quarters of the cine technicians' union, the ACTT. Seemingly, the club had already moved to these premises prior to the split. Among its regulars was Andy Irvine, subsequently a major figure in the reawakening of Irish music, then just another shy young man with a Woody Guthrie fixation.

Irvine was born to Irish parents in 1942 in Finchley in North London. His mother was a musical comedy actress and his older sister an actress too. Like Bert Jansch, Andy Irvine was something of a loner in his youth and aspects of his enlightenment are similarly comparable: 'I was brought up with a wind-up gramophone and a bunch of scratched 78s. I sat behind the sofa, where the machine was, all my childhood and listened to these songs [from the 1930s] – they were great songs. I was vaguely brought up as an only child, kind of secretive. But, in retrospect, when I began to grow up, or pretend to grow up, I was kind of searching for music that I liked. Then rock'n'roll came in about 1955 or '56 and my friends of the time thought that was great – Bill Haley 78s – but I wasn't into it. Then one day I heard *Backstairs Session*, which was an EP of Lonnie Donegan singing "Midnight Special", with Dickie Bishop and Chris Barber on bass, and I thought *that's* where it's at!'[40]

Irvine was particularly impressed with Dick 'Cisco' Bishop, largely on account of his nickname ('he made an EP himself, which sold about eight copies, one of which was to me'), and consequently purchased a Melodisc LP, the only one available in Britain at the time, of tracks by Woody Guthrie and Cisco Houston. As Irvine puts it, the record blew his mind, he began to learn the songs 'with all the mistakes carefully copied', and wrote letters to get to the source of this wonder. Remarkably – with postal addressing of the 'Woody Guthrie, America' variety – contact was eventually made. In an age when information and recordings to do with such matters were like gold-dust in Britain, an interest in Guthrie meant an equal fascination with his acolytes, one of whom, 'Rambling' Jack Elliott, was living in London at the time. The year was 1959, Malcolm Nixon had his new, improved Ballads & Blues up and running and one night the guest was Jack Elliott. Andy went to the club and followed Jack home on the tube to where he was staying. 'The next day I made up a tape of Woody Guthrie recordings I thought he mightn't have heard, as by that time I had quite a collection, and put the tape through his door. He rang me up and we became firm friends.'[41]

Andy was also fascinated with the Ballads & Blues, which he had been attending since at least May that year, a few months prior to the split. He was aware of the Soho scene, but this was something on a higher level. Besides, he had a crush on Peggy Seeger: 'I can see Ewan MacColl now,' he says. 'He'd get a couple of bottles of brown ale brought in from the nearest pub and he'd sit on a chair backwards – he was quite frightening – and sing these old ballads. I didn't like it much at the time but then Peggy would play something nice on the banjo and I'd like that, and I always enjoyed Stan Kelly's humour. In fact, when Ewan wasn't there it was like the mice playing when the cat's away. Everyone was a lot looser, Stan would be great fun – people would shout up witty remarks and Stan would answer them back. You wouldn't dare do that when Ewan was there! But, for good or ill, a lot of people followed him. I found him to be very intolerant. He certainly never spoke to me and I was happy enough of it.'[42]

It was not until he moved to Ireland in 1962 that Andy found other musicians of his own age with whom he could feel comfortable both musically and socially. There was, he believes, 'a middle-class aspect' to the early years of the folk revival. Elaborate parties in Hampstead are recalled, revolving around people on the wealthier fringes of the movement like cabaret singer Noel Harrison, the landed gentry Rory and Alex McEwan and Cy Grant, a lawyer and regular songster on the popular TV satire show *That Was The Week That Was*. Malcolm Nixon's Ballads & Blues set, Jack Elliott and all manner of American émigrés would also be on the guest lists. Even MacColl was not unknown to turn up at such frivolous events and sing something abjectly untraditional.[43] He made the rules. 'I was somewhat overwhelmed at the time,' says Irvine, 'because here were all these famous people and they were grown up and I was seventeen or eighteen and didn't feel grown up. I'd drink too much and collapse in a puddle.'

Nevertheless, he was certainly impressed with some of these people in performance at the Ballads & Blues – Long John Baldry, Rory McEwan and Robin Hall & Jimmie Macgregor. Macgregor had a Gibson mandolin, 'so he was God!' Youthfully impressionable as he may have been, Andy was also canny enough to realise there was something distinctly absurd about MacColl's preoccupation with rule-making: "I remember him introducing somebody who had an American accent and saying, 'Don't be fooled by this man's accent, he's actually from Portsmouth". And it was definitely a case of justifying this man coming along to sing songs from Portsmouth. People rarely got a chance to just get up and do a turn in those days but in any case you wouldn't have dreamed of getting up and doing anything other than songs from your own place of origin, although I do remember Long John Baldry being allowed to do one or two numbers as a fill-in. I don't see how Ewan could have justified that – singing the blues and coming from Kent or wherever it was!"[44]

Ewan was no longer master of the club he had created, the foundation of the whole British folk club explosion in the following decade. But he was only biding his time until, in June 1961, he could announce with war-mongering zeal his new command centre for the fight against mediocrity and commercialism: the Singers Club. Other people were getting on with the business of playing music, entertaining people and earning a few bob. 'With the folk movement,' says Chris Barber, 'and this applies to a certain part of the jazz movement, there were a lot of peculiarly narrow-minded people going around concerned with things that are absurd to have narrow minds about. With all these debates – what's cool, what's not, how you should do this or that, what's PC – the polarity of it overtook the opinions of the serious judges. The trouble was, as Big Bill always said, "All these things are folksongs. I never heard a horse sing one yet".'

It was not unusual for Big Bill Broonzy or any other visiting blues artist to play at the Ballads & Blues club when he was in town – there were so few places to play, and blues and folksong were still bound loosely together. 'In those days in the folk scene any American was God,' says Steve Benbow. 'Except Burl Ives – and he was the best of the lot! I remember some sort of get-together at Topic Records' place at 17 Bishops Bridge Road. Everyone made a record for Topic in those days and I guess it was a party for all their artists. Alex [Korner] was there, I think Cyril was there. But Ewan wasn't there. I met Brownie McGhee there, and played with him, but I've never forgotten old Sonny Terry said to me, "Could you show me where the toilet is?" So I led him across this room, round various tables and chairs, up some stairs and he said, "Right, it's okay baby, you can go now." He came back, followed exactly the same route, didn't bump into anything, got his harp out and blew. Incredible!'

With bona fide blues legends now stopping in town at regular intervals the young Wizz Jones had been presented with a golden opportunity. It was 1957, not long after he had discovered the Blues & Barrelhouse club, and he had been going across London with a borrowed machine recording two visiting American troubadours in the Woody Guthrie mould, Andy Irvine's new pal Jack Elliott and banjo player Derroll Adams: 'I met Ewan MacColl on the train one day and he said, "Come along to my house and record Big Bill Broonzy, he's staying with me." This was before I even played the guitar. And I passed up on that opportunity.'

Around the same time that Wizz was giving himself something to regret Martin Carthy, another legend-in-waiting, had discovered a coffee bar in Hampstead called the Loft: 'I'd gone down there having heard of this great Scottish singer, Robin Hall, who used to sing a song called "Down In The Mines". It was a new song to me. He was the big hero then for all of us. And I thought, "This is really fantastic, much better than skiffle." We worked the same coffee bars after that but not together – he was the idol.'[45] Hall, born in Edinburgh in 1937 and just arrived in London, was an extraordinary singer with a clear, soaring voice and flamboyant personality. At college in Glasgow he had become familiar with a local musician, Jimmie Macgregor, who was also now trying his luck on the London scene – initially as a member of the City Ramblers, subsequently of Steve Benbow's Folk Four: 'Robin would come to art school dances in Glasgow,' says Macgregor, 'and would always get up and sing. He had this kind of idiosyncratic attitude to the blues – he used to do thirteen-bar blues and seventeen-and-a-quarter-bar blues. Which was very interesting.'[46] No doubt. But fate had perhaps already decreed that there would only be room for one Scot in that generation with that level of idiosyncrasy – Bert Jansch. Instead, capturing the hearts of the mainstream and never venturing far off the beaten track in guitarish tom-foolery, Robin Hall & Jimmie Macgregor would become the British folk movement's first TV stars.

Rory and Alex McEwan had been the first to perform occasional folky spots on the BBC's popular magazine programme *Tonight*, closely followed by Cy Grant and Noel Harrison. But it was the newly constituted duo of Robin Hall & Jimmie Macgregor who truly nailed the gig and made it a platform to launch a very successful television-based career. Individually, Hall and Macgregor had gone to the 1959 International Youth Festival in Vienna. They ended up onstage together and found an unlikely and influential fan in the international bass-baritone opera singer and cultural figurehead of the American left, Paul Robeson: 'He was amazingly encouraging to us,' says Macgregor. 'He was particularly taken with what he saw as our promotion of songs from our own country. We were actually just enjoying ourselves. But I thought at the time if a man of that calibre gives you a nod of approval, maybe you should take yourself a wee bit more seriously. So when we came back to London we started to work on a repertoire and out of the blue we were asked to go on the *Tonight* programme.'

The offer was not entirely unsolicited. Bruce Dunnet, an Edinburgh Scot himself, had rung the producer in January 1960 and asked what they had planned for their Burns' Night edition on the 25th. Dunnet's ruse to get his protégés on was successful. Jimmy and his wife Shirley were members of Steve Benbow's Folk Four at the time. Steve had already appeared at least once on TV with a traditional song called 'Football Crazy' which he had learnt, in its Irish variant, from Ewan MacColl. MacColl had himself learnt it from the celebrated Irish broadcaster and uilleann piper Seamus Ennis. It subsequently transpired, as with all these things when an element of success is involved, that the song was not wholly traditional. But it was of no real consequence. Neither was the mildly out-of-joint nature of Benbow's nose. It had, after all, been 'his' big number. Robin & Jimmie performed a rousing version of the song in Scots dialect as their three-minute spot on *Tonight* and their careers were made. They released it as a single in August for the specialist label Collector and, presumably in response to demand, it swiftly reappeared with a picture sleeve on the more widely available Decca. They became regulars on *Tonight* and by 1964 were hosting *The White Heather Club*, a cheesy but popular Scottish television variety programme, and touring internationally on the back of it. 'I suppose we were quite snooty about it,' says Martin Carthy, 'but you got gigs where you could in those days. They did make an album called *Scottish Choice*, though, [in 1961] and it was something of a landmark because it was the first time one of the major labels had let people sing the songs they did the way they did without messing them about.'

Carthy himself was a man who could appreciate both the pitch-perfect quality of Robin Hall's singing and the raw excitement of live music in coffee bars. Born in Hatfield in 1940, he was a well-trained chorister and was also, for reasons that have never been made clear, learning the trombone. 'I could take a piece of Orlando Gibbons or a madrigal and sight-read it,' he once recalled. 'If you'd have put a folk tune in front of me I couldn't have sight-read it – my sight-reading wasn't terribly good. But because I knew how Orlando Gibbons worked I could guess the intervals.'[47] The life-defining moment for Carthy was hearing source singer Sam Larner at the Ballads & Blues and being bewildered, entranced and overwhelmed by music he could not immediately understand on a technical level but was inexorably drawn to. But that was a little down the line. In 1956 his choirboy's voice had broken and he had just heard Lonnie Donegan. A guitar that his father owned was about to come in handy. The young trombonist was likewise not unaffected by Bill Haley's 'Rock Around The Clock' and, as was everyone, by the outburst of colour that seemed to arrive overnight with Elvis Presley. 'Life is a lot more complicated now than it was then,' says Carthy. 'If you didn't wear grey trousers you wore brown or black trousers. And if you didn't have a pair of black shoes then you had brown shoes. When the song "Blue Suede Shoes" came out I actually didn't believe there was such a thing as blue suede shoes. I thought it was a joke – because it was all monochrome then.'[48]

Starting off with a skiffle-inspired repertoire, the Loft was the first coffee bar Carthy sang in, before moving on to Soho. It was 1957, he was seventeen, and things were starting to fall apart for him at school: 'I was taking my A-levels a year early and totally blew it out. I managed to leave before I was expelled, just for being a slob. I couldn't be bothered.'[49] Down at the Gyre & Gimble Martin found a like-minded soul. It was a scruffy-looking fellow called Jones: Wizz Jones. And his repertoire was as gloriously eclectic then as it is today: 'He wasn't playing skiffle then,' says Carthy, 'he was playing a real mixture of stuff. The first song I heard him sing was 'The Mole Catcher'. He could switch from that to Big Bill Broonzy at the drop of a hat – and did.'

So where did people get their songs – their English songs – from in those days? 'The Mole Catcher' was a music-hall number that had the intrigue and aura of a genuine traditional song. But Carthy was as yet more consumed with the music of Broonzy and Elizabeth Cotten, wronged author of Chas McDevitt's 'Freight Train' hit. They were passions that would still be declared forty years later in his own press material. The certified classic of the early Carthy repertoire, when it had found its feet by the turn of the sixties, was 'Scarborough Fair'. It would emanate, like the repertoires of many, from Ewan MacColl and Peggy Seeger. 'You got songs from wherever the hell you could,' says Carthy. 'I don't know where we got songs from. We just picked them up from each other I guess, but there was a feeling of pride in finding something nobody else had.' Publication of *The Penguin Book Of English Folksongs*, destined to be a seminal sourcebook for a generation of young singers, was just around the corner. Edited by Bert Lloyd and the composer Ralph Vaughan Williams, it was available by February 1961.

Some may be less certain of this but in the meantime, to Carthy's recollection, MacColl himself would delight in going down to the coffee bars of Soho in the company of Bert Lloyd, tapping into the energy of the patently frivolous skiffle craze and thrusting their performances of English traditional songs at the innocent punters. As Carthy concedes, 'Ewan always wanted to be in control of any situation he was in, and usually was,' so one can only speculate that his very presence, demeanour, age and authority were sufficient in commanding attention from an ill-educated crowd of musical thrill-seekers. But one situation the godfather of the folk revival could not and would not tolerate was to share a platform with a man called Alex Campbell – a denim-clad wanderer from Glasgow who was not only taking his degree in applied folk music entirely contrary to MacColl's syllabus but who was also, and not without intrigue, the recently-wed husband of Peggy Seeger.

There was a drama being played out there that few were aware of at the time, but of which many would speak in hushed tones over the years to come. For the moment, though, a more public drama was to be Martin Carthy's immediate way forward. With terrific luck he walked straight from school into a job as a prompter at the Regent's Park Open Air Theatre, and subsequently toured with the company – including a most illuminating trip to Glasgow – as assistant stage manager and cameo player in a production of *The Merry Widow*. For Carthy, the times were as exciting as they were for all the other young adventurers in music around London – Wizz Jones, Clive Palmer, Andy Irvine and many more who had effectively dropped out of conventional society to try their hand on the ethnic fringes of popular music. 'You're eighteen, nineteen, twenty – all balls and no forehead,' says Carthy, 'and you just go at it. As far as you're concerned it's all happening because it's all happening around you.' They had no idea at the time, but exactly the same thing was going on in Glasgow and Edinburgh.

CHAPTER THREE

Edinburgh: The First Days

Directly opposite St Giles' Cathedral at 369 High Street, it was no coincidence that the Howff was where it was. In a cobblestoned thoroughfare full of ale houses and vendors of tartan-tinned shortbread, a street winding right the way up to Edinburgh Castle – ancient seat of Scottish government and latterday magnet for tourism – and a street beating annually at August as the heart of the Edinburgh Festival, there would always be an opportunity for somebody staying open later than anywhere else. And increasingly, as the fifties turned into the sixties, there was a golden opportunity for somebody offering something with a dash of colour about it for a post-war generation that was trying its best to avoid the drab indignity of national service. Roy Guest, an individual almost as colourful as his own press material of the period would have had you believe, was about to become that somebody.

Born at Izmir in Turkey around 1934/35 and brought up in Wales, Roy was brilliant at the business of making things happen. One cannot say with assurance that Roy Guest's prime motivation was financial – there have always been easier ways to make money than folk music – but assessing the man who more than anyone else broke the ground for folk music as a viable, sizeable concert hall commodity during the sixties, the lure of lucre was not the least part of the equation. On the other side of the coin, in merging the polished public persona of his press appearances and his unquestionably self-written album notes of the period – a remarkable catalogue of self-aggrandisement in the guise of modesty – with his achievements and the pithier recollections of those around him, a near-reckless, steam-rolling bravado appears.

Roy had trained as an actor, teacher and film editor before finding his niche, and folk music was perhaps no more than a vehicle for his energies. Later career flirtations saw him promoting cabaret in New York, late sixties pop for Brian Epstein's NEMS organisation and chamber music as something akin to 'the new rock'n'roll' in the early seventies. In 1975 somebody booked the Royal Albert Hall for 31 December 1999, the eve of the millennium. Two years short of that date, Roy's will had revealed just who that giant of foresight had been. 'He was the most extraordinary organiser the folk scene has ever known,' says Martin Carthy. 'He worked very, very hard but he also had a magic touch – he had a genius for it. To give an example, he was out of it for fifteen years and was asked to organise a folk festival at the Fairfield Halls in Croydon – *the* impossible hall to fill. And he filled it. He broke the record. He walked back in, organised this folk festival and then disappeared again. And it was brilliant. Brilliant! Occasionally you got the feeling he was financially a little naughty, but one way or another he fired up all the people who were around him – either he'd anger them or he'd inspire them. As a singer he was crap.'

Roy had been passionate about acting since the age of twelve. Leaving Bedales School at eighteen – and there was always something 'public school' about his persona, on call as a tool of influence whenever necessary – he spent three years in the early fifties at London's Central School of Drama. A further two years were spent in repertory theatre at Ipswich and Bromley. 'The plays were mainly rubbish but I did learn how to run a stage, and I did learn discipline.'[1] Roy moved on to a teaching sojourn at Summerhill, where he first began singing and playing guitar, with the students, before opting, so far as the self-mythologising of his later published recollections can be trusted, to try a round-the-world singing trip. 'He would earn his fare to Canada by singing on the streets of London where he met many buskers and began the nucleus of a collection of songs and humour. He made the crossing to Canada in 1956, landing with a guitar and $5.'[2]

'It was in Montreal that I picked up the local paper and saw that at a meeting at the local Union Hall there would also be folksongs from someone described as P. Seeger. I went along and he absolutely blew my mind.'[3] Roy had heard Seeger previously on record, but at that time and in that culture Seeger's real-life impact would have been considerable. 'I was moved by the songs, the humanitarian message, but most of all by Pete's exhortation to us all to go out and sing: "It's easy – you can do it!" I was sure I could. With a battered guitar I was soon leading groups, rowing the boat ashore. After two months I was singing in public and getting paid for it. And I was artistic – a folksinger – part of the new youth who were going to remove the Establishment for good and all. My falsetto on "Wimoweh" had to be heard to be believed.'[4]

There is irony, of course, in Roy's published recollections of the period but something of the subversive nature of the whole folksong experience – widely pilloried by a scared America as the musical vanguard of Communism at the time – certainly appealed to his psyche. He later revelled in telling a story from this period of a 500-seater concert appearance with Guy Carawan at Seattle University becoming a 15,000+ rally based entirely on hostile pre-publicity. Hearing his records today, one cannot imagine the substance of such an event being anything less than the dampest of squibs. 'I sang bad songs because they had a message I believed in. I sang funny songs because they made people laugh. My hair was long and the image was an easy passport to success, financially and sexually.'[5]

Around 1958 Roy returned to London and wangled a recording deal with Saga, under whose auspices he ran a number of shows at the Festival Hall billed as 'Roy's Guest Night'. His absurd self-description as 'Britain's Burl Ives' reflected his promotional flair, and he inevitably secured exposure on TV and radio. By the time he appeared on the Scottish scene, Roy was able to tell people he had appeared on *Tonight* before Robin Hall & Jimmie Macgregor. The story was probably true and people were naturally impressed. The fact that Roy Guest could establish his reputation with a single nugget of information and an understanding of communication within a given context – a new city, new people, a compact scene – demonstrates a facet of what made him great. Just not as a singer.

Back in London, Roy became increasingly aware of the folksong revival: 'I didn't like it,' he declared. 'Hostile men with nasty stares and intense girls who didn't notice me. Middle-aged people too and people who asked where I got that version of that song. I began to feel insecure.'[6] The reference was thinly veiled. Roy's nemesis was one person, and one person who could certainly know a phoney when he saw one: Ewan MacColl. One night, seemingly in 1958, Sam Larner, one of the greatest 'source singers' of the era, appeared once and once only at the court of the folk revival. It was an evening that had a profound effect upon Martin Carthy and doubtless upon the many others who were there. And somehow Roy Guest, one of the most breathtakingly banal singers of any era, had talked himself on to the bill.

Sam Larner was an ex-herring fisherman from Norfolk who had first sailed in the 1890s and is remembered now as the star singer and story-teller of MacColl's third and most celebrated Radio Ballad, *Singing The Fishing*. 'What a wonderful person he was!' wrote Ewan many years after the event. 'Short, compact, grizzled, wall-eyed and slightly deaf, but still full of the wonder of life. His one good eye still sparkled at the sight of a pretty girl. We brought him to London to sing at the Ballads & Blues, and for several hours he sat and sang and talked to the several hundred young people, who hung on his every word and gesture as though he had been Ulysses newly returned from Troy to Ithaca.'[7]

And then there was Roy. 'I ought to thank him for dragging me along there,' says Martin Carthy. 'I saw Sam Larner and it changed my life. Ewan gave Roy this glowing introduction and it was clear that Roy had really done a job on him. He started his first song and I watched Ewan's face turn thunderous. He was furious, he knew he'd been had – and I don't think that would have happened too often. But Ewan's response was remarkable. He let Roy sing his allocated amount of songs in the first half and again in the second half, but he made sure people went away thinking only of Sam Larner. I doubt very much if anyone remembered a single song that Roy had performed.'

Credited on its sleeve to Roy Guest & the Tennessee Three – purportedly comprising a rather larger group of people including Robin Hall and Jimmie Macgregor – the Saga release *Cowboy* was, in Roy's subsequent spin, the product of a three-hour drinking session. A record of Wild West favourites, it went on, in the embroidery of Roy's recollection, to sell two and a half million and top the Austrian album charts for months. Implausible as the tale may be, if this material was the kind of hokum Roy was foisting on MacColl it is no wonder he went down like a lead balloon.

Nevertheless, like Steve Benbow, Roy was becoming something of an airwaves regular. Early in 1959, *Saturday Club* producer Jimmy Grant had thrown Steve and Roy together along with a few others – including Jimmie Macgregor and his wife Shirley Bland – as a group, purely for broadcasting, to be known as the Wanderers.[8] 'He wanted a folk group,' says Steve, 'so we were! Roy had declared he was Britain's answer to Burl Ives. He was a very good performer, a terrific showman. But not a very good guitarist.'

In August 1959 Roy was, in his own words, invited to the Edinburgh Festival. If it was becoming clear that he was not himself on any fast track to becoming a spokesman for a generation, he could still create the platforms for those who were. For both folk music and the man, it was a case of the right place and the right time. A cartwheel was rolling down a cobbled street. It could have crashed at the bottom. With a dose of 'enlightened self-interest' that would have made Alexis Korner proud, Roy Guest applied his melange of magic, risk and acumen and began forging by stealth a bandwagon of national proportions.

During the summer of 1959 the occupancy of 369 High Street was in the hands of a Scottish nationalist group called the Sporran Slitters. Their table talk was intriguing: 'They kept on saying that they'd see each other down at the Howff,' said Roy, 'and when I asked them what they meant they said they'd found the word in the poems of Burns, meaning a place of assignation, where rebels, drunkards and all sorts of rogues would meet. When we decided to use the place as a centre for folk music during the Festival I said, "Let's call it The Howff, with capitals." And so we did. It was meant to run for three weeks, but there was such an atmosphere going that it

ran for two years.'[9] Those 'two years' spanned 1959 – 62, peaking during the
Festival of 1961. There were few folk music entrepreneurs around in those
days and none in Edinburgh. Roy had discoverved a place where the
musical grass-roots murmured as vibrantly as London's and where the
position of 'big cheese' was still vacant. He effectively applied for the
job, got it and within two years he had turned a gaggle of disparate talents
into a happening scene and transformed the dank, derelict cubby-hole of
some ludicrous secret society into the talk of the town.

Owen Hand had stumbled across the Howff, just prior to being called up
for national service, in its first few days of being. 'A poet who rented a room
from my dad was a member of the Sporran Slitters,' he says, 'and told me
about the hippies who had rented their meeting rooms for the Festival
period, so I had to go have a look-see. My first impression was that Jill Guest
was gorgeous and I also liked the accessibility of the music. Due to local by-
laws they were not allowed to charge admission and got their money by
having a silver collection. I went along every night. After the Festival they
just kind of stayed on and so we had the makings of a club.'

Owen was perhaps the first of the future Howff regulars to discover the
place. Close behind him was the imposing figure of Len Partridge, the
godfather of Edinburgh folk-blues. Born in Dunkeld, Perthshire in 1938,
Partridge's interest in the guitar had been engaged in the early fifties by an
old lady in a neighbouring village called Meggie Rae, the grandmother of a
friend, who happened to play a number of instruments. 'She played none of
them very well,' says Len, 'but she had a remarkable ability to create
enthusiasm in others. I played, or tried to play, in isolation for a long time
because I didn't know anybody else who played guitar apart from this old
lady. Somewhere along the line I became aware of Huddie Ledbetter and
couldn't believe the sound he made, and of course discovered it was a thing
called a twelve-string guitar. One night, 1956 or '57 I'd imagine, I heard this
same sound emanating from the television and it was Rory McEwan, on the
Tonight programme.' Len wrote to Rory and received an immediate reply
saying 'Christ, amazing, you know Leadbelly . . .' and a distant friendship
began. 'He was an incredible help – all sorts of things I couldn't figure out at
all he knew, because he'd spent time in the States and was a fairly intuitive
musician anyway. He'd been to see Martha Leadbetter in the days when she
still had Leadbelly's guitar and he'd met and played with a lot of people.
Basically, he had the access and we didn't.'

Before even skiffle had made its presence felt, Rory McEwan would be
sending back to his pen pal Len reels of tape and discs of all sorts of
fascinating discoveries from his regular travels in America. Len was also put
on the trail of acquiring a twelve-string of his own. He had already tried

shopping for one in Edinburgh but received only blank expressions. McEwan himself had found his in a pawn shop in Galveston, Texas for $12. But a friend of his, Cyril Davies no less, was having one made by one Emile Grimshaw of Piccadilly, in London. 'Cyril wasn't at all bothered if I had one made out of the same design,' says Len. 'I learned quite a lot from Cyril but Rory was the biggest single source because he was totally free with his knowledge – all he needed was someone who was interested.'

By the time Roy arrived on the scene, Len had already made several trips to London, solely in pursuit of music. He had checked out Davy Graham at the Gyre & Gimble, and Cyril and Alexis at the Roundhouse, had bumped into Steve Benbow, and had made enough of an acquaintance with Ewan MacColl to know that it was not one he wished to take further. He had also met 'Rambling' Jack Elliott and his wife Jean and was consequently surprised, driving down Edinburgh's High Street one evening, to see a man with a stetson getting into a car, carrying a guitar case and accompanied by a young woman. 'I thought, "Good God, it's Jack Elliott," ' says Len. 'So we followed the car in an incredibly convoluted journey round Edinburgh finally ending up in a mews where there was nowhere else to go. I got out and walked forward, whereupon the window wound down a fraction and a voice asked plaintively, "Can I help you?" It was Roy. He'd obviously come north on a runner and thought we were whoever it was from London that he was on the run from. He was definitely very frightened. We thought it was hilarious.' The incident was brushed aside and Len, with his obvious interest in music, was invited along to Roy's weekly party on the High Street.

Bert Jansch was no more concerned with the history of the Howff than he would be in the coming years with the provenances of any other folk club. He would turn up and they'd be there. That was all he needed to know. Regarding the Howff, it was the early weeks of 1960 and a couple of people called Archie Fisher and Jill Doyle were offering guitar lessons 'and obviously, at sixteen years old, I fell madly in love with Jill Doyle'.[10] Jill, who had the distinction of being Davy Graham's half-sister, is remembered by her contemporaries more for a certain reputation with men than for any guitar playing of note. She had arrived up from London with Roy, using the name Jill Guest, and people naturally assumed they were married; in those days, living together was a rarity and people in Edinburgh did not ask questions. Bert took lessons from Jill for no more than a month, exhausting her knowledge and thereafter looking to Archie for further enlightenment. Archie consigns the whole business to the realms of myth: 'Bert came along, spent one lesson with Jill and learned all she knew and then spent two lessons with me. The reason it took me two lessons was I took him out and got him drunk during the first one.'[11]

Unfortunately for the story, Bert's first encounter with alcohol was much later – at Deacon Brodie's pub, High Street, aged seventeen and a half. Archie was nevertheless a major formative influence on Bert's playing and Bert has never shied from acknowledging it. Next to Len Partridge, Archie was the best guitarist in town. More specifically, he taught Bert the now commonplace, then revelatory clawhammer technique. These were the dark ages before instructional aids of any kind. You could barely get the records.

Many roads in the early days of the folk revival led back to Ewan MacColl, and so it was for Archie Fisher and his mastery of guitar. When Appalachian banjo/guitarist Ralph Rinzler accompanied MacColl at a show in Glasgow in 1958, it was the first time anyone in Scotland had even seen clawhammer technique: 'I went out on the stair and got taught a few banjo licks,' says Archie, who had developed a parallel interest in the banjo through Pete Seeger, 'and also got taught the guitar technique. Thereafter in Edinburgh they called me "the Clawhammer Jesus" – no one else knew how to do it. The idea was to have a moving, walking bass against a picked melody on the top strings. It sounded like two guitars – the hardest thing to teach. I think Elizabeth Cotten invented it. She played the guitar upside down, left-handed, playing the melody with her thumb and the bass with her fingers – so we were basically playing her style upside down.'[12]

The only two people of roughly Bert's age on the Scottish scene who were even close to making a living at music at that time were Archie Fisher, lean and smouldering, and a fellow of huge girth and jollity called Hamish Imlach whom he had met at secondary school in Glasgow. Archie gave Bert the rudiments of playing, while Hamish lived out the romance of the job: 'He was probably the first real folksinger I ever saw,' said Bert, 'storming away on his guitar. And I used to sit six inches away, watching his every move!'[13]

Born in Calcutta in 1940, Hamish had a colourful background. His paternal grandmother and great-aunt had owned a silver mine in Bolivia at the turn of the century, discreetly employing for some years a couple of characters known to legend as Butch Cassidy and the Sundance Kid – they never did have that shoot-out at the end. His father Herbert had played guitar at ceilidhs – Scottish dances – in the 1930s where he had acquired the name 'Ragtime Cowboy Joe', partly through playing guitar, partly through the family's fund of Bolivian outlaw stories, and all doubtless bolstered by a preference for Brazilian cigarettes containing one hundred per cent marijuana – available quite legally in Britain up to 1934.

Hamish's mother Margaret had a successful hairdressing business in Calcutta which allowed the family to lead a relatively lavish lifestyle. The Second World War was on and her husband, Herbert, having joined the RAF, was in Britain. Too late for the christening, a telegram from Herbert arrived advising Margaret to 'call him anything but Hamish – all the Hamishes I know are drunken wasters'. Perhaps true, perhaps not, but precisely the sort of tale Hamish would delight in telling against himself throughout a folk singing career unashamedly based on funnies first and music second. As a toddler, he had been bounced on Mahatma Gandhi's knee on a railway platform, as a child he had spent blissful weeks in the Himalayas recovering from TB, as a schoolboy he had gone through primary wearing a kilt (not, admittedly, through any preference of his own): rare beginnings for a fat boy who wound up in Glasgow in the fifties.

Hamish's parents divorced during the war and Margaret took her children first to Australia, homeland of her second husband, and then, for medical reasons concerning Hamish's younger brother, to Scotland. It was 1953. They had relatives in Glasgow: 'As the train came in up through the South Side and then the Gorbals I looked out at these blackened sooty buildings,' said Hamish, 'and thought this was war damage. My uncle and his family were living in a big old building on the top of a hillock dignified by the name of Broomhill, in West Glasgow. In the grounds was a small courtyard with stables, and houses which had been for the grooms. It was about to be auctioned off for back taxes. My mother went to the auction and bought it for £750, the price of a modern bungalow at the time. The value was in the land, but the house was a liability, a money-swallower. My mother proceeded to pour thousands into fixing the roof, getting the rooms divided, painting and decorating, furnishing and carpeting, and fitted it out as a boarding house.'[14]

Hamish had been intended for public school but wound up at a local establishment, Hyndland Secondary, where his combination of Palm Beach shirt and fez and a certain admirable though wholly unrequited swagger with the ladies were distinguishing features. 'It was in the playground that I first met Archie Fisher. I went up and asked if he would like to buy a lighter.' By the summer of 1958, Margaret had fallen out with her relations and was in any case spending a lot of time going backwards and forwards to Australia. Hamish, having finished school, was left to his own devices with the rare luxury of a large house and regular income from the rent. A year or two earlier it had been damaged by fire: 'Only half the building was salvaged in some sort of usable state, so rooms could be let out cheaply. I moved down to the little courtyard, to a flat in what had been part of the stables.' Determined to avoid national service as a squaddie, he applied to Sandhurst

Military Academy for officer training but then, halfway there by hitch-hiking, took cold feet: 'My mother wrote a letter saying my stepfather was dying in Australia and I had to be flown to his bedside. I got a nice letter back and was never called up.' Freedom, and a place to enjoy it, were his. 'I was the only one of our age to have a house, so the party was at my place. It lasted nineteen months.'

The 'Broomhill Bums', as they became known, were all keen on folk music and included Archie Fisher and his sister Ray, the eldest siblings of a large family that would later all make their mark on record; Bobby Campbell, a fiddler; and Ian 'Josh' MacRae, soon to become a recording artist of some local celebrity with 'Talking Army Blues' and 'Messin' About On The River'. During 1958 – 59 MacRae was appearing on Scottish TV's *Jigtime* as one of the Reivers, Scotland's answer to the Weavers.[15] Like Lonnie Donegan, he had acquired his professional forename from a musical hero (Josh White) and had attended Glasgow School of Art alongside Jimmie Macgregor. They were the first two students to play guitar at what was soon to be a hotbed of musical activity. Through national service MacRae had got to know Jamie McEwan, elder brother of Rory and Alex, who had once squired Princess Alexandra and who would, in the early days of the Broomhill party, bring along 78s of blues people the others had never heard of. People interested in the blues had a habit of finding each other in those days.

Ailie Munro, in *The Democratic Muse*, her study of the folk revival in Scotland, concludes that there are no reliable estimates for the proliferation of skiffle in Scotland but an accumulation of anecdotal evidence suggests its impact was immense. Even Ewan MacColl was obliged to reflect, with just a hint of exasperation, that 'oddly enough, the skiffle repertoire persisted in Scotland long after it had been abandoned elsewhere'.[16] Certainly, for Hamish and Archie the start of their interest in music was down to the skiffle craze, while the very nature of Glasgow – a major port and population centre – provided the other elements of what one could view in retrospect as a textbook progression through to the blues and, beyond that, to folksong from America and consequently to new forms of accompanying and presenting the indigenous music of Scotland itself:

'A lot of the kids played skiffle at school,' said Hamish. 'There were a lot of Dixieland jazz clubs around and we had very good record stores. I was buying blues records in 1955, before we ever saw any blues players. There were these six 78s on Vogue which had been done in Belgium by Broonzy, but there was very little else available. Then this guy called Cliff Stanton who had a record store started bringing them over from America, but they were very expensive and they'd take months – and he was ordering them and pirating them, using one copy to cut a metal master plate. It started with the well-known ones like Leadbelly, because of the skiffle connection, but then there was all kinds of things.'[17]

'Most of us at that time,' says Archie, 'were very heavily influenced by banjo and guitar aficionados from America. We were buying things on spec by mail order, instrument-led rather than song-led or tradition-led.'[18] For Archie, an unsuccessful attempt to buy the Jimmie Rodgers single 'Kisses Sweeter Than Wine' around December 1957 provided a revelation by default. The record was rising up the charts and the shop had sold out. The retailer pointed out a version of the song on an album by the Weavers, a group Archie had never heard of but, being flush with birthday money and not inclined to wait a few days for the release of yet another version by cabaret sensation Frankie Vaughan, he took a chance on it.

The Weavers, formed in 1949, are generally credited with kick-starting the folk revival in America, generating unprecedented sales – their recording of Leadbelly's 'Goodnight Irene' alone sold a million copies in 1950 – which continued even during a period of McCarthy-ist blacklisting for Communist sympathies during the early fifties. For Archie, the Weavers were his introduction to Pete Seeger: group member, author of the song, half-brother of Peggy and something of a whiz on the banjo. The following year, seeing Ralph Rinzler in action would be a turning point. For a start, it was the first time any of them had seen a capo or a thumbpick let alone clawhammer technique. Archie would learn an easy blues called 'Solid Gone' that utilised the technique and Hamish would have a crack at 'Railroad Bill'. For keen-eared youngsters in Scotland, as in London or anywhere else that played host to the visiting Americans, it was, in Archie's words, a case of 'guitar lessons by osmosis – you just watched and took it away with you'.

Hamish had gone along with the craze in trad jazz – buying the records, going to the dances – but his musical interests, right down to guitar playing, were in direct proportion to their social benefits. 'I was a very slow learner,' he recalled, 'had no natural aptitude for it. My reason for trying to learn was because everyone else was and they were my pals. I wanted a party piece. I had my own house at eighteen so it was a place to go back to with a drink and play, 'cos there were no gigs then. You'd occasionally get playing to the unfortunate people in an old folks home – but what had they done to deserve us!'[19] The next visiting performers to make a real impact on the progress of the Broomhill Bums were 'Rambling' Jack Elliot (an introduction to flat-picking) and then, most significantly, Brownie McGhee.

'When the boat landed in Southampton I didn't know what to expect,' said Brownie many years later. 'I'm getting off the boat and the bands was playin', the music was ravin' and the cameras were flashin' and I was ducking my head saying,"Excuse me, sorry, what do you want?" And they said, "You." "What do you want me for?" I thought I was in the way. They kept taking pictures of me. I said, "Nobody knows me here, who'd want pictures of me?" And when Chris Barber got to me he says, "Brownie, this is all for you." I says, "What for?" He says, "They're welcoming you here to the shore." I went for Big Bill, to tell the truth about it, because Bill says, "I won't be able to go any more, Brownie." Bill didn't tell me how they was going to react, he said, "They'll love you." That's all. I'd never been out of the country, and I just couldn't believe it could happen. I'd never been appreciated in America and nobody thought anything of the blues, which is American – the blues is America, America is the blues, and I *am* the blues – so I didn't think I should go anywhere else till America was understanding it. But when I got there it was altogether a different thing in '58.'[20]

Sonny Terry & Brownie McGhee visited Britain many times during the sixties. The first time they came it was April 1958 and, like Broonzy before them, they toured the country as guests of the Chris Barber Jazz Band. As if the culture shock wasn't great enough, by the time they appeared in Glasgow the following year, for a concert at the McClennan Galleries with Barber's band, they had to contend with a fat man living in a stable and hosting an endless party to which they were invited. Hamish produced his Philips tape recorder 'which Brownie and Sonny were watching like hawks. I didn't learn much but Archie did.'[21]

That summer, the party still raging, a touring production of *The Merry Widow* came to town. Among its personnel (and distinguished by the grand title of 'Assistant Stage Manager with Small Parts') was Martin Carthy. 'The master carpenter at the theatre was a folkie,' said Carthy, 'and he kept talking about the Glasgow Folksong Club, so I went along with him on the one night I had off. He took me to Hamish's place first. I met Ray and Archie Fisher and Hamish and Bobby Campbell there and then went to the club and met Josh MacRae, Norman Buchan, Gordon McCulloch . . .' Carthy was an emissary from distant London with knowledge to impart. He had been taking guitar lessons from Peggy Seeger and called her technique 'Peggy Seeger picking'. The Glasgow crowd had never heard of Peggy but any relation of Pete's was a friend of theirs. Carthy and Fisher traded licks. Slowly but surely, and only rarely by direct influence, the Scots were catching up on London.

The Glasgow Folksong Club was founded in the summer of 1959 by a committee led by a future Member of Parliament, and spare-time member of the Reivers, called Norman Buchan. Situated centrally at the Trongate in a lunchtime eatery, the Corner House, it was the first Scottish folk club open to the general public. 'The pleasantly pickled manager was quite tickled by the idea of an evening event,' wrote committee member and Broomhill Bum Ewan McVicar. 'He would charge a rent of £5 for the evening, and hope people would eat a lot of sandwiches. Drew and I reckoned that we could just about stump up the fiver between us if no one at all came on the night. They came in herds. I almost wept with relief.'[22]

'Drew' was Andrew Moyes, who would soon take over stewardship of the enterprise. It had been preceded, in spring 1958, by the establishment of a Folksong Society, under the wing of Hamish Henderson, at Edinburgh University. A Folksong Society at Glasgow University was established soon after. But the very earliest folk clubs in Scotland were those organised by enthusiastic teachers in two Glasgow schools. Morris Blythman's club at Allen Glen's Secondary for boys ran from 1953 to 1957. Robin Hall was among Blythman's pupils at the time and the teacher's home was a venue for visits by the likes of Lonnie Donegan, Peggy Seeger, Alan Lomax and elderly Scottish 'source singers'. He brought Josh MacRae, then at Glasgow School of Art, to the school to give guitar lessons and encouraged his pupils to envisage the worldwide fraternity of the folksong. The second inspirational teacher was Norman Buchan at the mixed Rutherglen Acadamy. Using skiffle as an incentive, Buchan founded a popular Ballads Club at the school in 1958 and the same year organised a 'Ballads & Blues' evening in Glasgow in aid of political prisoners in South Africa. It featured, almost certainly, Ewan MacColl.

Although MacColl was less Scottish in upbringing than he would have liked, he had established a solid affinity with Scotland since his time with Theatre Workshop. While that company, from its inception in Kendal in 1946 through to the respite of Stratford in 1954, 'lived on the brink of disaster . . . engaged in a war of attrition with a machine that wasn't even aware of our existence,' its tours to the working-class heartlands of Wales and Scotland drew increasingly large audiences. *Uranium 235* was performed for the second time in Edinburgh in August 1951 at the first of Hamish Henderson's 'People's Festivals' – an alternative to the high-brow Edinburgh Festival proper and the antecedent of today's Fringe. The following year MacColl's anti-US imperialism play *The Travellers* was performed at the event and, in MacColl's own analysis, proved so controversial that the Scottish TUC urged its membership unions to pull the plug on future funding. The People's Festivals collapsed under a cloud of debt in 1955, but MacColl had established a reputation and an audience north of the border that could only be developed as the folk revival took shape.

In 1954, on the back of his Stratford benefit concerts, a London agency had offered MacColl and some of his associates a national tour, of which he identified Glasgow as the most successful part. They played to an audience of several hundred teenage school children. 'From that gathering,' he believed, 'many of the early leading performers in the Scottish revival were later to emerge.' The same could be said of the membership of Blythman's and Buchan's school clubs and of the Broomhill Bums. Aside from being born there Bert Jansch had never been to Glasgow until he was fifteen, and he can still remember the journey on the bus. These were not cosmopolitan times. But they were interesting times.

Around October 1960, shortly after Bert had wandered into the Howff for the first time, Sonny Terry & Brownie McGhee returned to Glasgow and took a taxi to Broomhill, in search of the fat man and his never-ending party. But the party, alas, had ended. Hamish had run out of luck: 'I was attending lectures at Glasgow University – or supposed to be. In fact, I was watching cartoons at a film club called the Fred Quimby Appreciation Society, going to jazz clubs and drinking illegally. In the time-honoured fashion [my girlfriend] Wilma got pregnant and I married her. I was not quite twenty. Everything was going down the tubes. I was spending money as fast as I got it, running up bills everywhere. We were going to emigrate to Australia, and moved to Motherwell to stay with Wilma's parents till the papers came through.' Not finding Hamish, and discovering the house had been levelled in favour of high-rise flats, Brownie went back to the city centre, stopped someone in the street and quite remarkably scored Josh MacRae's phone number. That night, the party was at his place. A day or two later the whole team were in Edinburgh where the duo had a concert at the Usher Hall, and afterwards a session at the Howff.

Later illustrious visitors to the club would include Pete Seeger, Memphis Slim, Sister Rosetta Tharpe, and possibly even Muddy Waters, who first visited Britain in 1960 and whose uncompromising electric sound was too far ahead of a British audience just about educated to country blues. But for Bert Jansch the greatest and most enduring influence on his music, and on the course of his life, was Brownie McGhee. Many years later, not long before McGhee died, the film-maker Jan Leman brought Jansch to San Francisco to meet his hero one more time for the BBC documentary *Acoustic Routes*. His limp had got pretty bad, but as a raconteur and performer, McGhee was positively brimming with life, proud of his own history and willing to talk about it for as long as anyone cared to listen. In that sense, he was the very antithesis of his visitor. Bert, a man of precious few words at the best of times, was overwhelmed by the experience. Later on, gazing out over the bay, he had something to say:

'If I'd never known music, if I'd never gone to the Howff,' he declared,

'I'd still be a gardener now I should think. Because I was so entrenched in gardening, from the age of five right up till I was fifteen, and it was a way of life. I figure I'm a very solitary person anyway. I think you have to be to be a musician on the road. You have to be aware of yourself and your own solitude, 'cos although you like the experience and the atmosphere of the club, as soon as it's all over you want to be by yourself. But that may be a throwback from the gardening days, I don't know. Ever since then he's been an idol, he's been revered by me, and to play with him has been an extraordinary sensation. I never, ever thought I'd ever play with him in my life – and I'm very proud to have been able to have done so.'[23]

According to Owen Hand, back at the Howff at the very dawn of the sixties Bert Jansch sat there in front of Brownie McGhee, inches from his fingers, all night. He watched him play 'The Key To The Highway' and then asked, 'Could you play that again?' And the next morning Bert was playing 'The Key To The Highway'. It became a well-worn story of Hamish's that Bert had also played something of his own that night for Brownie, who conferred his approval with a question. 'How long you been playing?' he enquired. 'Six weeks,' said Bert. There would be many stories in Hamish's repertoire that were embroidered to the point of fiction. But that one was true.

Still employed as a nurseryman, the proud owner of a Big Bill Broonzy record and a first guitar in quick succession, Bert had been quick enough to realise his own limitations: 'I couldn't figure out how Broonzy played. I was fascinated with his technique.'[24] Broonzy's approach to everything, blues included, had been a happy marriage of pragmatism and diffidence: 'You just make the chords E, A or B,' he explained once, 'and just rack your finger across all the strings and sing the blues, and change from E to A to B just when you feel like changing. Any time will do. You don't have to be in no hurry. Just close your eyes.'[25] As a stage performer Bert has been doing something at least superficially similar from day one. From the wealth of idiosyncrasy apparent in an amateur recording of Bert made in Glasgow two years later, he might have been given the advice straight from the master's mouth. At best it had come first-hand from Brownie McGhee, who shared the same easy-going philosophy:

'Me and Sonny were together from the beginning of time to the ending of Sonny's life,' he told his visitor and his visitor's film-maker, 'thirty-five years to be exact. A long time to be with a man! We never had a contract between us. We made money, we had ups and downs, twists and turns, joys and sorrows but we never had a rehearsal. Why rehearse and play something else? Music is to be played, not read, and our best performances were when we were rehearsing on the stage! Two wrongs make a right, providing you make the wrongs at the same time, and that was a policy I followed. If he played the wrong chord, I played the wrong chord. That's *got* to be right. And we played that in life. Every mistake we made, we made 'em at the same time.'[26]

By the Edinburgh Festival of August 1960 the Howff had a regular clientele. There was Archie, of course, and Roy and Jill and a clutch of other musical talents who had been drawn out of hiding and into the sun: Len Partridge, the original guitar hero; Dolina MacLennan, a young Gaelic singer from the Isle of Lewis in the Hebrides; Owen Hand, born in Ireland and raised in Edinburgh, already the veteran of adventure as a teenage runaway, coal miner, boxer, hot-dog seller, South Atlantic whaler and fairground barker. Len would teach Owen guitar from scratch, and take Bert on from where Jill's knowledge had run out. For the new music and its acolytes, the Howff was a magnet. 'It was an awful place really,' says Dolina, 'but when it was full of people and full of music and full of joy it was a wonderful place to be. All this music had been going on but there hadn't been a focal point for it, and the Howff opening brought all those people together. There was nothing else like it at all.'

The previous year Dolina and her guitar accompanist Robin Gray had created a venue of their own, at the Waverley Bar in nearby St Mary's Road, where they would sing every weekend. While not a folk club as such, as a centre for live music it would roll on into 1963 and outlive the brief blossoming of the Howff. 'It was just a pub, but the first pub that had singing in Edinburgh,' she says. 'We sang there and gradually we would ask people to do a spot for us. I had to hide it terribly from my family because if they found out I was singing in a pub . . . This was forty years ago and women had only just started to be seen in pubs. We didn't know that our traditional singing was "folk music" – everybody took it that folk music was what was happening in the Howff. But there had always been an acceptance of traditional music around Edinburgh. There were ceilidhs every Saturday night – for music, not songs – and of course the School of Scottish Studies had opened and the collections had started by then. Hamish Henderson and Calum MacLean were the first collectors. And the American collectors had started coming round and gathering from the travelling folk. When I came to Edinburgh, by sheer chance I met up with Hamish Henderson and Stewart MacGregor at a party and somebody said, "Sing", and I sang a song and that was me, away – to this day!'

Stewart MacGregor was a doctor at a local hospital. On one occasion he stopped in the street to give first aid to a student nurse who had fallen off her scooter. The result of this encounter provides a fine example of the way word of mouth was the foundation of the new folk scene's rapid rise. The nurse in question, Maggie Cruickshank, was from a similar background to Dolina – from the north of Scotland where traditional song was a part of family life. MacGregor invited her to his next social gathering, at an isolation cottage in the hospital grounds. Dolina and Robin were there too. It was a revelation: 'Just in the middle of this party everything stopped and people started singing,' says Maggie. 'I was raving about this music and Stewart said, "Well, if you enjoyed that why don't you go up to the Howff?"' Bringing her little sister Liz along, Maggie did just that. She was immediately struck by Len Partridge's guitar playing – quite unlike anything she had heard before. The Howff at this stage was operating only at weekends, and Maggie became a regular. It was not only the music that made the place compelling:

'It was unbelievable,' she says. 'I've never seen so many characters in one place. There was a guy who was obviously into climbing and always seemed to arrive in his climbing gear, ropes and everything. Danced a lot. There was a young guy called "Wee George" who was like a gopher, went for everybody's fags. He'd been from a dysfunctional family and that's how he came to be at the Howff. All the odd bods in the world were there. Then there was Jim Haynes, a part-time stunt man who had a bookshop called The Paper Back just down the road where we'd all hang out as well. There was a guy called Highland Jim, an American with a big red beard who looked more like Rob Roy than Rob Roy, and had this Doberman Pincer called "Dog" that never sat on the floor – if it came into the Howff and wanted your seat, it got it. There was Mrs Mac, who used to make coffee and hamburgers, and an old guy called "Johnny the Basket Maker" who danced and made baskets and babies' rattles with beer tops inside them. People felt sorry for him so he would end up selling a lot of rattles! And then there was Bert's Uncle Wattie who had this banjo which was never in tune. It didn't stop him playing it.'[27]

The Howff was basically a coffee house, still open only at night as Maggie recalls: 'It was quite an innocent time but still quite bohemian. I took my parents along the odd time, and an old great-uncle from Canada. I'd been into jazz before and that was a bit bohemian, but it was just as if this was something new that I'd been looking for. There was a kind of natural progression from jazz to blues and folk songs.' Any time Chris Barber's band came to town, Maggie was there. She had all his 78s, and still has Bill Broonzy's autograph. Perhaps with her finals being in October 1960, Maggie missed out on Sonny & Brownie at the Howff, but her sister Liz was there and so too was this strangely quiet, unkempt fellow called Bert.

'My sister was about eighteen when she met Bert, who was seventeen,' says Maggie. 'He was very introverted – seemed to shuffle everywhere, shoulders hunched, always wearing this white raincoat. Somebody said he was like an unmade bed. He really was. I don't think he ever combed his hair. But he had this smile, and when he met Liz the next thing was they were sitting holding hands and seemed to just click. I can't remember how long the relationship lasted, but they remained friends for many years. It was off and on and off and on. She seemed to be madly in love with him but I think she realised there probably wasn't a future in it.'

Included on his first album some years later, Bert's first song was about Liz. Known as 'Courting Blues' on the record, and in its primal state as 'Green Are Your Eyes', it was an atmospheric, sensuous composition – simple in structure, subtle in execution and a piece of work that does not sound like the compositional debut it is. It was a blues of a sort but owed, on the face of it, very little to the sound of his blues heroes. 'I was knocked out when I wrote that and I used to go around singing it to everyone,' said Bert.[28] And as a result, he made a lasting impression on one passing stranger who would later become something of a soulmate.

Anne Briggs, perhaps the greatest English traditional singer of the revival, was a year younger than Bert, from a similarly complex family background, and would become increasingly similar in temperament as the sixties rolled on. Brought up by an aunt in Nottingham, Anne hitched up to Edinburgh with a school friend in the summer of 1960. They stopped at the house of a friend, Archie Fisher, and found themselves not alone in enjoying his hospitality: 'Bert was staying there for the weekend at the same time,' she says. 'He had just given up his job as a gardener and he was playing this guitar music. He hadn't been playing for very long but he was obviously a born guitarist. He was playing amazingly good music, very individual music. He had heard Archie Fisher and he had heard a lot of traditional blues, which had really influenced his playing. At that point he was playing an amalgam of that stuff plus he was starting to write one or two of his own songs. I think "Green Are Your Eyes" was in the process of getting together.'

Bert was still putting in time at the market garden when Maggie and Liz first met him, around August, but shortly after, drawn to the romantic notion of a life in music, he had packed it in. He did not, however, take an entirely direct route to the troubadour lifestyle: 'When I met him he was a grocer,' says Owen Hand. 'I remember Bert and I sitting at two o'clock in the morning, on the steps behind the Sherriff's Court, discussing the prospects of life as a grocer!' Bert worked in a supermarket for less than a month, but if it was meant to placate his family it was a half-hearted and ultimately fruitless excercise.[29] He left home and, becoming 'caretaker-cum-dogsbody', moved into the Howff. 'I used to sleep on the benches,' he says. 'Woke up every morning to the bells of St Giles banging away.' His mother was mortified. 'I went to talk to him, to try and get him to come home again,' says his sister Mary, 'but that didn't work. And although I bought records and everything I was still at a loss with the music people. I didn't know how to fit in with them. To us, you lived simply: you went out to work and if you liked music you bought records or went to the dancing, in groups with your friends, and that was it. But Bert's generation seemed to be completely different. There was a gap of over six years between us.'

'I think it was just a teenage thing,' says Maggie Cruickshank, 'like dropping out of school and finding his own feet. But I think he was comfortable with us. He was like a brother. He often came to our house at that time, my mother knitted him a jumper, did his washing for him. Liz was at his sister Mary's wedding [in 1962] but apart from Wattie I never met any of his family.'

Perhaps because of this close, family-like bond, Bert has come to think of Liz and Maggie as 'more from my home life' than fellow travellers in music. But within a year Maggie and Liz were both beginning to sing in public too, and as Maggie so pithily observes, 'I don't know what his home life was like – because he seemed to be around here a lot!' He was also a regular visitor at Owen Hand's flat in St Leonard's Street: 'I think it was just to play guitar,' says Owen. 'His own had been stolen, so he was usually around places where he could borrow one. He'd pick up the guitar first thing in the morning and he would play all day. You'd say, "Bert, there's a meal on the table," and you'd actually have to take the guitar off him to get him there. Come night-time we'd switch on the television and there was always this *'kerchunk, kerchunk, kerchunk''* going on in the background – "Bert, for God's sake would you shut up!" But he was totally dedicated. He spent almost his entire day playing.'

Bert lived at the Howff for what he recalls as between three and six months. Roy Guest, introducing himself to the best of Mary Jansch's memory as her brother's new manager, came round to the family home in West Pilton 'to reassure my mum that he was all right, that Bert was okay'. Bert himself would visit occasionally too but, although he loved his family dearly, making a clean break from their lifestyle and expectations for him was now paramount. He was good with his hands, and a self-sufficient individual. Whatever plans Roy Guest may have had for Bert's musical advancement, these qualities would come in very useful to his plans for renovating the down-at-heel Howff. In the meantime, Bert was merely the resident curio in a place where life's curios were abundant.

'Bert was a nuisance,' remembers Dolina with great affection, 'he was under everybody's feet. We used to try to clean the place up, get it ready for things and we made soup – soup was always going in the evenings when there was a function on. There was one wee toilet in the corner and this particular Sunday we were having a big night. Whoever was coming it was going to be a full house, and we were all getting the place together and the ballcock in the loo broke. There was no flush. You can imagine, sixty or seventy people and no toilet! So we gave Bert and Liz sixpence and a paper bag and sent them down to the Mocamba, a café on the High Street, to buy themselves a cup of tea and steal the ballcock!'

The day was saved and the evening, no doubt, a roaring success. What must be remembered, though, is that Bert, while very much a product of the Howff, almost never performed there. Only once, under the influence of drink, did he pluck up the courage to sing. But his guitar playing, at least, is remembered by all his contemporaries: 'He was just so young,' says Dolina, 'watching what everybody else did for hours to learn, learn, learn. And he would sit for hours with a guitar going *plink-a-plonk-plink-a-plonk* to such an extent that you wanted to break it over his head! He was like a dog with a bone. He would not give up till he got a thing perfect and then he would just go on and on and on with the same thing – that's my memory. But of course he'd just started playing.'

'He came on at a rate of knots,' says Maggie. 'The first time I knew what a good guitar player sounded like was when I heard Len, just prior to meeting Bert. Bert didn't have a guitar – he borrowed other people's. But he took to it like a duck to water. Within a short time we all realised, "My God, this guy can play." I've always felt that Archie has been a very underestimated player, but Bert was something else, like it was coming from inside him or something.' The following year, still with no guitar of his own, Bert bought one for Liz: a nylon-strung Martin Coletti. 'He taught her a few chords and was very encouraging,' remembers Maggie. Somewhere in Edinburgh, later that year, Liz made her public singing debut.

'Len Partridge would come to the club while I was living there,' says Bert, 'and he was a fantastic player. I used to go round to his house and take lessons.' Aside from his technical ability, through Rory McEwan Len had access to all sorts of material otherwise unknown in Britain at the time and which, alongside the Broonzy and McGhee canon, would make up the bulk of Bert's early repertoire. 'I think I was possibly more influential on Bert than Archie initially,' says Len, 'but I don't think so in the long term. No single person taught Bert how to play guitar – it was an amalgam. He came to me along with Harry Steele officially for lessons – officially in the sense that he paid for them. But at that time I would have said that Harry would have been the better guitarist. Harry was the diligent one. Bert was actually very slow, but then he suddenly took off exponentially. He was very withdrawn, but he was a laddie – five or six years younger than me.'

A tantalisingly brief amateur recording made at St Andrews University in 1963 confirms Len's reputation.[30] For unlike most of his Howff contemporaries, Len Partridge never pursued the big time. Owen Hand's view is one typically held: 'At the time of the Howff Len was possibly the most talented person there. But the other side of Len was his appearance. When he first came to the Howff he was over twenty stone in weight and only about five foot eight in height. He was so conscious of his weight that he seldom came out in the daytime and in the evenings travelled on an old Vincent motorcycle. He had a wild, long beard and long hair pulled back into a pigtail. Quite a formidable looking character. Unfortunately, his self-consciousness made him a bit stand-offish and gave him the appearance of being arrogant. He was fairly intolerant of Bert's youth, his appearance and his over-drinking and he tended to make a joke of him. But at the same time he was a massive musical influence on Bert. He was an amazing guitar teacher.'

Many songs in Bert's early repertoire, some of which have remained there ever since, can be traced directly to Partridge – among them Snooks Eaglin's 'Come Back Baby', Furry Lewis's 'Dry Land Blues', 'Betty And Dupree', 'Weeping Willow', the quasi-traditional 'She Moved Through The Fair' and the curious case of 'Hey Joe'.[31] As for Len's haughty demeanor, it was, he now admits, a defence mechanism. It was not the only way he stood apart from his colleagues: 'I remember Roy saying to me one night, sitting across the road in a coffee bar, "It's funny, Len, you're one of us and yet you're not one of us." I didn't know what he meant at the time. But I was living two lives: the life of a conventional sort of person who got up every morning and went to work, and then spent all night in subterranean bloody places playing guitar. Roy wasn't working at all – he just survived by free-loading, basically! He had it down to a fine art.'

Some time during the latter half of 1960, Archie Fisher and Jill Doyle/ Guest left Edinburgh for Glasgow. With Len unwilling to take on the responsibility, and a folk club swarming with eager pupils, Bert became aware that he was 'probably the most proficient player left – so I filled the gap. It was five bob an hour! The pupils used to attend the club regularly and I'd have a curriculum worked out. I reckon I'm a pretty good teacher actually. I could break it all down and go through the whole thing from A to Z.'[32] The money was good: Hamish Imlach recalls the fee for his own first paying gig, with Josh MacRae and Archie Fisher at a jazz club in Glasgow, as five bob each: twenty-five pence. Around the same time that Bert was finding his niche in Edinburgh, Hamish was teaching guitar every Saturday at Andrew Moyes's Glasgow Folksong Club: 'For thirty bob [£1.50] I'd teach guitar during the day and be resident singer at night. That would pay for a meal, my fares from Motherwell and enough to get drunk on.'

Hamish was already on the verge of becoming a professional folk singer. Never happier than when he was holding court, he was a natural entertainer. Short-lived enterprises as a travelling salesman and time-keeper on a building site would serve only as a source of farcical stories for his repertoire. Archie, another veteran of unsatisfactory employment – in his case turkey farming, milk marketing and the Merchant Navy – had been subsisting, as Hamish once put it, 'on porridge and curried rustled sheep' since the Howff had opened its doors. But the mushrooming interest in folk music, in both Edinburgh and Glasgow and very soon all over the country, was rapidly enhancing the prospects of people actually earning a living at it.

'Some citizens of Edinburgh are still amazed at the success of the Howff,' wrote Eric Winter in the *Melody Maker*, February 1961, giving the club its first national exposure. 'They are contrasting Roy's full houses with empty seats at the Lyceum and other theatres.' Surveying various aspects of the Scottish scene for the same publication in April 1961, Winter noted that up to two hundred people were regularly attending the Glasgow Folksong Club's fortnightly Sunday sessions. The evenings were being headlined by the Wayfarers: Archie Fisher, his sister Ray and fiddler Bobby Campbell. 'They have good style and voices,' wrote Winter, 'but they are wrestling with an urbanised and sophisticated audience – which is uphill work. Ray also sings with her younger sisters Cindy and Joyce. Jill Guest sings quietly but sweetly in her native English, brave lass. But the best voice in the Glasgow club is that of Doreen Laiolo, half Italian, lovely to look at and delightful to hear.' No doubt. Winter had opened his piece in praise of Dolina MacLennan, and it would not be the last time Dolina's name graced the paper: 'I had my tonsils out in 1962,' she says. 'Archie Fisher suggested I pickle them and send them to Eric Winter because Eric wrote about *everything* I did. He had a great fancy for me!'

The Wayfarers, in the company of left-wing playwright Arnold Wesker and Norman Buchan – who was, in addition to his various other roles, Scottish agent for the Workers' Music Association – had just completed a two-week tour of Scottish trades unions. There had always been a link between the new Scottish folk singers and the left – though it was a link that would have no influence on Bert. For others, motivational individuals like Buchan formalised the relationship. Nuclear Polaris submarines stationed at American Navy bases on Holy Loch, twenty miles from Glasgow, were a convenient focus for marches, demonstrations and 'ban the bomb' protest

songs during the early sixties;[33] the brief theft and return of the Stone of
Destiny – ancient symbol of Scottish kingship – from London to Scotland in
1953 had similarly ushered in a wave of nationalist polemic through the arts.
There had even been a campaign of blowing up post boxes with ERII, a
visible mark of English rule, on them. Morris Blythman, a staunch Re-
publican, was writing and collecting songs related to all these causes and
publishing them in songbooks. As Hamish Imlach noted diplomatically in
his autobiography: 'There are various accounts of who was posting the
bombs.'

'We all sang political songs,' says Dolina. 'We all sang the anti-Polaris
songs and anti-royalty songs.' Except Bert. But then Bert was not singing
anything much at all in public at the time. To some of the younger singers,
revolution was just another topic of pub conversation. 'Archie Fisher and I
were the first two folkies in Glasgow who weren't graduates from the
Young Communists' Choir,' says Hamish. 'That's not a joke, that's a
statement of fact!' He also recalled one occasion where he, Archie and
Josh sang for the Young Communists and the Young Conservatives on the
same night. Who knows, it may even be true. Around this time Hamish,
Josh and Bobby Campbell – on the back of Josh's 1959/60 chart successes,
and at the suggestion of Glasgow retailer Cliff Stanton – recorded a series of
Irish rebel songs for Decca. Appearing as three singles credited to the
Emmetones, a group that only existed for a day at a London studio, the
records failed to provide any of the group's members with long-term
recording opportunities. They were nonetheless among the earliest to
feature any of the young Scots.

Others were only just realising that not everything they could sing had to
be American or political. 'There was very little folk music on TV in those
days and even getting folk records was like gold,' says Maggie. 'A lot of our
earliest songs came from records. Then we realised that the stuff we'd
learned from our mum and dad was folk music so we sang that as well.'
Dolina MacLennan, coming from Lewis, had an additional stock of
American songs gleaned from seamen – country and western rather than
blues – that were unknown this side of the Atlantic. Even Roy Guest's
repertoire had a certain freshness about it: 'He'd sing things like "Everybody
Loves Saturday Night" and sing it in various languages,' recalls Maggie.
' "Michael Row The Boat Ashore", "Cumbaya" – that's exactly the sort of
stuff he was doing. Mind you, it was new to us, we'd never heard anything
like it before. He was quite charismatic. Not a great singer, but charismatic –
and he got us involved.'

Eric Winter, writing in that April 1961 *MM* piece, agreed: 'Last Friday
and Saturday I sang at the Howff,' he reported, ' whose Friday sessions,

presided over by Roy Guest, are largely trad nights with a sprinkling of topical material. The Saturday sessions, run by Len Partridge, a good twelve-string player, tend to be a little more American. Guest has nursed that audience carefully. It has never allowed itself to expect folk song to be an entertainment from the platform to the floor. Sitting where I could see them all, I saw five or six people joining in all the verses of long ballads such as "The Cruel Mother" and "Binnorie". In London you can't always find a soloist who can sing them all.'

As Dolina notes: 'Roy was the charmer of all charmers. He could embellish like nothing on earth and you would believe him.' Len Partridge is more forthright: 'He was a con man but in a nice way. As long as you knew he was like that you were fine. As an entertainer he had more class than any of us did. He had whatever it is that sells things to audiences. He made an audience join in whether it wanted to or not. I did a thing with him once at the Kelvin Hall and it was a bloody jazz event – the last thing in the world they wanted was us. How in the name of God he ever got on the bill I don't know, but that was Roy. I remember thinking as Roy went on, "This is going to be a nightmare," but when he came off he just handed me the audience on a plate. That's what he was like. The man has to be given his due: he was a tremendous entertainer.'

'Roy was like a floor singer,' says Maggie. 'He'd start the night off then you'd have maybe Ray & Archie, Bobby Campbell getting up and joining them as a group or maybe getting up on his own, Hamish Imlach, Josh MacRae . . . Loads of people came through for the weekend and we'd have them staying in our house for the weekend, sleeping on floors.'

The weekend trip from Glasgow to Edinburgh was becoming common-place: 'Quite a few of us from Glasgow would pile out of the pubs before they closed at 9.30 p.m.,' says Hamish, 'make a mad dive to catch the 9.30 train to Edinburgh – the last one, which had a bar still open. If the train was dead on time we could loup off at Haymarket and catch the last one back to Glasgow. If we missed it and it was a Saturday we could go up and get to the Howff just as it was warming up. Then we'd trust to luck we could find somewhere to kip until it was time for the first train home.' As often as not, the Glasgow crowd would sleep over at the Howff itself or at the Cruickshanks' place: 'It was an exciting time,' says Maggie. 'But it was all above board, there was no hanky-panky. My mum and dad were tolerant because they loved the music.' Dolina had come to Edinburgh in 1958 and then taken a teaching job in Fife from 1959 to early '62 – essentially the duration of the Howff. 'I used to come over at weekends,' she says. 'I was unusual among that crowd in having a job so quite often

fed everybody else!' The flat she had used while living in Edinburgh, at 19
Bristo Place, belonged to a friend. On Dolina's recommendation, the flat
was now let to Roy and Jill.

The truth of Roy's relationship with Jill Doyle is elusive. Steve Benbow,
who worked with Roy in the Wanderers in 1959, recalls the pair courting
during this period and believes there to have been a marriage. But there is no
record of any such marriage taking place in England or Wales, and if it
happened at all it was before they arrived in Scotland. All of which would be
of trivial interest were it not for the curious ménage à trois that developed
with Archie Fisher as the third party. 'She was quite promiscuous, but
likeable,' says Maggie, referring to Jill. 'I think she was the love of Archie's
life.' Maggie recalls a party she gave towards the end of 1960 to celebrate,
belatedly, her birthday in August and the passing of her finals in October.
Everybody from the Howff was invited. 'I've a funny feeling the sparks first
started to fly between Archie and Jill then. I seem to remember them
disappearing to one of the rooms . . . But there were no fights. Roy didn't
seem to have a problem with it, to my knowledge.'

Len Partridge often visited Archie Fisher's family at Easterhouses in
Glasgow, where he was always made welcome: 'One visit, Roy and Jill
had come along and when we left only Roy left with me,' he says. 'And I
remember so clearly Roy saying, "Well, Lennie, it's just as well I'm so tired,
otherwise I might be upset". That was one way of looking at it. There'd
obviously been something brewing for a while.'

It would seem that Jill left Roy for Archie; the pair of them then moved to
Glasgow for a short time, returning to live in Edinburgh again during 1961
and initially to the flat in Bristo Place. Their partnership lasted for two or
three years. Certainly, they were still together during the 1962 Festival,
several months after Roy had mysteriously disappeared from the scene. He
would reappear a couple of years later, marrying New York model Susan
Kohrs in London in July 1964. During July 1961, adding an unfathomable
twist to the matter, Roy formed a short-lived trio with Archie and Bobby
Campbell, causing quite a stir with a foray down to the Troubadour and
Partisan clubs in London. Archie was also still involved with the Howff
during 1961 and particularly throughout the Festival. In one photograph
from that place and time, there is a bandage on his right hand – evidence of
an episode that is widely recalled: 'What I heard was that Archie walks in to
his bedroom to find Jill with Roy,' says Dolina. 'He had to get out, and the
window was closer than the door. And of course there was a soft-topped car
supposedly full of pillows or something just below the window. Oh, life was
terribly exciting then! You just never knew what was going to happen next.'

The story made the local papers, the farcical element compounded by the captioning of Archie's name to a photo of one George Fleming, another Howff singer of the time. In fact it was a fellow called Giles Bristow, a friend of Bert's, who had been the third party. Archie's humiliation was made all the more public when George Fleming sued the paper and cashed in on his momentary celebrity.

Though Bert was still without a guitar of his own, another of his earliest songs dates from around this time: the rhythmically extraordinary 'Train Song', known originally by one of its lyrical motifs, 'Basket Of Light'. 'It was called that because when I was writing it,' says Bert, 'I was in a flat in Edinburgh after my first sexual experience with a lady. Shirley was her name. She was actually after Archie but she couldn't get him because he was involved with Jill, so she grabbed me one day. And that's how I remember sitting in this flat where the light shade had a basket hanging from it.'

Bert's domestic arrangements at this time were somewhat casual. He occasionally crashed at a flat shared by Giles Bristow and Harry Steele. John Watt, who founded the Dunfermline Howff in imitation and flattery of the Edinburgh one in October 1961, recalls that 'Archie, Bert and a whole gang' lived for a while at a flat in Rankeillor Street, a student area near the University. He also recalls an anecdote from the period, wherein Bert inadvertently becomes a car park attendant (a CV entry not recalled by Bert), which is a typical example of the generally absurd 'Bert story' possessed by many of those who have known him briefly at almost any point over the years – one favourite being the hardy perennial of Bert as the only person in the British Isles this century to go down with scurvy (also untrue).

Eric Winter had become an occasional visitor to the Howff during 1961. Even aside from the delightful Dolina, he was impressed with what he saw: 'Folk club? As a rule the term means folk club evening,' he told readers of his *MM* column in July 1961. 'Soon in Edinburgh it will mean more. Roy Guest, who runs the Howff, is to set up a round-the-week (possibly even round-the-clock) centre at 369 High Street. There will be facilities for playing records and tapes and a tape and disc lending library, informal and organised folk song evenings, chess and cards, and food and drink. Not least, there'll be regular visits from Jimmie MacBeath, Dolina MacLennan, Jeannie Robertson and other ethnic singers. Since Guest's partner is Jim Haynes, proprietor of The Paper Back shop where free coffee is always available, I imagine that song books and magazines will also be on sale. At £1 a year, membership sounds like a bargain.'

'Already the race for the quick pound note is on in the folk song world,' declared Ewan MacColl, with remarkable prescience, typical rage and only three weeks earlier in the same publication. He was setting out the stall of his come-back at the helm of a club, and he had naught but invective for the forces of mediocrity and profit: 'The only notes that some people care about are the bank notes,' he went on. 'The folk song revival can get so far away from its traditional basis that in the end it is impossible to distinguish it from pop music and cabaret. It has happened in some US clubs. True bawdiness is reduced to mere suggestiveness. The songs, sapped of their vigour, become "quaint". It's happening here too in the *Tonight* programme and I was scared when I saw what is going on in some of the clubs. We need standards. "Quaint" songs, risqué songs, poor instrumentation and no-better-than-average voices, coupled with a lack of respect for the material: against these we will fight.'

MacColl would not have entered into the spirit of the Howff. He certainly never played there although his name was well known to the Scottish folk fraternity. 'I didn't like him,' says Dolina. 'I loved his *Radio Ballads*. But him and Peggy, I found their public performances full of shit compared to people who sang the same songs naturally. They were "performing". It went against the grain.' Surviving live recordings from the period not only underline how exceptional a musician Peggy Seeger was but reveal a brighter and more likeable side to MacColl than his forays into print and the crushing earnestness of his commercially recorded work would have one believe. Great fun was to be had with a series of extracts from street songs and children's songs for instance, linked with wry commentary, in a style somewhat akin to music-hall. But MacColl's comedy was of a scripted rather than truly intuitive or improvisational nature and was still rooted in a belief that imbued worthiness to the oral tradition in all its forms, however vulgar. 'Ewan MacColl's polemical songs, on the contrary,' concluded one reviewer of a typical MacColl performance, 'have about them a self-righteous hectoring quality, unfortunately magnified by the attitude of magisterial condescension which he unwittingly brings to his stage presence.'[34]

In addition to his July announcement of Roy Guest's plans for the Howff, Winter could also report on the success of Dolina & Robin's recent tour of London folk clubs; on Roy, Archie and Bobby Campbell's debut as a trio at Aberdeen Folk Club; and on the opening night of Ewan MacColl's as yet unnamed new club 'with a shower of congratulatory messages from other clubs including Glasgow, the Liverpool Spinners' club and the Troubadour'. By the middle of 1961 the rise and spread of 'the folk club' as an instrument of the revival was gathering pace.

MacColl's new venture, in Soho Square, was grandly proclaimed but he was a leader of men, not an organiser of events. The launch had been left in the hands of Eric Winter, who failed to turn up on the night. Bruce Dunnet, a MacColl disciple from the Ballads & Blues days, was in a pub around the corner with Paul Carter, who ran the Collector label, 'and Ewan came in absolutely bloody furious and fuming because, he said, "We've got hundreds of bloody folk singers and no organisers." And Paul Carter says, "Well, here's Bruce. He's the best organiser of the lot." Ewan said, "Will you help us?" I said, "Yeah." They didn't know what to call their new club, so I said, "It belongs to the singers – call it the Singers Club." ' They did just that.

Focused around the 'godfathers' – MacColl and Seeger, Dominic Behan and Bert Lloyd – the Singers Club, initially operating only on Sundays, soon relocated from the ACTT building in Soho Square to the Plough in nearby Museum Street. It would move its premises on a more or less yearly basis thereafter: a particularly celebrated era at the Pindar of Wakefield from October 1962, open on both Saturday and Sunday; a financially fraught period at the Prince of Wales' Feathers from September 1963 (with an additional Wednesday night Singers Club operating from March '63 at the King's Head, Twickenham); a Saturdays-only relaunch at the Royal Hotel, Woburn Place, February 1964; a switch back to Sundays at the New Merlin's Cave, Margery Street, in January 1965; and a conscious move back into Soho, where a new breed of more liberated all-nighter folk clubs were by then thriving, in April 1966 at the John Snow in Broadwick Street. The venue may have changed with alarming regularity, but the Singers Club as a 'brand' became established across the land as the spiritual heart of the folk revival and its ever-expanding club scene.

In January 1961 Eric Winter had been able to revel in the break-through of a folksong event in London every night of the week – albeit only for one particular week filled out with a couple of special events at Cecil Sharp House, home of the English Folk Dance & Song Society (EFDSS). On a more regular basis, London's key venues at the start of the year were the 'Blues & Barrelhouse' at the Roundhouse on Thursdays; late night sessions of 'jazz, folk, blues and poetry' at the Partisan over the weekend with residents Martin Winsor and Redd Sullivan; the ACTT building in Soho Square with Malcolm Nixon's 'Ballads & Blues' on a Saturday (all of the above being in Soho); and Tuesday sessions with Martin Carthy's new outfit the Thameside Four at the Troubadour in Earl's Court.

The (Skiffle) Cellar in Greek Street had recently closed down, but the Partisan continued that venue's tradition of two Saturday night sessions, one running well into the early hours. The Gyre & Gimble coffee bar began a new club on Sunday afternoons in April. The Singers Club opened in June. Folk nights at the Witches Cauldron in Hampstead and the Red

Lion in Sutton announced their existence in September. By the end of the year there really was somewhere to go every night of the week, and a healthy choice come the weekend. And if Soho was the hub of all this activity, the suburbs were not far behind: from Streatham to Potters Bar, and Bromley to Richmond, venues were springing up in rapid succession.[35] There was nothing if not variety, and the spirit of adventure was abroad.

'Looking for and not finding a hall to hold 2000,' wrote Eric Winter in October 1961, 'Bruce Dunnet of the Singers Club took a deep breath and booked the Albert Hall for Pete Seeger.' The hall's capacity was 5000 and, bar the annual festival of the EFDSS – an occasion Martin Carthy recalls as 'just a pageant of country dancers in felt skirts and boring, boring shite basically' – had never been used for anything like a folk concert before. Co-sponsored and assisted by pretty much all the key club organisers of the day in the Greater London area together with stalwarts of the hard left Topic Records and Collet's Bookshops, the Seeger concert of November 16 1961 was the first great gathering of the folk movement. The hall was packed and the atmosphere electric.

'That was the first concert I ever did,' says Dunnet, who still displays a mixture of shock and pride on the matter. 'There was nothing of that size before it. The largest folk concerts had been St Pancras Town Hall [now Camden Town Hall], which seats 960 and it was very seldom full. But it was politics: Pete Seeger needed his passport back. I signed his work permit for the Royal Albert Hall. How we did it I don't know. It was the folksong people, the Communist Party, Labour Party, wood-craft folk from the cooperative movement – every bloody organisation you could think of.'

'It was a huge moment,' says Martin Carthy, 'because there had been this campaign to get Pete Seeger over to England. McCarthy was dead by that time but the House Un-American Activities Committee still lived on and they'd taken his passport away. This campaign had managed to get his passport back.'[36]

Prior to his Albert Hall triumph Seeger had been up and down the country, appearing in concert in Edinburgh on 1 November and later that same evening at the Howff. Around the country by this stage, though not yet mushrooming as fast as in London, there was a surge in folk club activity. Eric Winter, in a uniquely central position at the *Melody Maker*, had made it his business to gather information from the reaches. In May he could reveal the existence of 'a surprising number of folk clubs': nearly forty. By September he had noted forty-seven. By December it was seventy. Four months later it was eighty-one. Winter's figures may not have been comprehensive but they illustrate clearly the gathering speed of the revival's spread. Its breadth is revealed in what was happening in Scotland and the north of England.

Outside of London, a club run in Liverpool by the Liverpool Spinners – later achieving national fame at the light entertainment end of the folk spectrum as the Spinners – was widely regarded as the benchmark by those performers who were travelling.[37] The club had begun in autumn 1958, and the group's move away from skiffle to Liverpool folk songs, sea shanties and the like was taken on advice from London performer Redd Sullivan who thought they sounded like a bunch of schoolteachers singing blues. A handful of other provincial clubs had similarly emerged through and survived the skiffle craze while others could claim a lineage back to the first trad jazz boom of the early fifties. A latter-day folk club called the Wayfarers is believed to have originated in Manchester around 1953, and the Topic in Bradford around 1956. The first inklings of a circuit came in the wake of the Watersons' club in Hull, itself one of the very earliest in Britain: 'We started it off in a dance hall in 1958,' says Norma Waterson, 'with mirrors on the wall – the Baker Street School of Dancing. It was us and about sixty of our friends, and the woman who ran the dancing school used to make us sandwiches with biscuits and tea at the interval. We stayed there for about a year, and then the male members of the audience started to want drink. So from 1959 through to 1961 we moved between about five different pubs, finally finishing up at the Bluebell and that was "Folk Union One".' The Watersons themselves were alone among the early groups of the revival in eschewing the 'American model' of the Weavers and creating a largely a cappella, harmony-based approach to English traditional song. Their club lasted well into the 1990s, long after the reins had been passed to a committee.

Nearest to Folk Union One in the beginning was the Topic in Bradford; a little further north was the Newcastle Ballads & Blues, partly run by singer Louis Killen and strongly associated with the union movement. Immediately south, there was nothing at all until a club was opened in Grimsby, Lincolnshire, directly inspired by Folk Union One. By 1961 if not earlier there were contacts and occasional exchange visits between the North-Eastern English clubs and the Glasgow Folksong Club. Outside of any union influence, the Howff was not a part of this camaraderie. But its own influence was spreading and it was part of an increasingly thriving independent scene north of the border.

Inspired by what he saw at the Howff in Edinburgh, John Watt opened the Dunfermline Howff in October 1961. Roy Guest was, of course, among his opening acts. Further new clubs opened that same year in Aberdeen, in

Bo'ness, in Perth, and in St Andrews on the coast of Fife.[38] Two other Fife clubs, at Dundee and Kirkaldy, opened the following year and folk concerts in schools became regular occurrences in the region. Both Archie Fisher and Josh MacRae would come to enjoy a lucrative side-line as part-time teachers of guitar for Fife's education board.

The pinnacle of the Howff's existence was the Edinburgh Festival of August 1961. Literally by the eve of the city's three-week festivities the place had been renovated, redecorated and improved beyond recognition. Eric Winter, the man from the *Melody Maker*, was still tripping over paint pots and cables on the opening night. 'The Howff walls have been stripped,' he reported, 'almost by the bare hands of Roy Guest and Jim Haynes with a few friends, to reveal some dignified, ancient stonework.'

Most of the work had been done by Roy's 'friends', the most industrious among them being Bert Jansch. Thirty years later Bert re-entered the old Howff to film sequences for the BBC documentary *Acoustic Routes*. The premises were in the process of being revamped once again, this time to be used as a council office, and the dignified stonework was shortly to be covered with chipboard. Up the few steps from the street there was a sturdy wooden door leading into the first of the two main rooms nearest to street level. 'I made that door,' said Bert, as if reminding himself out loud. 'Really? Well you can take it with you if you like,' retorted a bemused workman, not quite understanding the resonance of what was going on. Bert was good with his hands.

'One room has been timbered to make an attractive coffee bar of the chicken salad and Danish pastry school,' continued Winter. 'Upstairs there will be books, tapes and discs, to form a king-size folk reference library with room to browse, talk, listen and sing.' 'We shall choose artists in or out of or on the borders of the folk field who have warmth and humanity to offer,' Guest told me. 'And we shall present them in the atmosphere and environment that suits them best."

Around June 1961 Roy had gone into partnership with Jim Haynes, a former USAF serviceman who had been stationed near Edinburgh and who had returned to open up The Paper Back, Britain's first paperback bookshop. With Haynes's money he could at last buy out the Sporran Slitters. The place had thereafter been transformed, to bring its physical character in line with that provided on a more atmospheric level by its clientele. 'You could go there in the early hours of the morning and there'd be somebody making soup you could stand your spoon up in,' says Owen Hand. 'In the afternoon you'd get all sorts of people dropping in. There were magazines and newspapers lying on the tables, you could play chess or draughts. It was a hippy club, open every day. Quite an establishment for Edinburgh at that point.'

The thrill of the new was not without its drawbacks: 'I was competing in the National Mod in 1961,' says Dolina, 'and I remember this headline in one of the papers saying "Dolina MacLennan, tipped winner of this year's gold medal, has been practising by singing Gallic songs in an Edinburgh beatnik club". I had a foot in both camps I suppose, but that was me stamped for life, a reputation absolutely gone!'

A published memoir by another Howffer, one Jeremy Bruce-Watt, paints an attractive picture of the venue's heyday: 'You were liable to meet anyone there. The membership of over two hundred ranged from a distinguished advocate to some very young persons ready to assail any of the world's most pressing problems for hours on end. Every Friday and Saturday for two years – and often other nights as well – a variety of colourful entertainers stood with their backs to the fireplace, facing the packed wooden benches and the massed flickering of candles stuck in bottles. The big room was lit, never brilliantly, by a row of narrow windows in the thick walls. You could go there after breakfast, dressed anyhow, and have a string of coffees, leaning in the window recess, watching the traffic and the people on the Mile, listening to St Giles' counting the hours, looking at the walls and beams trimmed with the adze. You could talk or listen to talk. You could play chess. Somebody always seemed to be tuning a guitar.'[39]

One could hazard a guess as to who that individual may have been. Bert's own memories of the Howff lack detail but he was very young, naturally withdrawn and happier to be a foot soldier than a general. Only much later, in the light of his success down in London, did anyone piece together mental notes of anecdotes or observations concerning this most shadowy of characters who had seemed, nevertheless, to always be around. 'He was very, very quiet,' says Dolina, 'and he hasn't changed at all. Very much his own person. I don't remember any angst, just quietness. I wasn't aware of Bert's importance for a long time. Bert an icon! I can see it, but I still have to chuckle because he's just "Bert" to me – and I still want to break his guitar over his head!'

He may not have been at the epicentre of its activities, but the whole Howff experience – Roy Guest particularly – would leave a strong impression on him. 'He was a very, very funny character,' says Bert. 'His primary role was an actor and, being Welsh as well, he used to act the folk singer rather than be the folk singer. A bit like Ewan MacColl. He had us renovate the place with a view to having it open for the Festival and then he booked all these amazing acts that had never been anywhere near Edinburgh. For some of them I'd be standing in the background, too in awe of

them – like most people in the place. I saw Pete Seeger there, and Sonny &
Brownie. With Rosetta Tharpe, I was there that night but it was too packed
to get in.'

Stranger still than any of these legends of folk, blues and gospel was the
week-long residency of Viennese cabaret diva Martha Schlamme: by all
accounts the runaway hit of the whole '61 Festival, and appearing exclusively at the Howff. Hamish Imlach was wont to recall that Schlamme 'could
sing in ten languages – badly'. Eric Winter reckoned it was 'tastefully and
entertainingly in sixteen'. A rave notice in the *Observer* diplomatically
described the singer as appearing at 'a room off the High Street, against
a dusty curtain of blue velvet' while 'disappointed crowds hang at the door
and listen at the window. Her audiences – already fanatical recidivists who
struggle back to hear her night after night – feel that their festival will taste
like ashes without her.' The writer marvelled that Schlamme was appearing
all week 'for fun and not for money'. But as Hamish recalled: 'She was
asking £1000 a night. There was all this publicity at the time of Roy getting
her for expenses – but there was a suite at the North British Hotel, a hired
Rolls, meals at the Festival Club, a fur coat . . .'[40]

'I remember collecting her from the airport,' says Len. 'There were no
Rolls Royces involved. The Howff was anything but quaint yet this
woman, who I take my hat off to for sheer professionalism, didn't bat
an eyelid. Every night she did these shows and I believe Roy had conned her
into coming for half the take. As it turned out, because of the amazing write-
ups the place was crammed and the take was better than any time before or
after. But it shoved out the regular audience. There were people standing
down below in the street looking very pissed-off. Suddenly all Roy was
interested in was the profit. He was willing to quite literally ignore those
who had put him where he was. I think that was the beginning of the end. I
don't think Martha Schlamme bankrupted him, I think he screwed himself
out of it.'[41]

Moral high ground notwithstanding, with a unique venue, a brilliant
publicity angle and a week of late-night shows to offer Roy had succeeded
in creating a buzz around Edinburgh that would strongly influence the
programming of folk music at the Festival and on the Fringe in years to
come. 'She has set the Royal Mile afire,' wrote Winter, 'and the critics are
talking about an official invitation to next year's Festival. Festival director
Lord Harewood has said he will look in at the Howff before Martha winds
up on Friday.' With all this attention, someone had noticed that the place
lacked the statutory requirements of two toilets and two exits: once the
Schlamme triumph had come to an end, an order of closure was served. As
the story goes, an eminent QC among the Howff's clientele drifted in that

night, in his bowler hat and pin-striped suit, to find a sea of glum faces. He heard the tale of woe, disappeared for a while and returned with the news that nothing more would be heard of the matter. Friends in high places. 'You couldn't say that people were folkies at the Howff,' says Len, 'because they came from so many walks of life and social backgrounds and were of a tremendous age range. And that, I think, is what made the Howff so different. Things were never the same after it. We were spoiled.'

For the second week of the Festival Guest had booked Dominic Behan, with two paragons of Scottish traditional song, 'source singers' Jimmy MacBeath and Jeannie Robertson, appearing subsequently, on three nights each, over the first two weekends in September. MacBeath, an old street singer from the north-east, was a 1951 'discovery' of Hamish Henderson's. He had been the very first guest at the Glasgow Folksong Club – astonished and delighted to have been paid a fee of £8. Jeannie Robertson, an Aberdeen housewife, was another find of the early fifties. Other specific dates remain lost in the mists, but both artists were frequent visitors to the club and would exert an enormous influence on the Scottish folk scene.

Dolina MacLennan & Robin Gray were now billed as the Howff's resident singers on Sundays, in addition to their ongoing performances at the Waverley Bar and the Nippon, a Chinese café run by students in aid of charity. Other venues were opening up to folk song in Edinburgh. A pub called the White Horse had started a weekly folk night. The following year, Archie Fisher would be fronting a popular Tuesday night club at the Crown. Folk music in Edinburgh was now quite a scene: 'We had such a busy life,' says Maggie Cruickshank. 'There was a continual round of socialising. It was hectic but it was also very relaxed – you wafted in and out of things and wove in and around each other. I don't think many people had phones in those days so it's amazing how anybody found out what was happening! It was a network. You saw people like Archie and Hamish and Josh MacRae as being high up in the hierarchy and us down below. But we didn't stay there for long – everybody was so encouraging to each other.' 'The thing was,' says Dolina, 'in those days if anybody got a gig you got as many of your friends in on it as possible to share. So if you got three quid for an evening you'd bring somebody else along and get thirty bob each.'

Few people actively involved in folk music in the early sixties owned a TV, but the medium still lent a sheen of success to those who appeared on it. Relatively few managed such a feat and fewer still got the opportunity to make a record. It was understandable that people believed there to be a hierarchy. Josh MacRae had enjoyed some notoriety as a recording and TV artist, under his own name and with the Reivers and the Emmetones. Ray & Archie Fisher were starting to appear regularly on *Here & Now*, STV's regional magazine show, and by the end of the year would have their debut EP *Far Over The Forth* available on Topic. Roy Guest was, of course, a veteran of *Tonight* and *Saturday Club* and was quite happy to make people aware of this. Robin Hall & Jimmie Macgregor – who are also known to have appeared at the Howff – were well on the way with their own TV career. By the end of 1961, even Dolina MacLennan & Robin Gray had their first EP, *By Morland Braes*, out on Topic and were lined up as guests on STV's new folk show *Alex Awhile*, fronted by Alex McEwan. Rory & Alex were both veterans of *Tonight*, and on *Alex Awhile* backing would be provided by Steve Benbow. Benbow himself was all over the nation's airwaves: on 22 December 1961 he appeared at the Howff in a performance broadcast by the Scottish Home Service. Within a year or two he was fronting his own series for STV, *Plectrum*: 'I was a bigger name in Scotland for a while than I was in England,' he notes. Maybe so, but his records were still not selling.

With such a wealth of talent in the city, it was inevitable that the beginnings of an industry would evolve. Bryce Lane ran the Leith branch of an Edinburgh soft-furnishings business called Jeffries. In some ways comparable to the beginnings of Brian Epstein's Liverpool empire, Lane first established a small hi-fi department at the store, then opened a dedicated branch of the business, named Audio House, in Home Street. The new store had the facilities to record people directly on to acetate. It was the beginnings of Waverley Records. Bryce left Jeffries and opened Craig Hall Studios – where in August 1963 Bert Jansch would make his first professional recordings, now believed lost. One of Lane's early acquisitions, with acumen redolent of Roy Guest at his best, was a Studer portable desk bought specifically to make annual recordings of the Military Tattoo at Edinburgh Castle: a perenially popular event, eminently saleable to the tourists.

Curiously, few of those involved in the Edinburgh scene remember Waverley Records, though a fair amount of product was released. Featuring his party piece 'Everybody Loves Saturday Night', one of the first was *Introducing Roy Guest*, an EP purportedly recorded live at the Howff with a West Indian Steel Band. Representing more obvious commercial nous was an LP, available in mono and stereo versions, of *The Edinburgh Military Tattoo Of 1961*. Catalogue numbers in the local press ads for these desirable items suggest at least one, perhaps two other records had already been released. The label had been flagged as 'imminent' in Eric Winter's brief *MM* piece on the Howff in February 1961, which also gave the distinct impression that the whole thing was Roy's idea. Perhaps if Roy had had the foresight to recommend Bert Jansch as someone for Lane to record, his name may have been secured as the Sam Phillips of British folk history. At the very least, the largely forgotten Waverley Records may have proved more memorable. One could not, however, suggest with any conviction that it would have guaranteed the venture a level of success more widespread than any it enjoyed at the time.[42]

'This time last year a great deal of folk was going on in Edinburgh,' wrote Eric Winter, in April 1962. 'A year later, by all accounts, the folk capital of Scotland has shifted dramatically to Dunfermline.' John Watt's Dunfermline Howff, situated in a disused cellar next to an optician's, had opened its doors on October 5 1961. Inaugurated by Hamish Henderson, with Roy Guest and Dolina MacLennan & Robin Gray its opening acts, the club was a success from the word go. Running on Thursdays and initially hosted, on alternating weeks, by Roy Guest and Robin Gray, by the time Winter came to his sweeping conclusion (not unreasonably used on club advertising for some time thereafter) Len Partridge and future MOR star Barbara Dickson were among the regulars and the membership stood at six hundred.

Two issues later, Winter let slip that the Howff in Edinburgh had closed. The St Andrews Society, 'regarded by some as the top people's cultural organisation', he wrote, had made an informal offer to reopen the club in new premises. More than that, in the pages of the *Melody Maker*, was never revealed. 'Roy went off quite suddenly,' says Maggie. 'He'd just done the Howff up, we'd all paid our membership fees and then he disappeared. The membership was like a pound each, so not a lot of money – he certainly wouldn't have been able to pay for a ticket to America on the proceeds!'

There is no concrete explanation as to why Roy Guest left Edinburgh when he did. His reputation secured, he could surely have gone on to still greater things as an organiser and promoter within the city's flourishing arts scene. One rumour had it that he signed up for a degree in sociology at Edinburgh University, pocketed the grant money and left for America. But any suggestion of money trouble is difficult to support: if Martha Schlamme had really compromised his financial position in August, he would surely have done a bunk nearer the time. The Howff was certainly still functioning by Christmas, when Steve Benbow broadcast from the place, and into the new year, when John Challis, a future flatmate of Bert's, happened by on a trip up from London. 'It didn't last terribly long after it was done up,' says Len, 'and part of the problem there was that Roy in many ways mistreated the regular clientele when he discovered, "Wow, there's money to be made here." A lot of people drifted away because of that. But he's a guy who I have actually quite fond memories of because anybody who is that much of a rogue is quite likeable. Provided you knew he was a rogue.'

By July 1962 Roy was running a Howff Mk2 in New York with none other than Martha Schlamme. Roy later accounted for his time after Edinburgh as 'the wanderlust returning', initially travelling all over Europe. During the winter of 1962 – 63 he drove from New York to Los Angeles to appear at the LA Troubadour with the Clancy Brothers. By the middle of 1963 he was back in London, promoting folk concerts on a grand scale for the Harold Davidson Agency. From January 1964 he was moonlighting as the host of *The Hoot'nanny Show*, a national BBC folk TV show broadcast live from Edinburgh – a strange move for a man supposedly 'on the run' from something in the same town. Bar the 'wanderlust', there are no obvious answers. But then Roy always was an enigma.

'A lot of people thought he was a little bit of a joke,' says Norma Waterson. 'I never did. He was one of the most far-reaching ideas men I've ever met. In the early sixties he was the one who put on all the old traditional singers with the young performers at all these big concerts at the Albert Hall and elsewhere. He went to the Arts Council and tried to persuade them to do what they do now in backing traditional music. That was Roy Guest.' Roy spent the rest of the sixties as the most ambitious, hard-working and successful folk music concert promoter and festival organiser in Britain, first with Harold Davidson, then the EFDSS, then his own Folk Directions agency. During the Folk Directions era he pioneered the promoter's now standard gambit of block-booking major venues on choice dates months in advance. Beatles manager and partner in the NEMS agency Brian Epstein, it is said, became so frustrated by Guest's ingenuity that he had no choice but to buy the company.

So it was that Guest worked two years, without a holiday, running the newly installed folk department of one the biggest promotions operations in the land. Burned out, he disappeared, to return once again in 1972 with a Howff Mk 3 in London's Chalk Farm area. He wanted to recapture a way of doing things, and run it on the model of what he declared to be 'the happiest times of my life' at the original.[43] It had taken a few years for him to realise what he had lost. 'The growing artistry of Ray and Archie Fisher, Bert Jansch and other serious performers was exciting to see,' he recalled at the end of 1964. 'But it was not a club that I ran responsibly enough. I didn't have the knowledge and experience necessary, although we had some good moments.'[44]

'The Howff was such a wonderful time,' says Maggie, 'but I'd say it was the beginning of something not the end. The Waverley had started by then, the White Horse was starting, and we soon found the Crown.' The premises at 369 High Street became, to Hamish Imlach's recollection, 'an upmarket tea-room', but Roy's venture had made a colossal difference to the perception and popularity of folk music in Edinburgh: 'After the Howff people stopped asking, "What's a folk song?" ' says Dolina. 'You could put on a folksong concert and people would come to it, whereas before they wouldn't have known what it was. People in their twenties who would go to the dancing on Saturday nights, they would come to the Howff or the Waverley first. It opened up a whole new world to people.'

CHAPTER FOUR

Three Dreamers

Under the archway, across the cold courtyard,
Up the stone stairway all pitted and worn
To a room in a shambles with orange boxes for chairs
Our lives all lay scattered, still yet to be born

Daylight would show you the cracks in the ceiling
Wallpaper hanging all tattered and torn
It looked like a junkyard of paraphernalia
Where three dreamers dreamed dreams still yet to be born[1]

Towards the end of the sixties Roy Guest would be established as the most successful folk music promoter in Britain. He would take an act like the Watersons, essentially unaccompanied traditional singers, and graft them seamlessly on to that most intangible and lucrative of things, the 'Swinging Sixties'. Two of his most successful clients would nevertheless be the two most innovative bands of the day to have emerged from the broad church of folk music: the Pentangle and the Incredible String Band. The key protagonists in both could trace their origins back to the Howff. One, of course, was Bert Jansch; the other was Robin Williamson who, by the time he had achieved national status, was the archetype of hippiedom. The same age as Bert, Robin had stayed on at school a little longer, missing out on the early days of the Howff but slipping in before the end.

'Robin wasn't bohemian at all when we met him,' says Maggie Cruickshank. 'He was very innocent in those days – quite ordinary, middle-class. The first time we heard him was at this concert during the 1961 Festival at a place called the Camera Obscura near the castle. He got up and sang this murder ballad, really into the whole act of it. That was the first time he'd sung in public, he told us.'

Robin would describe his own background as lower middle-class. But like Bert, whom he first met at the Howff, he was escaping from the drudgery of life: 'I left home with a fairly major thrust to get out of everything that I'd ever known and do something else. I could already play guitar – not very well, though. I took it up at school and played with two jazz bands, one of them an old-timey kind of band and the other a mainstream swing band in which I played electric guitar. And then I got interested in traditional music when I was sixteen-ish and got an acoustic guitar. I used to play the Waverley Bar when I was still at school, for ten shillings [50p] a night, doing traditional material. Archie and his sister were on the television weekly, during the last year I was at school. It was an evening news programme [*Here & Now*, STV] but they would do a song at the end of it. Jimmie Macgregor I remember being on there as well.'

Bert and Robin ended up sharing various dilapidated rooms in the less desirable districts of Edinburgh. 'Traditional Edinburgh tenement buildings in their last states of disrepair,' says Robin. 'Four flights down to the toilet sort of thing.' Robin recalls Bert both owning a guitar, though not a good one, and still gardening when they first met. One may concede that Bert and Robin could have met when both characteristics were in place, a year earlier, but their relationship in terms of sharing flats did not begin before the latter part of 1961. The dates may be gone, but Robin's recollection of Bert is still vivid: 'I seem to remember him as this sort of shambolic figure with a guitar permanently attached to one arm,' he says. 'He did own a guitar although he spent a lot of time playing on mine, which I'd been given by a man called Barney who was going off to become a Trappist monk. He had a very nice Levin which was better than anything that we had ever had a go at before.'

Accurate chronology is not possible for the period between the closure of the Howff in the early days of 1962 and the time that Bert would finally remove himself permanently to London, after a number of previous forays, in the autumn of 1964. Certain events can be pin-pointed with confidence, but as a whole the period is very much defined by the euphemism 'if you remember the sixties, you weren't there'. Bert and Robin certainly were, and shared accommodation for what both describe as 'two or three years' – certainly 1962, with perhaps a few months on either side and during which time Bert would enjoy various trips abroad. 'I am basically itinerant in all ways,' he has said. 'In life and in music, I must keep moving.'

Foreign travel would become integral to Bert's lifestyle, and a rich resource for his lyrical and musical inventions. Dope from North Africa was now becoming easily obtainable in Edinburgh. It was an exotic alternative to the heavy drinking that was favoured by some and was another aid to escaping the misery of life for those who chose it. In terms of Bert's increasingly accomplished if singular guitar playing there was also, at last, a benchmark by which it could be judged: that benchmark, for an entire generation of would-be folk guitar heroes, was a deceptively simple little tune called 'Angi'. And its maker was Davy Graham.

'Angi' first appeared on a Topic EP entitled *3/4 A.D.*, released around April 1962. The record's other pieces, '3/4 A.D.' and 'Davy's Train Blues', were instrumental collaborations between Davy Graham and Alexis Korner. Alexis could always spot talent, and had arranged for the session to take place. Somehow, he had also managed to side-step Bert Lloyd and his veto. Perhaps Lloyd had even approved the venture. But this was strange, innovative music with the dark muscle of Delta blues, something of the structural rigour of European baroque and the time signatures of modern jazz. 'Angi', a solo guitar piece written and performed by Graham, was short but effective. For those who could learn to play it, it would be their passport to folk club bookings nationwide for the rest of the decade. Bert Jansch took the piece, turned it inside out and made it his own. And he had never even bought the record.

Davy Graham was never a performing guest at the Howff but with Jill Doyle/Guest his half-sister he had a tangible connection to that scene, and some time prior to its release Davy sent Jill a tape of his new recording. Everyone would hear it and be dumbfounded. Bert unlocked the puzzle of 'Angi' and consequently introduced the new technique it held to all those around him: 'From the tapes, no one could work out how to do it, until I hit on the secret of it all, which was very simple. Our techniques are very different but I did learn a lot from him.'[2]

As had been the case with Broonzy, Bert figured it out and applied the new knowledge to his own work. After Big Bill, Brownie, Archie, Hamish and Len, Davy Graham was the final piece of the jigsaw. For the rest of the decade Bert would work on assimilating Davy's ideas into something uniquely his own, but the process of his musical education was now all but complete: 'The only three people that I've ever copied were Big Bill Broonzy, Davy Graham and Archie Fisher,' says Bert. 'After hearing Davy play, it was just all there.'[3]

Bert believes he first met Davy in Edinburgh, but only in passing. On one occasion he brought his girlfriend Angi, who had inspired the tune, to the Howff. 'We knew the song, so we were tickled pink to meet her,' says Maggie Cruickshank. Her immortaliser was a different prospect entirely: 'Extraordinarily intense,' is Dolina MacLennan's recollection. 'I wouldn't have spoken to him.' Davy Graham was indeed an eccentric and singular individual and right down to the present day one can sense from Davy, however subdued it may be, a feeling of antipathy or, at least, ambivalence towards Bert. Bert has always held Davy, as a musician, in the highest regard.

'At that time, my playing was influenced more by folk stuff like Pete Seeger and Archie Fisher,' says Bert. 'But certainly my playing now is taken straight from Davy. I first met him at the Waverley Bar but I got to know him really only later, in London. I already knew his brother Nick and his sister Jill – in fact, I seemed to know all his family except him. He was much more enigmatic than anyone else, and still is exactly the same. You still can't have a conversation with him.'

So where had this extraordinary man with his extraordinary music come from? Born in Leicester on 22 November 1940, his father Hamish from the Isle of Skye, his mother Winifrid from Guyana, Davy was brought up in the racially volatile Notting Hill area of London. The ages of ten and twelve have been given variously as the starting point of his guitar playing but either way he was, like Bert, sixteen before he owned one. And as with Bert, the individual and the instrument became inseparable: 'I started not doing homework and playing "My Baby Left Me", "Mystery Train" and Lonnie Donegan hits. I couldn't concentrate at school thinking of Lonnie Donegan.'[4] Davy left school in 1958 and became one of the first to follow in the footsteps of Alex Campbell and go busking on the streets of Paris. Wizz Jones would follow the same path: 'When I hit Paris [in 1959] it was late at night and he suddenly came round the corner. I remember seeing this vision of this tall, blond-haired, statuesque, deep-tanned, god type of person as he was walking towards me. I thought, "That's what I wanna be!" And he said, "I've just come up from Greece, man." He was so cool.'[5]

By the turn of the sixties, Davy Graham exuded an almost military bearing that contrasted perfectly his exoticism as an instrumentalist. But to a degree this was a studied cool, an affectation which he maintained and very probably grew into. It was, perhaps, a necessary part of coping with the rigours of life from an unusual background. As Duffy Power, one of Britain's earliest rock'n'roll recording artists, recalls: 'He lived on Westbourne Grove but he chose to go to a school south of the river, miles from where he lived. I get the feeling this might have been to keep his mixed-race background private. There were race riots around Notting Hill at that time, plus he'd damaged his eye with a pencil as a kid and he was slightly withdrawn anyway, so you don't know what kind of trials he had in the fifties.'

Others who recall Davy Graham from his pre-performing days affirm this picture of a shy, bookish and circumspect individual. But Graham was on a mission to become the master of his instrument. During 1959, Steve Benbow, Roy Guest and co. were appearing as the Wanderers on *Saturday Club*. 'We rehearsed in Old Brompton Road,' says Benbow. 'Davy, this kid, used to sit in the corner and watch and every so often he'd say, "Could you show me that chord?" And of course we did. We had no idea he'd become so good. It was unbelievable what happened. He went away to Morocco, came back and blew a hole through everyone.'

Andy Irvine's experience of the formative virtuoso is similar. Andy was not alone in hanging out with 'Rambling' Jack Elliott in 1959 – 60: 'I would arrive at Jack's bedsit and sit at the end of the bed till he and his wife woke up,' he says. 'But then Davy would arrive, at eleven or twelve o'clock, and Jack and June and myself would go out – while Davy would stay in the flat and play Jack's guitar. And when we came home Davy would quickly go. It was as if he could not be in the same space as the rest of us. The strings would be dead and Jack would say, "Oh, I don't know why I let that guy play my guitar." But he'd be there every day. He lived with his mother at the time and had a job pushing a broom somewhere and was an odd kind of guy. I thought he was very shy when I first met him, but the fact that he practised guitar six hours a day showed where his outlets lay.'

Over the next couple of years, the combination of natural shyness and dedication were apparent to anyone who cared to frequent the coffee bars and restaurants of Soho. Long John Baldry was Davy's sparring partner at the time: 'They had a feud going,' says Wizz Jones, 'but everyone used to say, "Wouldn't it be wonderful to see them play together?" 'cos John had such a great voice and Davy was such a brilliant player – a true innovator.' Long John and Davy did work together once on TV (*Hullaballoo*, 1963) but never on record.

Unlike Baldry, whose own fame peaked towards the end of the sixties, it was during his earliest and only sparsely recorded performing years that Graham truly secured his reputation. The real beginning of Davy Graham as a guitar legend, as an astonishingly advanced technician amongst a peer group of guitar pickers still happy to master the basic licks on Broonzy and Leadbelly records, was an appearance in Ken Russell's BBC film *Hound Dogs and Bach Addicts: The Guitar Craze*, first broadcast in June 1959. Budding guitarists the length and breadth of Britain watched Davy performing a complex blues and a fingerstyle arrangement of 'Cry Me A River' alongside contributions from Julian Bream, Bert Weedon and Lonnie Donegan. Martin Carthy was one of those whose jaw was on the floor: 'The twelve-bar blues he played seemed to have about three parts going at the same time. Contrapuntal blues! It was outrageously brilliant.'[6] Hamish Imlach had been equally impressed: 'It was okay when there was only one of him. But then Bert came along.'[7]

Bert Jansch, as a performer, did not exist before some indefinable point in 1962. Prior to that, he was an amazing player, but an amazing player in the corner of a room, on somebody else's guitar, and not readily inclined to sing. Bert would find his voice in due course. But in the meantime, Davy Graham

had single-handedly introduced Britain to the concept of the folk guitar
instrumental. It is often said that over in America John Fahey, in releasing a
short-run private pressing of his bizarre all-instrumental blues pastiche *The
Transfiguration Of Blind Joe Death* in 1959, invented both steel-strung guitar
music and the industry to support it, but Davy Graham could hardly have
known what was going on in the curious world of John Fahey. In Britain,
Davy Graham can claim the mantle of inventor.

'Davy was the first person I ever heard play more than one line of music at
once on the guitar,' says Robin Williamson. 'He'd kind of done a Big Bill
Broonzy/baroque thing because Bill used to go *thump, thump, thump* on the
bass string with his thumb – which Martin Carthy borrowed. But Davy took
the notion of making a baroque bassline, moving it slightly. The classic
example of that was "Angi". And Bert developed that considerably further.
But Davy was the man really – the first man to have a go at it in Britain. For
me, I was never so much into trying to do things that moved against each
other. I liked melody very much and alternate tunings. I explored tunings
very thoroughly at that point. Martin Carthy, who later developed a lot of
his own very fine tunings, was working mainly in standard tuning at that
time.'

Carthy, a regular visitor to Edinburgh by this stage, was indeed working
mainly in standard guitar tuning. But he had already started to look for
usable alternatives. By the end of the decade he had found, by process of
elimination, the note sequence that would most easily adapt to the demands
of accompanying English traditional song and consequently create the
distinctive Martin Carthy 'sound': CGCDGA. That tuning would remain
largely exclusive to Carthy's vision. But he had almost, before Davy,
stumbled upon the tuning that would become a cunning device in the
hands of Bert Jansch (who has employed it only sparingly) and something
integral to the subsequent careers of Archie Fisher, Jimmy Page and virtually
every future accompanist of Scottish and Irish traditional music: DADGAD.

'I met this old-timey band from Harvard University, the Charles River
Holy Boys, in 1961 or '62,' says Carthy, 'and I worked out this tuning that
was one step away from DADGAD: DGDGAD. I was trying to accompany
a particular song of theirs, and it sort of did the job but it wasn't very
adaptable. I remember showing it to Davy, and later Davy came up with
DADGAD. I'm not trying to take credit. I don't know if what I showed him
had anything to do with it at all. But he was the man. When he invented
DADGAD that was the moment life got interesting.'

To non-guitarists, the revolutionary new tuning can be described as
having the effect of adding hitherto impossible new chord sequences to the
player's armoury, opening up new melodic possibilities (albeit within a

limited range of keys) and creating a bigger, richer sound. Its invention can be dated roughly to June 1963.[8] By then, it merely added to Graham's enigma. 'He was the excellence,' says Archie Fisher. 'When he played, everything was incredibly simple. The economy of his style was what impressed most guitarists. Then, of course, we suddenly realised he wasn't playing in conventional tunings.'[9]

The holy grail of a truly successful alternate tuning was still on the distant horizon when 'Angi' appeared on record. Here was an exercise in standard tuning, but one that expanded forever the musical parameters of the folk form. 'Some of his style was more like piano playing than guitar,' says Archie Fisher, 'using big, massive sevenths, elevenths, things with funny numbers after them, but picking them cleanly with his right hand, imposing a classical or jazz technique on blues and then traditional music.'[10]

Moving swiftly on from his early obsession with skiffle, Davy was listening to the likes of Miles Davis, Wes Montgomery, Charles Mingus and Ornette Coleman. Regarding blues, Snooks Eaglin was a favourite and he would add a number of Chicago blues songs to his repertoire, but during 1962 the folk and blues scenes in London were at last going their separate ways. Davy Graham was, by default, falling on the folk side of the fence. Although involved for some months in Alexis Korner's new band Blues Incorporated (and indeed subsequently in John Mayall's Bluesbreakers), the godfather of British blues was not ultimately convinced that Davy was on the right wavelength: 'Alexis told me he didn't think Davy had a good feel for the blues,' says Duffy Power. For Davy, his admiration for Alexis was as much to do with his lovably rogueish tendencies as an operator: 'He was a terrific hustler,' says Davy, 'but he could charm you at the same time. He once asked me to do a gig for him that he couldn't do. I did it and got twelve pounds for it and he got the other twenty!'[11]

It was nevertheless Alexis who had realised the importance of getting Davy, and particularly 'Angi', on record, and who had arranged the session. Alexis's patronage and influence within British blues has long been recognised, but his patronage of Davy Graham would prove no less crucial to the development of British folk. 'Folk-baroque', in the terminology of Karl Dallas, may not have been a universally popular phrase, but in describing a music that blended folk, baroque, blues, jazz and other exotica together on an acoustic guitar it would come as close as anything to putting a label on Davy Graham. And, later, on Bert Jansch.

Davy Graham was not the only London devotee of the new music to have connections in Edinburgh. Clive Palmer had a friend in Kent who had been to Gordonstoun, an exclusive Scottish public school. That friend was going

up to Edinburgh to visit with an old school pal called Rod Harbinson: 'So
we followed him up, hitch-hiking, spending a couple of nights by the side of
the road,' says Clive. 'A couple of days after arriving in Edinburgh I got
asked to a party down the back of Princes Street and I met Bert at that party.
He was very much the same then as he is now – laid back, very relaxed.' A
few days later, Clive and his banjo turned up at the Crown Bar in Museum
Street. In the wake of the Howff, Archie Fisher was fronting a new Tuesday
night folk club at the venue. 'I met Robin that night,' says Clive. 'We started
playing together and through that I really started to get to know Bert.'

The 'three dreamers' – Bert Jansch, Robin Williamson and Clive Palmer
– became flatmates: 'We all shared lodgings in two or three different
buildings, all derelict,' says Robin, 'all of which would now be described
as squats. There was one of them in the Grassmarket, there was one in what's
now a car park opposite Greyfriars' Bobby [Society Buildings] and there was
another one in what's now really quite a trendy street near the university
[West Nicolson Street]. At that time it was a complete slum.'

The flat in West Nicolson Street was originally tenanted by Clive's initial
Edinburgh contact, Rod Harbinson. His family owned a whisky distillery,
which gave him the luxury of a private income, and an island near Oban,
which provided a place to take his friends periodically for a weekend's
adventuring. 'Rod was one of the early longhairs,' says Robin, 'long hair, long
beard and always wearing a kilt. Quite a distinctive figure.' Along with an
unidentified cohort, Rod was immortalised obliquely in Hamish Imlach's
memoirs: 'There were two young hairy freaks, classic ex-public schoolboys,'
declared Hamish, 'who had "gone to the bad" as they said in those days. They
lived in Society Buildings, a great name for a hovel, a horrible tenement
which had been posh 150 years earlier. They rode around in a vintage
convertible, wearing kilts, their sporrans stuffed with one-pound deals of hash.
I went to call on them in the middle of winter. They had one room, the size
of a tennis court, with a ceiling twenty foot high. They couldn't afford to heat
such a room, so they had erected a tent, indoors, and huddled inside wrapped
in blankets and heated by a paraffin heater. Their big hobby was poaching
sheep for the pot. One time they shot a prize ram. There were wanted notices
everywhere featuring this ram, which had already been stewed and eaten, and
was apparently very tough. You ate what you could. Archie was subsisting on
oatmeal. I remember he once tried currying it.'[12]

Money was short but the lifestyle pleasurable: 'You got up when you got
up,' says Clive. 'Rod put us up and bought the food when we didn't have
any money. But there were a lot of parties, and the Crown Bar was just
around the corner. So many things happening. To me, Edinburgh was really
going at that time. So many talented people around. I remember Bert

spending a lot of time on his own. There was a period when he was staying with a guy called Adam Parker-Rhodes. I think he was connected to the Cecil Rhodes people. I remember him staying there 'cos he was carving this chess set. He was very clever with things like that.'

By this stage, 1962, Dolina MacLennan was back from her teaching sojourn in Fife and had reclaimed the flat at 19 Bristo Place. Being situated across the road from the Crown Bar, it became a free hotel for travelling folk singers. It was also just around the corner from Bert, Clive and Robin: 'Robin wasn't as spiritual as he is now, he was just into music,' says Dolina. 'He was more effervescent than Bert. Clive was more like Bert. He had this very bad limp and was more into himself.' The common bond was the love of music and the emphatic rejection of a conventional lifestyle.

'It was a funny sort of time,' says Robin. 'I think most of us saw ourselves as some sort of bohemian. The Jack Kerouac era hadn't quite petered out and the hippy era hadn't quite petered in, so it was somewhere in between. There was a coined term at the time, "folknik", but that didn't really cover it. The notion was that there was an intellectual approach to a sort of "Zen life". Somehow it got around to bumming it with no money in a very stoned manner, and that somehow linked into the traditional music scene. A very curious mixture. But we seemed to spend an awful lot of time sitting around playing tunes, just fooling around with music – hours and hours and hours of it. There was so little money and there was very little time to do anything other than rolling up dog-ends and having a go at this or that tuning. I was interested in singing, Bert was interested in guitar riffs. He went through a brief period of carving wood. He tried to make a chess set, which became gradually more and more arcane. He did sing a bit, but mainly all I remember about Bert really is Bert playing the guitar.'

Robin was becoming particularly interested in traditional music, especially as performed by the older singers, many of them from 'the travelling folk' and now becoming revered regulars in the folk clubs: Jimmy Mac-Beath, who claimed descent from Macbeth, King of Scotland and namesake of the play that is not named; 'Old' Davy Stewart; Belle Stewart; Jeannie Robertson and their peers. In one of his earliest interviews, for *Melody Maker* in July 1966, Bert recalled that he'd 'done so many gigs with Jimmy MacBeath that we are quite old friends. I've worked with Belle Stewart and Davy Stewart too – a mad idiot but quite a guy.' Clive's passion was still music hall, but he was interested in the tradition and could read music: 'Clive used to sit there and sing all these old music-hall songs and I was absolutely amazed by it all,' says Bert. 'An absolute genius. From Clive I learned that real folk music is music that's around. It's not just traditional songs; it can be Vera Lynn.'[13]

Bert was soaking up whatever was around, including whatever music Robin and Clive were coming up with. Clive in particular would prove to be a major influence in his songwriting. Modern jazz was becoming a part of the picture too. 'There were certain favourite records,' says Robin. 'We never owned any of them or had any kind of record player, or any kind of possessions at all really. But there were records around in those days, and they were very influential because there wasn't a lot of them.' *Mingus Ah-Um* by Charlie Mingus and *The Night Time Is The Right Time* by Ray Charles and the Raylettes are recalled with particular fondness.

A new experience, in the form of dope from North Africa via Glasgow, was becoming widely available in Edinburgh at this time. Bert once recalled that 'in my circle of acquaintances we were getting through pounds of the stuff as early as 1961,'[14] but if so it was not common knowledge. 'It was only when Clive Palmer came on the scene that I began to be aware of it,' says Maggie Cruickshank.

'Drugs were very influential,' remembers Robin. 'Absolutely essential to the whole lifestyle then. It divided very clearly into those that smoked and those that drank. I recall pot being a major influence not only on how I thought about writing songs but possibly I would never have thought *about* writing songs had it not been for smoking. It was nothing to do with inhibitions, just opening up various corners of the mind. And anyway, growing up in Scotland after the war was such a crock of terrible times. I suppose it must have been the same in any other part of Britain. It was a bit grim. So there was a tremendous changeover when this blast of sunlight came in which, at that time, had a lot to do with drugs. It was another view on the world, almost like a fresh start. People were just trying to cheer up, basically. The songs people were writing were imitative and political and all of a sudden after drugs filtered in they were anything but imitative and not at all political – they were playful, discursive, quirky, elusive and involved the interchanging of modes and ideas. I'm not saying that drugs are a good idea. I'm just saying that that's the way it was then.'

'There was a wee bit of a quandary with Robin,' says Ray Fisher, 'because when people were writing songs, which was unusual at that time anyway, there was always a reason to write – like we needed a song to sing at the American sailors or something like that. I suppose his songs were just for fun. Him and Clive, they were a wee bit outrageous. People thought they were odd.'[15]

Along with Liz Cruickshank, Licorice McKechnie was one of a handful of girls Bert courted during his Edinburgh years. Licorice would eventually become, alongside Robin, a member of the Incredible String Band.[16] Bert's reputation as someone apparently instantly attractive to significant numbers of women, in spite of or because of his withdrawn personality, is an enduring quality. It was one element that contributed to making him the most charismatic performer on the London folk scene in the mid-sixties and, before that, in the clubs of Glasgow and Edinburgh. 'He had this "little boy lost" appearance,' says Dolina MacLennan. 'I was never affected by it myself.' 'To hazard an opinion,' says Robin, 'I think perhaps he brought out the maternal in women because he seemed to be always about to snuff out like a candle flame. He was like a kind of Scottish James Dean.' Comedian Billy Connolly, then an aspiring banjo player in Glasgow, puts it all into perspective: 'Women loved him,' he said. 'They were crazy about him. It was just extraordinary. They all wanted to be his mother – they all thought he was lonely and all that. He sounded so distressed and *alone*. So I would write songs like that: *"I'm lonely . . .!"* And nobody would come near me! "God, leave him alone, it's that lonely guy again!" '[17]

However Bert's character had evolved, it could not easily be faked. But was he really this lonely, angst-ridden character of legend? 'I think he probably was,' says Robin. 'But I think we all were then. He never discussed his family. But then none of us ever discussed our families. We must have travelled, off and on, hundreds and hundreds of miles together and I don't recall discussing pretty much of anything with him! We didn't get around to talking about God or how the world is or the meaning of life or anything like that – stuff that you normally talk about when people have a discussion. A man of few words.'

Bert's travelling, like the chronology of his domestic arrangements, is impossible to reconstruct precisely. But he had certainly been to France at least once before September 1962: the date of a live performance in Glasgow which remains his earliest extant recording.[18] In September 1963 Bert travelled to Morocco. He believes he had been to the South of France not once but twice before that: 'I had friends in Edinburgh who used to renovate people's houses in France and that's how I ended up going there,' he says. 'They had a place in Nanturon, near St Tropez, and I used to hitch-hike. We stayed there two or three months once. It was an absolutely gorgeous place, a Saracen village built in a circle with narrow streets and a centre like a village square. It was full of rich people. Every day a limousine would drive up, Brigitte Bardot would get out and sit outside this café. Every day – and I didn't have the courage to go up and say hello.'

Bert's first trip to France was undertaken during the lifetime of the Howff, probably summer 1961. He had set off from Edinburgh with a friend, 'a London guy who I'd met at the club. I remember getting caught with him on the railway. We were fiddling the fares – buying a ticket for threepence and travelling hundreds of miles. We stayed at his parents' house out in Buckhurst Hill, just outside London.'[19] The 'friend' subsequently absconded with Bert's 'Lonnie Donegan' guitar. Not a good start. The pair had travelled to London with the intention of finding some work on a building site to earn some money. On his own, Bert at least tried to see the plan through.

'I actually managed to get the whole squad sacked,' he recalls, 'because I refused to work in the rain. We were digging the foundations for a bridge and it started raining. I stopped work, went into the hut and drank tea – and they all followed me, all these big Irishmen. We were having a great time there in the hut until the foreman came in and sacked the whole lot of us. And that was my first day's work!'

While Bert was busy fiddling the fares down to London, a couple of young Londoners from Kingsbury County Grammar School were hitch-hiking in the opposite direction. Their names are forgotten and they play no part in Bert's story save to provide the first link in a chain that would lead, a couple of years down the line, to Bert's first base in London: periodically sharing a flat with a cheery art student by the name of John Challis and a philosophical man of leisure called David Blass.

'I started at Ealing Art College in September 1961,' says Challis. 'I'd done my first major hitch-hiking trip that summer, going across France with my girlfriend. So I think when someone suggested hitching to Edinburgh I might have said,"Yeah, I know how to do that!" Already there had been these other two friends who had gone up to the Edinburgh Festival that year and they had encountered the "New Departures" poets on the Fringe. They'd gone up as two nice little sixth formers to hear classical music and came back two raving beatniks. One of the people they'd got to know was a bloke called Adam Parker-Rhodes, a student at Edinburgh University. He was quite a major connection between us in London and the people up in Edinburgh. It was a base for a lot of us.'

Bert was of course also friendly with Parker-Rhodes. Just prior to the New Year, Challis, Blass and a third friend, George Tapner, hitched up to Edinburgh – lured not least by the attraction of a bohemian arts scene and the amazing availability of soft drugs. Like Challis, whom he knew from Kingsbury County Grammar, Blass had enrolled at Ealing Art College in September. He lasted six weeks before deciding it was not for him. Aside from Parker-Rhodes, the pair had another potential connection to Bert: a Glasgow drug dealer called Neil McClelland. Blass believes that he first met Bert, in Edinburgh, via McClelland, and recalls the place where he was living at the time: a room in a tall building on the Grassmarket, shared with another person, no doubt Robin Williamson. Through a combination of circumstances and his family's cosmopolitan, liberal values David Blass's home in London had become an open house to his friends and to their friends. In this context, McClelland had met Blass the previous year.

'McClelland was very intelligent and streetwise, but very dodgy,' says Challis. 'It might have been him who put us on to the Howff.[20] When I went to the Howff the first time, which was a few days before this big do which I believe was going to be the last night, it was during the New Year period. We knew *of* Bert but we may not actually have met him by then.' Strangely, although travelling to Edinburgh together, Blass became separated from Challis and Tapner and the two camps had consequently differing adventures: Blass did not visit the Howff but did meet Bert; Challis did not meet Bert but did visit the Howff.

On what was almost certainly his next trip to France, in the late spring of 1962, Bert and another long-forgotten travelling companion stopped at the family home of David Blass, in Wembley Park. John Challis also turned up at the Blass residence that evening: 'It was a place of far greater freedom and tolerance than we were used to in our own homes,' says Challis, 'so we were there a lot. I have this memory of the first time Bert appeared in the living room. I was sitting there having a drink, Bert came in with this other guy,[21] was introduced, sat down and within a short period of time he'd got a guitar out, started playing it and we were all just stunned! I had some idea of where he was coming from because I was already into country blues and we'd also, all of us, been to various folk clubs, like the Ballads & Blues. But that was all people doing Pete Seeger and Woody Guthrie stuff or traditional English music. Bert was around for a couple of days, but it was quite a while before I saw him again. The next time I saw him was when they were on their way back. By that time he'd written "Strolling Down The Highway". I think it was one of the first songs he'd actually written rather than just taking an existing song and adapting it.'

'I think I was semi-emulating Davy and a few others,' says Bert, of his wanderlust. 'The generation before me – players like Davy, Alex Campbell and Wizz Jones – had all done their fair share of busking around Europe, so I just naturally followed suit. You just busked wherever you went. I used to make just about enough money to get by. The best place I ever busked was in St Tropez with a blonde, buxom girl called Felicity, or "Fish" as she used to get called. We'd do an hour on the harbour front and make enough money for both of us to live for a week! We'd knock out Leadbelly numbers and anything else we could think of.'[22]

Of Bert's immediate circle, only Clive Palmer had already been to Paris, busking on the streets with Wizz Jones in 1960 or thereabouts. 'I didn't see him for years [after that],' says Wizz, 'and then I got a letter from Edinburgh, where he was living with Robin and Bert. I went up to see him.'[23] Bert would no doubt have been made aware, then, of Wizz Jones's adventures on the continent. He would already have been aware of Davy Graham's travels. He had few contacts and no money, but the prospect of getting out of 'Auld Reekie' for a while was becoming irresistible: 'I was open to the world,' he said. 'I just wanted to travel around and see a few places. But I also had this idea in the back of my mind that I wanted to be a folk singer.'[24]

Clive Palmer, Wizz Jones and Davy Graham all had experience of Europe to impart but the greatest role model of them all, the king of the road both then and for years to come, was a Glasgow man. A deeply charismatic, romantic figure who ricocheted off every corner of the embryonic folk revival, never stopping long in any one place, save perhaps his kingdom on the streets of Paris, Alex Campbell was some years older than the Bert Jansch generation but still one of them. An entertainer first, with no left-wing ties, Campbell knew all about Ewan MacColl and his views and disdained them. MacColl would have reciprocated in kind save for one complication: Alex Campbell was married to Peggy Seeger, the woman he loved.

'Alex married Peggy for Ewan,' says Steve Benbow, 'and the story is he never got paid. She couldn't work here unless she had a work permit or became a British citizen. I think they used Alex. I don't know why. A strange business.' Ewan had fallen for Peggy on their first time meeting, in March 1956, but he was already married to his second wife, Jean Newlove. They met again at the World Festival of Democratic Youth in Moscow in July 1957. Peggy returned to Britain to work with Ewan in the spring of 1958, but someone reported her expired work permit to the Home Office and she was given two days to leave. She went to France but was deported back and forth to Belgium and Holland, in a sequence of international buck-passing, before finally ending up, seven months pregnant, at a friend's flat in Paris.

'Alex Campbell broke the chain of events by marrying me in Paris on January 24 1959,' she later wrote. 'It was a hilarious ceremony. The American priest, in surplice and sneakers, lectured Alex at length on his forthcoming lifetime commitment to the poor girl whom he had gotten into such trouble. The following day I arrived, unimpeded, in London, six weeks before the birth of my first son. I swore allegiance to Her Majesty the Queen and settled down with Ewan, with great upheaval for everyone concerned.'[25] One must wonder whether the marriage was, to one of its participants at least, greater than a thing of convenience: 'Alex, whenever he got drunk,' says Bert, 'that was the one subject he brought up. You'd have to take that on board to assess Ewan's character.'

Born in Glasgow in the 1920s, Alex Campbell was a true romantic: a tearful sentimentalist, a ribald comedian, a troubadour, a legend in his own lifetime and perhaps in his day the most loved man in British folk. He would be the British blueprint for the Bert Jansch generation. Alex passed through all the key places at all the key times, played some songs, gave encouragement to the young up-and-comings, and moved on along the road. He is recalled, for example, as an early performer at Cyril Davis and Alexis Korner's Blues & Barrelhouse club in the late fifties; he was a regular at Malcolm Nixon's Ballads & Blues during its ACTT period; and he managed one visit to the Howff, enjoying the place so much, in Hamish Imlach's words, that 'he ended up staying for days, missing gigs all over the country'. Alex Campbell, in the early years of the folk revival, was everywhere. But who was he and where had he come from?

In response to what must now be viewed as the definitive Campbell interview, for *Folk News* in 1978, Dominic Behan wrote a lengthy letter questioning Alex's version of history, effectively his place in the folk revival, and his 'criticisms' of MacColl. In fact, Campbell had been both generous and philosophical about his old adversary: 'I don't think there'll ever be as good a writer as MacColl,' said Campbell. 'He's written some rubbish but his work on the *Radio Ballads*, that'll stand for all time. I went to see his show recently. After all the kerfuffle about him being him and me being me and never the twain shall meet, we are both doing literally the same kind of show. Because MacColl's now a showman. I don't know, perhaps he always was.'[26]

'Alex certainly met Peggy when he was in France,' wrote Behan, a tad mischievously in response, 'but did he know Ewan well too? I do not recollect Ewan talking about him and I do not remember seeing him except in the circumstances I have described.'[27] The circumstances Behan referred to were essentially those occasions, the earliest being the Edinburgh Festival of 1963, when Dominic and Alex worked together. Dominic was falling into the trap of believing that because he had not been aware of Alex prior to this (and Alex had initially been recommended to Dominic as an accompanist by Steve Benbow, otherwise engaged at the time), Alex had therefore played no previous role in the folk revival. He could not have been more wrong. In articulating a view held by many of those hundreds of younger performers – some destined for greatness, others to be no more than floor singers at their local club – a subsequent published response to Behan's revisionism, from one Michael Sutton, provides a compelling testament to Alex Campbell's place in history:

'From giving encouragement and instruction to young performers,' wrote Sutton, 'we saw him giving due acknowledgement and homage to the original sources of the songs he sang and, above all, we saw him reaching out to audiences, many of whom knew very little about folk music, and turning them on to it – planting a rich harvest for others to reap. In those days the folk scene was a very factional affair, full of splinter groups with chips on their shoulders. But while the scribes and pharisees were haggling over the finer points of doctrinal orthodoxy in small back rooms, Alex was going out among the folk, spreading the good word.'[28]

'What I do is so ephemeral, man, it's a nothing,' Alex once said. But he did not really mean it. 'In those days it was like being a missionary. I was at a party once. There were fourteen people and thirteen said I was the first folk singer they'd ever heard.' Alex Campbell reputedly made a hundred records in his lifetime. He never took them too seriously and, in any case, they never sold. As for himself, he always learned songs from people, not records, and only ever wrote a handful of songs himself. One of these, 'Been On The Road So Long', was penned in the early sixties and became his calling card, his ethos and his epitaph. Bert Jansch would record it several times during his own career.[29]

'Alex was larger than life,' says Dolina MacLennan, who put him up in Edinburgh many times. 'A total and utter romantic, totally outrageous and a wonderful entertainer – full of jokes but always close to tears as well.' 'He was good at getting himself gigs,' says Martin Carthy, 'but he didn't tour in the same way you do now. He'd come back from Paris in the winter, get himself some gigs and then go back to Paris. There were people who despised him, others who thought he was wonderful. In his way, he was a star.'

'When you're a young man you think you're going to be a poet,' said Campbell. 'I came into folk music from poetry, reading the ballads. I never realised they were sung. Then it must have been 1947 or 1948 I saw Jean Ritchie at the Festival Hall. It floored me. [But] I never thought I would sing folk songs in my life. The whole thing's an accident.'

Campbell's eventual embracing of music as a living and his near-invention of the troubadour lifestyle that went with it can be traced back to Baden-Powell, the 'gang shows' and the arduous country hikes that were part of a Glasgow boy scout's experience. For a slum kid, it was the only way to see what lay beyond the concrete. By the 1930s Campbell's family, originally from the Hebrides, were poverty-trapped city dwellers. His mother, father and two sisters had all died from TB in the same year. Alex was rescued from an orphanage by his grandmother who managed to bring him up on a meagre pension. Being involved in scouting's contribution to the war effort in Glasgow enabled him to mix with the various Polish, Australian and American servicemen based in the city, and to soak up their songs and culture: 'I knew Leadbelly songs during the war. I knew "Pick A Bale Of Cotton" before I heard it sung by anybody else. I knew "Goodbye Booze". These were all wartime songs. [But] Northern children in my generation, in any town in Scotland, were brought up with a whole background of folk music.'

Campbell got a job with the Civil Service and made his way up to Higher Executive Officer. One day, in 1955, he lost his temper, took it out on two of his clerks and was obliged to resign. Having already visited Paris and enjoyed the place, he returned on a whim and took a course at the Sorbonne. 'I went over with £800 which was a lot of bread in those days and I ran through that in a month. So there I am without any bread or anything at all except a guitar, so I started to sing in the streets.' It would be a way of life for the next six years.

'I was lucky being in the right place at the right time in Paris. How was I to know there was going to be a folk revival? It was so unusual then to see a street singer. There were the chain-breakers and the sword-swallowers and the fire-eaters but there were no folk singers in the streets. It was against the law. It was foreigners like myself who would do it. I was singing Leadbelly, skiffle numbers, occasional Scottish songs that I've known since I was a wee boy. Then again, I didn't consider them folk songs – I was just a skiffler.'

After a year or so, Campbell and a hard-drinking American called Derroll Adams secured a residency at the Contrascarpe, a popular cabaret café, which Campbell maintained for three and a half years on fifteen shillings a night, seven nights a week. He continued to work the streets, and to sell the New York Herald Tribune around the cafés at midnight. 'Paris at that time was a tremendous melting pot. We all mixed together: poets, painters, artists, writers. It became a sort of proving ground. Almost all the young kids like Wizz Jones, Malcolm Price, Davy Graham, they all came over. We had a system: the good cafés, the good theatre queues, that was for the residents, the guys who'd been there a long time. The new ones, you could tell them, "You work there . . ." I was called King of The Quarter at one time. I was more or less The Man.'

Alex would also make forays back to Britain. The sixties were approaching and the London folk scene rapidly growing. 'When I came back MacColl was a huge influence on the scene. I sang at the Ballads & Blues when he was still singing there. I think maybe we didn't get on too well because, maybe, I was more of a Scotsman than he was. I've a tremendous respect for the guy but I didn't like his approach to the people.' Campbell had first heard MacColl on record, and had assumed him to be an Englishman imitating a Scots accent. When MacColl's diktat of singing only music from one's own national or regional background came along, Campbell was having none of it: 'I was of the opinion that I loved Guthrie songs particularly, and I was going to sing Guthrie songs. Whether I was doing it authentically or correctly or not I didn't give a damn. So much so that it crystallised in an article in the *Observer* that said you were either a MacCollite or a Campbellite. I was put into a position that I never wanted to be in. [But] those days were good days because there was excitement and controversy on the scene. Josh MacRae called it "Schism & Booze". But it made me get to the point where I almost refused to sing any Scottish songs just in defiance of everyone expecting me to. If there hadn't been that controversy I would have developed differently. I would have been singing my own songs a lot earlier than I did.'[30]

When the spread of folk clubs around Britain began in earnest, Alex became a victim of his own generosity and reputation as an entertainer: 'I found I was being asked to open folksong clubs. There were very few pros in those days. I don't think anyone would ask Ewan MacColl to open up a club. For a start, he'd charge a lot more. I went on to open up maybe six hundred clubs. When I reached my nadir it must have been about 1962. I was getting fifteen to thirty bob a night from the clubs. I was sick and fed up with it all.' By this time Alex was living in London with his partner Patsy and the first of their children: 'There was one Christmas Eve, we had one egg in the house for the three of us. An egg, that was all. I said, "Fuck it, Patsy, I'm going to go out and busk." So I went up to Regent Street and it was marvellous. I really worked, I put on a show. I'd just got to the end of my second song and the police came up and stopped me. I said, "For Christ's sake, fellas, let me alone. I need the bread." "We can't," they said, "you're blocking the whole of Regent Street. There's no traffic moving." There were literally thousands of people there. I walked away disconsolately. I thought: "What am I going to do?" And I bumped into Bruce Dunnet. I told him the story and Bruce gave me ten quid. We got a chicken and everything else and that was a good Christmas. Then, of course, it picked up. I rolled along with the revival. But that's how low it was.'

By the 1962 Edinburgh Festival, the city's folk scene was firmly established and there was much fun to be had. Martha Schlamme, for a start, was back in town and performing this time at the Palladium. 'Alas there is no longer a Howff,' she lamented to Eric Winter, 'and Edinburgh will not be the same.' Bert Jansch, now on the verge of becoming a folk singer and actually performing his songs in public places at regular intervals, is conspicuous by his absence from any anecdotes of that year's shenanigans. It may be conjectured that he was off travelling in France at the time. Archie Fisher, meanwhile, was running a ceilidh with Jill Doyle/Guest at the Outlook

Tower, on hire from the Church of Scotland, and fronting an after-hours club in a disused toffee factory down by the Grassmarket.

'The sweetie factory operated on two levels,' says Hamish Imlach, 'two big rooms, where there were jazz bands and various folk singers like myself getting thirty bob a day to be there and fill in with songs when needed. We were able to doss on cattle mats in the chocolate room. It was a remarkable place. I recall seeing the conductor of the Berlin Philharmonic Orchestra, Cleo Laine and Geraint Evans all perched on the plastic cattle mats and Albert Finney riding in on a motorcycle. The Police hated the place because it was a club – you could pay for membership that lasted the three weeks then bring your carryout with you. In the second week they sold some basic food, then the police were able to close it down because of catering standards.'[31]

Eric Winter had a great time introducing three divas from the far reaches of folksong to each other at that year's festival: Martha Schlamme, Portuguese singer Amalia Rodrigues and Scots balladeer Jeannie Robertson. The venue was the Outlook Tower, and Owen Hand recalls the ensuing singing session, bristling with rivalry and one-upmanship, as one of the great nights of the revival. For the first time ever, folk events were accepted as part of the official Festival, with a series of shows at Murrayfield ice rink, hosted by Rory & Alex McEwan and presenting as guests the Clancy Brothers and Tommy Makem from Ireland (well-established in America, but rare performers in Britain); Carolyn Hester from America; London songwriter and broadcaster Sydney Carter, who brought with him a young West Indian singer, Nadia Cattouse; the classical guitarist and lutenist Julian Bream; and, representing the locals, Dolina MacLennan. Such a programme was indeed a concession to the new genre but the real breakthrough in presenting folksong to the masses in a festival/concert setting was going on elsewhere.

'Centre 42' was the name of the enterprise, emanating from Resolution 42 passed by the Trades Union Congress of 1960 which recognised 'the importance of the arts in the life of the community especially now when many unions are securing a shorter working week and greater leisure for their members'. The aspiration was to build a 'Cultural Palace' (to be constructed in London, of course) to be known as Centre 42. But before such plans got off the drawing board, Centre 42 came into existence as a touring festival, setting up in a given provincial town for a week, targeting 'deprived' working-class audiences, taking a week off and then moving on to the next town. As an attempt to devolve culture and art from London to the provinces it was a grand ideal. The playwright Arnold Wesker was at its helm, with Ewan MacColl and Bert Lloyd looking after the musical programme for the opening night concerts of each festival. A pilot event took place at Wellingborough in 1961 and was successful enough to be extended to cover five more towns the following year: Hayes, Bristol, Birmingham, Nottingham and Leicester. With a week off between each event, it was effectively a nine-week tour. Part of the brief was to involve singers from the areas the tour stopped in. At Nottingham, in August 1962, one of those to audition was Anne Briggs, who would become not only a travelling companion and early champion of Bert Jansch, but the greatest English traditional singer of her generation.

'I got a bunch of O levels and I was going to try and get into Durham University to do Fine Art,' says Anne. 'But after a year in sixth form Centre 42 came along and I thought, "Yeah, a bird in the hand's worth two in the bush – go for it."' Anne had been hanging round with a couple of lads from her village who had taught her a little bit of guitar, encouraged her to sing and accompanied her on a few coffee bar folk sessions in Nottingham. 'Woody Guthrie was a big hero,' she says. 'I used to do all his stuff.' It was nevertheless for English songs that Anne would become known, and even then there were recorded sources to learn from: 'I'd heard an Isla Cameron LP when I was fifteen and it was the first time I'd heard a modern recording of unaccompanied traditional singing. I'd heard field recordings on the radio of women from Barra bashing tweed around, but hearing Isla Cameron and then Mary O'Hara was a revelation. I had a tape recorder and I would record BBC folk programmes and learn the songs that way. There were other folk singers around Nottinghamshire, although the bias was very much American – even in the way they presented English and Scottish material. But I knew "my" songs as soon as I heard them, and I'd sing them my way.'

The night of the Centre 42 concert Anne sang at least two songs, unaccompanied: 'Let No Man Steal Your Thyme' and 'She Moves Through The Fair' – two songs, coincidentally, that she would record live in Edinburgh for Decca the following year, without a trace of American influence. Anne's entire recording career happened as a direct result of Centre 42: 'I think, in hindsight,' she says, 'it consolidated the woolly beginnings of the folk music revival. It made people in different parts of the country aware that they weren't just doing their thing in isolation. There were folk clubs in Nottingham, Bristol, Manchester, all over, and it brought things together and established a network. If nothing else, Centre 42 made the folk music revival coherent.'

Archie's sister Ray Fisher, who would later record with Anne and who performed on four of the five festivals herself, was intrigued to discover the extent of the musical activity around Britain that had developed with varying degrees of independence from London. The scene going on in Tyneside, led by the likes of Lou Killen and Johnny Handle, was particularly fascinating (Ray would subsequently marry Tyneside musician Colin Ross). Aside from repertoire, it was different in one crucial respect: 'They were linked somehow with London, by people coming and going, by records, by politics or whatever else,' she says. 'The same thing was happening in Birmingham with the Campbells and in Manchester with Harry Boardman. Wesker realised, "Look, we've got this musical activity going on in all these cities – we can utilise that!" It was all happening at the same time. We knew that it was going on because people would turn up in Glasgow and say, "Hallo, I'm from Manchester," [but] the interaction between each city had been minimal. Even between Glasgow and Edinburgh.'[32]

Wesker, whose play *Chips With Everything* had been a recent success, was bankrolling the tour largely from his own pocket. Among its key participants were the Ian Campbell Group from Birmingham. Alongside the Spinners and the Watersons they were among the earliest groups in the revival, none of whom was yet fully professional. Nevertheless, the Campbells had committed themselves so fully to Centre 42, undertaking three of the five festivals (those within travelling distance of home), that only Ian Campbell and fiddler Dave Swarbrick were able to hang on to their day jobs. Some years later Campbell wrote an incisive memoir of the experience: 'Along with the Clarion Singers we worked under Charles Parker in a group he had formed, called the Leaveners, to find a theatrical form for the techniques he had evolved in the *Radio Ballads*; we also appeared on the folksong concerts which were a highlight of all the festivals, and on the other six evenings of the week we were among those devoted enthusiasts who elected to bring Culture to the Masses by singing folksongs in the bar-rooms of selected public houses.'[33]

Bringing folksong to the pubs was a recognition by Wesker that his formal events were more likely to see audiences of middle-class, left-wing intellectuals than bona fide workers. Campbell concluded that the folksong concerts were a triumph, the Leaveners' performances a more qualified success and folksong in the pubs a disaster: 'I look back on those evenings with a distinct lack of nostalgia,' wrote Campbell. 'I can think of few tasks less rewarding than trying to present traditional music to a bar-room full of non-folkies who have not asked for your attentions and who have come looking for a pint with the lads and a game of darts.' Reactions ranged, he felt, from indifference to derision. 'Strangely enough,' he mused, 'although we were not being paid, we had undertaken to do the job and it never occured to us to give up and go home.'

Anne Briggs, having herself signed up for the rest of the tour, did not have that luxury. 'My family disowned me,' she says. 'I left home a runaway.

They couldn't understand what was happening, threatened to put a court order on me to keep me at home but as I pointed out, it was only four weeks to my eighteenth birthday. But for a couple of years I was out on my own. After the festivals, the Centre 42 movement felt a bit guilty about all this and offered me a job in their offices in London. I was a "go-fer" and I had a very interesting six months, nipping about all over London to theatres and galleries and such like, and I was getting gigs there on the back of it.' It was all experience that would later stand both her and Bert Jansch in good stead.

Bert Jansch was something of a prophet without honour in his place of origin. The transition from bedroom composer to performing musician was a vague one, although Bert recalls his earliest bookings around the Scottish Lowlands and North of England. He believes his first professional gig 'as opposed to just messing around' was at a particularly happening folk club in Rotherham: 'It was a huge club,' says Bert.[34] 'All the clubs in those days would hold up to four hundred people, and the universities too were incredible. You just don't get it now. People would just book you after a fashion and you'd hitch-hike to the gig. So I did a lot in the North of England, like Sheffield and other universities. I don't think you bothered about what kind of music you were playing at that time – anything and everything that came into your head. Prior to that, music was what you heard – the radio, your sister's influence, your brother's or whatever.'

Of all the clubs in Fife, he was only ever invited to play at one: the Dunfermline Howff. In Glasgow, he would quickly build an audience but it would not be a completely smooth process. Folksong was a working-class, increasingly young person's music and any young performer on the scene in those days would be expected to fit into one of two camps: traditional music or contemporary songs espousing the correct political values. Robin Williamson and Bert Jansch were unusual in being markedly non-political. Robin, whose traditional bent at that stage opened up many more bookings than would be offered to Bert in the Scottish clubs, recalls a lot of his own early work being promoted by the Communist Party. Bert was singing, composing even, in his own oblique manner, the odd civil rights song, but there was no great cause being followed. No cause, that is, beyond the desire to travel and play music for a living.

'You've got to remember that most of us in Glasgow were working in the shipyards or involved in trade unions,' said Danny Kyle, one of that city's earliest club organisers. 'Glasgow's industrial, Edinburgh isn't. It's as simple as that. There was intercity rivalry – we were the hard nuts of Glasgow, they were the poofs and charlatans of Edinburgh. Thank God that doesn't exist now. I remember Bert playing at "Saturday Late" in Cleveland Lane, in

Glasgow. Gordon McCulloch led a group of people that were against anything that wasn't either political or traditional. Bert went on and started to do his thing, which was very unusual then – excellent guitar work, obviously, but quite different from the "ban the bomb" songs everyone else was doing. I'll always remember Gordon McCulloch and the others made paper hats, like clown hats, out of newspapers, and then just totally sherracked him – heckled him to the point where Bert walked off. All of us had a narrow mind of some sort in those days and Bert was innovative, not doing the popular stuff like the rest of us. The sad thing is that Bert, given his head, would have played all the things that he'd written and all that he was getting into, but he would also sing traditional songs.'

The Glasgow Folksong Club had moved to 31 Cleveland Lane around March 1962, and that same month the club's regulars took the half-hour bus trip to the docklands district of Paisley to pack out the opening night of a new venture, the Attic Club. Ian Campbell's group were the club's first-night guests and Danny Kyle its organiser. On 22 September, the *Melody Maker* reported the Thursday night club's move to a Royal Air Force Association building in Abbey Street. What it did not report – and after all why should it – was the performance there a week or two earlier by somebody called Bert Jansch. Captured on a battered reel-to-reel by a fourteen-year-old schoolboy, it remains the earliest known recording of Bert Jansch and reveals beyond any doubt how extraordinary, for that time and place, his music really was.

Frank Coia, the schoolboy responsible, had become a regular at the Glasgow Folksong Club and was captivated by its atmosphere: 'You sat on the floor for the most part, no seating at all, no public address system as such, so any artist was totally acoustic. It was unlicensed, although you could get soft drinks. It was a very popular club, the little "in" place in Glasgow at the time. Somebody had told me Bert Jansch was worth going to see and there was a flyer saying he was one of two people from Edinburgh playing their own style of folk-blues, Davy Graham being the other. It would have been early '62 when I first saw Bert. It was totally mindblowing because nobody was doing what he was doing. As soon as I found he was playing again in Glasgow I did everything I could to beg, steal or borrow a tape recorder. I just had to put it on tape.'

Coia subsequently recorded Bert on several occasions: by his own testimony, all prior to the release of Bert's first album in April 1965. The matter of dating and dissembling the Coia recordings is, however, a complex one and a later date in 1965 for at least four of the songs now seems certain. There were perhaps as many as four public performances and a living-room session recorded during that three-year period, most of which have survived intact, albeit jumbled together on a single copy reel. The fifty-six remaining tracks, of which thirty have been issued on CD, provide an invaluable insight into Bert's presentation, style and repertoire at the dawn of his career. The presentation alone was something else:

'He had this sort of attitude,' says Coia. 'It was like he was cocooned in his own world of music – everything else was peripheral. He would just tail off one number and mumble into another. It wasn't professional in its presentation but it was a complete performance at one sitting. You could hear a pin drop when he was playing. It was usually a guitar which he wasn't familiar with and he'd put it out of tune after almost every number, because he was playing so hard – pulling the strings, which was his technique. The tape recorder was positioned beside him. When he actually started his set that was it – he was wrapped up in it and normally had to be prompted whenever there was a break. He was shambolic in terms of appearance and very introverted. I suppose you could say people were a bit scared to approach him in conversation – they would be a bit gob-smacked from his playing.'

'We were all trying to escape from something,' said Danny Kyle, 'and all of a sudden you could put on a backpack and bomb off to France – at least in your head you could – because of that music. All of a sudden, when I listened to Bert Jansch, I didn't have to be a shipyard worker. I could see "le continent". We were all reading Kerouac and here was a man saying through the guitar what Kerouac was alluding to in his books. That opened up poetry, guitar work, travel. With Davy Graham you could go and sit in total awe of the man. With Bert you would go and listen and look and you would say to yourself, "Here, perhaps I could do some of that," because he made it seem attainable.'

This curious perception of a common touch would carry Bert through the rest of the decade as a performer of unique, utterly uncontrived charisma. Audiences would multiply in inverse proportion to his non-existent skills as a conventional entertainer, communicator and exemplifier of text-book guitar styles. Where Davy Graham gave out an aura of aloof and unattainable brilliance, with poise and learning, Bert Jansch on a stage cried vulnerability, repression, the 'small man' aching for a better way through life – a man of the people. It was an extraordinary illusion: Bert Jansch was very different in character to Davy Graham, but he was every bit as much a loner and even more uncopiable as a technician.

'Davy Graham played a lot of bar chords whereas Bert never used them,' says Coia. 'It was just such a total diversity from normal, conventional playing – in tonality, in dissonance, in his ideas on chord progressions. He didn't play conventional chords – he played something that his ear wanted him to play, conventional or not.' Coia was not a guitar player when he first heard Bert Jansch, but in a manner that was to be repeated a thousand times and more in the coming years, Bert was his inspiration to take up the instrument. Having the man on tape meant he could imitate Bert's style and material at his leisure: 'Initially I thought there was no way you could do it, it was so far removed. It's his timing – his accentuation and the actual timing of his voice relative to the playing of his guitar which is so unique. They're almost two detached things put together. Forty or fifty people would have been the size of the smallest venue he played in Glasgow, but it was always full to capacity for Bert. It was exciting because it was so fresh.'[35]

There were songs from the repertoires of Broonzy and McGhee; there was a hint of Charlie Mingus; there was 'Courting Blues', his song for Liz; there was 'Strolling Down The Highway', with its enigmatic references to Algerian terrorists and garlic; and there was a quite extraordinary instrumental called 'Joint Control'. Never released on record, in Bert's own words it became 'the basis of about half a dozen other tunes'. It was certainly indicative of a style of guitar playing that would come to be instantly recognisable as that of Bert Jansch. Robin Williamson, on hearing 'Joint Control' for the first time in decades courtesy of Coia's recording, made an intriguing observation: 'It's years ahead of its time, and also years before anyone had ever heard kora. If you listen to African music – kora music and palm-wine guitar – it's got all those sort of rhythms going on. That music wasn't available in Britain then. It's almost like Bert had instinctively invented the ancestor of the blues.'

CHAPTER FIVE

Peregrinations

The winter of 1962/63 was unusually cold. Pipes were bursting in London, the Thames was frozen, the building trade was laid off en masse and some years later Kenyan-born light entertainment sensation Roger Whittaker could still recall it as his worst Christmas ever: 'I went to bed wearing a track suit and woke up the next morning with moisture frozen on my beard.'[1] It was hardly an opportune time for a couple of complete unknowns to trek down from Edinburgh in search of an audience. But so the cards had been shuffled. Anthea Joseph, running the Troubadour, had seen Robin performing in Edinburgh and offered him a gig, on Saturday, 19 January 1963. Bert came along for the ride: 'We went picking potatoes to get our bus fare to London – on the strength of that one gig,' says Robin.

They stayed with Davy Graham's brother Nick for a few days before finding a flat in the Earl's Court area. They had one other contact in London: David Blass. David's mother had by this time moved the family home from Wembley Park to Cresswell Place – just around the corner from the Troubadour. Anne Briggs, having left home to work for Centre 42, was already there. Blass had met Anne the previous year in Edinburgh, on a visit he had made by car. She had asked for and received a lift to London and, having made the connection, would return to stay with Blass at the family home on a number of occasions.[2]

Bert did not recall his previous encounter with Anne in Edinburgh some years earlier, but this time around the pair hit it off immediately: 'I remember that night well,' he says. 'And hopefully she does too.' There would be a lasting bond in terms of lifestyle and a shared interest in each other's music: 'By that time he'd got a lot more music together,' says Anne, 'but it wasn't recognised as folk music on the English scene, although people who knew their stuff thought, "Wow, what an original guitarist this guy is." Davy Graham was writing his own tunes, and he had obviously influenced Bert, but apart from Ewan MacColl, who was coming from a totally different dimension, there weren't any singer-songwriters at that point, as far as I'm aware.'

The Troubadour itself was among the earliest folk clubs in London – a tiny, unventilated cellar that held around a hundred people. Geographically removed from the other venues, at 265 Old Brompton Road, it operated independently of either Ewan MacColl or the Soho scene. Martin Carthy was a regular: 'It was started as a coffee bar in the fifties by a man called Mike Van Blumen, a Canadian Communist,' says Carthy. 'He had a folk club on a Saturday night but he also had poetry nights, jazz nights, basically anything that people would come to listen to and that people wanted to organise.' Jenny Barton and Anthea Joseph were the two organisers most associated with the place in the early sixties, and when Robin and Bert made their London debut Martin Carthy was in the middle of a lengthy period as the club's Saturday resident performer. Or was he?

'I'm sorry to bust those hoary old legends that both "Rambling" Jack Elliott and Martin were residents at the Troub,' wrote Barton, a tad pedantically, some years later. 'I owe them both a vast debt – the former originally put the Troubadour on the map back in '59, and the latter contributed very largely and for many years to our position near the top of the league. I can remember him when he had to dump a school satchel before hopping up on stage. My policy was always to book the best available, regardless of whether my audience had ever heard of them before. I was a rather reticent and inexperienced girl in my early twenties [but] the policy obviously paid, since the club remained packed like the proverbial sardine tin for nearly all the years I ran it. The audience paid the highest charges in Britain, endured quite the worst discomfort conceivable and most of them would cheerfully have admitted that they didn't know a traditional song from a cabbage; they simply had the ability to recognise quality when they saw and heard it – and indeed to give the bird in no uncertain terms when they didn't.'[3]

Robin was advertised, Bert was not; both played, neither remembers a thing about it. 'I'm not surprised,' says Carthy, 'they were both very, very stoned indeed! I'd met Robin before, in Edinburgh, and you couldn't help but be hugely impressed. I'd heard of Bert from various people. "Oh, he's amazing," they'd say, "he's only been playing guitar a year and he's miles better than anyone else, you gotta hear him . . ." And he lived up to expectations.'

Bert had already played on a stage in London earlier that week, upstairs at the King & Queen in Foley Street, at a blues session hosted by Cliff Aungier and Gerry Loughran. Again, his name was unadvertised. But the Troubadour experience was the watershed. Bert recalls Anthea Joseph remarking on his similarity to the previous week's guest, who turned out to be Bob Dylan. 'I asked her how much he got paid,' says Bert. 'It was thirty bob [£1.50].'[4]

Dylan, yet to make a significant impact on the world, was in Britain to appear in a BBC television play, *Madhouse On Castle Street*. The play, broadcast on 30 December 1962, was notable for the debut of a song he had just written, 'Blowing In The Wind'. A review in *The Listener* noted that Dylan had 'sat around playing and singing attractively, if a little incomprehensibly'. Nobody would have put any money on it at the time, but they had seen the future, and its name was Bob. While in London Dylan had been checking out the folk clubs. Brian Shuel, the only professional photographer to document that scene to any substantial degree over the coming decade, was at the Singers Club when Bob sang. By chance, he captured some now famous images of the young American surrounded by Ewan MacColl, Martin Carthy and the cream of British folksong at the courthouse of its burgeoning empire. Bob had been lucky to get through the door. Like Bert Jansch, Bob Dylan may not have made any records yet but his reputation was preceding him. It was a reputation that Bruce Dunnet – Communist die-hard, MacColl's doorkeeper, and a strident, imposing man at the best of times – was not impressed with:

'Bob had already been to the Roundhouse,' says Dunnet, 'and I think it was Martin Winsor had told him to fuck off [Dunnet believed this was due to a perception of Dylan as a drug user at the time]. And then, shortly after, he came to the Singers Club at the Pindar of Wakefield and Peggy Seeger told me we had to let him in. I said, "No, I don't want to let that shit in," because I knew he'd been at the Roundhouse and barred. But no, she insisted and I had to let him in.'[5]

Dylan subsequently appeared unadvertised at the Troubadour on 29 December and 12 January. The next time he appeared in London it would be May 1964 and he would be firmly established as 'the voice of a generation'. To the cognoscenti at that time Bert would bear briefly, and through no desire of his own, the mantle of being 'Britain's answer' to the guy. In the meantime, an intense focus on his own music was more than enough to be going on with: 'What he was playing,' says Carthy, 'you'd call it blues but it'd have to be a very, very loose definition of the blues. I can't remember the first songs I heard him sing but fairly soon after he came down here I heard him do "Strolling Down The Highway". That I do remember! It was just this drive, this incredible drive. His only concession to everybody else was to play "Angi" – and he played it all wrong! And still does. If I say Davy touched everybody it's true, but there are some people who could not have survived had it not been for Davy. Bert always had more than that. He never sounded like anybody but Bert.'

The Troubadour gig came and went and there were no other bookings in the can. Hustling around the frost-bitten scene, Robin secured a couple of further gigs in March but there was nothing for Bert. Bert maintains that, unlike Robin, he was not actively seeking gigs on this trip. Nevertheless, with his preference for traditional music, Robin was always the more likely of the pair to get work in the MacColl era. He was more acceptable. 'Eventually things really ground to a halt,' says Robin, 'and both Bert and I were finding it hard to get engagements. The folk scene per se had divided itself up very rigidly into a purist category, virtually run by Ewan MacColl, and a sort of international, neo-Israeli, peacenik thing which was a bit kind of "cabaret", and we didn't really fit into either. I don't think Ewan liked either me or Bert very much, and I think he actually tried to stop us being able to work in London that first winter we went there. That was the impression I got. I actually rather admired his *Radio Ballads*. Ideologically he wouldn't admire either of us. We couldn't have been described as either left-wing or right-wing – we were pretty much "wingless"!' In fairness, one of Robin's other London bookings during the trip was at a midweek off-shoot of the Singers Club alongside Joe Heaney, a man who would become one of his all-time heroes.[6] Possibly there was some incident or remarks made on the night, but Bruce Dunnet maintains it would have been out of character for Ewan, whatever the stringency of his views, actively to hinder the progress of other musicians.

By the end of March Robin was on his way back home. Bert would follow a little later. Perhaps not in the sense of a conventional relationship, he had nevertheless become close to Anne Briggs. Her record debut, singing two songs on Bert Lloyd and Ewan MacColl's thematic album of industrial folksong *The Iron Muse*, had been released on Topic to fervent acclaim towards the end of February. The album featured a number of other singers, mostly associated with Centre 42, but Anne had been singled out for particular praise. In part, the adulation was the surprise of hearing a stunningly beautiful new voice, but in part too it was the quality of a song to match. 'The Recruited Collier' was Anne's triumph. Her version – simple, unadorned and aching with poignancy – has never been bettered. 'She didn't sing like a little girl,' says Martin Carthy. 'She sang with real age, like she'd been singing for years and years. She was beautiful. She was a glorious singer and she just got better.'[7]

Though Anne was destined, largely of her own volition, to make precious few recordings thereafter, the wise hand of Bert Lloyd can be felt in the greatest of those that were to follow: 'Bert [Lloyd] was a friend first and foremost,' says Anne. 'But he was enormously generous in sharing work and his knowledge of songs with me. He wasn't a mentor, he was a giver.' Eric Winter declared, in *MM*, that on the basis of her record debut Anne could soon be 'a raving visitor to the London club scene'. The folk world still revolved around London, but Anne was the free-est of free spirits and her 'raving' was not to be confined: 'All the other traditional singers then,' says Bert Jansch, 'certainly all the ones I'd ever met, were old and rather staid. The thing about Anne was she was wild. She got drunk onstage and fell over all the time – it was a regular thing, along with a few others like myself. If she got fed up with a song she'd just stop in the middle and say, "Oh, forget that, I'll sing you another one." I had a similar approach myself. But at that time, her impact in that world, she was more akin to a punk than to anything that had gone before.' There was a softer, more vulnerable and solitary side to Anne too, a side of her personality that would bear comparison to Bert's. 'I remember thinking she seemed quite sad at the beginning,' says Ray Fisher, who had shared Centre 42 stages with Anne. 'She sang very mournful songs. She was certainly a lot quieter than I was. A much gentler person altogether.'[8]

Bert and Anne would maintain a loose connection for years – writing a handful of songs together, living upstairs and downstairs from each other in London for a period in 1965, appearing sporadically on gigs together right up to 1971. But their period of closest friendship and mutual support was here at the very start of their careers. Anne was the one with the record, the *Melody Maker* write-up and as a consequence the realistic prospect of getting some gigs around the country. Off they went.

'"Romantic" is probably the wrong word,' says Anne. 'Everybody used to think that we were brother and sister because we looked very alike at that stage. We were on the road together. If I had a gig and Bert didn't have a gig he'd come on mine, because he had nowhere else to stay. And the same if Bert had a gig and I didn't, because half the time we didn't have a roof over our head anyway. We were literally just dossing side by side. From my point of view it was great to be in Bert's company because he was a companion. Yes, he was a boyfriend but he was a very loose sort of boyfriend. He'd wander off and have an affair with a girl, I'd wander off and have an affair with a bloke, but we'd always sort of keep going back to each other. This went on for quite a long time. It was no great "I love you" kind of thing – we were just close: very, very close. Musically and in lifestyle.'

Ewan MacColl had been no more aware of Joe Heaney, a legendary old fellow from Galway of richly un-English accent, limited learning and a deep well of songs, than he was of Robin Williamson when both were granted the platform of his club's new (and short-lived) midweek gathering at the King's Head in Twickenham. How Williamson got the gig is anyone's guess, but Heaney had been recommended to Ewan by Bill Leader, who remembers the occasion purely for a moment of inadvertent comedy: 'Joe sang a couple of ballads, one of which was part English, part Gallic. Joe came off the platform, Ewan came over and said, "Nice to hear the old macaroni again, Joe" – a classic! Macaroni is a technical term to describe things sung in more than one language. I remember this because it seemed to be so inept but in a way so characteristic of Ewan, to start spouting grammarian jargon at some roots singer. It encapsulates for me the extent to which Ewan was not on the same wavelength as a lot of people he claimed to be close to.'

Bill Leader was something of a lone wolf on the folk scene. Coming down to London from Bradford in 1955 he had a keen eye for absurdity and a healthy disregard for the establishment – any establishment. He was, crucially for posterity and for the careers of so many British and Irish folk musicians, both technically minded and fascinated with the esoteric edges of culture. 'I always wanted to be a sound engineer as a kid. Instead of having daydreams about driving the Flying Scotsman I used to imagine myself recording in a film studio. I first got to London by getting a job in a film library. I was always interested in films. I got involved very slightly in the technical side of making English versions of foreign films but nothing ever came of it.'[9]

In parallel with this Leader became attracted to the ideals of the Workers' Music Association, which at that time was still involved with Topic Records, busily re-establishing the label after the impasse created by an inconvenient World War. They were stumbling around in an endearingly amateur fashion – one triumph was the release of a 'Rambling' Jack Elliott record on eight-inch vinyl, at a time when gramophone auto-changers set to seven- ten- and the new-fangled twelve-inch formats were all the rage. There was potential for a subsidised label, of which Topic was the only one of its kind in Britain, to make a profit on a small run with the new LP format. Runs of ninety-nine copies were a way for Topic, and the other specialist folk labels it inspired throughout the sixties, to avoid paying Purchase Tax. The gathering folk revival, the viability of the new format and not least the recent introduction of semi-professional tape recorders made an increase in record production both viable and worthy. But who would do the work? 'They got a few enthusiasts together to work on the idea of revitalising the label,' says Leader, 'and I was the only one who was keen on it and had time on his hands.'

Relying on rooms lined with egg-boxes, a microphone, a two-track tape machine and a good instinct, Leader initiated a process that would almost single-handedly, like the photography of Brian Shuel, document the folk revival. The judgement, breadth and tenacity of his work has possibly never been fully appreciated. Leader's first recording for Topic was of the Irish musicians Michael Gorman and Margaret Barry. He would later bring hordes of Irishmen back to his Camden flat, line up a crate of Guinness and press the record button. It was simple but effective. The late fifties and early sixties were the pinnacle of the London-Irish scene, centred on the pubs around Camden. Skiffle had run its course, Ewan MacColl had his thing going for the cognoscenti, his erstwhile associate Malcolm Nixon was trying to get something else happening with an expanding stable of more 'commercial' artistes and the blues scene patiently nurtured by Cyril Davies and Alexis Korner would only really kick in from 1963 on. At the dawn of the sixties, the Irish scene was musically the most visceral and exciting thing in town and, as a movement, the least ambitious of the lot.

Working for Topic in those days paid poorly, so in 1960 Bill took a day job as manager of Collet's record shop at 70 New Oxford Street. Collet's core business was as a publishing house, based in Wellingborough, with an overt left-wing agenda. They had several outlets in London, including a Chinese bookshop and a Russian bookshop, but the flagship was a political bookshop on Charing Cross Road. What became their folk, blues and jazz record shop had begun as a department of this earnest emporium around 1958. By 1960 it was in New Oxford Street where it would remain throughout that decade and beyond. With the escalation of recording opportunities, Bill's sojourn at Collet's was relatively short, around three years. As the sixties wore on and the magnetism of London's folk clubs became stronger, the place would become a virtual hostel, mailing address, meeting point and advice centre for all manner of musical road warriors. The person who would become most synonymous with the place, and with these aspects of community welfare over and above the job description, arrived shortly after Bill, and initially as his assistant. Her name was Gill Cook.

From a grammar school background, Gill had been a regular at all the folk and blues clubs in London, and had been a member of John Hasted's London Youth Choir. She took a job as a lab technician in Cambridge and found the good times in danger of stopping. 'It was a terrible job,' she says. 'I was half a student, which meant terrible money and having to go to evening classes every night. I got pissed off, went to work for a bookshop instead and while I was there got a call from Bill Leader up in London saying, "Do you want a job?" ' Gill had met Bill through Eric Winter. Eric, a full-time journalist and *Melody Maker* contributor, had been living in Cambridge and commuting to London, and in his spare time had helped run Stan Kelly's Skiffle Club at the Dog & Pheasant: 'It wasn't really skiffle at all,' says Gill. 'It was just a platform for Stan and he was wonderful!'[10] Winter and his family moved to London in the late fifties, and Gill would often come and stay while taking in the folk clubs – through all of which she inevitably made the acquaintance of Bill Leader. She took the job.

That same year, 1960, a zestful young man by the name of Nathan Joseph

– Nat to the world at large, though he never cared for the abbreviation himself – graduated in English from Cambridge University. With the offer of a junior teaching post at Columbia University, New York, he flew to the States and, for the first and only time in his life, 'freaked out'. It was a pent-up reaction against years of academic grind: 'I decided I really didn't want to do that any more. I decided to cut and run and bummed around America for the best part of a year, doing various things but earning enough money to get right round the States – which was a lot less easy then than it is now. Towards the end I was thinking, "Well, when I get back what the hell am I going to do?" '

Nat had always been 'mad on showbusiness' and harboured vague aspirations to be a writer. Words rather than music were his thing and in both script and performing capacities he had enjoyed something of a reputation on the university revue circuit. He and a friend, Stephen Sedley, later Lord Justice Sedley, had had a cabaret act that was purportedly the only one better paid than David Frost's on that scene at the time. 'I didn't have enough confidence in my writing or enough contacts to do that professionally but I could see, going around America, that something big was happening with gramophone records as we knew them then.'

Nat made contact with a number of record companies, particularly in the spoken word field, wrested ninety days' credit from them and, having no real capital whatsoever, shipped their product over the ocean, dashed back himself and feverishly trawled samples around the record shops of southern England, to whom he gave sixty days' credit. He did well enough to keep the process going, particularly with a language series *Conversophone*, but he nevertheless realised that real money would only be made through market-ing his own products: 'I had to come up with some idea that would not necessarily be what I wanted to record but would make enough money so I could start a bona fide company. I remember thinking, "What interests the British public?" and I put three things down: money, sex and royalty.'

The Queen was unavailable, money was dull, so sex it was. Nat recruited a controversial sexologist, Dr Eustace Chesser, under the pseudonym Dr Keith Cammeron, and recorded three albums in a series entitled *Live With Love*. Pressed up as catalogue numbers TRA 101, 102 and 103, they were the first three releases on Transatlantic Records. The scam worked: 'We got about a million pounds' worth of publicity for nothing,' says Nat, 'including the front page of the *News of the World*. There were discussions on the radio about sex records and how evil they were, but actually they were so tame it was unbelievable. Wouldn't cause a ripple in *Woman's Own* today but they sold what in those days was an enormous amount – nearly a hundred thousand records.'

One day in 1962 Bill Leader was behind the counter at Collet's 'and this little fellow with a squeaky voice came in'. It was Nat: 'He tried to sell me some albums on sex education which he thought were going to be a sure-fire winner and I seem to remember he had a EP on how to give up smoking. I remember he rang up the press agent in charge of getting the smoking EP off the ground and gave him such a mouthful of abuse it quite made my hair stand on end. He then suggested that maybe I should like to help him produce some records.'[11]

Leader also had vague aspirations to run his own record company, and would finally take the plunge in 1969 with Leader/Trailer – twin labels designed as outlets for folk music recordings of a highly specialised nature and for club singers respectively. When it came to the music business, Bill was a people person, a friend of the artist, a softly-spoken idealist with a well-developed mechanism for co-existing stoically alongside the more prepos-terous individuals and situations that life in the music game has to throw at one; Nat was a hyperactive pragmatist and businessman of cultured accent and literary bent who would make, by and large, the kind of records he liked and could retain a certain pride in releasing but who was nevertheless, within the confines of his determinedly non-pop music focus, always chasing the big return. For the rest of the decade, with Bill freewheeling along in a freelance capacity and Nat blustering ahead as the archetypal entrepreneur, the pair would build a unique catalogue of work by artists who in many cases would have looked long and fruitlessly to have found another outlet. Not least among them was Bert Jansch.

Songs Of Love, Lust & Loose Living (TRA 105) continued on the sex bandwagon, adding music to the equation with Shakespearian actor Tony Britton, Theatre Workshop veteran Isla Cameron and Nat's pal Stephen Sedley on guitar. TRA 106 was a quirky collaboration between songwriter/evangelist Sydney Carter and comedy actress Sheila Hancock, while TRA 107, released in March 1963, was the ingenious *Loguerhythms*, pitting jazz singer Annie Ross with the poetry of Christopher Logue. TRA 108, an LP by satirical songster Cy Grant, then enjoying a high profile on David Frost's TV show *That Was The Week That Was*, was the point where Bill Leader joined the team. He was shortly followed by photographer Brian Shuel.

Shuel had started working as a freelance photographer in 1960, working particularly with his father-in-law James Boswell who edited a magazine. 'The plan was for me to art edit and take photos for the magazine – a cosy arrangement which continued until he died in 1971, and which kept us alive very nicely while we got on with more important activities on the folk scene!' Boswell lived round the corner from Topic supremo Gerry Sharpe. He was asked if he would care to become a Topic director himself, and provide free sleeve designs while he was at it. 'He knew absolutely nothing about folk music,' says Brian, 'so he decided that he and I would go on a tour around Britain to dig the scene. I think he really wanted me to drive him but I saw it as an opportunity not only to get a few pictures on record sleeves but also, maybe, to work up a good magazine photo-story on the long-running folk "revival" which , incidentally, never came to pass though I'm still getting the pictures onto sleeves – and into books!'

The first stop was an Alex Campbell show in Croydon, May 1962. The jaunt continued through Teeside, Liverpool, Edinburgh and Dunfermline and back to London, where Shuel soon became a part of the scene he was documenting. He found himself largely on the 'Topic / Bert Lloyd / MacColl & Seeger approved side of things', and was bemused by the whole business: 'There was terrific factionalism. I was never quite certain what it was all about but I think most singers not approved by the above thought they were a load of pseuds who took themselves far too seriously. And I have to say, in retrospect, that they could well have been right.'

Brian became known to Bill Leader and consequently to Nat Joseph. It was still a small scene. 'Nat showed me the record sleeves he had already done,' says Brian. 'I remarked, in my tactful way, that they were complete crap, which had the surprising result of my designing all his sleeves for the next six years!' By this time Bill had also introduced Nat to folk music: 'I was soon hooked,' says Nat. 'Visits to Ewan MacColl's club in London and Ian Campbell's Jug of Punch in Birmingham made me into an immediate enthusiast. Particularly Campbell's club, where I sensed a more joyous and modern approach.'[12] The Ian Campbell Group, trademarked by fastidiously written harmonies and Dave Swarbrick's fiddle, would be Nat's first signing from the folk scene. Brian Shuel's first Transatlantic commission was the sleeve photography for *This Is . . . The Ian Campbell Folk Group* (TRA 110). It was also where the story of Transatlantic, as the home of contemporary British folk music, really begins.

In the early months of 1963, when Bert was in London for the first time casually trying his luck as a folk singer, Nat Joseph was busy setting out his stall with a series of eight Sunday night concerts at the Lyric Theatre, Hammersmith, running the gamut of folk, cabaret, spoken word and comedy. TV stars Robin Hall & Jimmie Macgregor topped the first night in March alongside Steve Benbow and the Thamesiders; the next one featured Tony Britton with Isla Cameron, plugging their own particular brand of love, lust and loose living; another one paired Benbow with comic surrealist Spike Milligan; there was a ceilidh night with step dancers (a good thirty years before *Riverdance*) on St Patrick's night and a 'ban the bomb' night on Easter Sunday, coinciding nicely with the annual march to the controversial nuclear facility at Aldermaston. There was no such thing as a bandwagon too far for Nat Joseph. As a businessman, he was a sharp operator. Less sharp, by all accounts, was Malcolm Nixon.

Following the fall-out with MacColl that led directly to the founding of the Singers Club for the pure of spirit and the all-new Ballads & Blues for the lovers of fun, Nixon had set himself up as manager of Collet's Chinese Bookshop opposite the British Museum. It would be little more than a front for running a folk agency. Hall & Macgregor were on his books, likewise Alex Campbell, Long John Baldry, Steve Benbow, Archie Fisher and an increasing portfolio of others. On the one hand Nixon's artists were getting a lot of work, but on the other he was running his operation like a lunatic. 'He had me in Thurso one night and Southampton University the next,' says Steve Benbow. 'It was ridiculous. I came straight off the stage, a bloke picked me up in a car, took me to Aberdeen Airport then down to Southampton, then back up to Scotland again, then back to London to do a broadcast. Every weekend I did this bloody broadcast from the Playhouse in Northumberland Avenue. My wife used to meet me with clean clothing and that was it, off I'd go again! So I was touring, doing two-hour concerts on my tod, and he had me coming backwards and forwards – and I just broke down.'

1963 could have been the year for Steve Benbow. He was regularly on the TV and radio, was fronting his own column in *Melody Maker*, had a contract with EMI/Parlophone and was enjoying a series of folkish novelty singles produced by George Martin. BBC light entertainment colussus Billy Cotton was covering Benbow's material on his big band radio shows, but as yet few were actually buying the records.[13] EMI were clearly chasing a particular gap in the hedge marked, as hindsight would reveal, 'Val Doonican'. A number of things started to go wrong: firstly, the Beatles came along; secondly, Val Doonican himself came along; thirdly, with a guy like Malcolm Nixon running your campaign, who needs enemies?

Steve managed his one and only Albert Hall appearance in September 1963, on an all-star bill of Nixon's folk finest, but by the time a BBC producer rang him up at the end of year to say, 'Loved your Lyric show with Spike, fancy doing his TV series next year?' Steve was laid up in hospital, stressed and overworked. By the time he did the series, *Muses With Milligan*, as musical resident, Val Doonican was fronting his own nationwide vehicle and having chart hits with the same kind of material Benbow had been peddling previously to no avail. Steve's fate was sealed: he had gone shamelessly down the path of schmaltz and not quite made the boat; it was too late to chase credibility. But then the option of becoming a successful singer-songwriter-guitarist by being 'credible' first and saleable next simply did not exist in 1963. Bob Dylan was arguably in the process of inventing the procedure. Though his momentum was of a slower-burning nature, in Britain Bert Jansch would be the next in line.

Some time in the spring of 1963, Bert Jansch and Anne Briggs made their way from London to Scotland. Anne had a gig at the Dunfermline Howff in May and organiser John Watt had been gracious enough to include Bert's name in the local press ads – possibly the first time it had appeared in print. Though flagged as a 'London based blues singer', he was not really based anywhere any more: the flat sharing-arrangement with Robin and Clive was in the process of dissolving, and in any case he was now of a mind not to limit his horizons to Edinburgh. As a guitar player he had already outstripped his one-time master Len Partridge and he knew it. So too did Len: 'Bert was the only person who ever apologised for being better than I was, which I thought was quite funny! I don't know how I was meant to take it, but he seemed quite concerned at that time that he was now better than I was. There were lots and lots of people better than I was, and there would continue to be ever more so.'

Drew Moyes's Glasgow Folk Centre had just opened for business at 45 Montrose Street, and Bert and Anne may well have played the new venue at this time. Certainly, one of the Glasgow visits recalled by Bert's young fan and tape recorder enthusiast Frank Coia was made in the company of a dark-haired girl with an English accent – both travellers road weary and in need of a bath, duly provided. By August, the Folk Centre was describable, in the words of Eric Winter, as 'a seven days a week mecca' for the folk buff, with folksong and poetry sessions on Wednesdays, late night Saturdays and Sundays alongside 'coffee bar, reference library, instrument lessons and rehearsal and recording facilities'. What Winter neglected to mention was the name of the young man almost certainly providing the instrument lessons: Bert Jansch.

Gigs were hard to come by and, like Hamish Imlach and Archie Fisher before him, tuition meant steady income and food on the table. As it happened, putting food on the table was not necessarily the concern that it might have been. Bert was now enjoying hospitality in Glasgow at the home of Archie Fisher's family: Morag 'Ma' Fisher and her many daughters. 'It was a convenience for me, being fed,' he says. 'It went on for months.' Bert had often stayed with the Fishers before, and by this stage Ma Fisher was providing welcome hospitality for anyone and everyone on the developing folk scene: 'There was always an open door,' she explained, many years later. 'My own favourite was Bert Jansch. He was the one really. He was one of the family. Some folk thought he was Archie's brother. He couldn't have had a better brother than Bert.'[14]

Archie at this time was over in Edinburgh with Jill Doyle/Guest, running a Tuesday night folk club at the Crown Bar. Anne Briggs certainly played there, and possibly also Bert: 'Archie was incredibly supportive of young singers and musicians,' says Anne. 'You'd never go hungry or never not have a roof over your head. In fact, his entire family was great in that respect.' Shortly after he had returned disconsolate from London Robin Williamson had initiated his own club at the Crown Bar, on Thursdays, with Clive Palmer and the initial involvement of their increasingly errant flatmate Bert Jansch. 'It was basically the only way to get a place to play,' says Robin. 'It was always full – ran for two or three years.' 'I think this is where the division started,' says Bert. 'Archie's club became very much more traditionally orientated, whereas ours went the other way – contemporary and more freaky stuff for the stoned heads, as you might say.'[15]

During the summer of 1963 Bert had been seeing Licorice McKechnie. Licorice was another acolyte of Edinburgh's increasingly identifiable 'hippy group', chasing after the dream of an alternative lifestyle: Moroccan cigarettes, Jack Kerouac and the music of Charles Mingus. 'Licorice's parents disapproved of what was happening to their daughter and sent a couple of guys looking for Bert,' remembers Owen Hand. 'Archie Fisher, running the Crown at the time, was terrified there was going to be trouble at the club and asked me if I would come along this night. When I entered the club the guys were sitting at the bar and Archie pointed them out. I went over and asked if I could help. They left, never to return. Being a mean-looking person has had its rewards.' It would not be the last time Owen Hand would rescue Bert from a heavy situation. But when the Festival finally came around, it was a situation of a more welcome variety that presented itself to all those in the city who had come this far with a bunch of songs and a battered guitar. The fairy godfather had arrived, and his name was Nat Joseph.

'Somehow I persuaded Decca to give me a lot of money,' says Nat, 'to go and record the folk music at the Edinburgh Festival. There was a wonderful man called Hugh Mendel who was head of A&R [Artist & Repertoire] there at the time, and who'd discovered Tommy Steele. He liked the idea of folk music "coming up" but didn't know anything about it. "Why don't you go and make some records for us?" I think I'd originally gone in there looking for some sort of distribution deal or something.' Never one to miss an opportunity, Nat got on to Bill Leader forthwith. Brian Shuel came too. On arriving in Edinburgh, the priority was finding out exactly what was

going on in the way of folk music. In terms of the programme proper, not a
great deal: a cheesy Edinburgh foursome called the Corries Folk Trio &
Paddie Bell (transmuted to the Corries the following year, when a career in
television beckoned) were appearing in a show called *Hootenannie*; Robin
Hall & Jimmie Macgregor were in residence at the after-hours Festival Club;
and Bruce Dunnet was promoting Irish raconteur Dominic Behan, accompanied by Alex Campbell and Nadia Cattouse, in his own show *Behan Being
Behan*. As far as the official programme went, that was it, but there was
plenty going on around it. Archie Fisher, assisted by Owen Hand, was
running his Outlook Tower ceilidh again. As Owen recalls, Bert and Archie
had fallen out: 'Archie was charging him money to get in.' He was probably
wasting his breath. For Ian Campbell, by this stage the only non-professional
member of his own group, 'it seemed that every folksinger in Britain had
made his way to Edinburgh, either to appear in one of the innumerable
fringe shows or to bum around for three weeks while taking whatever
opportunity presented itself to do his thing'.[16]

Rory and Alex McEwan, spurred on by the success of their Murrayfield
shows the previous year, had rejected the Festival committee's rather half-
hearted offer of a week in some minor venue and taken the plunge
themselves, hiring the Palladium Theatre for three weeks. It would stretch
even their own considerable resources and would effectively mean putting
on a 'Festival' show that would exist entirely independently of either
Festival or Fringe proper. Throwing caution to the wind, the brothers
rented a large house in Edinburgh, to provide accommodation for
themselves and the other artists in the show and, unwittingly or otherwise,
an essentially free bar for every other folkie in town. For the show, entitled
Straight From The Wood, Rory and Alex brought in a revolving cast for the
three-week run: from Ireland, the Clancy Brothers & Tommy Makem and
future members of the Dubliners; from America, Carolyn Hester; from
South Africa, the Manhattan Brothers; from England, jazz guitarist Diz
Disley, trad singers Martin Carthy and Bob Davenport and, not least, the
Ian Campbell Folk Group.

The show was a late-night affair: for the earlier part of the evening an
absurd man called Johnny Victory was running a variety show involving a
tap-dancing accordeon player, a contortionist, a chorus line of bored-
looking women in beehives and tartan bikinis and somebody with a
plate-spinning act. Writing about his festival experiences some years later,
Ian Campbell was still morbidly fascinated with this 'flint-eyed little man
who found it necessary to obscure his mafiosic face behind a red nose and a
lurid tartan Andy-cap. The prat fall and the custard pie ran the gamut of his
technique. I developed a sort of grudging admiration for Jolly Johnny

because it seemed to me that to expose himself to the public with material such as his took not merely courage but a suicidal heroism. I began to know why Andy Stewart became such a big deal. With competition like this he could not fail.'

An element of farce was endemic. Dominic Behan was effectively fronting a stand-up show, and standing up at all was the biggest challenge for those involved. 'The gig was done in darkness with a spotlight high-lighting the person performing,' says Owen Hand, who was running the door. 'It focused on Alex Campbell and found him asleep on his stool, completely drunk.' The lighting man switched to the other stools, now empty as everyone else – eager to fill the vacuum, singing different songs, bumping into each other and falling over – rushed towards Alex. 'Bruce fired Alex that night,' says Owen, 'and as Alex had no money we had to do a benefit night to get him the fare back to London. But the audience had loved the whole thing.'

Rory McEwan, buoyed up by ecstatic press reviews and the consequent skin-of-its-teeth success of his own show, hired Leith Town Hall for a party on his birthday during the show's run. The 432nd Light Artillery Regiment (Territorial Army), of whose boxing team Owen Hand was a member, were hired as waiters. Owen spent the evening in some embarrassment, explain-ing to the chaps that no, really, he was there as a guest. An after-party session at the McEwans' place was more memorable still: 'Imagine this as a scenario,' says Owen, 'Caroline Hester singing "Summertime" accompanied by Julian Bream on guitar and Larry Adler on harmonica. Sitting in a corner with an enormous beam on his face was Ravi Shankar.' Ian Campbell's fiddler Dave Swarbrick may also have been involved. 'As I remember it, the only one who lost his way was Bream,' says Campbell, 'but I suspect that was not so much a reflection on his musicianship as an indication of the amount of alcohol he had consumed.' HRH Princess Margaret, for whom Rory McEwan was official Scottish escort, attended the show and after-show party on another occasion, memorable to Ian Campbell for an incident with a temperamental trouser zip and for Dave Swarbrick exiting the premises to a camera-flash barrage from a squad of paparazzi who were obviously ex-pecting somebody else.

It was in this rarefied atmosphere that Nat Joseph, Bill Leader and Brian Shuel hit town: the entrepreneur, the engineer and the image consultant. They lost no time at all in manufacturing what the records would later present, in two gently disingenuous volumes, as *The Edinburgh Folk Festival*: 'There was a whole load of people up there,' says Nat, 'most of whom Bill knew, so Bill took me around saying, "This is the chap who's conned Decca, etcetera, etcetera," and everybody thought it was a huge laugh. They were wonderful people, and the parties were incredible. Somebody said there were a hundred different kinds of malt whisky and I seem to remember we got through fifty-two. It was a bloody good trip! I guess that's where I met Ian Campbell and the people who later formalised themselves into the Dubliners.' Nat and Bill put the word out and a host of the Edinburgh folk scene and its seasonal stragglers turned up for the session. Organising a venue had been the last thing on anybody's mind. Dolina MacLennan was off in Glasgow for the day. She came home to the flat at 19 Bristo Place astonished to find a hundred people recording live albums in her bedroom: 'I rang the bell and got hell from somebody because this recording was happening. "What the hell's going on?" I said, or words to that effect! I think I recorded something for it.'

Dolina was indeed recorded during the sessions, as were many others, but not all of them made the finished product. Those who did were Ray & Archie Fisher, Jill Doyle, Hamish Imlach, Owen Hand, Robin Williamson & Clive Palmer, Anne Briggs, Dolina MacLennan, the Ian Campbell Folk Group, Nadia Cattouse, Jean Hart, Lou Killen and Matt McGinn. Immediately conspicuous by his absence was Len Partridge: 'I was gradually pulling out of the folk scene,' he says. 'I had nothing against commercialism but I had everything against what it did to people. From a very, very happy band of innocents abroad, when money came into it people started climbing over one another's backs to get gigs. I'd enjoyed myself far too much to let that screw it. I just gradually began to withdraw.'

As they stand, the two *Edinburgh Folk Festival* albums represent a formidable and unique document of the Edinburgh scene more or less in its heyday – and the first time on record for many of those involved. But with hindsight, the opportunity had been there to create a document still greater. Two weeks after the event *Melody Maker* reported that Alex Campbell, Bob Davenport and John Watt's Tregullion Trio had also been taped, along with three great 'source singers': Jeannie Robertson, Jimmy MacBeath and Willy Scott. Martin Carthy was in town at the time, likewise the McEwans, the Clancys and the proto-Dubliners; Davy Graham is also known to have been around (memorably pinching a tartan hat from somebody involved in the Johnny Victory show); and so too was Bert Jansch.

After the farrago at Dolina's flat Craig Hall (Waverley) Studios had been hired, where Brian Shuel shot several reels of candid black and whites that capture a mix of elation, tedium, humour and trepidation. Strangely, none of Shuel's stunningly atmospheric images were used on the packaging. Instead, the sleeve fronts sported a nondescript graphic of an acoustic guitar while the flipside supplied suitably ambiguous information on the nature of the recordings and a few notes on each of those involved. No one remembers Bert Jansch being around, but there he is in the studio, playing his guitar at two angle-poised microphones on five frames of Shuel's film.

'It's a little unclear to me what exactly occurred,' says Robin Williamson. 'He was about to marry Licorice and they had gone as far as publishing banns, which you had to do before getting married in those days. Licorice's father was opposed to her marrying Bert and in the end, as it transpired, she didn't. Bert left with Lynda at the drop of a hat, and what happened after that I don't know. It didn't seem very heavy-duty. Seemed like a nice enough girl, but I don't remember what her second name was. Never saw her again. I lost touch with Bert round about there. But I've always been a friend of Bert's and he's always been a friend of mine.'

Bert had decided he was going off to Morocco: perhaps he simply could not handle the inevitable confrontation with Licorice McKechnie's family – and a tendency to walk away from conflict remains a hallmark of Bert's character – thus removing her from the equation. Bert recalls their relationship as not being as serious as the youthful talk of a marriage would suggest. In the event, he took up with a sixteen-year-old from Dundee called Lynda. Lynda wanted to go on the adventure and had nothing getting in the way of doing so save the law – she was too young to get a passport of her own. So on 4 September 1963 Herbert Jansch, 'general labourer and bachelor', married Lynda Campbell, 'shorthand typist and spinster', at the Registry Office of the District of Proven, Glasgow. Both gave their address as 42 Denbrae Street, Glasgow.

Bert could not even recall Lynda's surname, but then again it was purely an arrangement of convenience: 'I only knew her for about two months before this,' he says. 'We got married so I could get her a passport without her parents' permission: she was sixteen, I was nineteen. We hitched to Morocco. We were there about a month and then we came back to London and we split up. We didn't actually divorce then, but I've never seen her again. She went her way and I went mine. But it was a nice trip and it was good to be in a different environment – certainly an experience. The first time I'd ever been in a different culture completely.'

Once Alex Campbell had introduced the possibilities of busking in Paris, Davy Graham had taken the process a stage further in extending the adventure down to Morocco – 'the dope centre of the universe' in Bert's memorable phraseology.[17] But whereas Davy had soaked up the music of Arabic culture to inform his own compositions, leading directly to the creation of the DADGAD modal guitar tuning, Bert was largely there for the experience. Getting home had been particularly interesting: Bert and Lynda ran out of money and were shipped back to London by the British

Embassy. Bert's passport was consequently retained until such time as the cost of the process could be recovered. There would be no more strolling down highways for the foreseeable future.

The scale of the advance Nat received from Decca for what became *The Edinburgh Folk Festival Vols. 1 & 2* has never been revealed, but to this day those involved in the sessions still argue the toss about who among those performing received the biggest fee: figures range between a fiver and tenner. Contracts had been signed and there would be no royalties. Nat returned to London with enough profit to buy premises in Hampstead – acquired from Collet's and refitted as a record shop and distribution outlet – and to establish Transatlantic Records as a serious enterprise. They had a ready-made roster of acts just waiting for the call. 'I remember saying to Bill, "These people aren't signed up," ' says Nat. 'It felt like the basis of a label and Bill, I think, saw that he was running into a bit of a dead end at Topic.'

The great majority of those whom Nat and Bill had met during the Decca project would make at least some contribution to the Transatlantic catalogue over the following years. The first to be signed were the Ian Campbell Folk Group. Nat had developed a great affection for the group, most of all for Ian's 'spiky but very intelligent' character. Ian's preference for 'intelligent' songs with socio-political messages impressed Nat, who was himself, for all his capitalist instincts, on the left wing of the Labour Party at the time. Although sounding more dated with the passing of time than many of their soloist contemporaries, instrumentally at least the Campbells would be the blueprint for all the British folk-rock groups of the later sixties. Their Transatlantic debut (TRA 110) was followed with an album by Jean Hart (TRA 111), another post-Edinburgh signing, though of less consequence. A few notches down the catalogue at TRA 116 came the first and eponymous album by a group destined to enjoy massive influence and longevity: the Dubliners. Nat and Bill would make the trip to Dublin and from there to a pub in the Wicklow mountains, contract in hand, with the sole intention of bringing back the boozy balladeers to a civilised recording studio. Remarkably, their trip would be successful. Like the Campbells, the group would make several more albums for Transatlantic, all selling well and all going a long way towards allowing the label's A&R policy to expand into riskier, less obviously commercial areas – none more so, at TRA 125, than the eventual debut of Bert Jansch.

Bert and Lynda's marriage in Glasgow had been attended, and witnessed, by his friends from London: John Challis and David Blass. On their way to Morocco, Bert and Lynda had stopped off in London at the Blass family home in Cresswell Place. On his way back, and this time alone, Bert stopped at David and John's new address, 19 King's Avenue, Ealing, where he remained for some weeks. The attraction was not in the quality of the accommodation. The previous occupant of the dingy, cold and untidy two-bedroom flat was one Colin Thompson, whose estranged wife Sue was still living there with her baby. Although Blass had dropped out after six weeks, Challis was still embroiled in a Fine Art course at Ealing Art College and was friendly with Sue, a former college girl herself. In October Bert Jansch suddenly appeared looking for a floor to sleep on. The kitchen was available and so too, as the by-products of past-tense marriages, were Bert and Sue.

'I remember John Challis's mother made some remark like, "She can't go around with him, he's already married," ' says Sue. 'To which John replied, "That's all right, so is she"! We were lovers for a while and then it petered out, although we had a kind of ongoing relationship even after it finished, as it were. My impression is he was around a lot to begin with and then he was here, there and everywhere. During his later visits I was staying at my mother's about ten miles away, and of course I had a young daughter so I wasn't very free at the time. There was never any definite, traumatic ending as such. Occasionally I'd meet him somewhere and find myself saying, "Ah-ha, come home with me . . .!" '

Bert would use King's Avenue as his London base over the next few months until Blass and Challis were obliged to relinquish the tenancy during the summer of 1964. He would be a fairly frequent if irregular visitor. 'There were times we'd see a lot of him, times where he wouldn't be around at all,' says Challis. A handful of letters to Bert, from four regional folk clubs and a couple of personal friends, all dating from the first quarter of 1964 and preserved by John Challis's sister Anne, testify to his geographical state of flux. At least one reply from a club organiser was addressed to Bert care of Adam Parker-Rhodes, at 112 Nicolson Street, Edinburgh, while Parker-Rhodes himself corresponds with Bert in Ealing during the same period. The contents of the letters also reveal Bert's growing popularity by word-of-mouth: there are gigs confirmed or implied at folk clubs in Stoke (a repeat booking), Keele University (for expenses and door money up to £8), Sheffield University (£10 including expenses) and Leicester (£10 including expenses). The secretary of the Leicester club tells Bert that while he has clearly never played the club before he has 'been asked for so many times lately by the members'.

Given the nature of where everyone at King's Avenue was at in terms of their own personal development and ambitions, these were strange times: Blass, expelled from school, dropped out of college and coasting on private means, was working up to retaking his A-levels but was in no hurry to do so;[18] Challis was living on a student grant, attending a college where everything – music, art, conversation, lifestyle – was at the cutting edge; Sue, having already been through the same college and a disastrous marriage, was now a single mother trying to find her new role in life; Bert was perpetually broke, without a guitar but still determined to make music and some kind of living thereby. They were heady, intense times and all those involved have reflections that range from the profound to the bleak to the absurd.

'It was low,' says Blass. 'Neither Bert nor John nor I had any sense of housekeeping. I wouldn't say it was a terribly happy time. There were a lot of tensions – more, in hindsight, unconscious than conscious. Overtly we got on fine but I think everyone had a long distance to go before they knew "who they were". It was the early days of the social and sexual revolution so nobody was sure of anything. Everybody lived in groups, everything was out in the open – there was no such thing as a private life. It was like being part of a revolutionary cell: there was no sense of being able to withdraw into privacy, and this really wasn't down to the physical circumstances of living in a small place. So under those circumstances, where people haven't quite got everything together, there can only be so much support or affirmation for each other. We lacked a warmth, I think.' Sue is rather pithier in her assessment: 'We seemed to sit around a lot smoking fags and drinking cups of tea.'

Where Bert's head was at, after a whirlwind marriage of convenience, an eye-opening trip to North Africa and a brusque repatriation back to the penniless drudge of real life, is anyone's guess. Sue was just happy to be enjoying something close to the single life again: 'We'd occasionally go to the pub, the Royal Oak in Ealing,' she says. 'He was quite sociable but he did have this habit of withdrawing – he'd be in the same room, but he'd be somewhere else. I never actually went to any gigs of his, but I don't think he had many at the time. He was so talented and so sweet – that was the attraction for me – but one always felt that his mind was on something else, probably music.'

Back in Edinburgh a few weeks later, Bert moved in for a period with Archie and Jill, by now renting a top-floor flat, beside the Greyfriar's Bobby pub, from Owen Hand's father, who lived below. Hand senior was a bus driver, used to working unusual shifts, not used to coming home to find that somebody had raided all the food from his fridge. 'This went on for a while,' says Owen, 'until it was established that Bert was the culprit. We had an outside toilet on the stair and one day my dad was going down to the toilet and heard someone coming up. So he waited to see who came round the corner and it was Bert. "How you doing, son?" says Dad. "Fine," says Bert, and walks straight past him and into the toilet, closing the door in his face. Big mistake. "You fucking bastard! You eat my bacon and egg, you drink my tea . . .!" He worked himself up into this fury and whacked Bert in the face when he opened the door. Bert went upstairs with his nose broken, Jill comes down the stairs shouting, "You're a savage! An animal!" "I've never hit a woman in my life," my dad says. "Send your man down!" Archie had the sense to stay where he was. Later that night my dad's sat there with a bottle of whisky and Ruby from the Chinese restaurant and it's all fermenting in his mind. He hears all these people arriving at the door and going up the stairs. They're probably just sitting around getting stoned, but that's not what my dad thinks. "They're plotting against me!" he thinks. So eventually he got a hatchet, went up there and kicked the door in, brandishing this axe, to be viewed in horror by all these wide-eyed hippies. The relationship was over and Archie and Jill were asked to move out.'[19]

By the beginning of 1964, the lure of London on the musicians of Edinburgh was becoming hard to resist. It was an effect that would exert similar influence on individual performers and other little outposts of folk music activity all over Britain and, a little later, on the first shoots of revival activity in Ireland. Some performers, like Hamish Imlach, were so popular in their own regional territory that they would rarely accept the long travelling and derisory fees associated with performing in London. For others of a cannier disposition, like Bert, it was a means to an end. 'You didn't actually make your living in London,' he says. 'But I think we were there to get our names in the *Melody Maker*. That got you into all the clubs in the country.'

Having established a promising connection with Nat Joseph and Bill Leader through the Decca sessions, Owen Hand had removed himself to London by the tail end of '63. He secured his position with a few gigs and later a residency at a new club Leader was running with Gill Cook called the Broadside, at the Black Horse in Rathbone Place, Soho. Leader's plan for Owen was to position him in a band he was creating from scratch with political songwriter Leon Rosselson and two others, to be known as the Three City Four. They were destined to rehearse for six months, play two gigs and fold. For all his qualities, Leader never had much luck as an entrepreneur. Bert was as yet unknown to Leader, so his very first *MM*-advertised engagement was once again at the Troubadour, on 17 March 1964, a Tuesday, with another one two days later at a pub in Chelsea. He had travelled down a few weeks earlier and was staying at King's Avenue with John Challis and David Blass.

Challis, recognising his friend's music as something truly exceptional, was a tireless champion: 'Bert was covering a lot of ground at that that time – he was listening to jazz, country blues, modern blues and everything else. There were lots of people working in one area or another but nobody before Bert was actually putting them all together and blending them in that way. One of the tragedies about Bert is that he was so far ahead then that every bugger in the world copied him. People who've come later don't realise that there was that time when he was unique: there was nobody like him. He just appeared, fully formed. I was a little bit in awe of him. I mean, here's this guy, same age as me and I'm there trying to play Big Bill Broonzy's "Guitar Shuffle" – he could do it, sing at the same time, change it around, turn it into something else. I got him a gig in the college. I just asked permission to use the lecture theatre at lunchtime, printed up some posters by hand and stood on the door charging half a crown. He made something like 30–35 bob [about £1.50], which wasn't bad for a couple of hours' work. I'd got a couple of good friends by the lapels and said, "You've got to hear this guy!" '

One of John's friends, an eighteen-year-old by the name of Pete Townshend, had recently dropped out to pursue his own music full time. It was the talk of the college: 'Everyone was saying what a brave and risky thing it was to do,' says Challis, 'when he could very easily become an art teacher!' Invited by Challis, Townshend came round to the flat to see what all the fuss was about.

Born in Isleworth in 1945, Townshend had started in Ealing at the same time as Challis, in September 1961. Those who were interested in music at the college, particularly in the emerging sounds of rhythm and blues (R&B), soon found each other. It was perhaps no coincidence that Britain's first dedicated R&B venue – Alexis Korner's 'Ealing Club' – had located itself in the area from April 1962. The college music scene and the exchange of records, ideas and marijuana that came with the territory were formative influences on Townshend, Challis and their contemporaries. Although his father was a dance band musician, with the consequence that Pete had been brought up on Ellington, Basie, Ella Fitzgerald and so forth, he was 'a late bloomer' in terms of the depth of his musical knowledge. 'Folk for me was skiffle,' he says. 'I'd had a couple of introductions to skiffle but I had no idea about where it came from. I had no idea, for example, that Lonnie Donegan was poaching from people like Leadbelly and Pete Seeger.'

Covering Top 10 material and trad jazz, Pete had been a member of various school bands, with his classmate John Entwistle a constant feature on bass and trumpet. During 1962, the two friends had joined a band led by Roger called the Detours. Daltrey was at this stage on lead guitar and trombone. There would be a number of evolutions of name and personnel before they added Keith Moon on drums, in May 1964, and became The Who: the Greatest Rock'n'Roll Band in the World.

'It was in my second year, 1962, that I was first brave enough to get out my guitar amongst fellow art students and play it,' says Townshend. 'And very, very quickly I rose to some degree of notoriety at college. And in the early part of 1963 I landed very quickly into my "rite of passage". In the school band I was in we were copying the Shadows and Acker Bilk. I'd had my ears pricked up by Bill Haley rather than Little Richard or Jerry Lee Lewis; by Acker Bilk rather than Louis Armstrong. I was quite naive – my first year at college I spent talking to a girl that I fancied with absolutely no idea that she fancied me too. And with music, I never went into the soup, ever. I waited for it to come to me. What happened when I was at Ealing was that I was bombarded with all kinds of influences. Mainly what was inspiring to me was rhythm and blues. But John Challis was one of the most interesting friends I had then because he was one of the people who, like me, listened to jazz as well. He introduced me to quite a lot of new jazz, like Charlie Mingus. So I was very conscious of the fact that John Challis had something that me and my American friends, who turned me on to R&B, didn't have: he had a much broader knowledge.'

'One of the reasons everyone was amazed with Bert,' says Challis, 'was because we were all struggling to do creative work in our own different ways and here he was, appearing fully formed at the age of eighteen or nineteen and it was pretty fucking scary! Somewhat later I got a bit interested in Zen and the idea of the Tao, or the Way – which is to see the world as it is free from all your own illusions. Most people have to struggle to reach this state of enlightenment. But occasionally someone comes along who is already enlightened and that, I think, was Bert. There is a Zen statement about this which says, "Before I was enlightened I was the most miserable man in the world. Now I am enlightened I am still the most miserable man in the world, but I am enlightened." Part of his artistic endeavour was that he had somehow tapped into the Tao of misery, which is there in his music. What he was doing was as authentic as the traditional blues or folk music we were all listening to, but it was *his*. It was his thing. There you were sitting around with your mates, trying to play a Leadbelly number – and making a reasonable fist of it, because we weren't fools – and suddenly it was as if you had met Robert Johnson or Blind Lemon Jefferson, and he was the same age as you!'

John Challis had been tinkering around on both piano and guitar from at least the time when he would sneak in as an under-eighteen to the Blues & Barrelhouse Club in 1960 and 1961. He would eventually become a very fine pianist, in the barrelhouse style. Soon after meeting Bert he gave up on any notion of playing guitar. Bert was still without an instrument of his own but Challis could be of service: 'I had a Zenith, a dance band guitar with f-holes, and it looked very strange in folk clubs. It was a dog of a guitar, but Bert managed to make it sound like it was the most perfect Martin ever.'

Round at the Challis residence, in a haze of pot smoke, two guitars were swinging. When Pete chose to call, there was a second Scottish guitarist in town: Archie Fisher. Archie, a rare visitor to London in the sixties, was appearing at the Troubadour on 14 March, three days before Bert's engagement at the same venue. He had not long previously decided to adopt Davy Graham's revelatory new DADGAD tuning for his own work in accompanying Scottish traditional song, for which its modal thrum was ideally suited. There was a knock at the door.

'I remember that first meeting so clearly because it was so profound,' says Townshend. 'It's a pity that I can't remember subsequent ones. I found Bert very, very, very impressive. What I generally saw in the musicians I met at that time was competitiveness and ambition, and he didn't have that – he didn't have that sense that "I'm going to do something and you're going to be impressed." He's two years older than me and two years older when you're that age is quite a lot. But he just seemed to me that he was playing like a man twice his age, in a very fluid, eloquent style.

'What was extraordinary about that particular occasion for me was that there was something very mysterious going on between the two players. I think Bert was using a regularly tuned guitar but the other player, I think, was playing an open tuning. They were discussing chords, and obviously one or the other was translating. I've often thought about this: if I'd actually said to them, "What are you doing? What's different? Write it down." I was too proud. I was too afraid to ask for the secret, and if I had have done what it would have done to change my style . . . They sat and played for about an hour and I just watched, really. There wasn't a third guitar, although once or twice Bert gave me his guitar to play, but I didn't play very much. They played "Angi", I remember that – they were both playing that together. And that day I went and got a copy of the record, and I've still got it. The other thing that was quite popular at the time was *Jazz On A Summer's Day*. The Jimmy Giuffre Trio did "Train And The River" [in that film], which also had descending notes and which, I think, Bert played also on this day. And I went home and immediately learnt it – about as contrapuntal as I ever got on the guitar! But I could [later] play "Angi" quite well. What I also remember him doing on that particular day was extemporising: he was making things up, they were firing off one another, and I don't think I'd been in a room watching two people do that before. What I got was a sense that at that time he *was* the music: it sounds like a cliché, but that's who he was. When you come across a really great musician, what happens is you realise that they do become their music – it overshadows everything. My sense then was that I had met someone who was already on a path. I made an arrangement to see Bert play at the Troubadour but I couldn't go for some reason. Maybe we had a gig.'[20]

Following the *Edinburgh Folk Festival* sessions with Bill Leader and Nat Joseph, Anne Briggs had more or less opted out of music – or, more accurately, had been obliged to sideline any interest in that direction. She had taken up with one Gary Field, known to the denizens of Edinburgh as 'Gary the Archer'. 'Gary was a wild character,' says Bert. 'I used to teach him guitar, and he and Anne used to go out shooting rabbits with bows and arrows. Gary *was* Jimi Hendrix: he looked like him, dressed like him, had the same stance, everything – and this was before Jimi had ever appeared on the scene. And when I met Jimi Hendrix the first person I thought of was Gary, 'cos Gary was a very quiet guy but he was violent – and I got the same vibe off Jimi.'

While Bert had been away in Morocco, Gary and Anne had shared a flat with Robin and Licorice, but Gary was by all accounts on the very fringes of the fringes of the alternative scene. His father had enjoyed some honorary position within the gift of the Royal Family – Chief Bowman to the Queen, or thereabouts. To the recollection of John Challis, who harboured a wise instinct to avoid the man as far as possible, Gary was offered the title in turn and told them where to go. With Anne, he was an occasional partaker of the liberal hospitality offered by the Blass household. On one visit, probably during the summer of 1963 (Anne had a gig in London in July), the pair stayed for some weeks. Blass found Gary more fascinating than sinister: 'I liked him. He was very off the wall. Many people in those days had an ideal of country skills and music and these folky things, and he fulfilled these ideals with great accuracy. A very interesting person. Although he did have a shadowy, negative side.'

Field was in fact little more than a vagrant with an anarchic attitude, violent tendencies and a criminal lifestyle. He was eventually imprisoned for house-breaking. Anne herself is loath to recall the man: 'It was two years of hell,' she says. 'I know what it's like on the other side. A really, really bad time. My God, it sharpened me up.' Anne recalls those 'two years' (actually nine or ten months spanning two calendar years) as a period with no involvement in music. Shortly before Easter 1964 she met Hamish Henderson on the street in Edinburgh and was invited to a conference being held by his School of Scottish Studies. 'It was like a ray of golden sunshine in a really bad time. I decided to break out of the life I was living. It took some doing.'

'Anne came round to visit my wife and I, having been beaten up by Field,'

says Owen Hand. 'I was about to return to London on a bus organised by
the Edinburgh branch of Young CND, who were going to the Aldermaston
march. Anne was desperate to get away but had no money, so I arranged a
seat on the bus for her. Once we got to London, Anne went her own way.
Not long after this Field arrived in London with a crossbow over his back,
looking for her. He didn't find Anne but found the trad singer Lou Killen
who had been with Anne – and after a casual night drinking with him, stuck
a glass in his face.'[21]

With a lunatic like Field in town, wreaking revenge on anyone who had
enjoyed the remotest association with his girlfriend, almost nobody on the
folk scene was safe. Certainly not Bert. 'I was heading into Collet's one day,'
says Owen, 'when I met Alex Campbell who told me to watch out as Field
was in there looking for me. When I entered I saw Field and Bert standing at
the back of the shop. Bert looked terrified. I approached Field and said I
believed he wanted to see me. Field was as nice as ninepence and said it had
been nothing important. I gave him my phone number and told him to give
me a call if he later remembered what it was. Bert told me afterwards that
Field had said to him, "When I go for him it will be with steel." I guess he
meant a knife. Soon after that was the incident with Lou Killen and Field
took off back to Edinburgh. The next time I was in Edinburgh and came
across him – in the Crown Bar, with a group of his followers – I asked him if
he remembered what he had wanted to talk to me about. I then put it to him
about his intention of using steel and asked if he would like to try. I forced
him to back down in front of his followers. Field came from a similar
background to myself and knew me from days when I was considered a bit
of a hard man. I think he was frightened of my reputation, but he got his
own back later.'[22]

The EP Anne had recorded for Topic early in 1963 finally appeared in
May 1964. With remarkable pertinence to her own experiences, its title was
The Hazards Of Love. Recorded by Bill Leader, with a sleeve note from Bert
Lloyd and a now iconic cover shot from Brian Shuel, its four traditional
songs including 'Rosemary Lane', later recorded by Bert Jansch, were
unadorned and beautiful. Anne had been given 'Rosemary Lane' by Paul
Carter, who ran another traditional music label called Collector; the rest of
the songs had come from Bert Lloyd. Although she would not record again
until 1966 (four songs for The Bird In The Bush, another of Bert Lloyd's
thematic projects) and after that until 1971, there was already enough in the
public domain to secure her reputation as a singer of rare quality and instinct.
With Field having given up the chase, and her presence on the music scene
revitalised, Anne was free to use what influence she had not for her own
ambitions – for she had none – but on behalf of her soulmate Bert Jansch.

Like others involved in the *Edinburgh Folk Festival* sessions Anne had been offered a deal with Transatlantic by Nat Joseph. Her reaction was probably unique: 'I turned him down,' she says. 'He was flashing money about, but I felt a certain loyalty to Topic and, quite honestly, although they never had any money I felt they had discretion.' She nevertheless realised that Topic would never in a million years be interested in what Bert was doing, and so the only possible option was Transatlantic. Anne would be forthright in her championing of Jansch to both Nat Joseph and Bill Leader, who had engineered all three of her own record sessions to date, but the primary focus was on Leader: the most important thing, she felt, was to get Bert Jansch on tape.[23]

Anne had been staying not at the Blass family home, where Field would certainly have found her, nor indeed at the similarly welcoming flat off Gray's Inn Road tenanted by her friend Gill Cook from Collet's. Wherever the hiding place, in the free and easy manner of the times Anne was soon dating Bill Leader's recording assistant Seumus Ewans, described by Gill as 'quite an exotic character' with a huge Cadillac and no money, while Bert – an exotic character with neither Cadillic nor money – became involved with Gill, who had previously enjoyed a brief relationship with Owen Hand. Bert was soon acquainted with Bill Leader. The whole tangled web of connections would make the recording of Jansch by Leader a virtual inevitability, regardless of how uncommercial he sounded. But it would take a while yet.

Between Bert's first appearance at the Troubadour, in January 1963, and the second, in March 1964, popular music had experienced not one but two seismic shifts. The first and most celebrated revolution was in the wake of the Beatles, a foursome of ex-skifflers and rock'n'rollers from Liverpool whose transformation of American R&B muscle, rock'n'roll swagger and doo-wop harmonies into something singularly identifiable as British 'beat' was comparable to the transatlantic journey of jazz, folk and blues into skiffle a few years earlier. It would, however, prove to be a more durable, adaptable commodity. By way of illustration, on the very day of Bert's Troubadour debut the Beatles were enjoying their first ever national TV broadcast on *Thank Your Lucky Stars*; fourteen months later, on the day of Bert's second visit, they were picking up 'Show Business Personalities of the Year' awards at a Variety Club lunch and later appearing on a new TV show: *Top Of The Pops*. The second phenomenon, remembered less as a movement perhaps than as a clutch of momentarily successful groups and individuals, was folk.

The 'folk boom' was a phrase bandied to death in the pop papers of the middle sixties. It had first appeared in the wake of harmony trio Peter, Paul & Mary's US single successes during 1963 with two Bob Dylan songs,

'Blowin' In The Wind' and 'Don't Think Twice, It's Alright'. After appearing with Dylan and Joan Baez at Martin Luther King's 'March On Washington' in August, and given the unprecedented attendance figure of 46,000 for that year's Newport Folk Festival, this rather earnest ensemble were deemed to be blazing a trail for a new boom in folk amongst the young and reinvigorating a genre that had, in fact, been fermenting in the pop charts since 1958, with acts like the Highwaymen and the Kingston Trio. Dylan's manager Albert Grossman had created Peter, Paul & Mary as a more campus-credible version of the Kingstons. But Dylan was a one-off. His personal reputation, as distinct from the popularity of his songs in the hands of others, was being enhanced by hobo-ing along on the coat-tails of Joan Baez, floor-spotting at her shows as Bert Jansch had been doing with Anne Briggs. Cultural commentator Griel Marcus first encountered Dylan at a Baez gig and, in terms of the characterisation, one could almost substitute Bob and Joan with Bert and Anne in his account.

'It was the summer of 1963, in a field somewhere in New Jersey. I'd gone to see Joan Baez and after a bit she brought out a scruffy-looking guy with a guitar. He looked dusty. His shoulders were hunched and he acted slightly embarrassed. He sang a couple of songs. I was transfixed. I was confused. When the show was over I saw him trying to light a cigarette. "You were terrific," I said brightly. He didn't look up. "I was shit," he replied.'[24]

By August 1963 the scruffy guy in the field had sold 250,000 copies of his second album, *The Freewheelin' Bob Dylan*, which was not even available in Britain at the time. It included two songs which owed a great debt to the repertoire of Martin Carthy: 'Girl From The North Country' and 'Bob Dylan's Dream', based on the tunes of two English traditional songs, 'Scarborough Fair' and 'Lord Franklin' respectively. It had been Carthy who had first invited Bob, during his 1962 visit as a complete unknown, to sing at an English folk club, the King & Queen.

By the time of Bob's first return, for one night only at the Festival Hall on 17 May 1964, the concept of a 'folk boom' had been well and truly bought in from the American experience by a bandwagon-happy British media. Hindsight has demonstrated that 1963 was in fact the apogee of folk music as a social and cultural force in America, although given the very different social context the timescale of its rise and fall and the level of its impact in Britain are less easily defined. But back in 1963/64, Sunday tabloids frothed at the possibility of Communism poisoning the minds of the nation's youth, while the music papers simply made sure they were not wrong-footed by another explosion like skiffle without having predicted, examined and discussed the matter thoroughly beforehand. For *Melody Maker* the 'folk boom', the 'hootenanny' and 'protest' would be the currency of debate for the next couple of years, but nobody was putting a shape on what the breakthrough might be nor a date by which time it would happen. The *MM* columns attributed to 'Steve Benbow', and generally ghost-written by broadcaster and jazz man Ken Sykora, were quick to point out that if there was indeed a boom then it would all be down to the sterling ground-work of Ken Sykora, while sternly warning that 'to those whose real musical love is the sound of the cash register, folk music is becoming a bandwagon for selling cigarettes, soft drinks and cosmetics'.

This was no exaggeration: a low budget folk TV show in the States, called *Hootenanny*, had stormed the national ratings during 1963 while the title itself, a vague euphemism for a good-time gathering, became an all-purpose, non-copyright licence to print money. 'Hootenanny' candy bars appeared in New York with the added temptation to 'send in two wrappers and a dollar and get a folk record!'. By April 1964 the *MM* was able to report that 'the folk boom is beginning to pay off, with hootenanny discs flowing in thick and fast'. Streams of records were arriving from the States with that word in the title. Britain was not long in catching up: one wretched disc, *Hootenanny In London*, notoriously boasted a photograph of Anne Briggs in its sleeve montage yet not a trace of her on the record.[25] Clearly a pretty face will shift units. By June Malcolm Nixon had shamelessly renamed his Ballads & Blues club – by now occupying Saturday nights at the Black Horse – the 'Hootenanny, Ballads & Blues'.

The origins of the word may be, like skiffle, obscure, but the mid-sixties currency of 'the hootenanny' could be traced both in Britain and America very specifically to the increasingly popular medium of television. While America was tuning in to the folk music variety show *Hootenanny* on the ABC network in 1963, Scotland's STV were coincidentally running a series of ten-minute interludes with Rory & Alex McEwan called *Hootenannie*. In January 1964, fronted by Roy Guest and live from a jazz club in Edinburgh, the BBC nationally broadcast *The Hoot'nanny Show*. The hootenanny was anything one wanted it to be, so long as it was fun: the joy of the thing to the various purveyors of product was to be found in the infinite variety of its spelling. Occasional spots on national and regional magazine shows had been available to folk singers or, rather, to a handful of suitable representatives of the form, in Britain since the late fifties. Scotland had hinted at more substantial programming of the music with periodic series based around the Reivers, Steve Benbow and the McEwan brothers. But the first significant opportunity for folk music on British TV nationally came from BBC Manchester in July 1962, with a show called *Barndance*.

The station was taken unawares by the strength of audience reaction to *Barndance* and the series, fronted by Liverpool group the Spinners, was extended to six programmes. Produced by John Ammonds, who would go on to produce series with Val Doonican and Morecambe & Wise, *Barndance* was an old-style variety programme with a slant towards folksong its distinguishing feature. The Spinners, who were still very much an amateur group with day jobs, turned up at the auditions and sang, as Ammonds requested, two English traditional songs, 'John Peel' and 'The Mermaid': 'He said, "How many songs like that have you got?" ' one of the group later recalled. 'We looked at each other and said, 'Don't know – twenty, thirty, forty, whatever." "Well how would you like to do the series?" We were knocked out.'[26] The recording schedule was changed to reflect the group members' unavailability during weekdays and the resulting series was a quietly formidable step forward for both the presentation of traditional music on television and the career of the Spinners.

Easy targets for mocking in later years, by virtue of their Arran sweaters and ubiquity on television, the Spinners were nonetheless ground-breakers as the first public face of the British 'folk boom'. 'Uniform was a mortal sin,' said Tony, the group leader. 'But we were a weird conglomeration – a giant, two nondescripts and a black. You could say this was visually interesting but it wasn't because we all had such totally different tastes in clothes. There was no way we could all agree to look smart together or sloppy together. A uniform was the way to do that and I stand by it.'[27] In April '63, a second series of *Barndance* was launched, again involving the usual trappings of variety programming – female backing vocalists, a dance troup ('the John Peel Dancers', if you will) – and this time featuring the Ian Campbell Folk Group as the resident band. A third series began in May '64, this time with Steve Benbow resident. But the next significant breakthrough had already come, debuting in the autumn of 1963 and courtesy of the Birmingham-based ABC station. Its name was *Hullaballoo*.

Fronted by Rory McEwan and featuring as residents Martin Carthy and the Cyril Davies All-Stars, with weekly guests such as the Clancy Brothers, Davy Graham and the Ian Campbell Folk Group – *Hullaballoo* was no show in hock to the values of light entertainment. It was broadcast in several of the ITV regions, with London the most notable exception, at the very start of national 'folk boom' fever and with a longer-term vision might well have become that music's *Ready Steady Go!*. The Cyril Davies All-Stars, performing electric R&B, were Davies, Long John Baldry and a backing band poached wholesale from rock'n'roll novelty act Screaming Lord Sutch. Davies had opted to detach himself from Alexis Korner's jazzier direction with Blues Incorporated in November '62. Under the All Stars name he would release two influential singles, 'Country Line Special' and 'Preachin' The Blues', before succumbing to leukaemia in January 1964. The very presence of such a hard-line Chicago blues band on a programme with an otherwise folk bias reflects the communal 'bag' that folk and blues were still, in some quarters, being put in.

The first of *Hullaballoo*'s two series had been taped in June '63 and broadcast in October. In between, through meeting on the programme, the Campbells had been invited to take part in McEwan's Edinburgh Festival show during which they would take the plunge into fully professional status. Ian Campbell would not be alone in reflecting some years later that as a platform for British folk *Hullaballoo* had never been bettered. 'The programme sold well and was broadcast in many countries overseas,' he noted, 'and as a result we were still receiving congratulatory letters three years later from as far away as Australia.'[28] A concert at the Albert Hall on 21 September 1963, a week before *Hullaballoo*'s first transmission, featured most of the big names from televised folk and blues – the Ian Campbell Group, the Cyril Davies All Stars, Steve Benbow, Hall & Macgregor, the Spinners and others besides – and was both a sell-out and a watershed for folksong as a movement. 'The audience spread right across the age range,' noted a *Melody Maker* reviewer, 'and there was a genuine sense of occasion to which all the artists rose.'

The Hoot'nanny Show, transmitting from January 1964, was the BBC's response to both *Hullaballoo* and the folksong explosion that was just around the next corner. Its presenter would be Roy Guest.[29] Returning to Britain from his various adventures abroad Guest positioned himself wisely. From being simultaneously a brilliant entertainer, a performing artist of strictly limited consquence, a businessman of dubious repute and a promotional entrepreneur of inexplicable genius, within six months of his return he had talked his way into the Harold Davidson Agency, one of the biggest entertainment providers in the country, as the head of their new folk department.[30] It was a department they had not had before Guest's arrival. By the end of the year Roy could announce, with the gloss of humility and from the pages of a crusading new magazine called *Folk Scene*, that 'I shall accept no more bookings as a folk singer until I am entitled to call myself one'. He had already by then shifted his allegiance from Harold Davidson to Cecil Sharp House and the auspices of the venerable English Folk Dance & Song Society, which he would proceed, over the next twelve months, to drag kicking and screaming into the world of commerce, festivals, hootenannies and the ever-imminent folk boom. He would have little time of his own for folk singing, entitled or otherwise.

In April 1964, the *Melody Maker* announced a little over-excitedly that 'Peter, Paul and Mary mania' had arrived in Britain. Interviewed at the

time, the trio paid tribute not only to Pete Seeger and Woody Guthrie, but
to Peggy Seeger and Ewan MacColl, to Rory & Alex McEwan and most
tantalisingly to Bob Dylan and his third album, *The Times They Are A-
Changing*, available in America since January but not to be released in
Britain till May. It gave all the talk of a folk boom a tangible set of
personalities. It was also a scene-setter for the arrival in Britain the
following month of the one individual who most clearly embodied the
folk future: Bob Dylan.

Before Dylan hit town, there was a package tour embodying with equal
clarity the folk past. The American Folk Blues & Gospel Caravan featured
many of the individual artists who had toured Britain under Chris Barber's
patronage over the previous seven or eight years: Sister Rosetta Tharpe,
Muddy Waters with Otis Spann and Willie Smith from his own band,
Sonny Terry & Brownie McGhee, along with first-timers the Reverend
Gary Davis and Cousin Joe Pleasant. After the London show on 3 May,
there was to be a party at the bluesmen's hotel.[31] Gill Cook had invited
Owen and Bert along but as Owen recalls: 'The party was a bit of a disaster.
No one seemed to know about it but the blues men, Gill, Bert and I. I spent
most of the time sharing a bottle of vodka with Otis Spann, who was telling
me to come to Chicago where he would look after me. Bert spent his time
with his hero Brownie. After playing a few numbers Brownie asked Bert to
"play us a blues, man". Bert picked up the guitar and started to play one of
his pieces of the time, which was a blues but didn't conform to twelve-bar
type. "That ain't the blues, man," shouted Brownie. Bert lowered the
guitar. "Listen man," he said, "you play your fucking blues and I'll play
mine. Okay?" With that he picked up the guitar and continued.'

Bob Dylan arrived in Britain a week later, appeared on two TV shows,
gave a typically abstract interview to the *MM*, performed one concert at the
Festival Hall on 17 May and hung out with the Beatles and with Martin and
Dorothy Carthy. He also, to fill an otherwise idle night, went pub-crawling
with Bert Jansch. Bert liked Bob's first two albums and had performed
'Blowin' In The Wind' once or twice himself. 'Bill Leader seemed to have
got the job of taking him round London that particular night,' says Bert. 'I
was just dragged along. I was sitting in a car waiting outside the Savoy Hotel
in The Strand and Bill appeared with these three figures, all falling over.
They got in the car and apart from saying hello it was all "space" – that's
what they were talking about. You couldn't communicate with him – he
was totally out of it. We were basically there to take him round the clubs, so
we took him to the Black Horse and then we went to the Roundhouse in
Wardour Street and Martin Winsor was onstage. He was a pretty heavy guy,
a Soho face. The entourage came through the door and there was such a

racket going on Martin got angry. "Who the fuck do you think you are? Shut up or I'll throw you out . . ."'

It was the second time in two years that Winsor had badmouthed Bob from the stage of the Roundhouse. 'There were people who attacked Bob all the time,' says Carthy, 'people like Martin Winsor. As far as they were concerned, if a jazz musician like Charlie Parker or Coleman Hawkins smoked dope it was romantic, a really groovy thing. But all these scruffs come along from Minnesota and Edinburgh and it's like they committed sacrilege, spoiling his dreams. So they wanted to kick Bob out of the club and tried to make his life a misery. Bob just told him to piss off.'

Owen Hand heard all about it later on: 'Bert came back with a typical Bertian shuffle and I asked him what Dylan was like. "He's a drag man, a real drag," was the reply. Dylan had been full of himself, apparently. The highlight of the night as far as I was concerned was that Dylan would only drink red wine so one of his acolytes was despatched to get a bottle. The bottle was opened by pushing the cork inside and the contents poured into a half-pint glass. Meantime, upstairs comes the landlord of the Black Horse, sees the wine bottle and asks whose it was. "Mine," replied Dylan. "Where did you get it?" asks the landlord. "A little wine store round the corner," says Dylan. "Drink what's in your glass, take your bottle with you and get out. You're barred."'

Soho historian John Platt has described the Black Horse as 'a sombre Victorian pub which was the first to be reached up Rathbone Street but usually the last entered'.[32] Immediately after the Dylan incident, the Broadside was obliged to move on (although it did return to the Black Horse for a few nights during the summer). Ostensibly, the landlord wanted his upstairs room 'to run posh functions' instead. The club moved to El Toro in Finchley Road, at which point Bert was deemed worthy to grace its stage if not its advertising.

Owen meanwhile was in something of a dilemma: his wife, by this time with a baby daughter, had refused to move to London with the consequence that Owen had been travelling back to Edinburgh at weekends – just about the only time his much anticipated Three City Four group could rehearse. He arrived back home one weekend to find his marriage on the verge of collapse. The only way to save it was for Owen to give up on his hopes and dreams in London. It was a blow to all concerned: the group had just about got its act together, having performed two gigs – one at the Black Horse, one at the Golders Green home of Stephen Sedley's father, to an audience of 'rich Jewish Communists'. Owen took a few days to wind up his affairs in London and then cadged a lift for himself and Bert from a guy with a small sports car. It was at the end of May, straight after a gig Bert was doing at El

Toro: 'The trip goes down in memory as one of the worst of my life,' says Owen. 'The two front seats were taken by the driver and his mate, while Bert and I sat up at the back and froze. The journey took twelve hours, with numerous breaks to allow Bert and I to get our blood circulation going again. When we got to Edinburgh the wife had gone anyway, so what was the point? I didn't see either her or my daughter for over a year.'

Owen stayed on in Edinburgh for the next six months or so, but Bert was still travelling back and forth between his home city and London, where he had fallen under the wing of Alex Campbell. Campbell was also giving his generous patronage to another young musician, David 'Buck' Polley. Polley's passion was restoring old cars but he was also, most unusually for those times and for the folk scene, a user of heroin.

'When I could afford a new pair of jeans I'd give away my old pair to some guy who wouldn't have as much bread as me,' said Alex. 'Buck Polley, I was such a hero to him he used to *buy* the clothes I gave away so he could wear my clothes. I bought a black cowboy hat, so he bought a black cowboy hat. When we came back to this country from Paris, Buck and me, we had an old 1928 Morris Isis – beautiful car. We used to take Anne Briggs and Bert Jansch with us and they'd do floor spots and they'd get work, because nobody knew them then. Bert got my old jeans jacket, which I believe he has to this day. It's his sort of lucky piece, which Buck had bought off some other kid that I'd given it to in Paris. I said to him once, "Jesus, none of my records are selling very much, Buck." That was before we went to cheap LPs. "Well, Alex," he says, "die and they'll sell a helluva lot." '[33]

Campbell tried to get Polley off the drugs and thought he had been successful, but 'some bastard in Brighton turned him on again' and a week later, on 20 June 1964, he was found dead, aged twenty-two, of acute morphine and cocaine poisoning: an 'incautious overdosage', a suicide. 'He had a lot of trouble with his wife and kids,' says Bert, 'It was just the pressure, I think, of home life that got to him. He scored in the pub and the next day he was dead.'[34]

Bert and one of his Edinburgh friends had tried heroin once only, around the time of the trip to Morocco, but his general appearance and demeanor and the sheer incomprehensibility, to some, of his music would taint him with an unwelcome and wholly unjustified reputation for years to come. 'I'm sure whenever I saw him I thought two things,' says Pete Townshend. 'One, he was a really good musician, and two, was he carrying? My take at the time was that there was a possibility that Bert was a junkie. He did look like one. In hindsight, he actually looked quite poor, but I suppose how we interpreted that in middle-class West London was that he must have pissed it all away.'[35]

The greatest irony of all was that the song which would effectively make Bert's name, 'Needle Of Death', was an elegy for Polley and a stark reflection on the consequences of hard drugs. 'This image went around the country that Bert Jansch was a junkie and it was totally erroneous,' says Owen Hand. 'Because people knew Bert and I were close they would ask, "Has he given up the junk yet?" He wrote "Needle Of Death" and people automatically assumed he was junkie. As far as I'm concerned Bert never went near junk. Alcohol was his problem.'

It was not only the 'folk boom' that characterised 1964 in Britain; this was also year two of the 'beat boom'. The Beatles, who for Bert 'never entered my life', had made a pivotal impact the previous year, being followed not least by the Rolling Stones, whose originality may have been slow off the mark but whose sound was altogether tougher and more keenly influenced by the same kind of R&B that was doing the rounds in Ealing. The only pop/beat/R&B band with which Bert had enjoyed any personal connection was yet to make its mark on the national consciousness, but had certainly made its mark on his: The Who.

'I always remember going to one of The Who's first gigs in Ealing and being astounded, me as a folkie watching Pete smashing his guitar. The sheer volume and ferocity – I couldn't take that at the time. I saw them rehearse once at the Three Feathers [in Ealing], that's where I first saw them as a band. Pete would be rehearsing his windmills. What a thing to rehearse! I don't know if they were into the whole mod look at the time, but I wouldn't have said they were scruffy – but then nobody looked particularly scruffy next to me. I remember being round at Pete's flat in Ealing, with blue neon lights, the windows blacked out and piles and piles of blues singles. He was quite an expert.'[36]

'Pete's flat was a focus for quite a lot because of his big record collection,' says John Challis, 'and I can remember him experimenting with his sound system. There was one occasion everyone who came into the place had to lie down on the couch with a twelve-inch speaker on their chest while he whacked the volume up. Record wise, Pete had just about everything that was available at that time. One of the acts everybody loved at Ealing were Booker T & the MGs. I remember playing "Green Onions" to Bert. He really liked it.'

'I can remember Bert coming to Woodgrange Avenue,' says Townshend, 'where my mother had a house. We had the apartment upstairs and I remember him coming around, making him tea or coffee, rolling joints together, and I can remember listening together to a single on EP format that John Challis had bought of "Better Get It In Your Soul" by Charlie

Mingus which had just been released.[37] Bert had heard it the day before and he'd been playing it at John Challis's. I actually went out and bought a copy of it. A brilliant recording.'

This was a formative period for both Townshend and Jansch. In April 1964, The Who had failed an audition for a BBC radio broadcast. In May, they encountered Keith Moon and fate's hand was kinder. From roughly July to October they flirted with a new name, the High Numbers, enjoyed a twelve-week residency at the Railway Hotel in Harrow,[38] released their first single (albeit to minimal impact) and acquired the management that would eventually take them to a national level the following year. Bert was trying for the same thing, in a vague sort of way, but other than being in London and looking for gigs he had not the slightest idea how to go about it.

The Railway was a regular haunt of John Challis's and consequently, when he was in town, of Bert. The promoter of The Who's summer residency at the place, on Tuesday nights, was Richard Barnes, another of John's college friends: 'I remember one night they did a version of "Smokestack Lightning" which was very much, with hindsight, leading towards The Who sound,' says Challis. 'The amps were whacked up as high as they'd go, with this incredible rumbling filling the room. At the time I don't think I'd ever heard anything so loud. It felt as if an iron bar had been driven through my head from one ear to the other and I'd been lifted up!' As the public debut of what was to be his only real experiment with being a member of an electric band, Bert would find himself playing at the same venue, along with Challis and a host of dimly recalled others during the interval of a popular local act whose only national success would be winning a new bands competition on *Ready Steady Go!*: the Bo Street Runners.

'Because I was into the R&B thing quite heavily, Bert was toying with it,' says Challis. 'He didn't really like playing electric guitar. I think it was to do with the volume and because it was restricting his rhythmic and melodic freedom. I thought he was rather good at it, myself. The Bo Street Runners' guitar player was another guy from my old school, Gary Thomas. They were playing the gig and they let us use their gear to do an interval spot. They had an electric piano in the band and I was playing that. I'd abandoned my guitar to Bert, as you would.'

'I don't know why I wasn't more interested in electric guitar at the time,' says Bert. 'I think it was the paraphernalia that had to go with it, the amplifier and so on. Too much bother. Trying to get a gig was bad enough, without having to lug an amplifier around!' The very idea of Bert, the quintessential acoustic man, playing electric guitar in an ensemble situation at all was itself the by-product of a still more remarkable scenario. In 1962 Brian Knight, an early protégé of Cyril Davies's, formed Blues By Six. Credited as the second electric R&B group in Britain, coming between Alexis Korner's Blues Incorporated and the Rolling Stones, Knight's group were arguably more 'authentic' but certainly less successful than either. Various line-ups of Blues By Six came and went between 1962 and the band's dissolution by mid '65, and at one point around the middle of 1964 there was the very real possibility that either Blues By Six would take the electric blues world by stealth with an amazing and highly unusual new rhythm guitar player from Edinburgh or that the name of Brian Knight would feature in the footnotes of yet another career other than his own. In the event, it just about manages the footnote.

Challis and Bert had gone as a team to audition for Knight's latest line-up, somewhere in West London. As Challis recalls, it was memorable for all the wrong reasons: 'The drummer was a window cleaner and he turned up in his overalls and there was his bucket mixed up with his kit! The embarrassing part was they offered me the job playing piano but they didn't want Bert. Brian said, "Oh, the audience won't want to see you using a capo"! It was like the blues equivalent of a jazz purist. So I didn't take the job either. I rang him up and told him I'd hurt my finger moving furniture.'

Prior to the failed audition, Bert and John were already toying with the idea of getting their own band together. 'But being the sort of non-managerial people that we were and are,' says Challis, 'we couldn't get it together at all.' The interval jam at the Railway may well have been the first and last fumbled outworkings of the band idea, but somehow the notion survived a while longer, gaining a new lease of life with the addition of a third adventurer and remaining an option right up to the release of Bert's first album in April 1965. It was an album whose time for recording had now come.

'There was a big swell of opinion about the importance of Bert and what he was doing,' says Bill Leader, 'but it was Anne Briggs really who took me firmly by the throat and said, "Look, for God's sake you must do this record." At that time I was working mainly for Topic: bedroom recordings went to Topic, studio recordings were commissioned by Nat Joseph. But this was a bedroom recording and it was done on spec. I always think of Bert, and Annie Briggs too, as archetypal. I suppose there were people like that before them. There certainly seem to have been hundreds since, but they were the first. I don't quite know how to describe them.'[39]

It was probably in August or September 1964 that Bill agreed to make a record with Bert and to take on the onerous responsibility of persuading a record label, any record label, to release it. Bert and Gill had been regular visitors to Bill's flat at 5 North Villas, Camden. Indeed, having nowhere else

to stay, Bert was now temporarily living there.[40] During the summer
Challis's student grant had run out and the flat in King's Avenue had been
waved goodbye. What was to become the eponymous first album – the
'blue album' of legend – would be recorded in the kitchen at North Villas.
Leader had bought an old Revox machine while the room itself, sound-
proofed with blankets and egg-boxes, had what he believed to be a certain
magic in its natural acoustics. Like the home recording set-up of early sixties
British pop producer Joe Meek, this casual operation was both revolutionary
and absurd: 'He had a Revox set up in one room,' says Martin Carthy, 'and
you went and stood in the other room, with the microphone, and he'd give
you the signal, which was the light going on and off. It didn't always work,
so you'd be standing there and the door would open and he'd say, "You can
start now if you like", and the door would shut! I'm making a joke of it
because it's funny now, but at the time the opportunity for making decent
recordings just didn't exist. So when Bert went into a proper studio to make
his second album it was a giant leap forward.'

Give or take the ownership of a usable guitar, Carthy's scenario is exactly
how it was on the handful of sessions that would result in Bert's first album:
'Bert sat on the edge of the bed,' says Leader. 'We borrowed a guitar and he
just sang his little heart out.[41] I don't claim that I fully understood or
appreciated his music when I first heard it but I suppose I had my "junior
entrepreneur" kit on, because I was recording things that seemed to be
interesting and important at the time, and this fell into that category. We
took three tapes out that we wanted to use, took them along to a studio and
put some reverb and equalisation on to them and ended up with something
that was a bearable master. Technically it's dodgy – there's more dropouts on
some of those tracks that I'd care to admit to – but musically it's wonderful
stuff. So it still lives, in spite of all its faults.'

Bill had by now left his job at Collet's, in favour of running Nat Joseph's
new Transatlantic record shop near Hampstead Heath and being on call to
engineer recordings for the new label. But the Bert Jansch album was not the
only project he was doing on spec. He was also putting time and effort into
something equally strange: the Collins/Graham project. With the encouragement of Austin John Marshall, the entrepreneurial husband of Sussex
traditional singer Shirley Collins, the time was now right for Davy Graham
the maverick technician to take further the idea of eastern-influenced guitar
accompanying traditional music from the British Isles. Both *Melody Maker*
and the *Observer*, for whom Marshall worked at the time, had previewed a
'not to be missed' concert on 29 July 1964 at London's Mercury Theatre.
The performance marked the debut of an experimental partnership between
Graham and Collins, with the stated aim of merging traditional song with

modern jazz. 'The concert will have an Eastern flavour,' noted *MM* writer
Jeff Smith. 'For two years Davy's interest in oriental forms has led him to
experiment with different tunings, themes and rhythms (he recently spent
three months in the Arab quarter of Tangier, sitting in with the local
groups).' The following week, Smith had declared the concert both
musically successful and profitable, announcing a further concert date for
the duo in September and suggesting that Ember were likely to record the
partnership.

In the event, it would seem that Davy and Shirley began recording the
eventual *Folk Roots, New Routes* later that year with Bill Leader, and only
provisionally.[42] Through Alexis Korner's persuasion, Leader had recorded
Graham's 'Angi' in the basement of the Camden flat two years earlier. In the
intervening period, Graham had been enjoying a long residency at Nick's
Diner in Fulham which he had begun in 1961. In this context, he had
cameoed in the Joseph Losey film *The Servant* (1963), while an album deal
with Pye's budget label Golden Guinea, secured to some extent through the
influence of TV comedian Bob Monkhouse, had allowed the release of
Davy's first and least representative album. *The Guitar Player* (1963), garishly
packaged and boasting bizarre if dextrous six-string arrangements of such
middle-of-the-road staples as 'Yellow Bird' and 'Cry Me A River', was
Graham's bistro repertoire minus the clatter of cutlery. The album's chief
benefit to Graham's longer-term career was in introducing him to A&R
man Ray Horricks. He would subsequently record a series of albums, under
Horricks's direction, for Decca. The Collins/Graham LP *Folk Routes, New
Routes* was consequently optioned by the company. They would choose to
release it in February 1965 – one month after Graham's first album proper,
the remarkable *Folk, Blues & Beyond*.

Bert would sit in on some of the Collins/Graham sessions. It was the first
time he had had an opportunity to watch Graham playing although he was
already familiar with his techniques, mostly through Martin Carthy: 'Martin
was forever coming up to me and saying, "Hey, have you heard this one
yet?", and he'd show me something he'd picked up from Davy. I'd be
learning all his licks second-hand!' Midway through the sessions for the
Jansch and Collins/Graham albums, Leader enlisted both guitarists for
something quite extraordinary: they were to accompany, on respective
nights at Leader's Broadside Club, the Chicago blues legend Little Walter
Jacobs.

The originator of the amplified harmonica style synonymous with Chicago
blues, Little Walter was a man with a hard-drinking, tough-talking reputation who would die young in a street fight in 1968. Walter's best years as a

musician were already behind him when he toured Britain for the first and last time in the autumn of 1964. But amplified blues was all the rage, and the red carpet was waiting. A UK single would be released to coincide and there would be several appearances on TV pop shows, including *Ready Steady Go!*, the barometer of all that was hip and happening. Coming to prominence as harp player in Muddy Waters's band during the early fifties, Walter had struck out with a series of records under his own name that had been R&B chart hits in America. The last of the series, a brooding interpretation of Broonzy's 'Key To The Highway' in 1958, was just about the only thing in his repertoire with any possible connection to the repertoire of Bert Jansch.

Quite how the clearly incongruous duo of Jansch and Walter came to pass is unclear – conceivably Bill Leader had assumed that Walter, like previous bluesmen of his experience such as Memphis Slim or Brownie McGhee, was a self-contained performer, and only realised at the eleventh hour that accompanists were needed. Bert himself believes some other guitarist had failed to show up and that he was simply plucked from the audience to make the best of a bad lot. But Bert had been certainly booked and advertised a week in advance as the support act. It was clear from a preview by Jeff Smith that Davy Graham would be both accompanying Walter on his Saturday gig and also performing a solo spot with 'some of his recent oriental inspired compositions'. Smith's preview was the first time Bert had been mentioned in *Melody Maker* outside of the club ads: 'With Little Walter on Friday is young blues guitarist and composer Bert Jansch. Bert's new group may be doing a couple of spots too.' It was also the only time that Bert and John Challis's embryonic band would get a mention. The third member, Keith De Groot, had once gone by the name of Gerry Temple – a minor rock'n'roller in the 'stable' of pre-Beatles pop svengali Larry Parnes. Allegedly, it is De Groot's harmonica on Millie's 1963 novelty record 'My Boy Lollipop'. 'He'd fallen foul of Parnes ostensibly because he was taking drugs,' says Challis, 'but I think it was also something to do with Parnes being a bit of a dodgy character.' The only dodgy character Bert saw was De Groot himself: 'He was very shady,' says Bert, 'a drug dealer basically. The cops were always after him. He kept disappearing!'

De Groot's saving grace was his talent as a bongo drummer; he was also a fine Chicago-style harp player, clearly inspired by Little Walter. A tape of the trio rehearsing in the front room of Challis's mother's house survives and is a remarkable document of what might have been. Three numbers are played, all instrumental: a magnificent, mesmerising take on 'Angi'; a six-minute Chicago-style twelve-bar jam; and an extemporisation on an otherwise unknown but archetypal Jansch riff. Bert plays electric guitar,

Challis plays piano and De Groot plays bongos, harmonica and bass guitar. He was also to be the group's featured vocalist.

'I don't think we ever did a whole gig as a band,' says Challis, 'but we had spots at places like the Troubadour and the Scot's Hoose. It had to be somewhere with a piano. Bert was trying to get Bill Leader to front up some money to buy an electric keyboard, which would be portable. I'd bravely volunteered to play one, although at that time I hated electric keyboards. I was thinking in terms of an organ, like Graham Bond but more folky! Everybody at Ealing was into Chicago blues and I was also listening to pre-war city blues: Sonny Boy Williamson, Tampa Red . . . We actually did a Tampa Red number with the band.'

Bert was thus not entirely unfamiliar with the pantheon of electric blues, but on 25 September 1964 the immediate problem was not with Tampa Red's material but with Little Walter's. An additional problem was actually finding the gig at all – at an Irish pub in Willesden Green, temporary accommodation for the Broadside club. 'Nobody knew where it was and it didn't look like a folk club – it looked like a cheesy dance hall,' says Challis. 'It was all a complete dog's breakfast. Thinking back, I get the feeling Bill Leader was in a bit of a panic and had asked Bert to get him out of a spot. Bert was well versed in country blues but hadn't heard any of Walter's music. But it so happened that I had an album, *The Best Of Little Walter*. So Bert borrowed it for the afternoon, tried to learn some numbers off it – which couldn't have been too hard for him – and I arranged to meet him down there later in the day, where he gave me the record back.

'There were only about three people in the club when we got there, very early evening, and one of them was Little Walter, who'd just drunk his first bottle of whisky of the day and was starting on the second. He was still quite compos mentos, obviously used to it, but at the same time on a slightly different wavelength to where I was. On the other hand, I'd had several spliffs before we'd set out. So I became completely tongue-tied, thinking, "Bloody hell, it's Little Walter!" Bert and everybody else just cleared off and left me with him, and they were obviously having a row in the back room. So he's standing there going in and out of focus and I'm sure he was having the same problem with me, and neither of us could think of a thing to say. Suddenly I remembered this record which was in a carrier bag. So I took it out and said, "Would you mind autographing this for me?" "Sure, have you got a pen?" He sat down, licked the end of the pen – which was a biro – and spent about five minutes more or less *drawing* his signature from memory.'

The show itself was no less awkward. 'Jansch's gloriously slovenly playing was the stuff of nightmare for the formally trained but sweet dreams for the attuned,' as one commentator later put it. 'With unnerving instinct he might add or deduct a half bar or so from a twelve-bar blues, the dictionary definition of mistake expressed as style; he took risks with all the split second timing and casual aplomb of a high-wire act.'[43] Little Walter had no interest in the circus. 'It must have been so strange to him,' says Bert. 'He was trying to get me to play as simply as possible but of course I tend to play quite a few lines all at the same time. He was slightly thrown.' 'It was an embarrassing night,' says Gill Cook, 'but good fun in hindsight!'

A few days earlier Gill had put a little sign up in Collet's saying, 'Best Blues In Town: Bert Jansch'. It had a confirming effect on another young guitarist plying his trade on the club scene, John Renbourn. Chris Ayliffe, an accompanist for a young blues singer called Jacqui McShee, had been telling him how good Bert was and the card in the window was the final incentive. Renbourn went with Ayliffe to see Bert at Bunjies – a little coffee bar in Litchfield Street, unusual among London folk venues in rarely advertising – and came away suitably impressed: 'I heard the first set and he was just unbelievable, wonderful,' says Renbourn. 'We went to the pub in the interval and Bert was there having a drink, but although we went back for the second set Bert never came back!'[44] Bert's next gig was the one with Little Walter, whose desperate plea to Bert of 'Easy on the fingers, baby!' remains Renbourn's abiding memory of the occasion.

'They were chalk and cheese,' says Challis. 'It was obviously very hard going for both of them. They took a break, more drinking was done and the break got longer and longer. Never mind the stress that Bert was under trying to play this completely alien form of blues, by the time the break arrived I was completely out of my face myself because of all the stress I'd been through! Actually, I felt very sorry for Little Walter. Here he was 5000 miles from home, pissed out of his head in Willesden and trying to put a show together with a load of people who didn't understand him. What he must have thought of it all . . .'

Many years later an interviewer, Michael Watts, was surprised to find, amid the few furnishings and belongings apparent in Bert's then current abode, a copy of 'Green Onions': 'He laughed when it was remarked upon,' wrote Watts, 'and said he always played Booker T a couple of times a week.' There was a story behind it. In his early twenties he had lived in Ealing with a boogie woogie pianist from Ealing Art College and a friend of Pete Townshend's. There was a café next door to the college where they all used to sit and drink tea and share a joint, and on the jukebox would be Muddy Waters, Jimmy Reed and Booker T. 'And when I listen to that my brain goes bang, right back back to those days.'[45]

CHAPTER SIX

Nineteen Sixty-Five

' After only three weeks at Willesden Green the Broadside is moving back to town.' As the *Melody Maker* of 3 October 1964 could report, Bill Leader's club had been offered the Scot's Hoose, a public house on the northern fringes of Soho. The following week, the all-new Broadside was opened by Roy Guest, in one of his last engagements as a folk singer. Things were beginning to change. For both Bert's career and the British folk scene as a whole, the next few months would see changes to mark the ending of one era and the beginning of another.

If there is a line in the sand between the old order of 'folksong' epitomised by Ewan MacColl and his left-wing agenda and the new dis-order of individual 'folk singers' whose songs espoused largely personal politics, none more clearly in the vanguard than Bert Jansch, then it lies on Friday 16 April 1965: a date that would see both the release of *Bert Jansch* and the opening of a new club called Les Cousins at 49 Greek Street, Soho. In the period between the Little Walter gig of September 1964 and the point where he finally became a recording artist in the public domain, Bert would settle permanently in London, build a constituency second to none among his peers and a reputation to rival Davy Graham's. 'Swinging London' was just around the corner: by the time the summer of 1965 had passed 'the Sixties' had arrived.

'I was trying to find somewhere to stay,' said Bert, 'and I'd somehow got involved, possibly as a result of working at Bunjies, with Les Bridger. He had a pad and so I naturally attached myself to him.'[1] Bridger is recalled as someone who knew where it was at but could not necessarily do it himself. 'It broke your heart really,' says Bruce Dunnet, MacColl's organiser. 'A lot of the folk-singing people were not good singers but they had a good repertoire and got away with it on that. But Les was a lousy guitarist and a lousy singer.' Nevertheless, as a resident performer Les had been fronting numerous clubs from as early as September 1962. On 17 November 1964, with blues singer Jo Ann Kelly as co-host, Les opened a club dedicated to 'folk blues' at the Hole In The Ground in Swiss Cottage. Bridger's pad, shared with a cat called Tinker, was nearby and Bert moved in. He found his new flatmate fascinating: 'Les used to sing cockney songs – had the right accent. He made an album of these things which he was very proud of and it was dreadful. But you could never determine his age. He had grey hair when I met him. He now lives in Copenhagen and looks exactly the same.'

Earlier in November Bert had played two gigs with Wizz Jones, one of the godfathers of the 'folk blues' style who had already met Bert in Edinburgh in '63, in passing, and a year later in London. By then, like anyone else with their ear to the ground, he was aware of Bert's growing reputation: 'I was gigging upstairs at the Black Horse,' says Wizz, 'and I came down during the interval and was sat down at a table talking to somebody and there was this young guy sitting next to me in a combat jacket. I didn't know who he was, thought he was a labourer or something. But I'd seen him before, and suddenly I realised, "Hey, I'm sitting next to Bert Jansch." You couldn't get anyone more anonymous. But then if you saw him onstage he had everything, he had amazing charisma – a true original. When I first started playing I used to busk the streets with Long John Baldry and Davy Graham. I sat down and tried to learn Davy's songs. At the same time Bert was up in Edinburgh doing the same thing. Bert got to grips with it, perfected the style and went on to become a total original. When he hit London you wouldn't believe the impact he had. He was dynamite. Nobody had heard anything like it. If you're a young, good-looking guy and you're playing really well and playing something so different and so exciting you don't need any kind of stage personality, you can just be cool. The fact that you don't say much or you're very laid back – you can be like that. When you're older it's stupid, you can't do it. But Bert was a young, cool guy on the scene and he came alive onstage just by playing.'

The first of their gigs together was at the Buck's Head in Mitcham where Wizz was resident. Wizz Jones having a regular gig at all was something of a breakthrough. John Renbourn had been a devotee for years: if Davy Graham, the clean-cut 'retired colonel' with the incongruously mad music, was the instrumental excellence, Wizz represented the very essence of what looked to be such an attractive, bohemian lifestyle. 'Wizz was the main guy to listen to in the early days,' says Renbourn. 'But he didn't actually have any gigs, 'cos he had such long hair and bare feet that he wasn't allowed into most of the clubs.'

One Wizz fan at that Buck's Head gig was Ralph McTell: 'Unfortunately Bert was out of the game. He stuck a matchbox in his mouth, blew out the matches all over the audience, said, "That's an old folk custom", and wobbled off, which was all the sort of stuff legends are made of.' Ralph's brother Bruce, who would wind up managing both Ralph and Bert ten years later, was more intrigued with Bert's slurred, unintelligible diction:

'Needle Of Death' he heard as 'Need A Dad'. That same month Bert's first child was conceived. Its mother was Gill Cook.

Bill Leader dropped out of his role in the Broadside club shortly after it reopened at the Scot's Hoose in October. The mantle of organiser passed to Gill Cook. By the end of the year, finding it 'a bit of a struggle' on her own, Gill deferred to the most actively entrepreneurial Communist in town: Bruce Dunnet.[2] As 1964 passed into 1965, Bill Leader continued his periodic process of recording the strange and indefinable music of Bert Jansch.[3] A few years later Bert was able to recall that, in terms of material, 'about half the album was already there and I had to write the other songs while the sessions were going along'.[4] With Leader emphasising to Bert that the essence of what he did was in his own material, this was a creative period: a time when Bert's stage repertoire would increasingly shift from borrowed blues to original compositions.

'The trouble with recording,' says Bert, 'is that, as the word says, it records what you've done. A painting, once it's done, is there for all time, but music is not so. Music is an instantaneous thing that happens and changes. Anything to do with me – the writing, the material – it's now, it's not yesterday. Yesterday's gone. I never listen to the albums. Once it's recorded, it's past. I'm much more interested in the actual creation of songs, to create ideas and eventually put them down on paper or on tape, to record them in one fashion or another. It's an art form to me.'

Once Bill felt that his recording of Bert was representative and complete the problem became where to place it. 'There we were with this tape,' says Bill, 'and nobody was interested: Topic weren't interested in this "drug stuff" and Nat Joseph wasn't interested because he couldn't see that there was a market for it. People who were tuned into Bert were into the totality of text, music and performance – all three added up. Nat was a lyrics man. I came across this several times in trying to sell him ideas, that if I typed out the words I'd be more likely to get a contract than actually playing him a tape. He probably did recognise the quality of Bert's songwriting but he certainly didn't act very quickly.'

'Bill came in to the shop one day,' says Nat, 'and said "I've done this record, I'd like you to listen to it and I'd like to sell it to you." I remember listening to it and thinking some of the songs were terrific, really terrific. "Running From Home" was the first I heard. I was less struck than everybody else was on the guitar work. To me it was always the words that communicated. I don't think Dylan became great because he played great harmonica – Dylan became great because his words said something to his generation. The same could be said of Bert Jansch.' A period of time

elapsed and Bill became edgy. But it transpired that Nat had been lobbied by
the fearless Anne Briggs and was now aware of the 'word on the street'. He
was prepared to take a chance. The deal that was agreed, an outright sum of
£100 for the purchase of the recording with no royalties subsequently
payable, is perhaps questionable only in hindsight. It went on to sell in excess
of 150,000 by 1975, and remained on catalogue at full price until the label
was sold in 1978.[5] But in the early months of 1965 it was not a question of
what was fair but whether Bert wished to have a record released or not.
Nobody else was queuing up to do so.

'Perhaps if I'd been a cannier person, sitting on it for another six months,'
says Bill, 'we might have done a better deal. But there comes a time when a
record has to be released for an artist and if you miss that you bugger up his
career. So we did the deal and it was a hard bargain. I think Nat thinks I'll go
to my grave resenting that but I don't in the least: a deal is a deal.'

'Artists who recorded were very rare then,' says Bert. 'Bill said this was
probably the best offer I could get. I had no idea about royalties or anything
like that in those days and so I said yes. The songs on there are instant
snapshots. I was just fooling around doing gigs, not thinking about these
things. On reflection I was a bit annoyed about the deal that was set up
between Bill and Nat. They certainly took me to the cleaners.'

Subsequent to the deal Nat felt the record was a little short and asked for
three more songs, duly provided. When the record was released, Bert would
receive mechanical royalties for those three tracks alone. Nat arranged to
meet Bert in a pub and a long-term contract for his publishing was signed,
with Transatlantic's publishing arm Heathside Music. Some years later,
when the contract was examined, it was noticed that only part of Bert's
signature had been caught. Somewhere in London there is a bar table with a
reasonable claim on the minuscule Transatlantic publishing royalties of Bert
Jansch. 'The reason I didn't sign him as a recording artist at that time,' says
Nat, 'was because he was regarded as Bill's artist and Bill didn't have an
arrangement with him.' Nor would he.

Folk, Blues & Beyond was Davy Graham's manifesto at the very dawn of the
new era. Released in January 1965, three months before the first Jansch
record, it epitomised the sense of adventure abroad in all forms of popular
music at the time and crystallised ideas that other guitarists would explore for
years to come. Bert had already taken what he felt he needed from Graham's
playing, from the tape of 'Angi' years previous to the alternate tuning
DADGAD and the regular trickle of licks filtering second-hand through
Martin Carthy. *Folk, Blues & Beyond* would be a revelation to the wider
constituency but it would alter little the path which Bert was already on:

'There was something he said,' recalls Wizz, "You listen to other people and you copy but you don't do it for long – you find your own thing.' He got to the point where he didn't listen to anybody. He was very much on his own trip.'

Crafted and muscular as it was, *Folk, Blues & Beyond* did little to hide Graham's essential weakness as a vocalist. It was clear that some of the album's reviewers would prefer to regard Davy Graham solely, and be-grudgingly, as an experimental accompanist for the eminently more accep-table Shirley Collins. Curiously, the album of the Collins/Graham project, *Folk Roots, New Routes* was released only a month later, in February 1965. Welcomed perhaps more wholeheartedly for its ideas than its actuality, it was nevertheless a blueprint for what would later emerge as British folk-rock.[6] By coincidence or otherwise it also contained five songs that Bert would soon be adapting to his own more visceral arrangements.

By the time both albums were released Graham's lifestyle had taken a notorious turn. 'He lived with danger all the time,' says Martin Carthy. 'He decided to become a junkie. He did that quite deliberately because his heroes – people like Sonny Rollins, Charlie Parker, Bud Powell, all those guys – were heroin addicts. It was like part of the furniture: you were supposed to become a junkie to be a serious musician and Davy took all that in. At the time it was legal and you got it on prescription. I remember when it happened because I did a session with him at Lansdowne Studios in Holland Park the very day after he first took it. I think it was a session for Nadia Cattouse. We were walking down the road and he told me, "I had my first fix yesterday." He was a good man, but he was always a very strange man. I remember meeting Alexis Korner three weeks later and his opening remark to me was, "Do you know what that stupid bastard has done?" And it was basically bye bye Davy for four years.'

'The trouble is artists are self-indulgent,' Graham explained, some years later. 'It never occurred to me that art was self-indulgent. I always thought art was the product of self-denial. It seems to me you deny yourself something to acquire a technique over an instrument. When you've got the technique it's as if you've got a dog. The neighbours don't understand you.'[7]

Davy Graham's path became a thing of dark rumour on the folk scene, but mostly known only to his fellow performers. 'Dope was everywhere on the folk scene,' recalls Pete Frame, a wide-eyed fan turned club organiser. 'You were cool if you smoked dope. It was like a division from the Steve Benbow generation.' For audiences, the late Buck Polley was the only link between folk and hard drugs, and he was becoming an almost mythical figure. 'Alex Campbell was everywhere in those days,' says Frame. 'He'd get pissed and go on about Buck and give you a half-hour sermon on the dangers of drugs. He was like a schoolteacher that all the kids admired 'cos he could talk their language. He was older but he was such an incredible, romantic character.'

Bert Jansch was carving his own niche in the annals of romance too – less populist but no less arresting. His 'Needle Of Death', in memory of Polley, was a fragile but profoundly striking song for the times – a 'really outrageous, beautiful song', as another young songwriter called Neil Young would shortly discover, across the world in Canada.[8] Relatively simple in structure, it would be one of the very few Bert Jansch songs to be covered on record by another artist – in this case, later in the year by TV folk personality Julie Felix on her *Second Album* – and covered widely in performance among his peers.

'It was an incredibly popular song,' says Dave Arthur, who was performing then with his wife Toni as an English traditional duo. 'It was the only song we sang out of context with the traditional stuff. We had somehow linked into it because he was serious about it. He disowned it later because it became such a cliché, but at the time we believed it. It had an enormous influence on us and everyone else because it was of its time – very much music of the sixties but also very much to do with what was going on in London.'

Luton was thirty miles from London and the kind of town where everyone left school and worked at the local car factory. Growing up there, Pete Frame was 'one of those guys who found out about Bob Dylan through Peter, Paul & Mary'. By the end of 1961 he had taken a job in London, at the Holborn office of Prudential Insurance. Outside the office building was a prime spot for busking, regularly occupied by one Les Bridger. Frame gradually discovered the esoteric delights of Collet's record shop in nearby New Oxford Street. It was the only place in town where one could find Elektra and Vanguard imports.

'In February 1964 I went to see Pete Seeger at the Festival Hall with my friend Mac,' says Frame, 'and we came out completely blown away. We both worked at the Prudential: Mac goes into work on Monday, gives his notice in and clears off. He just couldn't cope with work any more after that. He wanted to be on the road, doing all that romantic travelling about. He went off and sold toffee apples on the beach at Cannes and never looked back. I was too insecure to do any of that. It would be another five years before I could summon the courage to "drop out and do my own thing", which had by then become eminently fashionable.'[9]

In a manner typical of many others in isolated little towns across the country, Frame became enraptured by the 'underground' feel and promise of the new folk music. For a start, there was a beatnik scene at a pub called the Cock in nearby St Albans: 'There were guys there with flared matelotstyle jeans. They'd noticed Dylan's leg on the front of *Another Side Of Bob Dylan* and had sewn big denim triangles into their Levis to be like him – though whether Dylan had flared his jeans or merely patched them was a matter for conjecture. Whatever, people were starting to copy him. By the end of the year, some of us had decided to start a folk club in Luton. I took on the administration: booking acts, taking care of advertising, handling the money. I had absolutely no idea what I was doing, of course, but I was on a mission to bring interesting singers to Luton – to enrich the lives of culturally deprived provincials like myself.' There was already a traditionally oriented folk club in St Albans, at the Peahen pub, and a regular at both this club and the Cock was an eighteen-year-old by the name of Donovan Leitch, known to his friends as Don and, very soon, to the world at large as plain Donovan: 'Britain's Bob Dylan'.

Donovan was born in Glasgow in May 1946. His family – socialist, self-educated and working class – had remained there until he was ten and then moved south to a newly-built council estate in Hatfield. Failing to acquire the right qualifications for art college, Donovan spent time labouring in factories and on building sites and sometimes helping his dad on a cake stall at Hatfield market. He bought into mod culture in a big way, riding scooters and following favoured R&B groups. In May 1964 he caught Bob Dylan's concert at the Festival Hall and folk became his new bag. That summer he trekked down to the West Country with a friend, Mac McLeod; they took waiting jobs at a hotel and busked in their spare time. More to the point, Donovan wrote 'Catch The Wind', in the vein of Bob Dylan: a beautifully simple tune with the abidingly intangible impression that its words might in fact be saying something important. Dylan had worn a black corduroy cap on the cover of his first album. In homage to Bob, Don returned from Torquay with not only a wonderful song but a Cornish fisherman's hat that would have to do. But he had not entirely lost interest in R&B. One weekend in November he joined a gang of friends on a rave to Southend to sleep on the beaches and support the Cops'n'Robbers, St Albans' very own Rolling Stones. During the interval, completely drunk, Donovan got up and sang maybe five songs including one of his own. A fairytale situation ensued: the group's manager Peter Eden was mesmerised, brought in local songwriter Geoff Stephens and arranged for Donovan to make a demo record at Stephens's publishers, Southern Music, in Denmark Street: 'Tin Pan Alley'. Stephens and Eden would be his management. The next step was introducing their discovery to the producer of hip Friday night pop TV show *Ready Steady Go*:

'They listened and they looked,' says Donovan. 'In retrospect I think they said, "This guy is going to do what Dylan did. We'll have him." And so I was on the show. For the first two weeks I wrote songs about the charts and about myself. I wrote "Talking Pop Star Blues" and I wrote a song about Tom Jones and Gene Pitney and sat with Cathy McGowan and talked about sleeping rough on the beach – it all happened in a period of weeks.'

Donovan was British pop's very own Dylan-hatted minstrel boy with pretty tunes, troubadour tales and a lifestyle to match. Not everyone was impressed. Andy Irvine, just returned from five years in Dublin, was one: 'I remember him sitting there telling the presenter he'd just hitch-hiked down from St Albans. "Yeah, right," I thought.' Others were of a similar mind. Donovan had become resident on *RSG* at the end of January and within a week he was a national sensation. Letters of outrage poured in to the pop papers from folk fans and Dylan buffs. For an inexperienced teenager, Donovan's reaction was admirably serene: 'I can't see anything wrong with adopting a style,' he replied to one detractor.[10] He would be justifying that position for the rest of the year. For the papers it was a godsend, the best controversy in ages and a shot in the arm for the rumbling 'folk boom' debate. Even his guitar was controversial. Echoing Woody Guthrie's slogan, 'This machine kills fascists', Don had taped 'This machine kills' to the body of his instrument. How, the *Melody Maker* wondered, did he justify that? 'Well,' said Don, 'I didn't think there were any fascists left – until I got into the music business.'[11]

Just prior to his TV debut, Frame had asked Donovan to be the resident singer of his new club, due to open at the Dolphin coffee bar on 20 January. Donovan was tied to his managers' game plan but he did recommend Mac McLeod. Another local player of note, Mick Softley, would also be a regular. The opening night was a great success. 'It was a small, claustrophobic basement with a huge supporting column obstructing the view of anyone who didn't get there early,' says Frame. 'But it was the coolest place in town.' McLeod was not long in recommending an amazing guitarist he had met called John Renbourn. Renbourn was duly booked for 24 February. It was a memorable night: 'Mick Softley had played,' says Frame, 'he was sitting down rolling a cigarette and Renbourn started playing "Judy" and as soon as Mick heard it he dropped his tobacco and just shot up to the front to get a view of this fantastic playing! I remember going to a gig in Borehamwood soon after that and it was Renbourn and Beverley, which was amazing – Renbourn, the stoned Julian Bream of folk guitar, and Beverley the most attractive art-school folk singer you could imagine. She was singing songs like "Wild About My Loving" and he was picking away behind her. At one point just before the solo she sings "If you want my loving, you gotta bring it with you when you come . . . what are you gonna bring John?" And John replies, "Les Bridger!" '

Shortly after Bert had moved in with Bridger, in November 1964, Renbourn called round with Dorris Henderson, an exotic young American he had just met at the Roundhouse.[12] John had recently decided to move up to London from Kingston while Dorris was not long off the plane from Los Angeles. Both were looking for a place to stay. Dorris wound up at Gill Cook's flat, where Anne Briggs was also staying at the time, while John moved in with Bert and Les. John had been born in Kingston in August 1944 – almost a year younger than Bert, and more middle-class in background. At school he had played electric guitar in a band by the name of Hogsnort Rupert & His Famous Porkestra. During the summer of 1962, however, he had hitch-hiked in the West Country and been intrigued by the acoustic musicians he stumbled across: 'I heard guys playing who said, "This is something from Davy Graham", but I didn't hear Davy till a bit later, when I was going to Kingston Art School and playing guitar all the time instead of doing art. Wound up in a club called the Wooden Bridge in Guildford; the R&B thing had started then and Davy was playing there with John Mayall. Davy was the one for me, as he was for just about everyone else – I used to follow him around after that and learn from him.'[13]

Renbourn was mentioned in *Melody Maker* despatches as a resident of the Guildford Folk Club as early as February 1963. A year later his name appeared again, this time as a guest at Derek Serjeant's Surbiton club. It would appear periodically thereafter in connection with the clubs in Surbiton, Woking and Richmond. Coming out of art school with no money, somebody had offered him a Scarth guitar in a backstreet for a fiver 'and fortunately the pub scene had started, so I drifted into that'. In September '64 he had twice seen Bert performing and the very day after the Little Walter gig he had performed in central London himself, bottom of the bill to Malcolm Price and the Country Cousins at Malcolm Nixon's Hootenanny, Ballads & Blues club. A month later Gerry Loughran, who had provided Bert with his first platform in the capital, gave John a more memorable gig at the Roundhouse. 'That was the first time I got paid,' he says. 'It was a fiver. And it was Scottish!'

Renbourn was a gifted musician. What he lacked, compared with Bert, in musical invention and individuality of expression, he made up for with an increasingly inquisitive approach to the nature and mechanics of music and a technical brilliance that was, like Davy Graham's, the product of relentless dedication. John's arrival in London as a young guitar slinger looking for opportunities was part of a pattern that would be repeated ad infinitum as the decade progressed; Dorris Henderson's story was a little more unusual. Americans were still, on the British folk scene, a rarity. Dorris had been working as a civil servant in Los Angeles, singing Appalachian mountain songs in her spare time. Her brother, in the USAF, had been stationed in Britain and recommended it. Dorris saved some money and got on a plane.

Dark-skinned and attractive, and vocally magnificent, she stumbled into the folk scene and was welcomed with open arms. On her second day in town she discovered the Troubadour, sang there and met Curly Goss, organiser of several clubs, including the Roundhouse. There she met Renbourn. Dorris was given a residency at the Roundhouse and, again through Curly, auditioned successfully for a new live music show on BBC television: *Gadzooks! It's All Happening.*

Bert, John and Les moved en masse to a new flat in King Henry's Road, between Swiss Cottage and Chalk Farm – still only half a dozen stops on the tube from the city centre. There would soon come a time when Bert and John would be all over the London scene but in these early days of their association, both were helped along by the extraordinary popularity of Les Bridger as a club resident and consequently as a patron to the potential guest artists sharing his flat. Bert and John would both enjoy bookings at the Hole In The Ground Tuesday club, while opportunities were tripled by the end of January with Les and Jo Ann Kelly taking the residencies of new clubs at the Red Lion in Borehamwood (Wednesdays) and the Black Bull in Barnet (Mondays). Jo Ann also took a Thursday residency at the White Hart in Grays, Essex, where Bert and John would similarly be among the early guests.

Either side of Christmas Bert tried out his new trio with John Challis and Keith De Groot on at least two bookings, at the Scot's Hoose and the Troubadour. There was a further trio gig at the Troubadour in May, but it was little more than a sideline for Bert. The solo album he had recorded with Bill Leader would appear on Friday, 16 April.

One of the band's gigs had been shared with Anne Briggs. Anne was more visible on the London scene at this time than she had been before or would ever be again.[14] Three Fridays in January she was on the bill at a new purely traditional club that Gill Cook was running with Roy Guest at Cecil Sharp House, but several of her other gigs in town would be shared with Bert. As both were in the same city with time on their hands, a roof over their heads and a friend with a flat that was empty during the daytime, they would also – for the first and only time – come together to write songs and learn from each other's music. It would be a remarkably fruitful period, whose achievements would have an impact on the work of both artists, and on many others besides, over the coming years.

'Bert would come around to Gill's flat during the day when there was nothing else to do,' says Anne, 'and we'd work together for our own personal interest on traditional songs, with his dramatic guitar playing. We discovered that they could really gel together. Once he started elaborating on what I'd come up with I had to move fast to keep up, so it really brought my guitar playing along. He'd write a verse, I'd write a verse. I'd come up with a tune, he'd play it, he'd elaborate on it. It was a very creative period but it only went on for a very short time.' The process was almost accidental, to Anne's recollection 'there was a lot of stuff that just drifted away – if it wasn't together by the end of the afternoon, forget about it'. But three original songs survived, to filter out on albums by both Bert and Anne individually between 1966 and 1971: 'Go Your Way, My Love', 'Wishing Well' and 'The Time Has Come'.[15] The last was composed by Anne alone, the others jointly, but all three combined otherworldliness, foreboding and melancholy and were quite unprecedented in any genre of popular music.

More importantly than the quality of individual songs however was the development of a new approach to accompanying traditional music that was superficially similar to that explored by the Collins/Graham project but free-er of form, looser in feel and as sensual and fresh as the content of the first song it was designed for: the one-night-stand Irish ballad 'Blackwater Side'. For all the rivalry that would develop between Jansch and Graham over the next few years, real or imagined, Graham would come to regard 'Blackwater Side' at the very least as 'a masterpiece of its kind, and I do not use that word loosely'.[16]

'All the traditional singers I knew at the time, like Jimmy MacBeath and Jeannie Robertson,' says Bert, 'were older people and you couldn't exactly say, "Could you just slow that down and repeat that verse?" But Anne, because she knew all these songs, I could quite happily get her to sit and go over the likes of "Blackwater Side" a few times until I'd worked out how to do it on the guitar. This was the first time I'd ever actually sat down and taken a folk song other than a Woody Guthrie-type song – a number that had a definite melody line that I couldn't change – and consciously created a backing to go with it.'[17]

'He had always had a real feeling for traditional music,' says Anne, 'but when I first knew him he just didn't think he had the right sort of voice and couldn't use the guitar in the right way to be a singer of traditional songs himself. By this time he'd become a much more sophisticated player, and I think he had the confidence to handle it. Everybody up to that point was accompanying traditional songs in a very Woody Guthrie, three-chord way. I was never happy with that – not in an academic sense, just aesthetically. It was why I always sang unaccompanied. I'd played guitar since I was fourteen or fifteen but seeing Bert's freedom from chords I suddenly realised that this chord stuff – you don't need it. "Go Your Way" was my first experiment with open tuning, my delight at discovering this wonderful sound.'

They were exciting discoveries: 'I was pregnant at the time but working very hard in the shop,' says Gill, 'and I can remember them ringing up and saying, "Hey, we've just written a song!" ' Bert and Anne never performed their new songs or traditional settings together at that time.[18] To Bert's mind they were simply 'too erratic to get it together'; to Anne's, it was a case of audiences perceiving them as entirely unrelated performers. For all her new-found freedoms as an instrumentalist using alternate tunings learnt from Bert – Graham's DADGAD and the DADGBE of 'Blackwater Side' – Anne would not have the confidence to use a guitar onstage for some years yet. It is not known when Bert debuted the ground-breaking 'Blackwater Side' onstage, but it would have to wait a year and a half to appear on record.

During the same period that Bert and Anne were writing together, in the early weeks of 1965, they were also appearing, individually, at gigs together. 'I remember going to the Singers Club a couple of times with Anne,' says Bert. 'If you were a Scots person you were expecting to sing Scottish songs. Anyone could sing. You'd put your name down, in a rota system, and Ewan would call you up. When I got up I played "Angi". But they didn't know me from Adam, so it didn't make any difference.'

As long ago as 1961, Eric Winter had dared to poke fun in print at the worthiness and pomposity of what were clearly the two towers of the folk 'establishment': the EFDSS and the Singers Club: 'To move from a Society event to the Singers Club,' he observed, 'is to swap the atmosphere of the vicar's tea-party for that of a cathedral. There are even one or two in the front row who appear to have rented pews.' MacColl was not amused. But in the face of changing times and the growing proliferation of young singers on the scene, the Singers Club was to take a stance of yet greater earnestness and controversy.

In 1964 Ewan concocted an idea for a modern 'bardic school' comprising young singers keen to learn the techniques of performing traditional song and more experienced individuals, such as himself, to impart such wisdom. It was to become known, in petard-hoisting fashion, as the Critics Group. In fact, it had been Ewan's *Radio Ballads* colleague Charles Parker who had named it, under pressure to do so on a live radio discussion, and it stuck. Anne had been asked to join and had declined, regarding the whole thing as absurd. Bert Lloyd and Lou Killen had also declined. 'Our original intention in taking on the group,' said MacColl, many years on, 'was to describe some of our own experiences, and to give warnings of the dangers and pitfalls which confront those who make singing folk songs a full time job. It didn't work out like that.'[19]

Still in its early stages, the Critics Group would become one of the great totems of the folk revival before an acrimonious dissolution in 1970. Good things would come out of the initiative. Ewan and Peggy had indeed a wealth of experience and knowledge to pass on, and Ewan's characteristic energy would fire up his young followers in countless specific projects – records, books, song research and most prominently a series of topical New Year shows known as the 'Festival Of Fools' that were innovations in pub theatre – but there was a fundamental flaw at the very heart of the group: 'Ironically,' as group member Frankie Armstrong recalled, 'we discovered that the founder of the Critics Group couldn't bear criticism of himself.'[20]

Blown away by the dazzling pyrotechnics of John Renbourn at his new club in Luton, Pete Frame was not going to question the great man's recommendation that he book Bert Jansch, and some time in March he duly appeared. 'I had never seen anything like it,' says Frame. 'I'd followed pop music and folk music and rock music assiduously since I'd been a kid and with everybody that came along you could tell their influences. Bert came along and I had no idea where it had come from – how he knew this stuff or how he played it. There was no precedent: it wasn't jazz, it wasn't blues, it wasn't folk, it wasn't classical but it was elements of all those. And that was just the music. The structures of the songs as well were just totally unprecedented. Renbourn had a kind of classical smoothness to him and you could tell where he'd got his material from, but Bert was just totally unique in my experience. He had a really jagged kind of guitar style and his image – no condescension to commercialism whatsoever. He looked like his clothes had just come out of the laundry basket – always wore a crumpled white shirt and black trousers – was always playing a borrowed guitar, his hair was always all over the bloody place, at a time when everyone was trying to copy the Beatles or Dylan – and his name even: it was unpronounceable! Anybody else would have called themselves "Bert Dylan" or something. Everything about him was a refusal to compromise.'

Frame had been lucky that Bert had turned up at all. As a surviving letter of apology regarding an engagement the previous month attests, the booker for Colchester Folk Club had not been so fortunate:

Dear Brian,

I am terribly sorry I could not make it on Monday. I ran out of money and couldn't find anyone to borrow from, and I'm afraid I was in no condition to hitch-hike. There was also the problem of finding a guitar.

Hoping this did not inconvenience you too much.

Yours sincerely,

Bert Jansch

'He was everything you wanted to be,' says Frame, 'a dextrous guitar player, footloose and fancy-free, attractive to women. Basically, all the blokes wanted to be him and all the girls wanted to sleep with him. He was almost like Kerouac and James Dean and Woody Guthrie rolled into one figure. He not only had access to his muse, but on a good night he could actually go into a netherworld when he sang. And that was very rare.'

'You need the buzz of playing to people,' says Bert on reflection. 'There's no other form of excitement that comes close to it. They need to be there, but in actual fact during the performance itself they cease to be there.' Like others who would be struck with the Jansch magic, Frame began to look out for Bert's name in *Melody Maker* ads and travel to other clubs to see him. The next one was a little unusual, an American themed evening at Cecil Sharp House on 19 March, promoted by Roy Guest, where Bert dutifully performed a by then untypical set of American blues and folk covers.[21] He shared a bill on that occasion with Jesse Fuller, author of the much covered 'San Francisco Bay Blues', and another newly arrived American, 'Spider' John Koerner, of the trio Koerner, Ray & Glover. Spider began dating Anne Briggs – they probably left London to travel together – marking an end to the carefree days of song-writing and musical adventuring with Bert. But enough had been achieved already.[22]

Anne Briggs had been tenacious enough to have Bert recorded by Bill Leader and signed by Nat Joseph. Periodic gigs at the ever-increasing number of clubs where Les Bridger held sway and through various word-of-mouth bookings at provincial clubs like Luton were fine but if Bert was to reach a mass audience there would have to be a regular place where they could reach him. For a third time, Anne knew somebody who could help: Bruce Dunnet. MacColl's lieutenant, an Edinburgh man like Bert and a man who saw no paradox in passionate Communism and fervent entrepreneurial activities, Bruce was forty-three – a good deal older than any of the young singers around town, and a good deal more experienced in business.[23]

Bruce's experience of running folk clubs and events was similarly vast. He had borrowed money from his employers at one stage to keep the Singers Club going, but was also running his own more commercially minded Folksong Unlimited club at the same time. In 1962, with organisers in short supply, he had run the door for the first six weeks of Alexis Korner's Ealing Club, conceding a floor spot to the Rolling Stones and subsequently passing on his unfavourable view of their music. In 1964 he had set up a national tour for Dominic Behan and a tribute concert to Paul Robeson; as 'Mary MacGregor' he was secretary of the Alex Campbell fan club; and by the end of the year he had a presence all over the London folk scene, well prepared to catch the new wave of performers and the oncoming fashion for late-night events. In December 1964, at Gill Cook's request, Bruce took control of the Broadside club at the Scot's Hoose on Fridays and announced two new projects for the New Year: a 'New Folksingers' club at the Prince Of Wales' Feathers on Saturdays and late-night sessions at Nicholas Hall on Tottenham Court Road, also on Saturdays. All three venues were in and around Soho, on the cusp of becoming once again the epicentre of musical magic and adventure.

Bruce had already heard of Jansch through Bill Leader, 'then Anne Briggs asked me if I would help him'. Bert was booked first for the Prince of Wales' Feathers on 30 January – a show that was attended by an impressionable young man called Ashley Hutchings who subsequently became, as founder of Fairport Convention and Steeleye Span, the godfather of English folk-rock. Hutchings was all over the London club scene during 1965 and '66, soaking up influences from Bert Jansch to Ewan MacColl and all points in between: 'Ewan was like the headmaster and Bert Jansch the naughty boy!' he recalls. 'But I was a great fan of Bert's and I remember, as a teenager, seeing him in various clubs around London. Very early on I heard a lot of talk, the kind of information that goes around audiences, that "he likes a drink or two". And this was always very evident in his performance. I saw some performances that were marred by drink but there was still a magic there, no question about it. He was a romantic figure – a one-off, a travelling rogue who spoke for young people. "Needle Of Death" I loved while "Strolling Down The Highway" was one which Fairport Convention had on its very first set list [in September 1967]. So the influence was most definitely there.'

Bruce was impressed enough with Bert's performance to institute a new Tuesday night session at the Scot's Hoose 'which was supposed to be Anne Briggs and Bert Jansch, and if I remember correctly Anne Briggs didn't turn up. We did six nights on Tuesdays and the maximum take over those six nights was two shillings and eleven pence ha'penny, because nobody knew him.' But the machinery was now in place for that to change. 'I would just host the evening basically,' says Bert, 'and anyone could get up and sing.' One night Steve Benbow dropped by: 'I thought he was very good,' says Steve. 'There wasn't much presentation, he'd just sit on a chair and play. A shy fellow. It was years later before I got to know him.' To all intents and purposes Bruce would fill the role of manager for Bert, although Bert would never formalise the arrangement. With the Scot's Hoose, and subsequent events that Bruce organised for Bert, 'the arrangement was Bert would have a third, I would have a third for expenses and a third would be put aside for the promotion of Bert but if he wanted the money he could call on it'.

Advertised as 'New Ventures', the Tuesday sessions very quickly opened
the floodgates for the Scot's Hoose as a venue. Initially a rival promoter,
Tony Shaw, launched 'Folk at the Hoose' on Wednesdays which became,
on March 3, the first club to advertise Bert Jansch and John Renbourn on
the same bill,[24] but very soon the venue was hosting folk events five nights a
week. Bruce would be running four of them, including Bert on Tuesdays;
the 'Broadside' name was quietly dropped from the Friday spot while he
decided what to do with it. The answer was Owen Hand. Owen had
returned to London at the end of '64 with a theatre group run by John
Antrobus, but had soon fallen out with the man and was consequently at a
loose end: 'One day I was going to Collet's to visit Gill Cook when I met
Nat Joseph, who asked me if I'd make a record for him. That's what kept me
around London and caused possibly the worst decision I ever made in my
life.'

Nat had a publishing interest in one Jo Mapes, and convinced Owen to
record his material for an album titled *Something New*, designed to project
Owen as a contemporary singer and songwriter and destined to be released
and promoted as such in tandem with Bert's debut. When the record came
out Owen hated it, and was consequently 'so intent on making amends that
I rushed into making my second album, and in doing so made all the same
mistakes'. Owen's career would take a more fruitful turn later in the sixties,
when he enlisted in the School of Scottish Studies and pursued the academic
route. But for the next couple of years he was to pursue, like Bert, the path
of the performer. Bruce offered him the vacant residency at the Scot's Hoose
on Fridays, providing a guaranteed income, and with Ruth, his new partner,
he took a room in Kilburn. From 6 April he was also being billed as co-
resident with Bert on Tuesdays.

'We saw quite a lot of Bert around then,' says Owen. 'At that time he
seemed to work on a "need to" basis and only did gigs that appealed to him.
The Scot's Hoose was amazing in that it attracted more musicians in the
audience than it could afford on the platform. On any night I could call up
floor singers of the quality of Martin Carthy, Andy Irvine or Paul Simon.
One night Bert and I were standing by the door when Pete Townshend,
who had started a folk club at Ronnie Scott's place, came in to see if he
could persuade some people to come and play at his club. He saw Bert and
came over. "Hey man," he addressed Bert, "do you want to earn a pound?"
Bert gave him a stare. "No man, I've already got one." '[25]

Bert's reputation as a live performer continued to spread with every
uncontrollable, unpredictable performance. 'I'm afraid there was this fascination,' says Nat Joseph, 'with Bert's character. His gigs were extraordinary. Half the performance was tuning up, grunting and mumbling,

sipping his beer, having a cigarette, playing a couple of chords . . . It used to drive me crazy. He was one of the most un-together acts I have ever seen. We'd have arguments about it. I'd say, "Look, you're a great artist but great artists have to be performers – you have an audience out there!" But I guess after my initial bewilderment, at how anybody could actually squander such marvellous material by performing live often so badly and without caring what an audience might think, I just realised, "Well, he's a one-off. He'll just do it his way and there is nothing anybody can do about it." '

The spring issue of a thrusting new journal, *Folk Scene*, polled the best-known performers on the scene with the question 'Who or what will be the major influence on the future of folk music in 1965?' The responses were telling: 'I will,' replied Dominic Behan; 'I don't care, it doesn't affect me,' said Donovan; 'I think this is a bloody loaded question,' offered Alex Campbell; 'Bob Dylan will continue to spawn hosts of imitators and pop-folk singers will rush out records of his songs in the hopes of denting the charts,' said Roy Guest, who was not to be proved wrong. 'No comment,' was Bert Jansch's response, while Ewan MacColl was 'regrettably too busy to answer the question'. Most prescient of all, though, was Sydney Carter: 'Byron, Shelley, Joan of Arc, Dylan Thomas – the image of the young poet / prophet / rebel: the image of the Hero as a Folksinger – this is the thing now. Pete Seeger and Ewan MacColl are too old – the Hero should be under thirty-one. It would help to be under-privileged or persecuted. "What has this to do with folk music?" Not much, but how "folk" or "musical" is the current folk revival? Doesn't it owe as much now to the Bomb and the Freedom Riders as to Cecil Sharp? And isn't it also, increasingly, as much a revival of song-making and verse-writing as of singing?'

By the end of February it was announced that Les Bridger and Bert were to become residents at yet another new club, on Sundays at the Marquis of Granby in Soho's Rathbone Street.[26] Within weeks, an after-hours meeting place for the whole scene would be found with the resurrection of the old Skiffle Cellar venue at 49 Greek Street. But for the moment, the coolest hang-out for the folksong cognoscenti was Bunjies, the little coffee bar in Litchfield Street. Colin Grafton, a travel agent who worked nearby, was one audience regular in that late '64 / early '65 period.

'Bert would often come in later,' he recalls, 'after playing somewhere else, I guess, and he would often be pretty full of beer by the time he appeared. One particularly memorable occasion, in early '65, John Renbourn came along and he was expecting Bert. Bert didn't show and we'd almost given up on him, so John was playing – and Bert finally arrived. Trouble was, he was totally blasted. It didn't affect his performance too much, though, at least not in a negative sense. They sat him down on a stool and he was hunched over his guitar, thrashing away like one possessed. It was extraordinary. He actually fell off his stool a few times, hardly appearing to notice, and John just stopped playing, put him back on his stool, and they carried on. I really can't remember what they played except "Angi", because Bert always played "Angi" at that time, but it was not so much the material as the spectacle and the energy in the music that was so impressive. I remember thinking they were such a great pair, not only musically but in the fact that John so good-naturedly picked Bert up and put him back on the stool as a matter of course.'

The very first time Bert had played with Renbourn had been during demo sessions at a basement studio in Denmark Street, shortly after they had met. Not intended for release, these tracks would nevertheless end up as the greater part of Renbourn's first, self-titled solo album (for Transatlantic, released in early 1966), including two spontaneous and not-wholly-in-tune jams with Bert, entitled 'Blue Bones' and 'Noah And Rabbit'. Amidst the largely derivative blues material that made up the bulk of the album, excellent though the playing was, the more adventurous, free-flowing nature of the two tracks with Jansch would prove indicative of a direction the two wayward virtuosi would pursue on subsequent joint appearances on record and on the relatively few advertised gigs they would perform as a duo.

Not only did Bert now have the exciting new possibilities opened up by the traditional music he had explored with Anne Briggs, he also had the possibilities of exploring further, with a like-minded instrumentalist every bit his equal if not greater, the ideas first suggested by Charlie Mingus and his contemporaries in modern jazz. In addition to his own powerfully individual songwriting, very broadly in the 'folk-blues' vein, here were two more strands to his musical personality which would ferment and rise to the surface to stunning effect within months. By the time his first album appeared it was already out of date as an indicator of where its author was headed next.

Transatlantic was by now operating from offices in Marylebone Lane in the West End. From the first Ian Campbell Group album at TRA 110 the label had progressed by leaps and bounds. Subsequent releases had included a second Campbell Group offering; two albums and an EP from the Dubliners; a second volume of Isla Cameron & Tony Britton's *Songs Of Love, Lust & Loose Living*; and the first widely available album from Alexis Korner's Blues Incorporated, *Red Hot From Alex*. More importantly than any individual release was the advent of a deal with Folkways Records in America, allowing Transatlantic to license their prestigious back catalogue exclusively for Britain.

Folkways had never conceded such a deal with any other label before and would not do so again. Nat Joseph looked to Folkways founder Mo Ashe as a mentor and later a friend, and was proud that vintage recordings by legendary blues and folk artists including Broonzy, Leadbelly and Brownie McGhee, previously either unavailable in Britain or prohibitively expensive as imports, would now be available to the masses at budget price. A new subsidiary label, XTRA, was launched in August 1964 to accommodate such material and to provide a home for contemporary British artists who Nat felt would find an audience more easily at less than full price. Alex Campbell, the most popular live act on the scene and yet a disaster in the record racks, was tailormade for such a wheeze. Alex's first British release, *Folk Session*, had only appeared in 1964, on Arco (a small-scale outlet born out of Arco Sound Services, an electrical store in Crawley). Ironically, his first of many albums for XTRA, released in February 1965, had been one of those licensed in from Folkways. But with Bert, there was never any question of under-valuing the product.

'People saw him as a rival to Bob Dylan,' says Martin Carthy. 'When his first album came out it really was a big day. People had been waiting for it like mad.' The LP *Bert Jansch* (TRA 125) was released on 16 April 1965 alongside Owen Hand's *Something New* (TRA 127). TRA 126, a compila-tion, featured both artists. Brian Shuel had designed promotional leaflets and adverts, taken out in a number of magazines, which identified Bert and Owen as 'two vast new talents'. While Owen was described as 'a warm, sympathetic singer, an interpreter of rare sensitivity', Nat was now confident enough to push the hyperbole boat out for Bert:

A remarkable, unusual, intriguing new talent with rare magnetism and originality, Jansch is a young writer-singer-guitarist producing some startling contemporary British folk-blues. His songs are mainly auto-biographical but always universally relevant. He writes of love, running away from home, drug addiction. He plays the guitar with incredible dexterity. He is probably the most original folk-blues guitarist in Britain (Davy Graham included). Around the folk clubs of Britain, Bert Jansch, his songs and his guitar playing are fast becoming the brightest legend of the more way out fans.

Like Alex Campbell, history has shown Owen Hand to have authored one truly outstanding song. 'My Donal', a whaling lament, was destined to 'enter the tradition' and outlive its author's own career as a musician.[27] That song was on *Something New* but reviewers at the time were ungenerous. 'Here is a competent singer with a not very exciting collection of songs,' remarked one, for *English Dance & Song*. 'But what is new about it?' They would not be saying the same of *Bert Jansch*.

Of its fifteen tracks, there was Davy Graham's 'Angi', taken at reckless speed and adding Cannonball Adderley's 'Worksong' as a middle-eight,[28] and fourteen others bearing Bert's name as author. Some tracks wore an influence on their sleeve: 'Smokey River' was essentially Jimmy Giuffre's 'Train And The River', while 'Veronica' (miscredited as 'Casbah') had started life as Mingus's 'Better Get It In Your Soul'. Mingus was echoed again in the title of a new and beautiful instrumental 'Alice's Wonderland', but if this had once been the Mingus tune of that name, it had long since evolved. Mostly, though, it was a record of very personal songs reflecting the lifestyle and world views of its author, from his earliest composition 'Courting Blues' through the swaggering imagery of 'Strolling Down The Highway' to the more recent, more poignant reflections contained in 'Needle Of Death' and 'Running From Home'. The sleeve notes, by Keith De Groot, and the moody, intense cover shot of Bert hunched over a guitar in a bare flat, staring straight at Brian Shuel's lens, completed the message that here was not only music to absorb but a way of life to acquire.

'That sleeve photo has so much character and atmosphere about it,' says Ralph McTell. 'And it wasn't an affectation. He really was this person who lived in student-type squalor, and didn't have a guitar, and could sometimes be drunk, and the girls would just fall over themselves for him. He had all that mystique and I guess everybody wanted to be like that.'

'His image was a non-image, an anti-image,' says Nat Joseph. 'It doesn't work for many but for him it worked. Audiences can spot phoneys, and the one thing Bert never was in his life was a phoney. He was incredibly intense. He felt everything too deeply, and I guess in the end that was the most damaging thing.'

Melody Maker carried a review that was largely descriptive in content, identifying Bert's influences and cautiously predicting a wider audience. Other publications – *English Dance & Song*, *Folk Music*, *Sing* and *Folk Scene* – were more clearly astounded: *Sing* marvelled at the listener-involving qualities of both songs and instrumentals, concluding that 'Bert Jansch is going to be a major figure among new writers'. *Folk Scene* went further: 'His work will touch youth with a force unknown to our present British artists.' But the most penetrating critique appeared anonymously in *Folk Music*:

In person Bert Jansch is not an impressive performer – unless one is a guitarist watching points. But on the basis of this record he may well be the sort of original talent one has been looking for out of the British revival. It might be objected that this is not folk music, and of course it's not. But until our categories expand to allow for this chansonnier, Bert must be included within folk in its broadest sense. Comparisons with Dylan are natural, but the similarities are mainly in theme – Bert's commentaries on the contemporary scene are quite individual in style and content. The guitar work invites immediate comparison with Davy Graham. But Davy's obsession with the exotic has passed Bert by, and if Bert is less adventurous his music is more of a piece. The delicate simplicity of his accompaniments is a nice contrast to the leaping about on Davy's recent two [and] the bite of Bert might be just what Davy's sometimes cloying music needs to make it more palatable.

By the spring and summer of 1965, word would be getting around back in the States that 'Swinging London' was the place to be. April saw the arrival of Tom Paxton, a recording artist for Elektra and, like Dorris Henderson, an immediate sensation in the clubs. Around the same time Jackson C. Frank appeared – an unknown quantity, but an inspiration of his time. Others would come too. They were all following in the footsteps of Paul Simon.

Simon had been all over the clubs since June 1964, and found himself on numerous bills with Bert Jansch: 'He was always telling me he was going to make it one day,' says Bert, 'and I didn't really take too much notice of him. He'd actually bore me. I'd been listening to "The Sounds Of Silence" for so long I got really quite sick of it. He was forever saying, "Ah, I'll make it some day, and when I do I'll come over from the States and I'll see you all right" – that kind of talk! I don't have a very high esteem for America as a nation so I always take Americans with a pinch of salt and with him I had exactly that attitude.'

'Simon was an arrogant, cocky, privileged little kid who could afford the air fares to come over here and groove about,' says Pete Frame. 'He was an amazing songwriter – but didn't he know it. He was also a magpie. The folk scene was all give and take, like a big family, and only the rogues didn't give credit where it was due.'

Simon's faith in 'The Sounds Of Silence' was nonetheless justified: as Bert's album was being released, the song was at No. 1 in the US charts. Returning to London for the summer with his recording partner Art Garfunkel, Paul Simon would continue to be a periodic presence on the English scene right up to 1968, when he would host a memorable party at the London Hilton for all his guitar-playing peers before disappearing off to stardom and America for good.[29] 'I remember the first time he walked into Collet's with Art and the single of "The Sounds Of Silence" in his hand,' says Bert, 'and Gill's bemused face on the other side of the counter. Paul stood just higher than the counter and Art was up on the ceiling! He was introducing Art and saying, "We've just got it back from America and they've put drums on it." I was always amazed at how that could actually be done.'

Though his was commercially the most enduring success story to have emerged from the British folk scene of the mid-sixties, Simon's reputation among his peers remains unenviable: a tendency to glean ideas, licks and arrangements from other artists and a perceived pushiness in his character have burned bridges with many of those he would once have shared a tiny stage with. 'Scarborough Fair' was Martin Carthy's 'big song' of the time, included on his first album, *Martin Carthy*, released on Fontana shortly after Bert's debut. Around the same time Tom Paxton was invited to the Carthys' for dinner and Simon arrived in tow. The song's words and arrangement were noted down over dinner and swiftly copyrighted to Paul Simon. Some years later Carthy, more than mildly aggrieved, did receive a one-off payment: 'The way I got it was comical,' he says. 'After splitting with my first wife, I rang Paul asking if the money had come through. I told him I wanted to buy a house for £1800. "That's amazing," he said. "The payout is exactly £1800." I thought it was great but I left with big donkey ears.'[30]

'Scarborough Fair' would not become a burning issue until its appearance on a Simon & Garfunkel EP in 1968. The following year Bert would be faced with something remarkably similar to his arrangement of 'Blackwater Side' on an album by a new 'underground' rock group called Led Zeppelin. But the question of plagiarism within the supposedly public domain world of traditional song was nothing new. As early as July '62 Eric Winter, reviewing American folklorist Oscar Brand's book *Folk Songs For Fun*, observed its 'ludicrous sounding claims as to who wrote or arranged what'. Brand's response was simple: 'Recomposition is better than decomposition.' The issue was brought firmly into the arena of public debate in March '65 when Dominic Behan let it be known, via the letters pages of *MM*, that the tune to 'With God On Our Side', a track on Dylan's third album, was not traditional but registered with the Performing Rights Society to himself. A fortnight later, in the same letters pages, Gordon McCulloch pointed out that a remarkably similar tune had been collected and published decades previously by Cecil Sharp, the godfather of English folklorists. Clearly Mr Sharp, he concluded, had been guilty of 'ante-natal plagiarism'. The phrase stuck, and though Behan (according to one bemused newcomer to the scene, Roy Harper) 'spent the next eighteen months trying to enlist people to help him take the guy to court and have it out', it was an idea without legs. Dylan, as far as Carthy was concerned, always credited his sources. And once again, from 30 April to 10 May, with a documentary film crew in tow, Bob was back in town.

Dylan's return to the UK was a big event: publicly lauded by the Beatles, flattered by the 'imitation' of Donovan and in his element as a 'spokesman for a generation', his every utterance was being viewed with a gravitas unprecedented for any previous product of the pop process. Whether Dylan actually had any message is unimportant: the perception that he held the key to the universe dictated the agenda. Outwitted at every turn, bedazzled with Bob's relentless irony and gobbledegook, unable to keep up, the world's media were wholly at the mercy of a mischievous enigma. Bob's new album, *Bringing It All Back Home*, would be released in May to coincide with the tour. Kicking off with the meaningless, genius word-association litany of 'Subterranean Homesick Blues', it would contain Bob's free-est, most expansive imagery to date. If the concept of Bob-as-Messiah was a garden path, this one led right past the shed to the fairies at the bottom of it.

The Dylan visit precipitated an intensifying of the folk boom debate. Ray Coleman had written a diligently researched piece for *MM* back in February headed 'Can There Ever Be A Boom In Folk?' For the first time, the folk scenes in the regions of Britain were dissected with facts and figures. For the London region, Roy Guest suggested forty clubs, twenty professional artists and one hundred semi-professionals. No other urban centre was yet quite on that level, but many were thriving and provided the mathematics to confirm it. Coleman estimated three hundred clubs around Britain, denoting a mushrooming grass-roots movement. But he could also conclude by noting what appeared to be an in-built destruct mechanism that could never allow a folk boom on a truly commercial scale: 'Immediately a folky record reaches the best sellers or gets mass exposure,' he wrote, 'purists often insist it is "not real folk music". Folk in Britain has never had it so good. Ironically, fervent folk fans seem concerned at the prospect of the music being discovered by too many.' And therein, with snobbery and factionalism, would forever lie the problem.

'The term "underground" was borrowed later on by other people to talk about Pink Floyd, Fairport Convention, Jethro Tull, stuff like that,' says Martin Carthy, 'but there had been an "underground" going on since 1960/61. When this "folk boom" took shape and gained momentum by the mid-sixties you're talking about millions of people going to clubs. You're actually talking in millions. It was never, ever reflected in record sales but it has to be true. Every sizeable town in England at that time had a choice of folk clubs, every night of the week. It was huge.'

'The Times They Are A-Changing', Dylan's pertinently titled first British single, was released in March, in tandem with Donovan's debut, 'Catch The Wind'. Both went Top 10. Sensing a bandwagon, Nat Joseph had released the Ian Campbell Group's version of 'The Times' three weeks earlier. It was not a hit, but the concept of British folk groups, singles and credibility was firmly established. A couple of weeks later the Spinners released a single of Alex Campbell's 'Been On The Road So Long', declaring it a protest on war. Not to be outdone, Transatlantic issued Alex's own version of the song on a single. Neither was successful. At the same time, in a piece headed 'Dylan v. Donovan', the two artists at the centre of all this activity were asked to comment on each other and the imminence of the 'boom'. 'I don't really know what a boom is,' said Bob, by telephone from the States. '[But] would you please say hello to Martin and Dorothy Carthy.'

Donovan would step confidently into the den of irony that became *Don't Look Back*, the ground-breaking documentary of Bob's 1965 British tour. Renbourn, Dorris Henderson and Alex Campbell would provide their own cameos too, gate-crashing Bob's hotel suite after a typically boozy Campbell gig. For the next number of months, Dylan, Donovan and the folk boom would be a question for every music writer to bring up with every pop person who crossed their path.

'When Woody Guthrie's in the hit parade I'll admit there's a folk boom,' was the no-nonsense view of Chas Chandler, of the Animals. 'It's only two people,' pointed out Manfred Mann's Paul Jones. 'There are lots and lots of folk records coming out and not meaning a thing.' The subject of Donovan was less equivocal: 'I don't particularly like Donovan's records,' said chief Animal, Eric Burdon. 'But I like him so much as a guy. I know he's genuine, so I'm a Donovan fan.' 'Bit of an enigma,' suggested Spencer Davis. Dylan's 'enigma' was less tolerably endorsed by others: 'I can't stand it when people say he's a genius,' raged Tom Jones, Welsh beefcake and balladeer. 'I don't like him. Don't like his attitude or his records. I just want to forget about the fellow.' 'I look forward to the Graham Bond Folk Four,' suggested one wag, in the *MM* letters page. Mick Jagger poured his bile on the whole movement as 'folk fakers' and Ian Campbell responded with his view of the Rolling Stones as 'phoney Americans'. The music papers were having a field day. By the end of the year Beatles manager Brian Epstein, asked for his view on traditional music generally, summed up the pop nation's mood on the whole debate: 'On the whole, I find it boring.'[31]

This was all fluff, surface-controversialism that fed off itself. But Ewan MacColl, the man most widely viewed as having created the monster in the first place, had yet to have his say. He was far from amused: 'Dylan is to me the perfect symbol of the anti-artist in our society. He is against everything – the last resort of someone who doesn't really want to change the world. He doesn't say anything President Johnson could disagree with. He deals in generalisations. His poetry is punk. It's derivative and terribly old-hat. This boom has been artificially created and it won't be over until big money has been made by the people who created it. We're going to get lots and lots of copies of Dylan.' Dylan and those who followed him, he continued, had 'missed the point of Woody Guthrie',[32] had no real anger or passion in them. He himself, he wholeheartedly admitted, had taken to railing against even his own audiences of late: 'I've been doing it quite purposely, on the assumption that art which only produces an emotional response is bad art. My function is not to reassure people. I want to make them uncomfortable, to send them out of the bleeding place arguing and talking.'

MacColl's vitriol in print had precisely the result he had doubtless intended. Letters poured in to the *Melody Maker*, pages were devoted to pop and folk personalities giving responses, with phrases like 'sour grapes' and 'ivory tower' endlessly repeated. But there were many who conceded that the godfather of the British folk revival may have had a point. The most telling observation was from Marianne Faithfull: 'In a way I think he is right, but he is the wrong person to say so.'[33] If anyone had been a pop product of the 'folk boom' it had been Marianne. In May '65, her record label had released two debut albums simultaneously: one a pop record, the other folk. Her next album, *North Country Maid*, would feature a cover of Bert's 'Courting Blues'. A 'pop-folk' artist like Donovan and Dylan, Marianne was somebody else for MacColl to despise. But MacColl's time was over: his rant against Dylan and the populism of folk music was his valedictory address.

Robert Shelton, later a Dylan biographer, summed up the sadness but also the determination to move forward felt by many for whom folk music was an exciting and ever-evolving adventure: 'I have enormous respect for MacColl as a singer, writer and philosopher of the folk revival,' he wrote at the time, 'but he is so thoroughly out of touch with Dylan's generation that it was ill-advised of him to pontificate from his lofty and distant eminence. The Dylan generation is making its own rules in belief, political commitment and literary and musical style.'[34] They were indeed, and in London their centre of government would be a tiny little cellar in Soho, seemingly owned by somebody called Les: 'Les Cousins'.

Pronounced *Lez Cuzzins*, universally abbreviated to 'the Cousins' and almost never recalled or referred to at the time by anyone in the intentional French pronunciation *Lay Coo-zan*, the proprietors of 49 Greek Street were a likeable middle-aged Greek couple by the name of Matheou, anglicised to Matthews. They ran a restaurant on the ground floor; the floor upstairs was rented out to an illegal gambling club; and downstairs, operated initially by one Phil Phillips (agent for Irish entertainer Noel Murphy) and subsequently by their son Andy, in the cellar that had once been used by Russell Quaye for skiffle sessions, was the most extraordinary new folk club in town. Remembered as the very cradle of the singer-songwriter-guitarist explosion of the mid to late sixties, the Cousins' existence spanned April 1965 to the early weeks of 1970, though its origins remain shrouded in myth.

'Around the Christmas season Les Bridger used to disappear,' says John Renbourn. 'No one knew where he went but he was always drunk when he came back. Turned out he was in a pantomime, crowd scenes in *Peter Pan*. Anyway, one night he was weaving back through Soho and actually fell down into a basement doorway where there was a room full of young girls – some sort of student establishment. So Les told them he was the world's greatest guitar player and that was just what they needed. So then and there the Cousins started and we had a regular place to play.'[35]

Whatever the truth, it could never have been anticipated that such a tiny, uncomfortable, unremarkable, unlicensed and almost certainly unprofitable place would become such a legend. Accommodating perhaps one hundred and fifty people at a pinch, it had membership and entrance fees measured in shillings, a backroom bar serving tea and sandwiches, and decor comprising a giant wagon wheel on the wall and fishermen's netting draped from the ceiling. The facilities for making music were sparse: a small stage, a piano in the corner, one electrical socket and a microphone. It was, if nothing else, the only 'folk' club at that time with a microphone.

In retrospect, the list of residents, regulars, the advertised and the unexpected who passed down the narrow steps of the Cousins provides a virtual roll-call of folk music's contribution to the 'Swinging Sixties'. For many of the performers it was a rite of passage, an experience that has created a lifelong bond to that time, that place and those people and to the shared values it represented. Many of those whose careers effectively grew out of an exotic apprenticeship at the Cousins still talk in terms of a brotherhood: there are no class reunions, but it shall always be the 'Class of '65'.

In that year, and on into the next, a time-traveller could pick at random any all-nighter session at the Cousins and see any number of extraordinary musicians take the stage: the three kings – Bert Jansch, John Renbourn and Davy Graham; the heirs to the thrones – Paul Simon, Al Stewart, Ralph McTell, Roy Harper, Jackson Frank, Dorris Henderson; the king and queen of 'pop-folk' – Donovan and Julie Felix; future legends of folk-rock taking floor spots – Sandy Denny, Trevor Lucas, Cat Stevens; emissaries from the living tradition – the Watersons, the Young Tradition, Anne Briggs, Dave & Toni Arthur; emissaries from Outer Space – the Incredible String Band; the godfathers – Alexis Korner and Alex Campbell; stalwarts of the scene –

Owen Hand, Les Bridger, Noel Murphy, Martin Winsor and Diz Disley; Hamish Imlach, the clown prince of Scotland conceding occasional visits to the capital; Wizz Jones, the original hippy; Long John Baldry, still with a foot in every scene going; Duffy Power, rock'n'roll survivor and the best British blues singer there was; drop-in Americans of the quality of Doris Troy, Sandy Bull, Arlo Guthrie, Danny Kalb, 'Spider' John Koerner, Derroll Adams, the Reverend Gary Davis and Bill Monroe; once-only visitors of the mythic variety – Bob Dylan, John McLaughlin, Eric Clapton and Jimi Hendrix. The booking policy would be the broadest in town. Steve Benbow was an early headliner, but the audience were unkind: 'They thought I was commercial,' he says. 'I wasn't!' Even Ewan MacColl & Peggy Seeger came once, typically fearless in the very crucible of the new order.[36] All of them, and many more besides – 'goodly knights of the guitar, riding their instruments like warhorses through the neon world of Soho'[37] – played the Cousins in those first two calendar years.

This was the Swinging Sixties in its essence: you had to be there. There was nobody taking photographs, no one with a tape recorder in the corner of the room, nobody writing down set-lists, almost no one shooting film and not a single piece of contemporaneous reportage of any length.[38] When amazing things happened, they happened without warning and only for the benefit of those in the room at that time. Only the part-story of the press ads and the fabulous memories remain – memories which, by and large, forget the dull nights and telescope the great ones into one endless, unrepeatable party.

'It was an alienated sort of place,' wrote Karl Dallas, grasping for perspective some years later, 'which didn't fulfil the promise of the Young Tradition blow-up over the stairs as you descended into the heat and the fug, which seemed to suggest some sort of cross-cultural ferment. For though the mix was there, undoubtedly, it was often hard to distinguish anything at all through the grass-smoke and general stoned-out, crashed-out, all-nighter sheer unconcern of its audiences, who seemed to be there less for the music than the whole phoney ambience of the place. It was a time of polarisation, when the young Turks were about to wrest the folk revival from the hands of the Old Left pioneers who ran the Singers Club and *Sing* magazine, a schism which is remembered today, wrongly, in terms of attitudes to traditionalism and national culture but which was, in reality, more concerned with lifestyles and a reaction against the puritanical neo-Calvinism of Marxists like Bruce Dunnet and Ewan MacColl, for which the new band of what we were later to call singer-songwriters were to substitute something a great deal more anarchic, more hedonistic, more instinctual, less rational. And yet, something was so obviously happening there, despite the squalor of the place and the blasé uninterest of the audience compared with the rapt, almost religious concentration of the dedicated students at the Singers Club, that one kept returning, and even Bruce Dunnet found himself managing Bert Jansch for a while.'[39]

It is difficult to explain conclusively why the Cousins carved its name in the annals while other venues – some with advantages of priority or quality of artists, some even momentarily just as popular – are now all but forgotten. Overambition, geography or other factors now obscure may explain the faltering progress or relatively short lives of the Mercury Theatre club in Notting Hill, the Centre in Balham and many others.[40] What is less easily explained is the rise and fall of the one venue to offer everything that the Cousins would, and to do so more than three months earlier: the Student Prince in D'Arblay Street. Opening at midnight on Saturday, 2 January 1965, it was the very first of the folk club all-nighters. Soho historian John Platt has sourced the origins of all-nighter music events to a series of 'raves' spanning 1951–53 and organised by jazz singer George Melly at Cy Laurie's club in a basement in Gerrard Street. 'Although today the idea of spending a whole night in a crowded, airless basement appears extraordinary,' as Melly explains in his autobiography *Owning Up*, 'it was very exciting then.' Having lain largely dormant for a while, the idea was still exciting in 1965.[41]

The Student Prince was run by Curly Goss, whose experience of running folk clubs went back at least as far as the King & Queen at the time of Bert's first visit to London. The winning combination of Alex Campbell, still the biggest draw on the scene, and Dorris Henderson guaranteed the opening night. Two weeks later the *MM* could note a 'big turnout' for the new venue, this time for Dorris with Paul Simon, with other 'names' in the audience. Curly was simultaneously running a late-night revue called *Two In Folkus*, with Dorris and Martin Winsor, at the Little Theatre Club, St Martin's Lane. Problems at the Prince began on 30 January when the proprietors of the premises had what Goss described as a 'change of policy'. A month later, on 27 February, it resurfaced as the New Prince at 23 Gerrard Street with an all-nighter featuring Long John Baldry. The next week it was Long John with Dorris, by now a TV star from regular appearances on *Gadzooks!*; on 27 March, it was Dorris & John Renbourn, now working together as a duo.

The Cousins had opened on a Friday, 16 April, initially advertising a 3 a.m. closedown. For several weeks it avoided going head to head with the Prince, which was only operating on Saturdays. On Saturday, 15 May, having already expanded from one to four nights in the week, the Cousins took the plunge on two fronts: opening on Saturday and advertising as an all-nighter. By this stage the Prince had moved again, to 43 Wardour Street, and had now become the Allnight Folk Prince. The first night of competition pitted the unknown Weston Gavin and Bob Thornton at the Cousins against the unassailable Alex Campbell with Martin Winsor at the Prince. The following week it was Gavin and Thornton against Owen Hand and Joanne Hindley-Smith, again established names. And then there was nothing. The Prince, in all its guises, simply disappeared. Two weeks later the Cousins could celebrate with the first and rarely repeated double-billing of Bert Jansch and Davy Graham, and could announce Jansch as its first weekly resident, every Thursday. With the only real threat to custom having somehow lost its way, through too many changes in place or name or whatever else, and the hottest act on the scene having signed up for the long haul, the Cousins could hardly fail. And nor would it.

'I was resident at the Scot's Hoose for about a year,' said Bert, 'and then also at Les Cousins, which had just started up. I was resident at both for a while, which was mad on the face of it because they were only about a hundred yards apart. But it seemed to work. Often I'd do a night in Bunjies, one in the Scot's Hoose and one in Les Cousins in the same week. Les Cousins took off at that point and pretty soon people were coming from all over the country to spend the weekend sleeping on the floor of the place. It was run by Andy Matthews, but he didn't do anything – his parents, who ran the restaurant upstairs, they did most of the work. They were beautiful people. Every wayfaring folk singer would always get fed. That's why his business went down. It looked a very classy restaurant – the food was superb – but he used to feed any folkies that wandered in, which put all his ordinary customers off. He saved a few people's lives, did Mr Matthews. Cousins was much more of a meeting place. The Scot's Hoose was my thing. It was just me and occasional friends, like Sandy Denny, who dropped by. I was usually drunk and either played brilliantly or dreadfully. There were no restrictions – you could play for three hours if you wanted to. Those were crazy days.'[42]

Bert's residencies at both the Scot's Hoose and the Cousins were the making of him as an artist of national reputation. Both residencies would run to the end of 1965, with, on average, one other advertised Greater London gig per week, let alone the sessions at Bunjies (which almost never advertised). There would, of course, be innumerable other shows, at clubs and universities in the regions: 'Apart from playing the Cousins or dropping into places like that,' says Bert, 'you didn't actually make your living in London. You were travelling to gigs all the time, all over the country.' The geographical extent and quantity of these gigs is impossible to know now, although Bert rarely if ever worked the long-established club circuit in the

South and South-West of England, favouring instead the venues to the
North. There are photographs from a gig in Chelmsford in '65, the letter of
apology to the Colchester club, and a handful of reminiscences from here
and there. Two provincial clubs Bert did play regularly were at the
Blacksmith's Arms in St. Albans and the Green Man in Old Harlow –
both opening in June '65, under the auspices of Bruce Dunnet's 'Associated
Folk Clubs'. By that stage Bruce had enough faith in Bert's drawing power
to put him on in both clubs as featured guest for their first and second nights
running. Another regular booking was Leicester, where one committed fan
was Steve Tilston, who would be recording for Transatlantic himself by the
end of the sixties.

'I remember seeing Bert and Martin Carthy in 1965 within a week of
each other at the Leicester Folksong Club,' says Steve. 'At that time Martin
wasn't playing anything remotely recognisable as the style he's got today,
whereas with Bert it was already all there – all those pull-offs and slurs and
legatos and trills. It was unmistakably his guitar playing, and let's remember
he was the first real British songwriter on the scene. The very idea of writing
your own songs in the mid-sixties was really quite revolutionary. For me,
sitting in my folks' front room in Leicestershire, playing his first album, a lot
of it seemed to typify London – which is why, as soon as I was nineteen or
twenty, I left for London to be part of the Cousins scene. By then, of course,
it was on the way down.'

Interviewed in print for the first time in August 1965, in *MM*, Bert gave
his considered view, maintained in subsequent interviews, that 'the audiences for folk outside London are very good, and those inside London are
very bad'. However much he disliked the London scene personally, and
however much he was gigging elsewhere, to a very great extent Bert's career
and reputation would be founded on his inextricable association with Les
Cousins, the coolest venue in the country, and by the continued appearance
of his name in the *Melody Maker* London club ads. It is not insignificant that
the first club to advertise its guest attractions in large bold type, leaping out
immediately from anything else on the page, was the Cousins; it is also
worth remembering that the one act it was promoting more regularly than
anyone else in 1965 was Bert Jansch.

'I'm sure they got a lot of out-of-town audiences because people would
see the ads in the *Melody Maker*,' says Ian Anderson, subsequently editor of
Folk Roots, but at that point just another kid in the provinces. 'You already
knew that people like Bert and John were the going thing, and after you
looked enough weeks and had seen their names in big print at the Cousins
you'd want to go there. You would immediately believe that the Cousins
was the place to go in London, so it became it.'

'I'd be up there pretending to be a beatnik with John Steinbeck novels hanging out of my pocket,' says Pete Frame. 'I was a provincial hick basically, looking at people and thinking, "Cor, they're real beatnik kind of people," and they were probably just up from Bromley thinking the same thing about me! There was tons of posturing going on. We were all bloody weekend beatniks, holding down day jobs.'

It was not only bearded men with duffle coats who found the new scene attractive. As Maggie Holland, a provincial cohort of Ian Anderson's, observed: 'Parents seemed curiously untroubled by the thought of their teenage daughters spending Saturday night in Soho, if it was sitting on a cold hard floor listening to some long-haired guitarist.'[43] 'It was a different world completely,' remembers Val, another regular, 'there were no rapists or mad people around. There was a trust between people that is gone now. Soho was a safe place. You could spot the prostitutes, the villains, the sex people, but they didn't want anything to do with young hippies – they'd got their own world. Of course, if we'd been wearing mini-skirts and beehive hairdos we might have been in trouble.'

Never actually calling itself a folk club, the Cousins very quickly developed a culture and etiquette all its own. As a teenager growing up in the West Country, Ian Anderson was typical of the Cousins' weekend clientele: 'It was the cheapest hotel in London,' he says. 'At some point we twigged that because of the Cousins all-nighters you could go up to London and it wouldn't cost you – you could hitch up on Saturday morning, do all the running around places like Collet's in the afternoon and go to the evening session at Cousins, or even stay in the pub across the road. There was a place near Covent Garden called the As You Like It coffee house – a gay, vegetarian place. The waiter would always be trying to persuade you to try his "divine trifle"! The all-nighter never really cracked into action till one o'clock, so quite often we'd go over to this place after the evening session and then go to the all-nighter. Coming out at dawn, Judith Piepe would throw her doors open for breakfasts. She had the famous flat where Al Stewart and Paul Simon stayed, but she also ran some sort of mission hall nearby. At the end of an all-nighter she or her boyfriend Stephen Delft, a guitar maker, would get up on the stage and say, "The tubes don't start running for another hour. If anybody wants a cup of tea, come with us."'

Coming from Bournemouth, where he had played lead guitar in beat groups, Al Stewart was one of the first wave of blow-ins to the Soho singer-songwriter scene. Arriving in London in February 1965, one of Al's first gigs was at Bunjies, where he proceeded to play, in correct order, the entirety of *The Times They Are A-Changing*. 'I wasn't a folk singer at the time,' says Al, 'I just happened to own a couple of Bob Dylan albums. But all these singer-songwriters I met in London seemed to be doing something very fresh, very exciting. And the folk scene seemed a little more intellectual than the rock'n'roll scene, and that was appealing. Wearing a corduroy jacket and living in a coffee bar when you're nineteen and discussing Sartre with like-minded people was a long way from being in Bournemouth talking about how the Surfaris got that great guitar sound!'[44]

Bumping into Paul Simon, who was rooming with Judith Piepe – a social worker with a charitable weakness for folk singers – Al moved in too for a period. When 'The Sounds Of Silence' became a US hit in April Simon moved temporarily back to the States, leaving what Al observed to be a fortuitous hole in the scene: 'People booked me who'd previously booked Paul Simon. They could have me a lot cheaper and I knew all his songs, plus Dylan songs and the odd Bert Jansch like "Needle Of Death". Like everyone else, I'd had to learn "Angi", because they didn't take you seriously unless you did at least one guitar instrumental. [But] I was a compendium of contemporary folk songs.'[45]

Also staying with Piepe by the dawn of the Cousins era was a strange young American called Jackson C. Frank. One of the most tragic but revered figures in the story of British folk, Jackson's mythic status is secured by the brevity of his rise and fall – delivering one monumental song, 'Blues Run The Game', recording only one album and never really outliving as an artist the scene within which he thrived. 'He was an absolute genius,' says Bert. 'A lot of the music that came out of that period was most certainly due to him. "Blues Run The Game" influenced just about everyone who heard it. You could say that it changed the face of the contemporary songwriting world. He was the ultimate.'[46] Characterised by a certain pathos and sense of doom, Jackson's work was no bedsitter affectation, it was the real thing.

Born in Buffalo, New York, 1943, Jackson (the 'C' was for Carey) had suffered serious burns in a fire at school when he was eleven. Eighteen of his classmates had died, and for Jackson the physical and psychological injuries would stay with him for the rest of his life. During a period of several months recuperating in hospital he learned to play guitar and in 1957, on a trip with his family to Memphis, he met Elvis. It was another pivotal event. By the time he was sixteen, Jackson was performing rock'n'roll, but developed an interest in older songs and became involved in the local coffee-house folk scene. Inspired by the success of Buffalo contemporary Eric Andersen, Jackson and future Steppenwolf star John Kay decided they too could make it big as folk singers. Jackson also applied to college as a failsafe but turning twenty-one in 1964 there was suddenly a whole new side to the equation: an insurance payout of $110,500 (minus legal fees) for the fire. 'Living for today' became the new ethos.

'I left my job on the *Buffalo Evening News* and went to England,' he recalled.[47] The motivation was not music but, now 'able to indulge the propensity', car-buying: 'At one time in England I had a 1950 one-off Bentley, a new Land Rover and an even newer Aston Martin DB-5.' But he had also brought his guitar, and on the boat trip over, around March/April '65, Jackson wrote what is believed to have been his first song, 'Blues Run The Game'. Tinged, as much of his work would be, with melancholy and not a little strength in adversity, it encapsulated the lifestyle, dreams and fears of those who had chosen the uncertain path of singing songs for a living. In England, he would find many of his new peers more than willing to perform or record it. Expecting nothing but welcomed with open arms, as Dorris Henderson had been before him, these were exciting days: 'Bert Jansch, Donovan, Sandy Denny, Al Stewart and many others became associates and dear friends.' Courtesy of Paul Simon, Jackson Frank joined the crowd at Judith Piepe's.

'I led a very charmed life at that time,' says Bert. 'After the first album I was never down and out. I was lucky I had the outlet to put down all these experiences at the right time, at a time when most young people don't have the opportunity.'[48] In this crucial period in Bert's ascendancy, during the summer of 1965, he had the field almost totally to himself. On the acoustic scene, there was simply no one else in town to touch him instrumentally or to rival his drawing power: Alex Campbell would be touring America from July to December; Davy Graham would be off around the Middle East in search of exotica; John Renbourn, inexplicably, would be absent from London from the beginning of June until the end of August (Dorris Henderson left for America at the same time, not returning till September); while Jackson Frank, perhaps the only man to equal Bert in terms of songwriting promise and singular charisma, would disappear from July to October. All this was coincidental – it was the free-and-easy nature of the scene, nobody was thinking of 'building careers' – but with two weekly residencies in the most happening quarter of the most swinging city in the world, during its peak period of tourist activity, the legend of Bert Jansch was set to explode. By this time, again with Les Bridger and John Renbourn in tow, he had moved to yet another flat: 30 Somali Road.

Situated, to the great amusement of all concerned, near Shoot Up Hill in the West Hampstead/Kilburn area, Bert, John and Les occupied the upstairs, while the Young Tradition – a new harmony trio comprising Peter Bellamy, Royston Wood and Heather Wood – were downstairs. The Young Tradition had formed under the wing of Bruce Dunnet at the Scot's Hoose earlier in the year. 'Revival singing', in the hands of people liable to appeal to both the Soho set and the more conservative traditional music clubs around the country, now had its duo, trio and quartet: Dave & Toni Arthur, the Young Tradition and the Watersons. Anne Briggs, an honorary 'fifth Waterson', would often stay with the downstairs crowd at Somali Road. All in all, it was quite a scene. 'They got all the gigs, we got all the visitors,' says Anne, of the guitar heroes upstairs. 'They were earning a great deal of money by then. In fact, I suspect they paid our rent quite a lot of the time.'

Having shared a bill with the Dubliners in a concert at Cecil Sharp House in May, Anne had been encouraged to visit Dublin and meet a friend of theirs called Johnny Moynihan – a traditional musician of similarly free-spirited outlook to herself. Having done so, and begun what was to be a long-term relationship with Moynihan, Anne's life for the next few years would revolve around the desire to spend time in Ireland, where the revival of folk music on a widespread commercial level had yet to happen, and the need to return periodically to England and earn some money gigging to finance the next trip. There would always be a place for her at Somali Road: 'Downstairs was a folk haven for anyone who had nowhere else to stay,' she says. 'It was packed with bodies like sardines, it really was.'

The following year Moynihan would form a band in Galway called Sweeney's Men. Including Andy Irvine in its fluctuating line-up, it would provide a blueprint for the future direction of Irish music and its eventual revival in the seventies as a young-person's music on a scale comparable with Britain's 'folk boom' in the sixties. Andy, disillusioned with his life as an actor in Dublin, had been making occasional trips back to England before settling in London again in 1965, and thereby getting sucked into the life of the full-time troubadour.[49]

Friendly with both Anne Briggs and the Young Tradition, Andy would soon be one of the regulars at Somali Road: 'I always thought of it as the harder drugs upstairs and the softer drugs downstairs,' he says, never more than a drinking man himself. 'But I'm sure that wasn't true. The fact that Bert had had that early record, when most people didn't have a record out, boosted his status enormously. There was a certain awesome, semi-legendary quality about him, even as he sat there and played. I would put him in the same bag as Davy Graham on that, although Davy had a mystery about him that was kind of scary, that you didn't want to get into. With Bert, it was a little different. You could say, "Hi, Bert" – "Yeah . . .", but you wouldn't go any further. You could go into a place and he would be there and so would Peter Bellamy and his crowd, talking loudly and showing off – but Bert was a little bit distant from them as well. Because he was silent and they were loud there was a kind of awe.'

Another resident of the upper floors at Somali Road, during the spring/

Left: Cyril Davies and Alexis Korner at The Roundhouse, c.1957.
(courtesy Len Partridge)
Middle Left: Steve Benbow, c.1962. *(courtesy Steve Benbow)*
Middle Right: Ewan MacColl and Peggy Seeger, 1965. *(Brian Shuel)*
Bottom Left: Dominic Behan referees as Alex Campbell picks a fight, Edinburgh 1963 *(Brian Shuel)*
Bottom Right: Chris Barber, mid-fifties.
(courtesy Phil Smee)

Above: Len Partridge dazzles while Archie Fisher looks on, c.1960. *(courtesy Len Partridge)*
Below: A rare glimpse of The Howff, c.1960. Roy Guest holds court with Hamish Henderson, far right. *(courtesy Ian Anderson, Folk Roots Magazine)*

Top Left: Bert Jansch (middle left) with brother Charlie (middle right) at the nursery in Edinburgh, c.1960 *(courtesy Bert Jansch)*
Top Right: Big Bill Broonzy *(courtesy Phil Smee)*
Middle Left: Clive Palmer, Robin Williamson, Bert Jansch and *that* chess set, Edinburgh 1963 *(courtesy Rod Harbinson)*
Middle Right: Bert Jansch at Chelmsford Folk Club, early 1965 *(courtesy Stuart Wallace)*
Above Left: Bob Dylan at the Singers Club, December 1962. Ewan MacColl far right *(Brian Shuel)*
Above Right: Gill Cook, c.1970 *(courtesy Gill Cook)*

The Edinburgh Festival, 1963 *(all photographs, Brian Shuel)*
Top Left: Archie Fisher at Waverley Studios
Top Right: Bert Jansch - the lost recording
Above Left: L-R: Bill Leader and Nat Joseph
Above Right: Dolina MacLennan at Waverley Studios
Left: Rory McEwan in concert
Below: Owen Hand, Hamish Imlach and Alex Campbell in blissful harmony
at Waverley Studios

Above: Bert Jansch with Anne Briggs, c.1963 *(courtesy Anne Briggs)*
Left: L-R: Anne Briggs; John Challis; Jill Doyle, Edinburgh Festival, 1963 *(Brian Shuel)*

Bottom Row: The flat at King's Avenue, Ealing, late 1963 *(courtesy David Blass)*
Left: Bert Jansch
Middle: Sue Thompson
Right: David Blass

SHIRLEY COLLINS & DAVY GRAHAM
FOLK/BLUES HAPPENING
CECIL SHARP HOUSE
2 Regent's Park Rd NWI   GUL 2206
7.30 SUN 17 JAN '65
tickets 7/6

Top Left: John Renbourn and Dorris Henderson, 1965 *(Brian Shuel)*
Top Right: Pete Townshend - possibly not in a folk club, 1965 *(courtesy Phil Smee)*
Above Left: Donovan, 1965 *(courtesy Phil Smee)*
Above Centre: Andy Irvine, 1965
(Brian Shuel)
Above Right: Duffy Power, 1965
(courtesy Duffy Power)
Left: Davy Graham and Shirley Collins, 1965
Below: Liz and Maggie Cruickshank, 1965
(courtesy Maggie Cruickshank)

Top Left: Bruce Dunnet, c.1967 *(courtesy Bruce Dunnet)*
Top Right: Bert Jansch with unidentified admirer, Somali Road, 1965 *(courtesy Kieran Bracken)*
Middle Left: Judy Cross and Bert Jansch, February 1967 *(courtesy Bruce Dunnet)*
Middle Right: Bert at Newcastle City Hall, March 1967 *(courtesy Neil Brown)*
Above Left: Outtake from *Sweet Child* sleeve, 1968 *(courtesy Mary Jansch)*
Above Right: First Pentangle photo session, Tottenham Court Road, late 1967. L-R: Thompson, McShee, Renbourn, Cox, Jansch *(Brian Shuel)*
Bottom Left: Pentangle publicity shot, 1971 *(photographer unknown)*

Top Left: Recording *LA Turnaround*, 1974
(Charisma publicity shot)
Top Right: Bert with Terry Cox and Nigel
Portman Smith live at the Half Moon, 1984
(courtesy Bert Jansch)
Middle Left: Bert with Davy Graham (left) and
Wizz Jones, 1990 *(courtesy Bert Jansch)*
Middle Right: The final Pentangle line-up:
Bert, Jacqui, Nigel, Peter and Gerry, 1990-95
Above Left: Bert Jansch and Peter Kirtley,
BBC Northern Ireland, 1992 *(Colin Harper)*
Left: Bert Jansch and Loren Auerbach, Isle of
Arran, 1999 *(courtesy Bert Jansch)*

summer of '65, was Bert's friend from Ealing Art College, John Challis: 'This time it was me who was sleeping in the kitchen,' says Challis. 'Having left Ealing I'd tried to get work as an illustrator and failed miserably, ending up working at the income tax office at Lisson Grove.' Necessarily a little detached from the scene at Somali Road, Challis was in a position to observe Bert's changing fortunes:

'He never looked ahead, but he was very focused on what he was doing. If you saw him without a guitar it looked like there was something missing! The romantic idea of the tortured artist is a bit superficial. But there is a sense in which actual possession of a creative ability of that order is as much of a penalty as a benefit because you can't switch it off – it's with you all the time. I think at the time what really bothered him was that what seemed so obvious to him was completely obscured to most other people. There are two things about Bert: one is that he was at times very fragile and vulnerable but there was also steel inside him. There were these two sides and they co-existed. Bear in mind I was the same age as him – I was very young, very bewildered by life myself and he was the first seriously creative person I'd ever encountered. I found it quite hard to understand, but I did try to understand and I think that was part of the basis of our friendship: I wasn't laying stuff on him and expecting him to respond in a certain way.

'Renbourn was much more the "professional musician". He was much more together than anybody else. Whatever conflicts there were between him and Bert weren't played out in public. There was obviously a huge amount of mutual respect. Renbourn was more of a technician: more theoretical knowledge and faster fingers. But Bert had this blinding origin-ality, and Renbourn was good enough to be able to keep up with that.'

To Challis's recollection, downstairs did not have all the visitors. People like Alex Campbell, 'Rambling' Jack Elliott and Derroll Adams would drop in on Bert and John. There was also someone rather more familiar to the teenage population: 'It must have been the early part of 1965 that Donovan was hanging around,' says Challis. 'He aroused a good deal of suspicion amongst John and Bert and their friends. He seemed far too friendly. It subsequently transpired that his management were trying desperately hard to get Bert to sign up with them. I remember Bert saying to me once, "I've just spent a day with Donovan and been chased all over the place by teenage chicks – what's that all about? I can't live like that!" '

'I was an overnight success,' says Donovan, 'and if I entered a folk club afterwards half of the room would be mumbling about how I'd done the dirty on them, sold out, gone over to the other side – all this ridiculous stuff! When I met Derroll Adams he took a shine to me, and he saw that I was being hammered like crazy by the Dylan/Donovan thing in the press and everybody taking the piss out of me because I'd gone on television – "Don't sing any popular songs, don't make any money out of it, don't buy any good clothes" – all this bullshit. Now the only reason I wore rough clothes, and I suppose Bert too, was because we were cold, we were poor and we actually might have to sleep rough or on somebody's sofa without any heating, and you didn't want to freeze. So Derroll took me and he introduced me to people like Bert Jansch.'

Donovan had almost certainly first seen Bert performing at Pete Frame's club in Luton, on 28 April 1965, where Bert, to Frame's delight, had brought along Dorris Henderson and John Renbourn for the ride. Donovan was fascinated by Bert's playing, his songs, his strange charisma and his apparent lack of ego: 'Nobody would teach how to play the guitar in my group,' says Don. 'But when I went to Bert I saw things that I wanted to learn – this descending pattern of "Angi", this seminal song that opened up "Stairway to Heaven" for Jimmy Page, "Sunny Goodge Street" for me, probably thousands of songs. The descending pattern can be taken back to Johann Sebastian Bach, but when it finally arrives at Bert Jansch he's doing things with it and he becomes a kind of doorway for lots of people, and what I found when I would go to Bert's place was that he didn't mind showing you. And that is the great magnanimity of the artist: Bert Jansch shared.

'I tried to play exactly like him to begin with, until you realised that Bert didn't play exactly the same thing every night. It was a "genre" of picking that you could improvise on. He was doing something extremely sensual, and yet you got this impression from Bert that he didn't really care whether you liked it or not, and if he didn't want to sing it too loud you wouldn't hear the words. But it was magic. He had the power – the power of the bardic voice. He was actually writing a new tradition and that was exciting. I followed him around when I wasn't working myself. He was a hero. When you go to see a figure like Bert you're going in the hope of hearing a new song which is going to explain some obscure emotion. That was the fascinating thing – you might hear something that he might never play again, because he'd forget it or something. So there was this anticipation. And the girls in the room would fall in love with him.'

Bert liked Donovan as an individual and enjoyed his early recordings. Two singles had now been issued and by May there was an album, *What's Bin Did And What's Bin Hid*: 'He was already world famous,' says Bert, 'but he would come down to Cousins and mix with the crowd. In those days you felt rather awe-inspired by this "television character", as I used to call him. My friendship with him was a Cousins job – we used to meet there, drink there and play there.' What Bert was less inclined towards was the nature of the pop game of which Don was a part, and particularly his management, Stephens and Eden, 'a couple of mad, pushy geezers who put a hat on his head, stuck him on the telly and made a million pounds out of him. They did a "sign your name here, lad" scene on me and, being a kid, I put my name to some publishing thing involving a couple of songs Donovan wanted to record. The album subsequently got into the charts, but I wasn't exactly showered with royalty cheques.'[50]

'Donovan's management used to come round to get songs from Bert,' says Renbourn. 'They'd make a field trip to darkest West Hampstead! The thing was, they didn't know who Bert was, and there'd always be loads of people asleep on the floor. So the guys would come in saying, "Bert! Bert!" and someone would say, "Yes, that's me" and foist these songs on them. Les Bridger claimed to be him most of the time. Bert was quite happy for it to go on.'

'Oh, Deed I Do' was a genuine Jansch song recorded by Donovan for his second album, *Fairytale*, released later that year, but never recorded by its author. Donovan was also championing Bert to the press at every opportunity and featuring a number of Bert's songs in his live repertoire: 'Needle Of Death', 'Running From Home' and 'Do You Hear Me Now?' Around that time Bert was involved with Beverley Kutner, a singer who later married and recorded with John Martyn, a singer-songwriter from the later Cousins era. But during 1965, Bert's only competition for Beverley's affections was Donovan: 'We had a triangle at one point,' says Don, 'and my recollection is that it may have cut us all up at the time. "The House Of Jansch"[51] was written about that triangle, and I wrote another one called "Sweet Beverley" because Beverley was about to become famous and get a record deal and I was trying to give her some advice. How could I give her any advice? I was getting ripped off right, left and centre!'

'I think Beverley might have been putting herself about a bit,' says Challis. 'At one point she asked me to go on the road with her, but because I knew she was involved with Bert I kind of backed away from it. But she sang with me a couple of times at the Scot's Hoose – an excellent blues singer.' By the end of the year, Bert was involved with a young woman called Jan Cole, but Beverley was around long enough to appear in the background on the sleeve photo for Bert's next album. It would also be Transatlantic's first-ever colour cover. Nat Joseph had quickly realised Bert's potential and had signed him to a long-term recording deal before the first album had even been released. He was also keen for Bert to start touring internationally.

'Having done the album for Nat,' says Bert, 'I remember him wanting me to go to Denmark. But I didn't have my passport, having not paid back the fare from Morocco [after being repatriated by the Embassy in 1963], so the

record company paid it for me. I was king over there. I only had to arrive in
the country and I'd be plastered all over the place, all the front pages. Why, I
don't know. They had their own folk singers who sang in Danish – they
tended to put music to poetry by famous national poets. It was all very
straight. How I got involved I've no idea because when I first went there
everyone spoke and sang in Danish. There were very few English singers.
The Danish style of folk clubs – it was more of a booze-up really.'

After that first trip to Denmark Bert would tour the whole of Scandinavia
roughly twice a year. In the seventies and eighties, when Bert's star was on
the wane in Britain, the regularity of work in Northern Europe would serve
him well. Both Alex Campbell and Les Bridger would end up living in
Denmark. But for Bert, explaining his popularity there remains elusive: 'For
some reason I used to know all the generals – all of them – in Denmark. It
was a very exciting time to be living in, the sixties. Not stopping to think
about things – that was what was more exciting about it than anything else.
Even to this day I still know some of the Danish generals. But the scene's
changed: for me worse, for them probably better.'

'I don't know what Andy Matthews wanted in the first place but it soon
arrived,' says Roy Harper. 'It was like a song that writes itself. And pretty
soon he was surrounded by these people who all wanted to play at night and
all roughly in the same style. It was like a synergy. I remember the first day I
went to Cousins. It was all down to Peter Bellamy. I think somebody had
told me he was planning to get his own record label together so I went to see
him. He sat me down and said, "Okay, play me your favourite song." So I
played him "St James Infirmary", plucked straight off a Snooks Eaglin
record, to which he said, "Pretty good – you ought to come down to a place
I know tonight and play some songs there." And that was the Cousins. I
didn't look back – I knew this was the place I ought to be.'

Born in Manchester in 1941, and brought up in Blackpool, Roy already
had a colourful past. This would not be unusual amongst those who would
gravitate to the Cousins. Joining the RAF in order to leave school at fifteen,
he stayed there two years reading poetry incessantly, eventually feigning
madness in order to leave. Between 1959 and 1964, when he finally drifted
into London, Roy had spent time in a mental hospital and in prison and had
busked all over Europe. His first paid gig had been a poetry reading in
Newcastle, but through Dylan the pursuit of words and music became
suddenly more attractive. Once out of prison, he had married a zoologist
called Mocky. Along with Ralph McTell, married to a Norwegian girl,
Nana, and Wizz Jones, whose wife Sandy was an ebullient banjo player,
Roy would be among the very few performers on the Cousins scene to hold

down a marriage, although his would not prove as enduring as the rest. The only other performer of note to maintain a successful marriage was also one of the first people Roy saw performing in London: Alexis Korner.

Around May 1965, Alexis, his wife Bobbie and their family moved to a flat at Queensway. A more or less washed-up pop star by the name of Duffy Power was living nearby in Cleveland Square, in a uniquely elegant rooming house for musicians that had once housed the likes of Gene Vincent and Billy Fury and was now populated by hard-up jazz people. Born Ray Howard in 1942, 'Duffy Power' had been discovered in the fifties by pop svengali Larry Parnes and had been part of the same stable of carefully groomed British rock'n'rollers as Billy Fury, Marty Wilde, Johnny Gentle, Vince Eager and Gerry Temple (nee Keith De Groot). Some were successful, some not: Duffy, like De Groot, was of the latter category, although he had enjoyed numerous singles releases between 1958 and 1964.[52]

Once free of the teen-pop circus of package tours and lightweight material, Duffy would discover and embrace the blues and prove himself to be among the greatest R&B singers, harp players and songwriters of the sixties – unassailably powerful, sensual and in no small way driven by various traumas in his personal life. Duffy's recurring mental problems, essentially paranoia and violent tendencies, would at least produce tangible artistic results in a series of peerless folk-blues-jazz fusion recordings cut during 1965 – 67, though mostly unissued at the time.[53] The chilled-out atmosphere of the Cousins would become a constant source of solace to Duffy through the ups and downs of his professional and personal life during the latter half of the sixties. He would even meet his future wife Val there. But in May 1965, having determined that R&B was the way he was going to go but still unsure about how to make it viable, Duffy got an introduction to that perennial godfather of opportunities, Alexis Korner.

'I knew of Alexis,' says Duffy, 'I'd seen him, I was a great admirer – used to copy him, sat on a high stool, bought a capo. I was just short of tying a strip of cloth round my head! So I went around to Alexis's place and he says, "Here, Duff, we're gonna work together." Duffy and Alexis would work together for ten or twelve months, mostly as a duo around the folk clubs. They would also record an album later that year with bassist Danny Thompson and drummer Terry Cox as the latest version of Alexis's Blues Incorporated.[54] Duffy's introduction to the Cousins was also through Alexis – the pair of them taking American singer Doris Troy there around May/ June, assured of an opportunity to get up and have a blow.

'She'd sung "Maggie's Farm",' says Duffy, 'and I can remember sitting in the cab on the way home saying to her, "I'd like to work on Maggie's Farm," and she said, 'You would!'. It really pissed Alexis off because he really envied innuendo, couldn't get it together himself! I played there with Eric Clapton one night as well. John Mayall played too, I think. We'd been at a party at Alexis' and we all went down there. It was very interesting. A guy came up and said, "Could you turn it down?" I was playing harp, Eric had his electric guitar. "No man, I can't turn it down," he said, "it's just not how it's played." I remember at the party we'd been playing and someone had asked Eric could he play "Fly Me To The Moon" and he'd turned to me and said, "No, we don't do that sort of stuff – do we Duffy?" And I'm going, "Well, I'm not so sure about that . . ."'

'I remember Duffy from hearing his rock'n'roll singles on Radio Luxembourg,' says Ian Anderson, 'and was dead impressed when this bloke showed up down the Cousins. He was just blowing everybody away, coming down and borrowing a guitar – and the monstrous amounts of energy and emotion he would wring from those songs . . . This was the only person I'd ever come across who gave me the impression that this might have been what it was like to have seen one of the old blues guys in their youth, in full flow with the devil in hot pursuit.'

Alexis was already a revered figure on the various club scenes, and respect was due by association to anyone he brought with him. Besides, Duffy Power – with a tendency to go ballistic at the merest hint of derision, and a performer of rare intensity – was not someone to mess with. During the Little Walter tour the previous year he had been so incensed at the quality of playing coming from one unfortunate individual on guitar – not, on that particular show, Bert Jansch – that he had taken to the stage and wrested the instrument from him. Walter, enjoying the opportunity for a break, had simply taken a seat in the front row and watched 'the Duffy Power show'. These were the sort of people the Cousins was made for. It played home to all manner of tortured artists: depressives and eccentrics like Jackson Frank and Roy Harper,[55] a drug-sozzled Icarus like Davy Graham and the dangerous-to-know Duffy Power. All, in their own way, troubled but brilliant.

'Bert was a wild young lad, six years younger than me,' says Gill Cook. 'Our son Richard [Cook] was born in October 1965. He was very supportive but he wasn't taking any responsibility then. Just one of those things. I was very fond of him and he was delighted I was having a kid, and when he started to earn money he'd send some. He's still supportive like that.'

Released on 11 November 1965, Bert's second album *It Don't Bother Me* (TRA 132) featured songs that were very much reflections on his recent life in London – alternately tougher and lazier in feel and more self-assured than the vulnerable ballads and angsty guitar vignettes that characterised his

debut, and even looser in composition. It had been produced by Nat Joseph
and recorded as far back as April, in a real studio – the product of two or
three afternoon sessions and several bottles of wine. Hinted at in the brief
song-by-song sleeve notes, it was full of oblique allusions to the various
comings and goings in Bert's love life: 'To be imprisoned by someone's love
can be as painful as not being loved at all,' as he put it in a commentary on
one composition. Both Jan and Beverley were mentioned by name in the
notes; the situation with Gill was doubtless embedded deeply in the songs
too; as indeed may have been Liz Cruickshank, who had stayed in London
that summer, performing with Bert on occasion, before heading off to work
in Canada for a time.

There was also a brief flirtation with politics on the new record, in 'Anti
Apartheid'. Bert had joined Donovan, Joan Baez, Tom Paxton, Roy Harper
and others at a Vietnam protest march back in May, but in contrast to his
peers, politics would be a rare topic in his work: 'I couldn't be attached to
one party or another,' he says. 'I didn't know enough about politics at the
time, and if I didn't know about something I'd stay away from it.'[56] There
were three instrumentals: 'Tinker's Blues', in honour of Les Bridger's cat,
and 'The Wheel', inspired by the Cousins decor, were both solo, while
'Lucky Thirteen' was a mesmerising Renbourn composition involving both
players. Comprising theme and improvisation on an unresolving chord
pattern, it very clearly pointed in a direction that would be explored more
fully on *Bert And John*, their first and only joint album, the following year.
Bert's original cyclical guitar epic 'Joint Control' had been recorded for *It
Don't Bother Me* but shelved, along with the otherwise unknown 'Just Like
You'.

Two other pieces that did make the cut, 'Been On The Road So Long'
and '900 Miles', acknowledged a debt to Alex Campbell and Derroll Adams
respectively. Indeed, the former 'recycled' instrumental ideas from Bert's
arrangement of 'Blackwater Side', which had itself yet to appear on record.
It is very possible that Nat Joseph had insisted on repeating the first album's
formula of contemporary songs and instrumentals which were Bert's trademark. Recording traditional songs at this stage was, he may have felt, an
absurd idea. As it transpired, the new record was always going to suffer in the
shadow of its predecessor. 'In the short term this LP will sell exceptionally
well, as it has every right to,' wrote Dave Moran, in *Folk Scene*, 'but in the
long run it will add nothing to that first LP.' This was a typically held view,
although floor-singers around the country were ready and waiting for it.

'The first one had permeated out slowly,' remembers Ian Anderson, 'but
by the time the second one came out he was famous enough that people
wanted to grab it immediately. It was like Dylan – after an album or two you

got it the day it came out and you learned the songs or else all the other local singers had learned them first. There was a guy in Bristol called Tim Clutterbuck with an amazing memory for words. I remember one Dylan album came out and he had the whole thing down in forty-eight hours. So in Bristol Tim was the man to beat, and I'm sure there were people like that around the country!'

It may have been felt that this was a more drug-influenced record than before, but while dope-smoking was abundant among the residents and visitors at Somali Road, Bert had ceased to be an active partaker. 'A lot of my writing is down to just imagery,' says Bert. 'That's exactly how Bob Dylan works: it's just putting words together, just the sheer imagery of things flashing through his mind. They don't mean anything at all. I am a songsmith of the same ilk. I dream up imagery that can pose questions, questions that bother me, therefore I put them into a song. But I don't think I've got anything that's of value to other people's way of life or anything. All I hope to do is to give something to people that they can think about.'

'I never saw Bert smoke,' says Roy Harper on the question of marijuana. 'I don't know why he didn't. It might have helped him. To me it's always been a tool for writing.' A year or so later, in an interview for Danish television, Bert was pressed for his own views on drugs. In spite of his personal stance and the tragedy of Buck Polley, Bert was not to be cornered into dogma: 'It depends on the individual,' he said. 'The world's been using drugs ever since it was created. It's up to your own self to determine whether drugs are a good or bad thing. But also it's up to the individual if it helps him to do whatever he wants to do.'[57]

'I'm not a believer in "the drug created the song",' offers Donovan. 'A lot of people say, "Was it all those drugs you took that made you write all those wonderful songs?" and I say, "Yeah, sure – why don't you go out and buy some drugs and write some lovely songs yourself?" Having said that, fair enough, "Strawberry Fields Forever" wasn't written on a cup of tea and a biscuit.'

Nobody was writing about Strawberry Fields at Somali Road, but the scene there was typical of student life in any generation – crazy and fun for a time, perhaps, but not something any sane person can tolerate forever. John Challis, for one, had been a student long enough: 'It was getting a bit decadent to my way of thinking,' he says. 'Most of us had been smoking an awful lot of weed for something like five years without a break, and there was a constant stream of people going through the Young Tradition's place downstairs. I was starting to feel that I needed a change of air. I eventually decided to go back to college and do a postgraduate year which began in January 1966. I moved in with my girlfriend in Ladbroke Grove. Hanging around on someone else's scene doesn't really progress you in getting your own shit together. I'm one of the world's great hangers-out, but there comes a point where you really do have to buckle down and do some work.'[58]

During November, the EFDSS were running a conference of regional folk club federations. Danny Kyle, organiser of the Paisley club, was one of the delegates and being in town was invited to a party at Somali Road: 'It was the first time I'd smoked hash,' said Danny. 'I had my guitar with me – a three-chord merchant, playing my wee Scottish songs, and in the room there was Bert, Davy Graham and all that crowd. They started chopping up this black stuff, cooking it and smoking it, and I had a go of that. Then the guitar work started and I just quietly put my guitar away!' Roy Harper, who lived only a few streets away, was at the same party. It was something of a rare contact, either socially or professionally, between Davy (who had just returned from four months in the Middle East), and Bert and John. They were, at the same time, both his devotees and his rivals: 'Suffice to say I didn't even pick my guitar up,' says Roy. 'Bert put his down after about five minutes and five minutes later so did John. Davy never managed to turn his talent into a brand that people could go out and buy and enjoy, but in those days he was just amazing. He would turn up and play the entirety of Ravel's "Bolero", which is a pretty strange thing to do, but you could tell where each instrument came in – the clarinet, the trombones, the bassoons – all in one guitar.'

In January, Andy Matthews could tentatively announce that Davy Graham had agreed to a Cousins residency on Fridays. But it was not to last. Davy was not one to be pinned down, although every time he did appear there queues down the street are always recalled. In retrospect, though, Davy's moment had passed. Future recordings would be patchy, if occasionally brilliant, but with everyone from the Beatles down discovering India, the novelty value of Davy's easternisms could no longer be relied upon. He was no songwriter, either, and his releases would appear less prolifically than those of either Bert Jansch or John Renbourn, while his presence on the domestic scene would be constantly interrupted by trips abroad. Live recordings from the period testify to moments of brilliance, but by all accounts the drugs were making his performances and behaviour unpredictable.

'If you were a casual listener you were hardly aware of Davy,' remembers Ashley Hutchings. 'Regular club-goers in London obviously knew Davy well but the casual listener would have known Bert Jansch, and Davy hardly at all. Because Bert was the man on the road. That was my impression. As a guy in the audience I was told I should go and listen to Davy; Bert was the one you went to see because you wanted to see him. He was a romantic figure, a figurehead. Insofar as the audiences were concerned, Davy was a shadowy character and Bert was a hero – and that is a very big difference.'

'We only kicked in in 1956,' says Duffy Power, 'into what you could call rock'n'roll, and that includes the folkies. And the first one to pop up who was decent, who was quite bright and inspirational, using world ideas, was Davy Graham. But then along comes another bloke who's better. He may not have had Davy's original fashions, but he had much more of it in the fingers – and that was Bert. And then up comes another one and another one. I think for Davy that must have been a bit of a blow. He was an inspiration of his time. He was inspired, but not a genius. Then again it's maybe a kind of genius once, when it's your moment. There are lots of things like that in life, when there's somebody who for a certain moment will fly, will burst into flame. He was ahead of his time.'

'When he was on this planet, Davy definitely had an aura,' says Ian Anderson. 'He was a legend in front of your eyes. You could hardly believe that you were lucky enough to be in the same room, he was that good, and talking to him offstage he was a lovely, unassuming bloke full of enthusiasms. He liked to cultivate a bit of an image but he was basically all right. John Renbourn was also very approachable and we became friends. But Bert seemed to throw up an aura of "Don't come near me". Even in the back room at the Cousins you wouldn't approach him. It wasn't that he was unfriendly – you just wouldn't go and strike up a conversation with him. It wasn't the done thing. Whether that was something he erected, or we erected in our own heads, I don't know. But I wouldn't say I was unique in that view.'

Bert wound up his Cousins residency on 23 December 1965, handing Thursdays over to Alexis Korner for the following year. No doubt in the spirit of Christmas, that final night was a treat for the regulars and something symbolic for all those on the stage and for the venue itself. Appearing together for one night only, in the heart of Soho, the three kings: Davy Graham, John Renbourn and Bert Jansch.

CHAPTER SEVEN

Pentangling

B y the dawn of 1966, Bert Jansch was unassailably a star of the 'folk' underground. He had never been played on the radio, had never appeared on television and had given only one interview to date, but his reputation was spreading. The name alone was memorable, and out in the provinces thousands of kids were inspired and intrigued.

'The name evoked something,' remembers John Wilson, a young drummer in Belfast who would shortly rise to prominence with the blues–rock trio Taste. 'We read the *Melody Maker* religiously, from the price on the front to the printing information on the back. You'd read his name in the *Melody Maker* so you assumed he must actually be somebody, and that when he walked around London everybody would be nodding and saying, "Wow, there's the great Bert Jansch!" The same with Alexis Korner. It made you feel that if you were in London these were the sort of people you would meet, which was all total rubbish but for a young kid sitting there day-dreaming that's what it was all about. Bert was an inspiration to a lot of musicians in Belfast because he was a lone wolf, the good player out on his own. I must admit, in those days the man's music helped me through all that period of getting away and doing it in the real world. He represented to people like me all that was good about the music business.'

Wilson's testimony is not unique. All over Britain individuals were discovering Bert Jansch. Rab Noakes, a young Scot, later a successful songwriter and producer himself, vividly recalls the moment he made the connection: 'It was the summer of 1965. I was on holiday in London and came across the first album in a shop window display. I remember being entranced by the photograph and intrigued by the name. I went into the store and played the record in a little booth and I can honestly say I'd never heard anything like it. I bought the LP and brought it back to Alloa and spent much time trying to play it all. I had limited success but much of it remained, and remains still, out of reach. Bert became something of a hero, and the first album was played endlessly until the second one appeared. I had no idea then that he came from Scotland and had been part of the Edinburgh scene. That scene was already a bit mythological to people of my age anyway, and we would travel far to catch performers from that era, particularly Owen Hand and Archie Fisher.'

Like so many others, Rab Noakes made his way, in 1966, to London: 'I spent many evenings at folk clubs to listen, learn and get up for floor spots,' he recalls. 'By this time I could play a few Bert numbers. I saw Bert play a couple of times and won't ever forget one night at the Scot's Hoose. I was asked to do a floor spot and had opted for an unaccompanied song from Scotland, "The Merchant's Son", a narrative about the guile of the poor pitted against the naivete of the wealthy. As I was singing I recognised Bert standing over at the bar beside Bruce Dunnet, who ran the club. When I finished the song he wove across the room towards me with a pint in his hand which he gave to me with a compliment. I was dumbstruck and delighted, and really quite surprised to see someone I admired acting in such a down-to-earth manner. It was, though, as I found out later, very typical of his generosity.'

Bert had brought an end to his residencies at Les Cousins and the Scot's Hoose in December 1965, although he would still perform at both venues periodically throughout 1966 – 67. Established as he now was, if Bert did not feel, in a given month, like playing at the Cousins, the Scot's Hoose or even in London at all, he would simply not do so.[1] The new year would see other significant changes for Bert. He would release two more albums, one in full collaboration with John Renbourn, both very different from his previous work. He would only rarely now allow himself to be booked for all-nighters, at any venue. As the year wore on he would become increasingly viable as a concert artist. And at some point in the spring he decided that the scene at Somali Road had become intolerable. Along with John Renbourn, and without Les Bridger, Bert moved into a flat at 23 St Edmund's Terrace, in St John's Wood. There would, at least, be no more interruptions from Donovan's people looking for songs. Indeed, things were beginning to go momentarily awry for Donovan, who spent most of 1966 in litigation with his management and/or in America, preventing the release of any new product for the best part of a year.[2]

Bert had been wise to have remained semi-detached from Stephens and Eden and the 'ducking and diving' side of the music business they represented. Aside from anything else, his personality was not equipped to deal with public recognition on a par with Donovan's. 'Bert was never somebody who was going to be marketed,' says Martin Carthy. 'He was unacceptable. Nobody could get their heads round the way he played guitar and sang, not in a commercial sense. That's not an insult to Bert, that's just a fact.'

There was nevertheless a clamour of expectation surrounding Bert, manifest from his earliest interviews: 'Everybody asks me what my message is. The answer is that I'm not trying to do anything in particular,' he had told the *MM* in August 1965.[3] At the beginning of 1966 his views appeared in print again, in an Oxford University magazine: 'When I record I'm not recording for anyone, just myself,' he told his questioner, Robin Denselow. 'I'm not in the record business for money. I don't sell much but I'm quite happy: I mean, I sold about 1,500 in two or three months, then Donovan brings out an LP and within a week he sells 8,000.' Of more interest to Bert was his new direction: 'I do a lot of work with John now and we dig doing it,' he said. 'Words mean a lot but you've got to have a reason for writing them. You receive more from hearing a sound than you do from working out words, that's why I'm now mainly interested in instrumentals. You should leave words alone until you've something to say.'[4] For the moment, Bert Jansch had nothing more to say.

There You Go, the debut LP from Dorris Henderson and John Renbourn, jointly credited, appeared on Columbia in February 1966. John's solo debut *John Renbourn* appeared on Transatlantic the following month and suffered greatly by comparison. Some of the material was similar, but less polished (the recordings were year-old demo sessions), lacking the character brought by a vocal stylist of Henderson's stature. The two instrumentals with Bert Jansch, 'Noah And Rabbit' and 'Blue Bones', were quite beyond some people: 'They seem to have no hatstand upon which to hang themselves,' declared *Folk Scene*'s reviewer, Dave Moran, adding that 'if John Renbourn is to progress artistically then he must stop being delighted with his own ability'. This was a harsh view but one that perhaps needed to be expressed, not only of Renbourn but of Davy Graham (especially) and Bert Jansch (potentially). All three were now perceived as a quite distinctive by-product of the folk revival and their technical accomplishments were now taken as read. 'They've proved that they can exist as an independent "third stream", influenced by both folk and jazz,' wrote Karl Dallas in *MM*. 'They've now got to produce some really memorable music that stands up on its own account.'

While no folk venue, barring the Scot's Hoose, managed to establish a lasting presence in a Soho dominated by the Cousins, the latter's success influenced existing clubs nearby. The Marquee, the premier R&B venue in London and at that stage owned by Chris Barber, was just around the corner in Wardour Street. Ken Colyer's Studio 51 was another R&B spot, in nearby Great Newport Street. Within a few months of the Cousins opening, both would be running at least one folk/blues night a week – at Colyer's club a Saturday all-nighter. Bert rarely played the Marquee but was regularly featured, as a soloist, at Studio 51.

Bert was also now performing sporadically with John Renbourn. Their London platform was always the Cousins, with John joining Bert almost every week in the last three months of Bert's Thursday residency. The collaboration continued well into 1966 although opportunities were less regular, partly because each artist now commanded, individually, the highest club fees available. As a duo they were in theory unaffordable, but in practice the partnership was too engrossing to let finance get in the way.

The strange fusions of styles and influences that marked *Bert And John*, their inevitable joint recording, paved the way for a more fully realised exploration of ideas in a full group context, though at the time the record did little to assuage those who felt this was all just virtuous noodling by the technically impressive. 'On the whole this is a pleasant, unmemorable record,' concluded Karl Dallas, 'which will be required listening for everyone interested in well-played guitar. But very little of it sticks very long in the mind.'

'It was one of those albums me and John did virtually in an afternoon,' says Bert. 'We did actually put some thought into it but a lot of it was a jam. The album itself is only fourteen minutes long – seven minutes a side – but there's probably twenty-four tracks on it!' Bert's memory is a caricature, but only just: the album is twenty-six minutes long with twelve tracks. Some of the material and arrangements delivered on the promise of 'Lucky Thirteen' (the pair's sharply focused duet on *It Don't Bother Me*), while others fooled around with arpeggios and produced nothing of consequence.

Barring two vocal tracks, a dishevelled crack at Anne Briggs's 'The Time Has Come' and 'Soho', a brooding Jansch original destined to be covered on demos by both Sandy Denny and Nick Drake, the album was instrumental and very much of a style. It brought the modern jazz influence to the fore and displayed on its cover a couple of cool young hipsters smoking thin cigarettes in a darkened room and playing some inscrutable and doubtless eminintly fashionable board game (its name was Go). The iconography of sleeve design was desperately important in those days, a broken vase from which entire civilisations could be built in the minds of the followers of such cult celebrities.

Having found the 'real studio' work for *It Don't Bother Me* a pressurised experience, *Bert And John* had been recorded by Bill Leader in the front room at St Edmunds Terrace. It was one of three albums involving its namesakes which Leader recorded in the summer of 1966. Among the others was Renbourn's second album, *Another Monday*, recorded in Leader's Camden flat – infinitely better than his debut and, as with *Bert And John*, tentatively pushing forward with new ideas. The rudimentary blues covers were still in evidence, with vocal colouring from Jacqui McShee, but

Renbourn's interest in Early Music had now risen to the surface with the beautifully crafted Elizabethan pastiche 'Ladye Nothing's Toye Puff' and the inspired combination of guitar and oboe in 'One For William', a remarkably original trek along the borders of jazz and baroque.

The third album in this restlessly inventive trilogy was the most astonishing of all. Credited to Bert Jansch, though featuring Renbourn prominently on four of its eight tracks, it too had been recorded at Leader's place and its title was *Jack Orion*. The ideas had been brewing in Bert's mind and fermenting in his playing style for the previous year or more, and this was consequently the most focused, taut and energized product of the trilogy. Its impact was immense. Bert had at last committed to record the first fruits of his explorations with traditional music, relying exclusively on DADGAD or 'dropped D' tunings, that had begun with Anne Briggs before even his first album had been released.

'*Jack Orion* really turned people upside down,' says Martin Carthy. '*Bert And John* not so much. At the time, *Jack Orion* was the one where people just sat back and thought, "What *is* he trying to do?" It was just so outrageous and different, so unlike anything else that anybody else had ever played – and the title track was nine minutes long! For us twenty- to twenty-five year-olds ballads were still boring things which you had to get down to as few verses as possible. We didn't actually understand this idea that it's not a question of how long a ballad is, it's the fact that it does so much in such a short space of time: so it's thirty verses and ten minutes long – that's two and a half hours in a film. And if you give it just as much concentration as you give a film you're going to be just as excited.'

'Jack Orion' itself was the vestige of a traditional melody, reconstructed by Bert Lloyd as a narrative on the sexually charged adventures of a demonic fiddler. Bert Jansch's version succeeded more through the intensity of performance than through any great accuracy in execution: this was a relentlessly dark, dense assault upon the hallowed tradition. Other tracks, however 'Trad Arr.' in their credits, were vehicles for the scattergun imagination behind Bert's instrumental work. His interpretation of 'The Gardener', a song learned from Owen Hand, was wildly impressionistic – a wordless vocal scatting some rumour of the song's melody atop a cyclical, string-snapping riff which reappearred in the arrangements of Ewan MacColl's 'The First Time Ever I Saw Your Face' (sensitively performed, and a moment of light in the modal darkness) and the immortal 'Blackwater Side'.

That song at least, by far the most crafted piece on the record, had already been played around the clubs. Al Stewart had been following Bert around, keenly observing this revolutionary new playing style and determined to master it. A few weeks before *Jack Orion* appeared, Al had booked a studio and session players to make his own record debut. Jimmy Page, an established sessioneer, turned up to play guitar and during a tea-break Al played him what he believed to be Bert's accompaniment for 'Blackwater Side'. It was possibly Page's first acquaintance with the DADGAD tuning, and the seeds were sown of what would later become a distinctively folky, eastern-influenced but very British element in mainstream seventies rock that would have wide-ranging reverberations in that world.

In his subsequent capacity as a member of Led Zeppelin, the biggest rock group of the seventies, Page would be enthusing wildly on the topic of Jansch for years to come: 'A real dream-weaver,' he said. 'At one period I was absolutely obsessed by Bert Jansch. His first album had a great effect on me. It was so far ahead of what anyone else was doing. That was what got me into playing acoustic. I watched him playing once at a folk club and it was like seeing a classical guitarist. All the inversions he was playing were unrecognisable. He was the innovator of the time.'[5]

'I don't recall being shocked,' says Nat Joseph, on checking out Bert's new sound. 'I was never shocked when I heard anything other than when it was very bad. Bringing in the traditional material was something that seemed to me extremely interesting because everybody had thought of Bert as a kind of Dylan-esque character. He was going back to the roots and I couldn't see why not.'

'The treatments may not be trad but they're fantastic,' agreed the reviewer for *Sing*. 'At first sight the idea is horrifying,' cautioned Karl Dallas in *MM*, 'a bluesy guitarist who has hitherto concentrated on contemporary subjects singing the big old ballads of the true traditionalist. In fact, Jansch's interpretations illuminate the songs from a completely new angle. As sung by him, the brutal world that created the old ballads doesn't seem so very far off from the world of the "Needle Of Death".' And if anyone needed reminding, Transatlantic were repromoting that one as lead track on an EP. *Jack Orion*, *Bert and John* and the *Needle Of Death* EP were released simultaneously in early August 1966, the last comprising five tracks distilled from Bert's first two albums for the delectation of impecunious students, the unwaged and the casual buyer.

From mid-1965 the opportunities for folk music on television had exploded, and a little earlier in the year Bert had sneaked on for the first time to perform 'Needle Of Death' on a topical religious show called *Hallelujah!*[6] A twenty-minute Sunday night broadcast for the Birmingham-based ABC, the show was screened in all ITV regions except London. Its presenter was Gill Cook's neighbour Sydney Carter, with Martin Carthy and Nadia Cattouse as resident performers: 'It was the weekly God slot,' says Carthy, 'and basically we would take a subject and do songs on that subject.

Mainly it was confined to British traditional stuff, but we also did American stuff and bits of Kurt Weill and Bertolt Brecht. The week Bert was on the subject was drugs. It was close on being controversial.' Being nervous, Bert recalls nothing of the experience: 'I don't know how it went down,' he says, 'but they seemed to think it was in keeping.'

Around the same time as Bert and John's flurry of recordings were being made, in June 1966, Indian sitar virtuoso Ravi Shankar was in Britain for a Festival Hall concert, a groove-in on BBC Television's *A Whole Scene Going* and a series of recitals at provincial folk clubs, pubs and public libraries. On 12 June his entourage arrived at Bardswell Social Club, a tin hut in Brentwood, Essex, where the support act was Bert & John.

'We weren't allowed to smoke,' says Bert, 'which I found a bit weird because they were burning all this incense. I'm not quite sure how we got through the night without a cigarette. Probably disappeared outside every now and again. But it was great fun. After the gig they had to get back to London so we all travelled together in the train. There was a whole load of them, all with long black coats and sitars and the like. We were on the platform of this station and for some reason they were fascinated with this speaking weighing machine and kept jumping on and off it. When we got to Liverpool Street at the other end they ordered this taxi, all seven of them, and started to get in one side and out the other. The taxi driver didn't know what to make of it. They were all just a big bunch of kids!'

From the summer of 1966 onwards, plans were afoot in the camps of Bruce Dunnet and Nat Joseph to establish Bert as a concert hall artist. The two men had little in common, but Bruce admired Nat's integrity: 'He was only interested in commercialisation,' says Bruce, 'making money out of the records, and to that extent he was honest. He never pretended to be a folksong enthusiast although he enjoyed some of it and he certainly came to the clubs on occasions.' There was no great strategy at work, rather two individuals who realised that Bert's audience was growing and that in terms of the club scene, one could only play more venues, not bigger and better venues. The obvious answer was concerts and festivals.

The folk festival in Britain had become a serious proposition in 1965 with the first Keele and Cambridge events, although it was still a fragile concept – potentially large, organisationally complex events run by amateurs. The first Beaulieu World Folk Festival on August 6 1966 aspired to be Britain's Newport: Phil Ochs, Tom Paxton, Bert Jansch, John Renbourn and Julie Felix were to share an open-air platform with the Spinners, the Dubliners, the Watersons, Ian Campbell's group and others. Poor organisation, torrential rain and a number of cancellations, including Bert, in hospital with

what was reported as 'suspected rheumatic fever', did not assist the potentially momentous occasion. It was nevertheless enjoyed by the 3500 who
turned up, and highlights were broadcast on BBC television and radio.

Two months earlier Bert had also failed to appear at the Newport Folk
Festival itself. Nat Joseph had flown to the States to negotiate the appearance
and a licensing deal with Vanguard for Bert's recordings. No explanation
was given for the Newport deal falling through, but the first of three Jansch
albums specially compiled for the US market[7] soon appeared on Vanguard.
Entitled *Lucky Thirteen*, it was a twelve-track distillation of his first two
albums. Bert's reputation in the States had already been growing on the basis
of import albums and namedrops from Donovan and others. The scene was
now set for his first North American tour, and it was reported in *MM* to be
'99.9 per cent certain' that Bert and John would be touring clubs and
colleges on the East Coast and in Canada from 16 October to 30 November.

'It'll be down to audiences of thousands if I do it,' says Jansch, speaking
generally to Karl Dallas in July 1966 on what were then only rumours of an
American tour. 'It rather frightens me. To do a tour you've really got to go
through the mill.'[8] Bert was taking it easier after the insane pace of the
previous year: 'I was doing five nights a week but that's too much. It stops
me from working on new songs. Now it's all down to work, shopping,
decorating the flat, all sorts of wild things like that.' Then, with no real
explanation, the American tour was cancelled. 'The arrangements didn't suit
me,' was all Bert said at the time, 'and anyway I didn't figure they'd let me in
now that I've signed a petition about Vietnam.'[9]

By the summer of 1966, Bert was the veteran of at least seven concerts,
mostly organised by Bruce Dunnet and all of them multi-artist affairs with
his name rising gradually up the billing. He had recently endorsed the
'Folksingers Committee For Peace In Vietnam', another of Dunnet's many
guises. On 1 August 1966, on a bill topped by the Dubliners, Bert Jansch
took the stage directly after Ewan MacColl & Peggy Seeger in the
committee's first 'Peace In Vietnam' concert at London's Unity Theatre.
If nothing else, the concert brought under one roof all sections of the folk
community and introduced, in Karl Dallas's words, 'an interesting new girl
singer called Sandy Denny'. Later that month, with the Beatles' *Revolver*
topping the mainstream UK album chart, *Bert And John* and *Jack Orion* were
at Nos 1 and 2 in the *Melody Maker* folk chart, compiled from sales at the
major specialist stores. The time was now right for Bert to try the concert
halls on his own.

'I will never forgive him,' says Bruce Dunnet. 'We formed a company,
Jansch Enterprises Limited, because it was beginning to look as though he

was going to make a lot of money. My wife, who is not a Communist, agreed that she would run the financial side of the business for Bert to protect him from rapacious fuckers, that was my social attitude. My wife registered the company with £100. She had one share, Bert had one share, I had no shares. I wasn't a money-grubber. We formed a company, he agreed, then he disappeared. I could have sued him, but what's the point?' The full story of Bert's fall-out with Bruce Dunnet, his manager in all but name, may never be known. Although the company registration document of Jansch Enterprises Ltd. (signed by Jansch) survives, it is undated. The timescale of the situation is probably October 1966 to March 1967, the backdrop Bert's remarkably successful transition from clubs to concerts and the consequent attention of bigger fish in the music management business. Complicating matters further, just as his solo stature had risen to unprecedented heights, Bert was forming a band.

The facts of Bert's watershed concerts are simple: performing at the 860-seater St Pancras Town Hall on 15 October (a Bruce Dunnet promotion) and two weeks later at the 350-seater Jeanetta Cochrane Theatre (a Nat Joseph promotion), he not only made history as the first British soloist of the folk revival to attempt a solo concert, but sold out both venues. At the end of November he topped the bill on a benefit concert prompted by the Aberfan mining disaster, when a slagheap engulfed a Welsh primary school, and in December he headlined another 'Peace In Vietnam' concert. In the first three months of 1967 there were at least seven more concerts including an unprecedented tour, organised by Dunnet, of four major venues: Birmingham Town Hall, Glasgow Concert Hall, Manchester Free Trade Hall and Newcastle City Hall.

Described briefly in the *Melody Maker* as a 'triumphal progress', a few flyers, a couple of photographs from Newcastle, a press release describing Bert as 'a master of the casual presentation so loved by folk fans' and a set list from Birmingham are all that remain of this ground-breaking achievement. Dutifully recorded by a fan, Richard Lewis, the set list provides a unique insight into Bert's repertoire of the period. Never before had he had to assemble such a large body of work for a guaranteed listening, paying audience. Whatever they expected, Bert had a wealth of new material to be heard. In a thirty-two-song performance, in two hour-long sets, Bert featured only ten songs which had thus far appeared on his records. There were a handful of unnamed instrumentals and blues covers dating back to his Edinburgh days, and up to five notated titles which may indeed be otherwise unknown Jansch originals.[10] But Bert left the material that can be identified as his work-in-progress for the second set: seven songs that would shortly be recorded for his next LP, *Nicola*.[11]

Bruce Dunnet remains justly proud of the tour. Bert had become a national force by word-of-mouth alone: 'He got over a thousand people at Manchester,' says Bruce. 'Bert Jansch, solo and un-fucking-known. Now, pardon me, but who created that audience? And this is what down-hearted me when he said he'd got a manager. It was my time, my effort, my money that went into promoting him. Booking those halls was a commitment financially, and he turned his back on me.'

The 'manager' that Dunnet refers to was Gerry Bron, a member of the family that owned Bron Orchestral Music Services in Oxford Street. Here, memories become irreconcilable and the evidence confusing. To Bert's mind, he had only ever been courted by Gerry Bron: 'I remember going up there to the Bron agency and chatting to Gerry and his wife Gillian but beyond that it never got anywhere. No contracts were ever signed.' From 3 December 1966, however, adverts began appearing in the *MM* declaring Gerry Bron to have 'Exclusive Representation' of Bert Jansch. A press release authored by Bruce Dunnet for the Birmingham concert on 18 January 1967 refers to Bron as Bert's current manager. Bruce himself cannot explain this, recalling his association with Bert ending dramatically on the very day he was told of the supposedly formalised relationship with Bron: 'They'd had this discussion, and Bert had agreed that Gerry Bron should be his manager. Bert Jansch came to my flat and asked would I be his concert promoter because now he had a manager. He had never wanted a manager before. And I said, "Bert, you can go out the door or out the window. I don't want to talk to you any more." And that was the last time I saw him.'

Bert can only recall the managerial machinations of 1967 in a generalised blur, involving not only Dunnet and Bron but also Jo Lustig, a sharp-talking New Yorker who had previously wrested Julie Felix from Dunnet's management and was to do so again with Bert. It seems clear, however, that this arrangement was only confirmed in the early weeks of 1968. To Bert's recollection, Bron was even then still an option. As to the confrontation with Dunnet, he simply cannot recall it.

'I don't think I would simply up and leave anybody like that,' he says. 'I don't know who approached who with Gerry Bron, but Gerry wasn't interested in the band. That was the choice: to go with Gerry solo or go with the band. I was in a bit of a dilemma about the whole thing. One thing I would say about Bruce, though: he didn't lose any money through me. I did the concerts and filled them up with people. We didn't have a contract that bound me to him. If I wanted to change direction I could, and I did because he wasn't that interested in the Pentangle which was my main concern at the time. The only point which Bruce could possibly feel aggrieved about is that I went with the band and eventually signed with Jo Lustig. I certainly didn't

turn my back on him, because he was still running the Horseshoe for a
period. This company certificate – I don't remember anything about it. He
probably turned up one day and said, "Here, sign this." I didn't know the
mechanics or structure of how everything was placed in the music business
then – like managers, record companies. To me they were all just one thing.
As far as I could see, Bruce was helping. I asked him to run this club at the
Horseshoe and he did. He was never out of pocket because of me, that's for
sure.'

In addition to the solo concert tour Bruce had set up a Sunday night club,
designed as a regular London platform for Bert Jansch, at the Horseshoe
Hotel, opposite Tottenham Court Road tube station. The hotel's function
room was a plush, 400-seater venue which had only rarely been used for
folksong events. Bruce believes the journalist Robin Denselow brought
Gerry Bron to the Horseshoe, but Denselow recalls nothing of the matter. In
any event, the 'Exclusive Representation' ads had been appearing for some
weeks before the club opened. Dunnet has perhaps a tendency to believe in
conspiracies, but all that can be said for certain is that around March 1967 his
professional association with Bert Jansch came to an end. By the time they
parted company, and due at least partly to Dunnet's promotional work, Bert
had increased his profile and commercial standing substantially and was in
possession of a thriving Sunday night club in the centre of London. He was
also in possession, against the better judgement of Gerry Bron, Nat Joseph
and any number of sceptical fans, of a five-piece band.

Back in March 1966, Dorris Henderson had returned to the States for a
while. Possibly John would have asked Dorris to help out on *Another Monday*
had she been around, but instead he had asked Jacqui McShee. Jacqui had
been active on the folk scene since 1960. Performing initially at the Olive
Tree in Croydon, and later on advertised dates and floor spots in the London
clubs, Jacqui had been part of a duo with guitarist Chris Ayliffe. 'Chris
worked in a music shop in Balham, and he knew Bert and John,' says Jacqui.
'It took me years to realise it but he introduced me to Bert and then John. I
think he did it on purpose.'[12] By the end of 1965, Jacqui was running a club
at the Red Lion in Sutton with her sister Pam: Bert and John were both
booked, for a top-whack £8 each, and the friendship established.

After recording *Another Monday*, John wondered if Jacqui might fancy
doing some gigs together. 'At that time he and Bert were at St Edmund's
Terrace,' she recalls. 'It was a great flat, always lots of people there. I started
going there quite a lot, working on stuff with John. He and Bert were
playing together anyway, and they decided they wanted to start up a club
and we would play there every week and have other people along to

play.'[13]   John & Jacqui's first advertised gig as a duo was at the Cousins in
August 1966. They performed together thereafter, although Jacqui continued to run the club in Sutton and hang on to her day job. Renbourn,
similarly, was still performing as a duo with Bert and as a soloist and was also
following Bert as a solo concert artist. With the popularity of both players
now confirmed as beyond the capacities of any folk club, it was inevitable
that the musical explorations begun on *Bert And John*, *Jack Orion* and *Another
Monday* would be taken further. Jazz, blues, traditional songs, original
material, medieval influences, unusual time signatures and potentially three
vocalists – all the ingredients necessary to create, in theory, the front line of a
truly unique and outstanding group. But where could they find a rhythm
section? The answer was: 'straight out of somebody else's band'. And that
somebody was Duffy Power.

On 5 November 1966 the Marquee played host to the first and last public
appearance of Duffy Power's Nucleus. The band comprised Duffy on vocals
and harmonica, John McLaughlin on electric guitar, Danny Thompson on
string bass and Terry Cox on drums. Thompson and Cox had worked with
numerous names on the London jazz scene but had most recently been part
of Alexis Korner's circle, working with him as a trio on *Five O'Clock Club*
and in his residency at the Cousins. But they had also been involved in an
extraordinary series of demo recordings with Duffy Power and his songwriting partner John McLaughlin. A guitar prodigy from Yorkshire,
McLaughlin had known Duffy since 1963 when both were doing package
tours of Gaumont cinemas – Duffy as pop star and McLaughlin as sideman to
Jet Harris & Tony Meehan. For all his virtuosity, McLaughlin admired
Duffy's raw talent and by 1966 they went back a fair way. 'I took him down
the Cousins once,' says Duffy. 'One guy said we sounded like Junior Wells
and Buddy Guy! It was just me and him. But he didn't want to know about
that scene.'

Only four of the remarkable R&B/jazz fusion recordings that Duffy and
McLaughlin recorded, with various rhythm players including Thompson and
Cox, surfaced at the time: a Duffy's Nucleus single in Britain and an EP in
France. It was a pioneering sound on fragile foundations: 'Duffy's Nucleus
wound up because I was totally freaked out and paranoid,' says Duffy. 'Exposed
to the possibility of fame at an early age, I became disconnected from reality. I
was very insecure, and drug-taking didn't help.[14] I wasn't looking for the gigs,
and when I turned round and had a chance to book some gigs and start
something they were all gone. I brought them together, but they were running
around picking up jazz gigs for themselves. It was as simple as that.'

During the period of his illness, Duffy found solace in the unconditional
camaraderie of the Cousins. 'Duffy should have been one of the greatest

heroes this country has had in the blues game,' said Thompson years later. 'A lot of people, phenomenal musicians, don't get the credit they deserve.'[15] McLaughlin and Thompson recruited sax/flute/clarinet player Tony Roberts and simply carried on as the Danny Thompson Trio, specialising in modern jazz standards and holding together, in tandem with its members' other projects, well into 1968.[16]. Danny, meanwhile, had been asked along to the Horseshoe by John Renbourn, whom he knew from working on TV shows together and from the Cousins scene. He jammed a few tunes with Bert, John and Jacqui, enjoyed himself and came along the next week with his favourite rhythm partner, Terry Cox. And now they were five.

Beyond the conclusion of five individuals 'drifting together', the beginnings of the group that would come to call itself the Pentangle are obscure. Rehearsals took place at the end of 1966 with a bass player and drummer whose names are not recalled, while Renbourn believes that drummer John Marshall played some of the early Horseshoe gigs before moving on to Soft Machine. But by the Horseshoe's fifth week, 5 March 1967, press ads that had initially named only Bert, John and Jacqui were now including Danny and Terry. Bruce Dunnet, still on the scene, was advertising the Sunday sessions in *Melody Maker*, the *Morning Star*, *Tribune* and the *Observer*.

John Renbourn was the visionary behind the new band: 'I guess I was the catalyst in getting all these people together,' he concedes. 'But there wasn't one mind dictating. It was Bert's idea to get the band to play in a regular place, to knock it into shape.' There was very quickly a shared feeling of excitement about what their union could achieve. 'It was very much John's thing,' says Wizz Jones, a regular guest at the Horseshoe. 'If you spoke to Bert about it he'd always shrug it off and say, "Oh, I'm only in it for the beer." But in fact he was equally excited about the whole thing.' No one had anything to prove and nothing was in the balance. This was purely a Sunday night get-together: if the group failed or fell apart, everyone had their 'day job' to go back to and nobody could possibly hold the experiment against them. Which was just as well, as the first night of the club had been a disaster.

'I went there with my wife,' says Pete Frame. 'I thought it was a bloody shambles. There was absolutely no cohesion between any of the instruments or any of the voices and they obviously had no idea how to play electric guitars. The drums were (a) too loud and (b) not in sympathy with the music at all. Bruce Dunnet was there, and whatever gig you went to where he was the promoter he always put a downer on the atmosphere by being officious. This time he was making a scene with some poor innocent guy who happened to be sitting a seat reserved for John Renbourn's wife. He was always complaining about something.'

Before long, however, the magic that was to create a wholly new and intoxicating sound, and which would eventually provide the group with its ticket to critical and commercial success, clicked into place: 'We started off with traditional songs that John or I knew, Bert's songs, just anything,' says Jacqui. 'We would play or sing something, and if it was liked we'd decide to do it. There was no big deal about it – it was basically music we all liked and nobody was told how or what to play. Those Sunday nights at the Horseshoe were actually more like rehearsals Sometimes we'd rehearse a song in the afternoon and not have it quite ready but do it anyway, just to see how it would work out.'[17]

Danny had considerable recording, performing and broadcasting experience with an array of blues, jazz and folk people. He had played on Davy Graham's *Folk, Blues & Beyond*, and the Horseshoe group was effectively building on that kind of fusion. 'We'd play these folk tunes,' says Danny. 'I'd always add my improvised bits and I'd say to Bert, "Instead of playing the regular pattern why don't you repeat this little section while John does a solo?" That's how those improvised bits came in, which was pretty new. That became the Pentangle sound. Then we'd have extended sections of solos and whoever was soloing would give a little lick that we all knew and that would be the cue for everyone to come back in. It worked really well. I'm amazed that [later on] we used to do three hours at the Albert Hall, sold out a month before-hand – every gig was the Horseshoe really.'[18]

Bert and John's domestic arrangements had developed in tandem with their new group and club. In November 1966 John had married his long-term girlfriend Judy Hill, whom he had met at Kingston Art School. Judy had a friend called Judy Nicola Cross (for clarity, referred to here as Nicola) who had attended the same college: 'John and Bert were both living at St Edmund's Terrace and then John moved Judy in,' says Nicola, 'and I met Bert through them. The first time I realised that Bert was interested in me was at John and Judy's wedding, at the party after, where I was actually with a long-term boyfriend. Bert wasn't at all outgoing but when he made a play for a woman he did it very nicely and it was very attractive. I fell deeply in love – and dumped my long-term boyfriend rather hastily!'

Nicola's relationship with Bert was to last until Christmas 1967: 'The first six months of our relationship I was in heaven,' she says. 'The second six months it wasn't so good. I seem to remember we broke up in the middle and then got back together. I pursued him and that was probably my mistake.' The union was finite, but Nicola and Bert were close during a significant period in his career. Nicola gave up her commitments as an art teacher at two girls' schools outside London and took a job in the capital,

moving in at St Edmund's Terrace. On occasion she would travel with Bert
to his gigs in the regions. The surviving documentation from a show at
Bedworth in the Midlands in February 1967 indicates Bert's relative worth
at the time: he received £40, the once indomitable Alex Campbell £25 and
everyone else between £5 and £15.

From Nicola's recollections, this was a period when Bert was working
continuously on his music. He was very much open to widening his
horizons, gleaning anything of value from the pop charts and taking Nicola
along to see Pink Floyd at one of their earliest gigs. The tools of Bert's trade
were expanding too: having owned a John Bailey acoustic for a few months
(his first personally owned guitar since 1960), Bert had recently acquired an
experimental Bailey electric, for use with the band, and a twelve-string
acoustic. He was also the co-owner, with John Renbourn, of a sitar. 'Alexis
Korner phoned up one day,' says Renbourn, 'and said, "Would you boys
like to buy a sitar?" And we said yes, we would. "Well, the man's probably
outside the door now," he says. This guy knocks on the door with peroxide
hair and black sunglasses, with a sitar not even in a case: "There you are.
Lovely, isn't it? Ten quid." And suddenly we had a sitar!' Bert, incidentally,
recalls the price being somewhat higher at £30.

Photographs taken by Val Wilmer of Bert 'playing' the new toy appeared
in the music papers during 1967, but only John would have the courage to use
it on recordings. Bert was having enough to do with his battery of guitars: 'If
he was in the flat, he was playing the guitar,' says Nicola. 'I remember some
girl at a gig saying to me, "Oh, you're so lucky to be able to listen to him
playing all the time." And I said, "Well, he doesn't sit around playing 'Needle
Of Death' all day, you know!" He always played beautifully, but it was always
just something in the background. I never heard him say, "Listen, I've just
written a song", although he did sit with paper and pen and write songs. Anne
Briggs would come around occasionally. They both tried to teach me how to
play guitar and got very frustrated when I couldn't!'

Bert, Nicola and the newly wed Renbourns spent some time as a quartet
at 23 St Edmund's Terrace 'until Bert got John and Judy to move out
because Judy was pregnant', says Nicola. The Renbourns moved to
Camden. By April 1967 Bert was recording his next album. Released in
July, its name was *Nicola*: 'I should have felt terribly honoured,' says Nicola,
'but it's different when you're in the middle of these things. I was a bit blasé.
I suppose it felt like a natural progression.'[19]

The album was recorded over several studio sessions with Nat Joseph as
producer and David Palmer as musical arranger, and its concept – folk singer
meets orchestra – was of the moment: both Judy Collins and Al Stewart had
just released similar works and to great acclaim. 'I think it was his least

successful album,' says Nat, 'but you have to try. You can't just go on making the same album. It got a lot of knocking at the time, but it was an interesting experiment. We had a comparatively limited number of artists in the earlier days, and I always felt that they shouldn't stand still. I always tried to push them to do something different and tried to introduce them to new talents coming up in other areas, like David Palmer.'

David Palmer, a recent graduate of the Royal Academy of Music, would go on to become a member of Jethro Tull in the seventies. *Nicola* was his first commission and he took the bull by the horns. Ultimately, five of the album's tracks saw Bert fronting a fifteen-piece orchestra and coming out of the experience with something at least tolerably accomplished: 'These were live sessions,' says Bert. 'It wasn't as if they put the orchestra on later. But it was wrong of them to do it with me, because I'd do anything at the time, just out of interest.'

Bert's romantic streak is to the fore on *Nicola* and while it remains unsatisfying as a unified album, it has its moments. The instrumental title track was a stylish pseudo-baroque marriage of woodwind, cello and guitar, wearing the influence of John Renbourn boldly on its sleeve: 'I haven't got the ability to quite comprehend what John is on about,' said Bert, a few years later, 'because I've always been so far behind him musically. But I think he's learned a lot about actually living from me whereas I've learned a lot of interesting things from John which I hadn't been interested in before.'[20]

At one stage Bert had felt that the eventual *Nicola* should be a blues-oriented album. 'Come Back Baby' and 'Weeping Willow', powerful solo performances originally learned from Len Partridge, were the survivors of this notion and were the first 'traditional' blues songs Bert had committed to vinyl. The brooding 'Go Your Way My Love', retrieved from the Jansch/Briggs collaborations, was similarly arresting. On the other end of the scale 'Rabbit Run' was a delightfully impressionistic piece, inspired by *The Wind In The Willows*,[21] which cleverly utilised, for pace and atmosphere, the double-tracking of Bert's vocals. Alongside the use of electric and twelve-string guitars, double-tracked voice was another Bert Jansch first and last on *Nicola*.

The Palmer/Jansch collaboration yielded one real triumph: 'Woe Is Love, My Dear'. A masterpiece of pathos and execution, Palmer's arrangement of Bert's paean to unrequited love was lavish but wholly sympathetic to the tenderness of Bert's sentiments. Recorded a month after the release of the Beatles' 'Penny Lane', the piccolo trumpet solo can hardly be coincidental. Prompted on the question of singles by *Beat Instrumental* in December 1966, Bert had revealed himself to be sympathetic to the principle but, given

Transatlantic's promotional ability in this area, believed it to be a waste of time.

'I have to say we were pretty bloody useless at promoting singles,' says Nat Joseph. 'But I always thought "Woe Is Love" was a potentially major song. I remember saying to everybody, "That's a hit single." The principal problem was the title.' Hardly an opportune flagship for the 'Summer of Love', 'Woe Is Love, My Dear' had nevertheless the same inscrutable poignancy as Procul Harem's 'A Whiter Shade Of Pale' (a UK chart-topper in May 1967) and was announced in some music papers as a forthcoming single. Inexplicably, the single that finally appeared coupled 'Life Depends On Love' with 'A Little Sweet Sunshine', two further Palmer/Jansch concoctions that diluted the essence of Jansch while lacking, as compensation, the full-on swagger of a successful pop singer. The record did become DJ 'Baby' Bob Stewart's 'single of the week' on the influential Radio Luxembourg, but the public stayed home in droves. 'Rather than jumping direct from solo folk artist to pop star with lush backing,' concluded Karl Dallas in his *MM* review, 'it might have been more advisable to have stopped at the transitory stage of the Pentangle.' In retrospect, he was right.

The group's name had come from John, inspired by the Arthurian tale of *Sir Gawain And The Green Knight*. The 'pentangle' was the sign on the inside of King Arthur's shield: 'So we decided that that would be a good name,' says John, 'because it was valuable to protect us from evil as much as anything else! Of course, when we went to play in America later on we hit up against the California culture which was very much into tarot cards and the occult and all things esoteric, and almost by coincidence our stuff slotted right in with that.'

The first concert appearance of the Pentangle, and the first appearance of the name, had been at the Festival Hall on 27 May 1967. The rest of the bill had featured Ottilie Patterson, with Chris Barber's band, and 'Spider' John Koerner. But it was essentially the Pentangle's show, and it was sold out. A surviving set list from a concert at Birmingham Town Hall three weeks later – comprising an eight-song John & Jacqui set, a five-song Bert set and an eight-song group set – indicates that the group were still in the process of defining their repertoire. Material from the solo sets would eventually settle into the group's repertoire while, conversely, the group were still dabbling in arrangements of material from Bert and John's solo repertoires, with a bluesy emphasis. The instrumentals 'Waltz' and 'Bells' were the only group originals at this stage.

As the Pentangle were becoming a formalised unit, so the Horseshoe club, a 400-seater venue many times plusher than the average folk cellar, was

gaining the ring of permanency. From June the Pentangle would invite their
friends each week as guest performers: the likes of Wizz Jones, Anne Briggs,
Ralph McTell, Alexis Korner, Davy Graham and Clive Palmer.

'During late Sunday afternoons,' says Kieran Bracken, a club regular, 'the
band would set up, and could later be found partaking of their Sunday tea
across the road in the Wimpy Bar until about 6.45. In those days pubs were
strictly closed between two and seven on Sundays. They would then make
their way back to the Horseshoe and ring the doorbell for admission. Bruce
Dunnet had membership cards printed, and memberships were sold for ten
shillings. At one point he even took to selling photos of Bert! He also kept
the evening running to schedule which gave it all a very professional feel.
The audience covered a broad spectrum – students like myself, bohemians,
young couples and a few older "professional" types. Entry was five shillings
[25p] for members, seven and sixpence [38p] for others. Usually this left me
nothing for beer. Indeed, many sat through the evening without consuming
much at all, band members excepted!

'The music started at 7.30 prompt. The hotel closed sharp at 10.30, so
there was no time to waste. After some rapid infusion of refreshment in the
bar John would always start off the night, usually joined by Jacqui. John's
cigarette-smoking ability was so fascinating as to be of almost equal interest
to the music. This is the only man I have ever seen who could light up
before the start of a piece and play it from beginning to end while smoking a
cigarette down to the butt without removing it from his mouth. Bert would
take the floor at eight and play a solo half-hour. The audiences of the day
were very tolerant of the effects of alcohol on performers. Frequently Bert
would appear to be well gone, unable to focus on the proceedings, and yet
his charisma alone seemed to carry him through. In retrospect, I suspect the
guy was nervous as hell. Looking back now, I can recall a sort of
determination on Bert's part to make the whole thing work.

'After Bert there would be a short break, a long queue at the bar and then
the floor-spot, maybe Sandy Denny, Clive Palmer or Les Bridger. But time
was short and Pentangle really had to be on by 9.30 to give the audience full
measure. My last train home was 11 p.m. If the band was on form and
overshot the 10.30 closing time there was a real possibility of an uncomfortable night on a station bench. This did happen to me a few times. To this
day I still feel it was worth it.'

One Sunday in July, Tony Wilson went along to investigate the phenomenon for *MM*: 'It's some months now since the Pentangle made their debut at
the Horseshoe Hotel,' he wrote. 'Then they were ragged, uninspired and
generally lacking in confidence – now that has all changed. They have
become a much tighter unit. Musically the group has widened its horizons

and is performing folk songs like "She Moved Through The Fair"[22] and "Let No Man Steal Your Thyme". They appear to be cutting down on the blues stuff, which is an improvement as in the past they were top heavy with blues songs and this created monotony. The real test, however, will be when the group moves out of the sympathetic environment of the Horseshoe and they have to face a cold, un-blues un-folk oriented audience.'

On 13 August the group had to do just that, appearing as 'The Pentangle with BERT JANSCH' alongside Jeff Beck, P. P. Arnold, John Mayall, Fleetwood Mac and Cream at the seventh National Jazz & Blues Festival at Windsor. 'There was a guy in the audience who had the biggest teeth I've ever seen,' says Jacqui, 'and he just stood up and pointed at us and laughed and laughed and laughed! It was very disconcerting. He'd obviously never heard anything like us and thought it was funny. We shouldn't have been sandwiched between all those people. We were definitely on the wrong bill.'

'It was nearly the end of the band,' says John. 'A guy that Bert was very close to, Simon Bouchant, had just been killed in a car accident, and his girlfriend was there. Bert was trying to look after her plus think about playing, and I'm afraid it was just a disaster. Nat Joseph had been against the idea of the band doing it, but Bert told Nat that the band must definitely do it, for the publicity. But the publicity was terrible! The review simply said, "Bert Jansch was dire".'[23]

Nat Joseph had not been enthusiastic about the group: 'I had long felt that Bert and John could become the nub of a folk-rock band,' he says, 'but the kind of music the Pentangle turned out was just the kind of music I didn't think they would. It was far too bland.[24] I'm not denying that it wasn't successful or good, but I always felt they could have done something much more exciting.'

Immediately after the Windsor débâcle the group flew to Denmark for their first-ever tour, organised by Bert's Danish agent Walter Claybell who had inexplicably billed the Pentangle as Britain's newest rock sensation. It was another disaster: 'The first night, it was a typical rock club,' says Bert. 'The stage was quite high and the audience were "down there". It was full and they were all kids, fifteen- to sixteen-year-olds, all expecting rock'n'roll. The Pentangle show at the time was that John would go on first and do a solo set, and then John and I would do one, and then I would do one, and then the whole band would come on. But that night John lasted two or three songs. They were throwing coins. It was really quite dangerous.' 'In the end,' says Jacqui, 'we all went on, turned everything up as loud as possible and played the normal set, just very loudly. They thought it was great.'[25]

Shortly before the Danish tour, Bert had debuted his electric guitar onstage: 'I could never handle it,' he later admitted, 'although John

Renbourn was also starting to play electric guitar at that time. We always kept solo spots, partly to appease folk guitarists. We were greeted with shouts of "Sell-out!" because we had bass and drums, even though it was a double bass.'[26] Bert's brief use of an electric guitar had been simply a response to the amplification problem. If he had ever harboured any thoughts of exploring the instrument further, these were swiftly forgotten in the wake of a momentous concert on 25 September 1967: a 'Guitar In' at the Festival Hall with flamenco player Paco Peña, the classical duo Tim Walker & Seb Jorgensen, Bert Jansch and the Jimi Hendrix Experience.

Bert was already aware of Hendrix by then. His version of 'Hey Joe', which Bert had himself performed years earlier, had been a hit at the start of the year and prior to that he had turned up at the Cousins.[27] 'I'd read some poetry he'd written,' says Bert, 'and also I'd heard a tape of him playing acoustic guitar and I've never heard that since. It was magic. We were onstage when I said hello, at Jimi's soundcheck. I did meet him but he didn't open his mouth once all evening. I enjoyed his soundcheck more than anything else. It was quite extraordinary: he walked on, plugged into one of his pedals, turned the whole volume up as loud as possible, smashed [a chord on] the guitar once, and that was it.[28] Paco Peña that night was actually in the artists' bar handing out leaflets for flamenco guitar lessons! But Jimi's show itself that night was stunning. Unbelievable.'

Only two papers had sent reporters along: *Melody Maker* and the *Financial Times*. Tony Wilson, for *MM*, marvelled at Hendrix's full array of performance tricks, clearly redefining the possibilities of the instrument. Bert Jansch 'ambling on stage with two guitars', his six- and twelve-string acoustics, was in marked contrast. Bert was 'well on form' and new material was aired including 'A Woman Like You' and 'Birthday Blues'. 'I was standing in the wings,' says Nicola. 'It was fabulous. I know afterwards that Bert went out and bought different strings for his guitar – whatever Hendrix used. I remember John rang and I told him Bert was off buying new strings and John said, "Oh, he's not is he? I've just done that!"'

Bert would share two further bills with Hendrix and would remain in awe. Yet today other iconic players regard both men as being of equal stature: 'As much of a great guitar player as Jimi was, Bert Jansch is the same thing for acoustic guitar,' was Neil Young's view; 'He tied up the acoustic guitar in the same way that Hendrix did the electric,' was the conclusion of Jimmy Page.[29] Many more, Johnny Marr and Bernard Butler among them, have since agreed.

The group was by now dominating Bert's performing life. One of the very few solo engagements he managed before the end of the year was a Saturday night at the Cousins with Anne Briggs; he also appeared at an all-star concert at Manchester's Free Trade Hall in a duo with Renbourn, alongside Dorris Henderson, Al Stewart and the Incredible String Band (by now psychedelic paragons on the Elektra label). In November the Pentangle, misbilled as 'Bert Jansch & the Pentangles', undertook their first British tour, arranged by Nat Joseph and jazz impresario Pete Burman: 'I only remember bad things about it,' says Renbourn. 'Pete Burman would take a long time in the dressing room getting decked out in a dinner jacket, with throat spray and all the rest of it, and then he'd run on stage and give this incredible introduction. And then we came on. It was ridiculous.'

The group had done two or three town hall-type concerts before but this was their first serious venture into the provinces, mostly to university venues. At the Queen's University Festival in Belfast they represented the world of pop with, incredibly, Les Bridger, Jimi Hendrix and the Watersons. For the Watersons, after two years of Roy Guest's management, it was the final straw: 'We'd been on the road solidly for about a month,' says Norma Waterson, 'and we were asked to host an evening in some sort of cellar in Belfast, and the place was absolutely packed out. The format was we sang for about half an hour and then it was an open mic. We sat there until everybody had finished and walked back to our hotel, absolutely shattered, at nine o'clock in the morning. We all just looked at each other and said, "What on earth are we doing?" We decided that night to stop singing.'

The Watersons had first heard of Bert at Bill Leader's flat in 1965: 'We were round there recording something,' says Norma, 'and Bill said, "I've just recorded this young guitarist. Do you want a listen?" He played the tape and we all just thought it was brilliant, and that's when we started booking him for our club in Hull. Bert played the club loads of times. After a while we handed it over to a committee, because we were touring so much. Bert said to me only recently, "From the day you left that club, I never got another booking!"'

In February 1968 Bert was featured as a guest artist on two of the Watersons' farewell concerts: at Manchester Free Trade Hall and Newcastle City Hall.[30] That same month, his own group acquired a manager of formidable reputation, had its first of many sessions broadcast on BBC Radio 1 and began recording its first single and album for real. The manager's name was Jo Lustig, and from now on the ramshackle, happy-go-lucky progress of the Pentangle was going to be a streamlined machine of purpose and efficiency.

Jo Lustig was a New Yorker who had first come to Britain in 1960 as Nat 'King' Cole's publicist, settling there and transforming Julie Felix, a vocalist of questionable quality, into a national television celebrity. Danny

Thompson and John Renbourn had both worked with Felix and knew Lustig. At some point Bert invited him down to the Horseshoe: 'I went to see the band and I liked them very much,' said Jo. 'My philosophy is simple: if you can apply commercial techniques to crap, it can happen. Why can't you apply it to fine music? I have a strange way of managing: I like to get a group of musicians who know their way. I let them handle their own way artistically, I handle their business. I'm not out to make friends with my bands. Bert once said to me, "Jo, you never hang out." I don't like hanging out – that's not my scene.'

Lustig's manner was abrasive and his fee substantial but his instinct was sound, his energy fearsome and his contacts seemingly inexhaustible. One obituary in 1999 characterised him thus: 'Mention almost any name of significance in the arts, music or post-war Anglo-American culture in general and his response would be the same: "He's a friend of mine." He had the stocky build of a sawn-off shotgun (and sometimes the temperament to match), his steel grey curls and Roman nose lending him a magnificently leonine appearance. His Brooklyn accent, gravelly laugh and habit of punctuating his conversations with a jabbing finger could sometimes lead people to mistake him for a rough diamond. But he was an immensely cultured man, a canny operator who delighted in being an American at large in the world of British culture.'[31]

At the time Jo was introduced to the Pentangle the only act he was managing was Roy Harper. In later years, Jo would manage a stream of successful acts but the Pentangle were the making of his reputation and he, in turn, the making of theirs. Almost overnight, they were transformed from a cult folk-club act to a bona fide concert act with an extraordinary appeal across the social spectrum and massive, sustained media coverage. 'Most of the band had fairly rough things to say about Jo,' says Bert. 'But I quite liked him. He very, very rarely made mistakes.' Where everyone agrees is that Jo Lustig was the best PR man there was. To build a campaign around his new charges he would need something to sell: exclusivity. The club demand for Bert, John and the band would have to be starved to create the possibility of a concert relaunch. By the end of March 1968, the Pentangle and Bert and John as solo performers were withdrawn from circulation. Although they would continue to record albums, Bert and John's solo careers were effectively stopped and would remain so for the next five years. The group's relaunch as a concert act was scheduled for 29 June 1968 at the Festival Hall. The first album and single would be out by then, and the concert would be recorded for the second.

The first casualty of the Lustig regime was to be the Horseshoe. The club had, in truth, already served its purpose. The supposedly resident group had built up its repertoire and confidence and were itching to move on, increasingly accepting outside bookings. Although it ran on till March 10 1968, the club's apogee coincided on Christmas Eve 1967 with the ending of Bert's relationship with Nicola. Wizz Jones, Alexis Korner and Sandy Denny were all guests. It was Jacqui's birthday the next day and she and Sandy, the worse for wear, sang 'Make Me A Pallet On Your Floor' – and fell over. Nicola had come with two college friends, Maggie and Chris. 'Everybody was buying Bert drinks,' she says, 'beers with whisky chasers. And on the bar was this enormous line of drinks. We all went back to my parents' house where Bert and Chris finished off another bottle of whisky. That night was a disaster and on Christmas Day Bert was ill. Even he couldn't take that many whiskies. I don't think Chris got out of bed all day. The next day Bert caught a train and left and that was it. We didn't fall out as such: he just left and it broke my heart.'

'The departure from the Horseshoe in early '68 was rapid and final,' recalls Kieran Bracken. 'The announcement went along the lines of "due to overexposure this has been the last evening". The next time I saw the band was at the Festival Hall relaunch, after which they departed on a seemingly endless tour. Watching and listening to the Pentangle through that year at the Horseshoe was very, very exciting and one was aware of being part of something the like of which had not been seen before. Many saw their first album as a "beginning", but in reality it was the end of a long process. Folk, jazz and blues all rolled into one! And we had been around to see it come together.'

CHAPTER EIGHT

Rosemary Lane

'Pentangle is at a standstill at the moment,' said Bert, surveying his career at the end of 1970. The interview, conducted during the course of a marathon drinking session around the pubs of Soho with *Sounds* writer Jerry Gilbert, was the most comprehensive Bert had given to date. Aside from exploring the detail of his long ascendancy, Bert was open in acknowledging that the Pentangle were at last experiencing artistic differences: 'I think the problem is that the group has been working for such a long time that it finds it hard to get together to produce something that's of value to everyone in the group,' he offered. 'I don't want Pentangle to split up but it must be a lot free-er in what it does; I'd like the original concept of the band to remain there. In doing the Horseshoe I think we all got the satisfaction we wanted and I think we're missing that at the moment. We ran the club and we had the freedom of playing together or not at all. I mean, if we just wanted to get drunk and fall about then we could do so. After that came the serious thought that we could maybe take the whole thing a stage further.'

The 'whole thing' had in fact been taken almost as far as any pop, jazz, folk or rock group could ever expect to get. With the release of their long-fêted first album and single in May 1968 the Pentangle's profile had mushroomed virtually overnight. 'I did like that first album,' says Pete Townshend. 'There was something fresh and innovative about it, although the Pentangle never really engaged me as such. But I was amazed with their success, which as far as I could see was instant. They seemed to be playing the Royal Albert Hall almost immediately.' Certainly, the Pentangle were doing something new and exciting, but equally in Jo Lustig they had a manager who was the best PR operator in the business.

In 1968 alone Lustig secured for his group at least eleven BBC Radio 1 sessions and at least eight television appearances. The potential appeal of an act that was pigeon-holeable nowhere but could squeeze in pretty much anywhere made them at once more saleable and simultaneously more exotic as a 'product'. They could move seamlessly from college gigs and Edinburgh Fringe residencies to folk festivals, jazz festivals, the biggest and most unforgiving rock festivals of the day, stylised set-ups in country churches, cathedrals and casinos, and major auditoriums such as Carnegie Hall or the Paris Olympia. If coverage on the airwaves was impressive, in print it was relentless: this was a group, like the Beatles, whose members were all distinct individuals and all capable of providing good copy.

But by the summer of 1970 Bert's life of being endlessly whisked around the world with a bunch of colourful characters had lost its novelty. The boredom of travelling, the arguments, the pressure and the intake of alcohol that had become daily routine were no longer being adequately compensated for by the music. The social contact, invariably in pubs, that had hallmarked the group's beginnings was becoming rarer. For a start they were all living much further apart: Bert had moved to the little village of Ticehurst in Sussex, John was still relatively nearby in Surrey, Jacqui was in Reigate suburbia, Danny had a manor house in Suffolk and Terry was in the process of moving to Minorca.[1] Pete Frame interviewed his old hero for his pioneering new rock magazine *Zigzag* in October 1969, during a tour in support of the group's third and most commercially successful album, *Basket Of Light*. Bert was now, to all intents and purposes, the rhythm guitar player in a pop group. Frame put it to Bert that the Pentangle were unusual among their peers in not living together:

'We live totally different lives,' said Bert. 'The group gets together when it has to, when it's forced to. Like when we have to do a record we get together and create some numbers, but apart from that we do no rehearsals at all. We just get onstage and play.' Frame also noted that Bert was not getting much opportunity to sing his own songs these days: 'I'm given a section in the programme, as everyone is, to do whatever I want,' he replied. 'But yes, it's so long ago since I did solo performances. I was just about the first folk singer to successfully do a solo concert in this country, and that was doing a two-hour show, just as we're doing now [with the group]. But that too was a far cry from those folk club days, when I never had a programme but just went in and sung whatever was in my head. Nowadays there has to be a bit of organisation because there are so many of us involved.'[2]

For Bert, the desire to create and be a part of a genuinely cooperative, democratic unit of five creative individuals had to be balanced against the inevitable compromises. In theory it was the same for each member, but in practice Bert was always the least vocal in making his presence felt. The live half of the group's second LP, *Sweet Child* (a double), was recorded at London's Festival Hall on 29 June 1968 – the first of the concert and festival dates that summer that effectively relaunched them as a concert act. At this period the five members of the group were at their live peak, complementing and collaborating with each other in various combinations and giving space for purely individual contributions. The balance between the constituent parts, onstage at least, would never again be so perfect.

Among all the many concert reviews and surviving set lists from the summer of 1968 to the summer of 1971, there is not one reference to Bert performing a solo spot. His only solo outings in that period were two BBC radio sessions around the January 1969 release of his first truly Pentangle-era solo LP, *Birthday Blues*.[3] Bert dismissed claims at the time that he was short of material but it was a ragged affair, a handful of well-honed songs and instrumental ideas fleshed out with bluesy jams and wordy vamps on matters spiritual and metaphysical. 'Some numbers have taken me years to write, others have taken me two minutes,' said Bert, hardly countering the criticism. 'But I'm not out to become the greatest solo artist in the world.'[4]

Recording the album around the time of his twenty-fifth birthday in November 1968, Bert had been joined on half the *Birthday Blues* tracks by fellow Pentanglers Danny Thompson and Terry Cox and by Ray Warleigh on saxophone and flute plus Duffy Power, an inspired choice, on harmonica. The highlight of the ensemble tracks was 'Poison', a powerful if oblique reflection on pollution, but these were little more than spikier extensions of the Pentangle sound. Bert's future direction as a solo recording artist was to be glimpsed more clearly in the baroque fascinations of 'The Bright New Year', a song for his mother, and the instrumentals 'Birthday Blues' and 'Miss Heather Rosemary Sewell'. The latter indicated the current woman in Bert's life. In this case they had married.

Heather Sewell was an art student from London, strikingly different in background and personality from her new husband. Previously the girlfriend of Roy Harper, Heather had actually met Bert through Roy, probably early in 1968: 'I was familiar with his music on record,' says Heather, 'although I didn't know of the existence of Pentangle at that time. The first time I heard him perform was when I went with him and Roy down to a gig in Bristol. They were playing on the same bill. It was a classic case of love at first sight.' Heather's inevitable 'defection' to Bert resulted in what she recalls uncomfortably as 'a duel of songs' and an understandable degree of angst from Roy.

'She was a lovely girl, very good-looking,' says Roy. 'Bert was more well known than me at the time and I think that Heather was rather more conscious of that than she should have been, although Bert did have this boyish charm. Every woman who ever met him wanted to take care of him and so it was with Heather. The presentation in Bert's stage performances was always awful, same as it is now, but it did somehow pull women in. But he never took advantage of that because it wasn't an act – he was like that off the stage too. I think Bert was careful about the way he treated the whole subject with me. He took good care of me that way, in his own silent way. He didn't ever do anything maliciously. I would have loved Heather to the end of the world, but she chose against me. What can I say? I was a bit mad at the time. Then again, in her own way she's a screwball too – and her match in life was not Bert Jansch.'

When Heather met Bert it was on the eve of the Pentangle's most rigorous two years of touring, and they were consequently prompt in marrying, at Lewes, in Sussex, on 19 October 1968. The touring lifestyle caused problems for some of the other marriages within the band and it must surely have contributed in some way to the eventual failure of Bert and Heather's. 'I've always been happy in my own company anyway,' says Heather, 'but I think the first time that it was difficult was when they first went to America [January – March 1969]. I was still adjusting to life away from London. But life was very good for me because there was plenty of money. I had a lovely house, a few acres of land, I could paint. But it left me time to myself, without the compromises that are inevitable when you live with someone. What I did object to was things like him not letting me go to the Isle of Wight Festival that year, because I wanted to see Bob Dylan. He was worried I might get molested in the crowd. He was a very jealous man. I'm sure he thought he was being protective. What he said about that particular incident was that it was a big gig – the Pentangle were playing too – there was a lot going on and he didn't need the tension and anxiety of wondering if I was all right. I felt perfectly able to take care of myself. After all, I'd been a student in London, and I hadn't exactly led a sheltered life. But he was a very conservative man in many respects.'

Aside from painting, Heather had decided to occupy herself in other ways during one of those early tours: 'I renovated the house,' she says. 'That was how I expressed my creativity at the time! I just knocked the guts out of this beautiful seventeenth-century cottage that we'd bought. All the original features had been obscured, so I did the classic thing, wiping it all off and exposing the beams. Bert was horrified actually. He was away in America when I started that project, and when he came home there was only the bedroom that wasn't affected. The roof was off, the floors were up, the builders were in . . . He went absolutely spare. I hadn't thought that he'd be tired when he came home and wouldn't want to live on a building site! But I certainly feel about him that he was a very great teacher to me, just in life. He's incredibly perceptive and he's also very gentle and caring, and he doesn't mince words – and I needed a bit of a shaking up, I think. I was a bit of a spoilt brat. I couldn't allow myself to indulge in generalities, and platitudes were not acceptable. And I hadn't realised that until I met Bert.'

'If you passed Bert Jansch in the street it is doubtful whether you would give him a second look,' observed David Hughes, an interviewer for *Disc* who met with Bert in April 1970, typically, at the Capricorn Bar in Soho. 'Jansch is a humble soul who seems unaware that musicians and audience alike hold his playing in great respect. He is a self-contained unit. He knows what kind of person he is – and wants to stay that way. His life is simple. If he had pursued his solo career he could, he says reluctantly, have become a latter-day Donovan. But he didn't want that. "I'd rather prop up a bar somewhere with nobody knowing who the hell I was. I like my beer and I don't like people staring and pointing their finger at me when I just want to enjoy myself and be an ordinary human being. I'm just an ordinary, average guy like you. I watch *Tomorrow's World* and *Doctor Who*." He has an obvious affection for humanity. He cares about people; he cares about peace but, superficially anyway, he doesn't seem to care about himself. "I'm not very stable – if I wasn't married it wouldn't really worry me where I slept. I thought I should buy the house as some security for my wife. I suppose I am a country person but I do like the city. I need the country to off-set the pressures of work. But I don't want to tell you about the house; I want to keep it a secret." '5

'He liked to keep a very clear division between his private life and his public life,' says Heather. 'I can remember one time we had somebody come to do an interview at home, which was very unusual. The guy started to ask me questions about how it was for me when Bert went away, at which point Bert started to get extremely angry, cut the interview short and threw the guy out. He felt very keenly that that wasn't any of his business. The curious thing about Bert is that as a man he has very little to say, as a poet he has a great deal to say, and that's how it should be, I suppose.'

Hughes's article for *Disc* explored the poverty of Bert's childhood alongside his current status as something approaching a pop star, and certainly now as a man of comfortable means. Bert's responses had been prickly concerning his early years and most particularly on the topic of stardom and normality. He was nonetheless proud of what the Pentangle had achieved and delighted to have the best of both worlds: popular success and, as a group member, relative anonymity. During the first six months of 1970 the group was commercially at its peak. *Basket Of Light* had charted at No.5 in November 1969 – largely on the back of 'Light Flight', a song that was concurrently featuring as theme music for the BBC's first-ever colour drama series, the hugely popular *Take Three Girls*. Invariably whistled by visitors to the gents at Bert's local, it was the key that had opened the Pentangle's door to mainstream consumers.

The year opened with soundtrack recording sessions for an ultimately unsuccessful film, *The Devil's Widow*, based on the traditional ballad 'Tam Lin'. At the same time the BBC were broadcasting a series of four half-hour radio programmes dedicated to the group. In terms of television, from January to June there were at least twelve appearances, spanning Britain, France, Belgium, Holland and America and ranging from *Top Of The Pops*[6] and tea-time variety shows to half-hour concert broadcasts. Printwise, the Pentangle were everywhere from solemn analyses in broadsheets to the centrefold in teenage girls' magazine *Jackie*. In terms of live work, from February to April there was a seven-week British tour followed immediately by another seven-week tour of America – their third and longest there, opening at Carnegie Hall and routinely playing college campus venues to audiences of eight thousand or more. One *Melody Maker* headline from May, 'Hysteria and exhaustion for Pentangle in the States', said it all. 'We've been on the road since Christmas and we absolutely need a break,' said Danny. 'We come back in a couple of weeks' time then we go into the studio to start recording our next album, then we take a couple of months off.'[7]

That June – July rest period became sprinkled with odd concerts and TV dates and then it was into August with four festivals, climaxing with the mammoth Isle of Wight Festival, an event chiefly memorable to Bert for the privilege of lying under the stage listening to Jimi Hendrix perform in Britain for what was to be the last time. There were a handful of further shows in September, more recording sessions for the new group album, and then another full-scale tour of Britain in October – November. Bert's family would delight in seeing him during such tours, when the group would generally play Edinburgh's Usher Hall. The family had collected Bert's records from day one, but going to Pentangle concerts was the first time any of them had seen him performing: 'I'm sure our mum was very proud of him,' says Mary, Bert's sister. On Boxing Day, the Pentangle members and their extended families could all relax and watch themselves on prime-time BBC2, pre-recorded at the ancient Trumpington church in Cambridge-shire, for a broadcast entitled *Songs From A Country Church*: this was what success was all about. And Bert was rapidly losing heart with the whole business.

Discontent, disillusionment and frustration, on both business and musical levels, would eventually come to consume the Pentangle, but at the very height of their commercial celebrity it was Bert who first experienced the malaise. Danny and Terry were pro musicians revelling in the trappings of success. John was basking in the limelight as a studious adventurer in medieval music and all things esoteric. Jacqui, without any children at this stage and with her husband Jock in conventional employment and occasionally travelling with the band, was free to enjoy the trip without getting quite so detached from real life as the rest. Bert, also married, was finding it more difficult to adapt to the responsibilities and to living away from London: 'I think it was okay for a while,' says Jacqui, 'but he still had to have the pub across the road. I won't say his life revolved around the pub, but he spent an awful lot of time in pubs. He's an observer.'

During their time at Ticehurst, Heather recalls that Bert 'rarely thought of anything except escaping the pressures'. During the odd free moment, they might visit Anne Briggs, living relatively nearby with Johnny Moynihan and subsequently with her new partner Pat. 'When I saw Bert,' says Anne, 'he would often say, "Oh shit, I wish I was you, just travelling around singing what you really want to sing and doing what you want to do." He often said that, and I can see why now.'

Arguably the most creative but also the least vociferous member of the Pentangle, Bert was finding his role increasingly marginalised. While much of the group's music was still challenging to play, Bert's delicate, magical touch was often lost in the overall sound, especially in concert, and he yearned, as Anne observed, to relive the freedom of earlier days. If he could not have it in actuality, he could still have it in music. The clearest evocation of that yearning would also prove to be the finest single work of his career: *Rosemary Lane*.

The making of *Rosemary Lane* was a throwback to happier times in itself. It was recorded simply, on portable equipment, by Bert's very first producer and engineer, Bill Leader, over the course of periodic visits to Ticehurst. 'It took a year to make,' says Bert. 'Bill used to come down to the cottage and spend the weekend, and sometimes he'd just spend it with me and Heather, not actually recording. We'd set the gear up and then we'd go for a pint, discuss it, and if I felt like recording we did it. The songs were just whatever I had at the time, wherever my head was. I was losing interest in the band at that point, wishing for other things to do.'

Fuelled by a sense of longing for times past – his own not too distant past and an Olde England more of the imagination than of history – *Rosemary Lane* was romantic in aura, serene and reflective in tone and breathtaking in its starkness and simplicity of presentation. The dearth of tangible, discernible contemporary references, save for the dark observations on America – a place he now loathed – in 'Nobody's Bar', and the undatable nature of Bert's instrumental techniques produced a work of timeless quality. Everything one needs to know about Bert Jansch, in support of the notion that he is an artist unique in his art and whose art is of great worth, is demonstrated on this record. It reveals an unmistakable personality yet at the same time a transcendent quality to the work implying that, at its heart, the work itself is the foreground and its creator a barely visible presence facilitating the construction of something magical. Enigmatic, as a judgement of the whole, is too short a word.

In the context of Bert's circumstances and state of mind at the time of its execution, *Rosemary Lane* can be seen to reflect each with piercing clarity. But the listener is offered more than one man and his troubles. 'Wayward Child' is observation becoming parable; 'Nobody's Bar' takes the idea of metaphor on to the doorstep of the metaphysical; 'Bird Song' rings the bell and goes right in. And who could fail to hear an echo of John Donne in 'A Dream, A Dream, A Dream'? Like that of the metaphysical writers of a previous age, Bert's writing – in general, but particularly on his three solo albums of the Pentangle era – displays a marked preoccupation with 'the soul', and with the nature of true love. On his previous album, *Birthday Blues*, it had been clumsily expressed; on his next album, *Moonshine*, it would be almost too clever by half. *Rosemary Lane* was where less became more and everything was in balance.

'A lot of my writing is just throwing up questions that I might think about myself but not come up with the answers,' says Bert. 'You get a lot of the same thing in each song. I write from personal experience. I do bring in, in all my songs, God, and I often bring in instances that happen to me in everyday life. This applies to all my songs. I cannot distinguish between one song and another. To me, they're all just one big song, almost like a diary. I don't write because I think, "Ah, I've got an idea for a song." I'm not that kind of writer.'

Imagining is the key to understanding on *Rosemary Lane*. When Bert sings, on the traditional English title track, 'When I was in service in Rosemary Lane . . .' one does not hear Bert Jansch singing a song from the early seventies: one hears the story as if straight from a fireside story-teller in some indeterminate place and time. It is of no relevance that Bert is singing from the point of view of a woman, the subject. The same is true of 'Reynardine': the accompaniment alone is a masterpiece, a distillation of all that is definable as the contribution of Bert Jansch to guitar playing. After years of being more concerned with the guitar than the voice when recording, Bert had now reached a point where he was viewing both with equal care. There would come a time, in the mid-seventies, where the balance would swing momentarily towards the presentation of voice and songs alone, with Bert in virtual denial of his status as an instrumentalist. But on this album, with that unmistakably rough-hewn vocal displaying a new poise and clarity and with that inimitable, highly individual guitar work honed to perfection, the songs and tunes were accompanied by an open invitation to the mind's eye. And the view was breathtaking.

As Bert was proving with words and music, and as Anne Briggs had already proved with words alone, in the late twentieth century the very best of the English and Irish traditional canon could still enthral and communicate without contrivance. The style of accompaniment Bert used was not synonymous with 'the sixties' or 'the seventies', but had been honed to the demands of the song. If troubadours of the eighteenth century had played guitars, it would only be a stretch of academic credulity, and not of the listener's imagination, that this might be how they would have sounded.

'I always felt that it was very sad that somebody who should reach a position of fame so young should feel so at odds with it,' says Heather, 'because he did. Although the whole flavour of the sixties had allowed him to come to prominence it was so far away from who he is and what he was. He was an enigma, and still is. He stood outside of the sixties because he was part of something much older. There was much more of the bard in him than anything else. He actually lives the myths and legends inside himself and makes them real. What he writes is of legendary quality but concerned with contemporary society, or so it appeared to me.' Drawing upon old and new, in the form of traditional songs, baroque interpretations and masterful pastiches, and his own contemporary writing, *Rosemary Lane* encapsulates the view that great art comes out of a refusal to accept existing boundaries, but not through a refusal to acknowledge the past.

Very little of the material on *Rosemary Lane* would happily have survived a transition into the Pentangle's repertoire, and as a consequence very little of it was ever revealed onstage at the time.[8] One or two pieces, perhaps more, were only ever performed for the recording and then forgotten. 'I'll probably have to re-learn this one back from the record,' read Bert's brief sleeve note on his delicate instrumental 'M'Lady Nancy'. It is likely that he never did.

Given 1970's workload, the following year must have felt like a holiday to the Pentangle. There were a handful of gigs and recording dates in the first quarter, with an American tour scheduled for April – May. Ostensibly, the tour was cancelled at the last minute because Heather was having a baby. Prior to the group's previous US tour in April – June 1970, Bert had gone into print labelling the place 'the most violent country in the world';[9] after it, his view was even more dogmatic: 'Under no circumstances will I return. All that madness and insanity, no thanks!'[10] With the tour cancelled and with few summer festival dates – a consequence of certain open-air disasters the previous year – the group members were left with a swathe of free time

until the autumn. Bert and Heather used a little of it to move house: 'We
were very happy in that place,' says Heather. 'But it was too small. Kieron
was born while we were still living there. Bert's mother wanted to come
down from Scotland, so we gave her the house and we bought another one
nearby. Bert's like that – an incredibly generous man.'

Discontent was now endemic in the group. Their fourth album, *Cruel
Sister*, released and promoted with a full British tour at the end of 1970, had
been a commercial disaster. The relative freedom of 1971 must have given
everyone time to reflect. They had come together in a spirit of adventure
that was sufficient to fuel the first three albums, but the energy had almost
tangibly expired by the time album number four came around. Musically
low-key, it was based largely on John and Jacqui's vision and contained only
traditional material. True, it showed aspects of musical development,
particularly with John's use of low-volume electric guitar, but it was not
the right way to maintain the momentum of critical and popular success.
Bert's contribution was limited to co-vocalling with Jacqui a side-long and
less than gripping revamp of 'Jack Orion' and adding a little concertina to
John's atmospheric 'Lord Franklin'.[11] On the group's subsequent albums the
balance would be redressed, and previous heights reconquered, but with the
definite science of hindsight their moment had passed.

The one-time darlings of the media became a whipping boy, a byword for
tedium and lethargy. The pressures of touring and each member's changing
social and personal circumstances were factors in the 'magic' waning; a
diminishing of commitment from their manager, increasingly busy in developing new acts, may also be conjectured,[12] as can a lack of financial will on the
part of Transatlantic to see the project through. Relations with Jo Lustig, their
manager, were definitely deteriorating. His contract would come up for
renewal in February 1971, and begrudgingly everyone would agree, in the
absence of any better ideas, to re-sign. In a way, this lack of any imagination in
providing for their own best interests is illustrative of what Jo viewed as a
tendency towards complacency in the group. But any group under the
spotlight of critical interest can only bask in the glory for so long. The
Pentangle had enjoyed more than three good years, and those who are built
up by the media must surely be torn down by the same.

Reflection, recorded over three weeks in March 1971 at a promising but
technically problematic new studio called Command, in Piccadilly, was the
Pentangle's fifth album. Bill Leader, as producer, was especially well placed
to observe their disarray: 'If the Pentangle were the sort of people who could
have hung together, realised groups have difficulties and that they'd got to
somehow handle that, then they would have gone on to make more music.
But at the same time, if they were the sort of people who would have

appreciated that, they wouldn't have been the sort of people they were – and they wouldn't, in the first place, have been producing such interesting music. My memory is that the two pros, Danny and Terry, would be there on time; Bert and John would arrive at different times, depending on how much they'd had to drink and where they'd managed to lay their heads the night before. And it seems to me, in retrospect, that each day a different member of the group had decided that this was it: "Sod this for a game of soldiers, I'm leaving the group!" And we'd spend the rest of the day either trying to get him back or doing the best we could without that particular member. I don't think Jacqui threw that sort of tantrum. She was just very disappointed that this was going on. But certainly with the rest of the group, it was as if they'd drawn straws before coming in to see which one today was going to throw a moody.'

For all the angst of its creation, *Reflection* would prove to be not only the best recorded Pentangle album (the only one to use sixteen-track facilities, exploited to the full) but arguably their most satisfying. John brought 'So Clear', his only self-written vocal contribution to the group's canon, and furthered his distinctive explorations of the electric guitar; Terry offered 'Helping Hand', a funky, intriguing little tune; Jacqui's singing was better than ever, atmospherically double-tracked in places; the traditional selections, 'Wedding Dress' and 'Rain & Snow', were more sensual, less austere than before; Danny's contribution was rarely more powerful than on his triple-tracked bowed and plucked intro to the album's stunning title track, an eleven-minute epic based on Bert's old 'Joint Control' riff; and, not least, Bert's contribution was once again the equal of his colleagues. It was, in a sense, the follow-up that *Basket Of Light* had demanded. But by the time it came out in October 1971 it was too late to make a difference.

Rosemary Lane was released in May 1971, the same month, by way of context, as Carole King's *Tapestry*, Paul McCartney's *Ram* and Mountain's *Nantucket Sleighride*. It was a month later than scheduled. 'Those who have waited patiently for this album have in it a reward deserving of their endurance,' declared the *MM*. The most penetrating observations came from Jerry Gilbert at *Sounds*: 'The thing with Jansch is that you cannot compare him with anyone else, you can only draw the comparison between the man as he was and the man as he is today,' he wrote, establishing a truism that still stands. 'The aesthetic pleasure derived from listening to Jansch these days is based on quite different merits from, say, the Jansch of five years ago, despite the fact that he has gone right back to the traditional songs which were his starting point. And although his own material is far more tranquil these days it is a sublime tranquillity which is totally uncompromising.'

Gilbert believed that Bert 'would have arrived at this stage with or without Pentangle'. Aspects of the Pentangle experience had certainly informed the content of the original songs on *Rosemary Lane*, but the overall mood and musical stylisms of the record were utterly independent of it: this was never a collection of pieces designed to be repeated on the concert stage. Which was unfortunate, as for the first time in over three years Bert had a solo engagement looming.

Jo Lustig had promoted Lindisfarne, a hot new folk-rock act from Tyneside, at London's Festival Hall in March; he had booked the same venue for 30 June, for the similarly up-coming Belfast singer-songwriter Van Morrison. In May Morrison's manager cancelled the arrangement and Jo was left threatening writs, with a large room to fill at a month's notice. John Renbourn had already established the precedent, having played the more compact Queen Elizabeth Hall in February in support of his Early Music album *The Lady and The Unicorn*. Now it was Bert's turn: 'I let John do his first, because I'm a coward,' said Bert, three weeks after the event. 'It took about a year to talk me into doing one. To start with, I didn't have a repertoire. I couldn't sing songs I've done on my albums because they were done so long ago I'd forgotten them. And I prefer to use new material for a concert. [But] I think it's a good thing for us to do musical things on our own. It brings in fresh ideas. The group needs new life.'[13]

'Bert Jansch has a gift for the understatement,' wrote Andrew Means, reviewing the great event for *Melody Maker*. 'He strolls on stage, head bent towards an introspective world of jeans and plimsolls. Just as casually he exits. It was hard to believe that last week's Festival Hall concert was his first solo since Pentangle was formed. In retrospect it was equally surprising that he should concentrate on the contents of his recent album *Rosemary Lane*. But if his choice of material could have been more representative of his past, Bert's performance was an undeniable success. Sure there were bum notes and cracked vocals, but the result was merely to intensify expectations. The legend fled in the face of something more positive – live music.'

Also on the bill, at Bert's insistence, were COB – Clive's Original Band, the latest in a series of esoteric ensembles fronted by Bert's old pal Clive Palmer – plus a heavily pregnant Anne Briggs. Both Clive and Anne had been key influences on at least the content, if not also the style, of *Rosemary Lane* and a little earlier in the year they had also been part of a package of one-off album deals arranged between CBS and Jo Lustig.[14] Anne had already released an album that year, for Topic: her self-titled LP debut and her first appearance on record at all in five years. Mostly traditional and unaccompanied, it did feature the Jansch/Briggs composition 'Go Your Way' and, somewhat after the event, her first recording of the troublesome

'Blackwater Side'. *The Time Has Come*, appearing later in the year on CBS, would mop up the remaining songs from that collaborative period in 1965: 'Wishing Well' and 'The Time Has Come', adding many other new, self-written and instrumentally accompanied songs. It would prove to be the public swansong of a singular career.[15]

The return of Anne, as a now legendary, mysterious figure from the early years of the revival captured the reviewers' imagination, all but over-shadowing Bert's performance. Words like 'beautiful', 'uncompromising' and 'compelling' were lavished on the typically nervous goddess of trad, though to Andrew Means 'more so than Bert, her music taxed the patience of the uninitiated, balanced between monotony and fascination'.

'I was stone cold sober when I did that gig,' says Anne. 'I was pregnant and I didn't have anything I could actually wear and Jo Lustig's wife Dee gave me this bloody awful pink maternity thing. I think Jo was so gob-smacked he sent somebody out to give me a bunch of flowers. He didn't know what else to do and I didn't know what to do with the flowers. I was so embarrassed.' As Jo remarked after the show, having comically botched the job of compere: 'I fired myself on the spot. But it really was the best concert I have put on since the first Pentangle concert three and a half years ago.'

Bert's set, after the novelty and revelation of Briggs and Palmer, was short and understated – seemingly no more than forty-five minutes. Most of the material performed had been relearned from *Rosemary Lane*, for this sole event, with only 'Oh, My Babe' to remind people of who he was before the Pentangle. 'There was a great sense of occasion at that concert,' remembers one fan, Mike Fox. 'When Bert finally came onstage he seemed nervous and ill at ease, although still able to joke with the audience – "As long as it's not one of mine," he said, when a baby started crying! As a fifteen-year-old I was staggered at the intensity of the performer and his level of involvement with the music. He finally left the stage half-way through "Veronica", which was going badly wrong, only to return resignedly for an encore – "They wouldn't let me out!" '

True to form, however, Bert had debuted some 'new' material at the concert: a new vocal interpretation of Ewan MacColl's 'The First Time Ever' and 'Twa Corbies', a Scottish traditional song long in the repertoire of Archie Fisher. Bert would make the latter his first solo spot in years during the next Pentangle tour, at the end of the year. It would also be the featured item in his only solo TV outing of the entire Pentangle era, on BBC 2's *Once More With Felix*.[16]

Rosemary Lane was a minority interest album, even at the time of release. Bert Jansch, the solo artist, was no longer at the heart of the British folk scene. Besides which, the scene itself had changed markedly from its heyday in the mid-sixties. The *Melody Maker*'s Folk LP of the Year award for 1971 would go to Steeleye Span's *Please To See The King*. A triumph of electric 'folk-rock', it was indicative of the direction British folk music was now expected to embrace. The best of the Cousins-era singer-songwriters – Al Stewart, Ralph McTell, Roy Harper and so on – had all graduated to the thriving college circuit, on an equal footing with the middle-to-top division rock bands of the era. Others, like Sandy Denny and Dorris Henderson, had joined bands with a folk-rock sound. Duffy Power would that year make an entire album with progressive rock luminaries Argent, while Alexis Korner of all people had jumped whole-heartedly on the bandwagon with a series of bands including the Mickie Most-produced pop-rock 'big band' CCS and, with various refugees from King Crimson, the stadium-filling Snape. The Cousins itself, ultimately overrun with would-be guitar heroes to the exclusion of any audience, had simply run out of steam. Steve Benbow had become a taxi driver.[17] Ewan MacColl, having inadvertently destroyed his own Critics Group from the inside, was about to enjoy a more positive new celebrity as author of Roberta Flack's worldwide hit with 'The First Time Ever I Saw Your Face'. Alex Campbell, the godfather of all troubadours, just continued to do what he did.

While *Bert Jansch, Jack Orion* and the rest, for all their rough edges, had challenged and captivated fans and contemporaries alike, they had been recorded and released during a time of musical development and discovery in popular music as a whole. 1971 was no longer that time. In any case, who was Bert now but a vaguely anonymous member of the Pentangle – a modestly successful pop group whose members indulged in periodic solo projects of little interest to the uncommitted? There was, of course, a contractual obligation for both Bert and John to carry on delivering solo albums alongside the group work. John was happy enough in having the best of both worlds; Bert was growing weary of one. Nat Joseph observed that once Bert had been caught up in the machinery of the band he was 'somehow never a free soul again'. It would appear, from the weary interiors of 'Nobody's Bar', that Bert had begun to agree with him.

'The success of the band meant that we were all able to buy places in the country,' he explained some years later, 'and to some extent my bohemian existence stopped. But John was living in Surrey and I was in Sussex, and we'd often end up after a Pentangle concert at Waterloo Station waiting for our trains at a dossers' pub called the Hole in the Wall which sold ale at a shilling a pint. We'd invariably end up talking to these amazing tramps, missing our trains and staying all night.'[18]

One memorable insight into Bert's lifestyle during the mid-Pentangle era is provided by David Cartwright, a singer-songwriter who joined Transatlantic in 1970. 'After recording and mixing my first album in a day and a half,' says Cartwright, 'I went down to see Nat Joseph with a view to getting him to spend a bit more money and doing the job properly. Needless to say, Nat's smile and guile talked me round, and I was never to recover. Anyway, that very afternoon I was introduced to Bert who was wandering around Nat's Marylebone offices cadging ciggies. In the sixties I'd booked him four or five times at Stourport Folk Club, overlooking the River Severn: a beautiful, intimate little club hosted by genuine, though somewhat elderly, Woody Guthrie devotees. Bert's impact on all the Harmony Sovereign "learners" in the audience was spellbinding. He didn't remember me. Why should he? But he shook my hand and we had a little chat. As I made to go, he sprang after me and we left the building together. It was a warm summer's afternoon. We went for a drink, as you do, then another, then another. By ten o'clock we were bosom pals and very, very drunk. I was new to London but I loved it. In those days you did. Bert knew a club in Soho where they served really late.

'At about midnight he suggested moving on, to "somewhere with a bit more life". So we found a night club, where we sat huddled in a corner, . looking at the ladies. I put my arm around a pretty waist, who immediately went and told her boyfriend. He came over and told me to stand up, so he could hit me. Bert suddenly adopted the warmest, friendliest American accent and intervened on my behalf. We were just tourists, "a little drunk but meanin' no harm, buddy". And that was that. At about two in the morning it really was time to go. Bert assumed I'd got a pad somewhere; I thought that he had. We realised then that we had nowhere to sleep. But Bert had friends, and at three o'clock I found myself giggling into a rhododendron bush as he knocked, rather loudly, at a door somewhere in Fulham. Eventually a man wrapped in a large multi-coloured blanket answered the door. No questions, no aggro. We were invited in, shown a couple of dog-eared sofas, and slept log-like till mid-morning. Ralph McTell made us a hearty breakfast, talked to me about "good old Transatlantic" – he was just joining Warner Brothers – and we left about midday. I've not met Bert since.'

> *I don't know what my baby's gonna say when I get home –*
> *I really should have gone but the booze keeps flowing on.*
> *But right now, feel like staying on here,*
> *Let the booze flow out of my ears –*
> *But I really, really, really should go,*
> *'Cos I know that my baby's back home*

'When I Get Home', one of the stand-out tracks on *Reflection*, the Pentangle album recorded in March 1971, is Bert's most transparently

confessional song of the Pentangle era and clearly explores the dilemmas
of his life at this point. A married man with 'clipped wings', he was torn
between the responsibilities of home life and a partner he loved and the
relentless pressure to escape it all through nihilism and drink. Bert is
no complainer by nature, but this song was as close to a 'cry for help'
as he ever came. Perhaps most tellingly, a verse is devoted to his Uncle
Adam who, to paraphrase, worked hard all his life, never married and
came home drunk every Saturday night – 'and I wish that I could be like
him'.

For all its problems, Bert's marriage would outlast the Pentangle, but John
Renbourn's would not be so fortunate. Bert and John, still friends as well as
colleagues, would go off adventuring around Ireland together at least twice
during the Pentangle era. In the summer of 1971 they went with Sue
Draheim, a recently arrived American fiddler with whom John would return
and set up home in Devon. For Bert, the Irish trips were remarkable in that
Luke Kelly from the Dubliners seemed to appear in every pub they ventured
into. Bert's hope for the summer '71 trip was to seek out the celebrated
uilleann piper Willie Clancy. The first step was to make for his home village,
Milltown Malbay[19] in County Clare:

'We went to the pub that we knew he always played in,' says Bert, 'a pub-
cum-post office-cum-grocer's shop, and they said, "Oh, he doesn't come in
till eleven o'clock." So I think we just wandered about until half past ten and
went back to the pub. Quite a few people were gathering – Americans,
people with tape recorders and all that – and come eleven o'clock they shut
the pub. Willie arrived with his mate and that was it: we were there till
dawn. He sang and he played and then somebody else played and then Sue
played, and they were all knocked out because she knew all the tunes. It was
a great night. In fact, we became Willie's roadies for about a week after that,
went to about three or four gigs with him. And the funny thing is, money
didn't seem to be involved. Food, drink and general hospitality seemed to be
the system.'[20] Later in that holiday, the three adventurers made it to the
Cliffs of Moher, on the western shore, among the highest sea-cliffs in
Europe. Taken by the experience, Bert came back with a song for the next
Pentangle record: 'Jump Baby Jump'.

Jo Lustig's 'stable' of artists had expanded significantly during 1971, and as
Jacqui McShee notes: 'Everybody was more or less in the same musical vein,
and we were all playing more or less the same venues. We began to feel that
he was getting bored with us. It just seemed that he would book us out to
places and we would be on the road all the time, and occasionally we'd meet
up with Steeleye Span and find that they were complaining of the same

thing. We'd been saying, "Don't sign with Jo!" But of course they did. They saw our success and they wanted the same.'

The Pentangle's relationship with Jo soldiered on into 1972 but with the release of Renbourn's solo album *Faro Annie* in January the association with Transatlantic had reached its conclusion. Aware that a change was coming, Renbourn had recorded the album – deliciously out of kilter with the solemnity of his recent instrumental work – shortly after the Irish trip as a kind of celebration, with old friends Dorris Henderson and Pete Dyer, Danny and Terry and Sue Draheim guesting. 'I remember with quite a lot of fondness and gratitude the fact that I made any records at all,' says Renbourn. 'I saw Nat as being quite a benefactor and I developed a genuine respect for the type of music that came out of Transatlantic as a whole. Our contracts were all about to expire and the American company that had been leasing the group's stuff from Transatlantic for American release, Warners/Reprise, wanted to take them up: Bert's and mine as solo artists and the group's. I had one more record to do for Transatlantic and in a moment of some wistfulness decided to make a record that was like the first one, just to make it a complete cycle.'

The Pentangle's exit from Transatlantic was characterised by a sense of bitterness. Members of the group differ in their opinion of who was to blame. Bert has no doubts: 'Nat's the villain in the whole thing,' he believes. 'If you sign a contract with anybody you take it as read that you get paid. You don't afterwards, having signed it, look through the thing to find any flaws in it, which is exactly what he did. What else was he doing with it – looking for some bedtime reading?' An eavesdropping employee at Transatlantic told Jacqui that Nat was 'jumping up and down, hugging himself with glee' when he realised through examining the contract that he was by now, through whatever proviso or mechanism it was,[21] within his rights to stop paying the Pentangle record royalties.

'It's perhaps worth explaining that we put up a lot of money,' says Nat. 'Nearly always we paid the recording costs and we never sought to recoup them. We did pay lower royalties than some companies, but instead of, say, paying £10,000 worth of recording costs, not paying the artist a penny until that £10,000 had been recouped in royalty earnings and then giving them a ten per cent royalty rate or whatever it was in those days, we paid for the recording and then gave the artists a royalty from record one – although that royalty may only have been five per cent.'

With nobody in the group understanding how or why their royalty tap could be legally switched off, they were looking for someone to blame. 'Nat was saying, "Well, you signed the contract and your manager okayed it – why don't you sue your manager?"', says Jacqui, 'while Jo was saying,

"Look at my contract." It said on the bottom, in very small print, "You cannot sue me for anything under any circumstances"!'

As a man who was taking twenty-five per cent 'off the top' as manager and an additional twenty per cent off mechanical royalties, Jo Lustig must undoubtedly accept some blame for the failure to ensure against a contractual situation that left his artists in a position where the flow of royalties could be simply curtailed after a given period. With no more mechanical royalties and a large part of their concert income going straight to their manager, before expenses, the group established their own publishing company, Swiggeroux, in 1971, as Jacqui recalls, 'to try and actually make some money out of all the work we were doing'.

'The amount of work and travel the Pentangle had to do was horrendous,' says Ralph McTell. 'Because there were five of them, and let's say they didn't skimp on anything, they often came back with absolutely nothing to show for their labours. They had the most terrible fights and rows on the road and an unbelievable amount of drink went down.'

If Nat was absolutely within his rights in the case of the Pentangle, still his major artists at the time, then the only criticism must be his judgement as a 'man manager'. Transatlantic had blazed a trail in providing unique opportunities to talented artists at a time when there were few other outlets. But it is telling to consider that Transatlantic artists of the calibre of Billy Connolly, Gerry Rafferty, Mike Oldfield and the Dubliners, to name but a few, achieved significant commercial success only after they had left the label. Nat was scrupulous as a businessman and daring as a pioneer, but was he also wise and pragmatic enough as the builder of what could have been an empire as critically and commercially brilliant as those created by Chris Blackwell at Island or Richard Branson at Virgin?[22]

'Everybody eventually fell out with Nat and left him,' says Dave Arthur, of the duo Dave & Toni Arthur. 'It's a shame because I love Nat dearly. He's a really sweet guy but a very, very hard businessman. Friendship doesn't come into it with Nat. He would send you a bill for 25p. He was our agent for a while, and if some ancient TV thing we did is being repeated the fee goes to Nat: he takes his twenty-five per cent and sends on a cheque for £8.35! You'd think nobody would do that, but he does. He's very good, but he's utterly businesslike. The folk people, of course, weren't.'

Solomon's Seal, named after the oldest known rite of magic, was the Pentangle's final album. With the advent of full-scale electric folk-rock, let alone their own troubles, individually and collectively, the group's increasingly fragile music was on borrowed time and everyone knew it. 'Pentangle beat the boredom barrier,' had been the damnably faint praise lavished by *Melody Maker* on *Reflection*. That album had failed to chart, but the seeds of an artistic renaissance were definitely there, and the signing of a new three-album group contract, plus Jansch and Renbourn as solo artists, with Reprise in the early weeks of 1972 resurrected a sense of hope.

Recording began promptly and, after a low-key 1971, the new year also saw a touring schedule to rival that of their glory days, with tours of mainland Europe, Scandinavia, Australasia, Britain and possibly also America. Bringing along pals like Ralph McTell, Wizz Jones and COB as support acts wherever possible was a conscious attempt to bring some camaraderie back into the picture, but by this stage it was all papering over cracks: 'Various members had personal troubles at the time and there was a lot of drinking going on,' says Jacqui. 'It was hard to cope. It just wasn't enjoyable any more.'

In hindsight *Solomon's Seal* is a record of people's weariness, but also the product of a unit whose members were still among the best players, writers and musical interpreters of their day. Everyone wanted it to work, and said as much to interviewers at the time: 'It's probably my favourite of our albums,' says Jacqui, 'but we worked on it in the studio as much as anything. There wasn't much rehearsing – there wasn't time.'

Musically less adventurous and sonically drier than *Reflection*, the new album was released in September. Of its content, the group had been playing Cyril Tawney's 'Sally Free And Easy' (sung by Bert) in concert for years; 'No Love Is Sorrow' was a rare and striking song contribution from Danny; while Bert offered two compositions, 'Jump Baby Jump' and 'People On The Highway'. The latter, sung in unison with Jacqui, was a beautiful melody and guitar figure softening a desperate strength-in-adversity lyric that reflected Bert's current creative viewpoint: 'It's better to be moving, better to be going, than clinging to your past'. The rest of the album was traditional: 'Willy O'Winsbury', a song inadvertently 'created' by Andy Irvine cross-referring a set of lyrics to the wrong tune in a folksong manuscript, had previously appeared on *Faro Annie*, but the most powerful and delicate of the trad arrangements was 'The Snows', a chilling song of loss recorded previously by both Anne Briggs and Archie Fisher. 'You get the feeling they'll go on for decades like this,' concluded one reviewer, 'making pretty, well-played, unstartling albums, enjoying themselves in their own mild way and not causing any commotion.'[23] He was wrong – on both counts.

The British tour of October – November 1972 became the Pentangle's valedictory parade. A number of live reviews from odd shows around Britain during the summer had been surprisingly positive, deferential even, with commentators now realising that here was a real rarity, a group of five individuals in their seventh year as a creative unit. But there were still those who marvelled at how strangely soporific the Pentangle concert experience could be. Even Bert, the group's staunchest apologist at the time, will not on reflection deny it: 'Oh, the Pentangle could be dull, absolutely boring,' he says. 'I wouldn't go to one of their concerts! The tuning up was horrendous. People used to fall asleep on stage, quite regularly – me and John, because we had the guitars to lean on. If we didn't have anything to do we'd be hunched over them with our arms folded and before you knew it you were asleep, getting a gentle nudge from Danny or somebody letting you know your part was coming up soon. It got too into its own self, that was the problem.'

'We knew things were getting tired,' says Jacqui. 'We knew it was beginning to fall apart. We'd signed the deal at Warners' offices and it was like a big champagne party. There was a lot of positive talk, but there were internal politics that we weren't aware of at the time and not long after we signed the guy who signed us was moved sideways or something and I think then the interest waned. We actually did have thoughts about folding, to get rid of Jo, and then reforming as something else.'[24] As it was, prior to the October – November tour they came to an arrangement with Jo that their relationship would conclude on New Year's Eve. Holding things together till then was the problem.

'It had really gone sour for them,' says Wizz Jones. This was the Pentangle's only British tour to include support, and though it was never planned as a farewell, they were going out in style. 'The management chose to send me and Clive Palmer's COB along on the same bill, to give us both a leg up,' says Wizz. 'But it really was an incredibly shambolic affair. Danny Thompson had this sport that he insisted on every night of persuading, bribing, the night porter to open the wine cellar – and he cleaned out every hotel wine cellar on that tour. I mean, God, the kind of stamina you needed to do that! But everyone was involved really, it was the classic "rock tour syndrome". Jacqui was wonderful, she was just so used to working with these people. I don't think any other woman would have put up with it. I remember on one occasion saying to someone at a hotel at about one in the morning, "Have you seen Bert?" and they said, "Well, the last time I saw Bert he'd just gone into the lift with a tray of drinks." The last thing the guy saw was the doors closing, the lift starting and Bert toppling over with this tray of twenty or thirty drinks, crashing in a heap. I'd love to have been there at the other end when the doors opened. A wonderful vision, and it really sums up what that tour was like.'

Solomon's Seal had been strongly exposed, with two BBC radio sessions and TV concerts for Granada and BRT in Belgium – appearances that, though barely months apart, show a group with new life and a group with its life visibly extinguishing. The Belgian show, a half-hour live in a dismally bare studio, was broadcast in January 1973, though recorded before the British tour. It was notable for the Pentangle becoming a rhombus: Renbourn had been too drunk to make it to the end of the show. The British tour was of a lower key than before, but nonetheless well received. Bert had regained sufficient confidence or interest to take regular solo spots, and both 'Reynardine' and 'The January Man', a Dave Goulder song learned from Martin Carthy, were featured. The tour was scheduled to finish up in Barry, Glamorgan on 8 December, but Danny became ill with heart trouble and the final three dates were cancelled. The Pentangle, launched in a blaze of publicity at the Festival Hall back in 1968, would appear to have played their last note in public at a civic hall in Barnsley on a cold Wednesday night in November 1972.

'I think it was the evening of New Year's Day,' says Jacqui. 'I got a phone call from Bert. It was really late at night and he was pretty drunk. "I can't take any more," he said, "I really can't take any more. The band has split." I phoned John the next day and he said, "Bert can't split the band. It's not his to split, it's a five-way decision." So he came to see me the day after that and said, "What shall we do about it?" And then there were phone calls all round. And just somehow nothing happened.'

CHAPTER NINE

After the Goldrush

'Pentangle Split' was the front-page headline in the first *Melody Maker* of the new year. 'It's been on the cards for six weeks, but we haven't got round to sorting out the details,' said Jo Lustig, the only person quoted. *MM* writer Andrew Means commented that the only surprise was the five members managing to hang together so long. Rumours and denials of splits had been around for two years. The straw that broke the camel's back, Means speculated, had been Danny Thompson's illness. News of the Pentangle's dissolution, he concluded, was 'an anti-climax'.

The following week the *NME* could judge the reported split as 'the biggest non-story of 1973'. Lustig was denying that he had put the story about, while acknowledging that the group had been due to leave his management 'amicably' on 31 December – an arrangement that had been agreed before the autumn tour. The group's new manager Roger Myers, an accountant for the Rolling Stones with little experience at the front line, led the damage limitation exercise but conceded that Danny's illness had put any group plans on hold: 'You can say that the others will be pursuing their individual careers for the moment,' he stated. Renbourn was writing material for what would prove to be his first and only album of original songs – part of the group/solo deal with Warners/Reprise: 'We're all pottering about doing bits of music here and there,' he said, 'getting it together until it works.'[1] A group tour of America was being pencilled in for the autumn, while it was hoped that Danny might be well enough to allow the group to record a new album within a couple of months. Terry Cox was in Minorca, Bert Jansch was 'in bed with the flu'. His new album *Moonshine* would be released at the end of the month.

To Bert's mind *Moonshine* was 'an album that never surfaced – I don't think anyone knows it exists'.[2] He could say that only two years later. For this was an album out of time: promotionally unsupported by the record company, by then undergoing an internal shake-up, and musically an artefact of the now moribund Pentangle era. Produced by Danny Thompson, arranged by Tony Visconti and clothed in the rich visual foil of Heather Jansch's sleeve art, it remains a delightful curio in Bert's canon. With an atypical wordiness, unwieldy in places and not retained on later work, a renewed vigour jostled for attention amidst an aura of serenity carried over from *Rosemary Lane*.

An array of guest musicians were featured throughout: a flute consort adding Elizabethan poise to the dark tale of 'Yarrow', a traditional song salvaged from the last days of the Pentangle; guitar and harp weaving a delicate web around 'The January Man'; Shetland fiddler Aly Bain scatting through the tumbling wordage of 'Night Time Blues'; Ralph McTell blowing harmonica on 'Brought With The Rain'; jazz guitarist Gary Boyle blistering and burbling his way through 'Oh My Father', doomed to oblivion as a single. Most striking of all, perhaps, was the reappearance of Ewan MacColl's 'The First Time Ever', sung as a canon with Visconti's wife Mary Hopkin, and featuring Charlie Mingus's drummer Dannie Richmond.[3] First covered by Bert as an instrumental on *Jack Orion* it had since been an international hit single for Roberta Flack and was destined for the repertoire of Elvis Presley. Bert later met the author of the song and was damned with faint praise: 'He said, "Oh, Bert Jansch. My son's got a lot of your records. He's a big fan of yours." "Thanks a lot, Ewan, that's really great," I thought.'[4] Curiously, Roy Harper remembers Peggy Seeger saying exactly the same thing to him.

Critical reaction was cool. *Let It Rock*, a new monthly, viewed the album as 'precisely the way not to bring folk into rock or rock into folk'. Andrew Means, for *Melody Maker*, was philosophical: 'One has to make allowances for his style. But he does what he does well and with sincerity.' In *Sounds*, Jerry Gilbert was less equivocal. For a start, he felt, nobody did 'The January Man' as well as Archie Fisher. 'Gone are the beautiful romantic ballads of *Rosemary Lane*,' he concluded, 'and in its place we have the old harsh Bert: but whereas his voice once went hand in hand with the music it now sounds a little incongruous.'

Moonshine was a brave experiment with outside musicians, intricate arrangements and a mixed bag of material but it still felt like a product of the sixties. If Bert was to remain relevant as a creative force he needed to make a giant leap forward. How that would ever have happened in the context of remaining a part of the Pentangle, a group viewed widely as having been long since stuck in a rut of wispy inconsequence, is difficult to imagine. Within weeks of *Moonshine*'s release, that problem was resolved: the group finally imploded.

'Pentangle dies with a whimper' was the *Melody Maker* headline of 31 March 1973. Karl Dallas interviewed four of the five members and this time the facts were right. Studio time for a projected group album had been booked for April, but Terry had decided to leave. Danny, unhappy with the circumstances of Terry's departure, followed suit. The other three had lost the will to deal with it. Ralph McTell's brother Bruce May was following the situation with interest:

'Roger Myers just couldn't believe it,' he says. 'The Pentangle had walked out on Jo but they still had a binding contract with Warners, under the terms of which they only had to deliver an album to pick up, I think, £5000 – in those days a fortune. All they had to do was spend another few days together and pick up £1000 each. But they just flew apart.'

For Dallas, the dissolution of the Pentangle marked 'five years which had begun in the excitement of exploring new musical territories and ended in something close to tedium'. Jacqui was talking about a solo album; John, doing odd gigs with her as a duo, was recording his own solo album for Reprise and thinking about moving abroad; Danny too was talking about a solo album, feeling musically rejuvenated and 'looking forward to the next gig, whatever it may be'.[5] He had also just recently returned from Paris where a holiday with Mr and Mrs Ralph McTell and Mr and Mrs Bert Jansch had turned into a recording session with one George Chatelain.[6]

Like John and Jacqui, Bert had been using the enforced lay-off since January to play some low-key club gigs but 'I certainly don't want to do it for the rest of my life,' he told *Melody Maker*. 'I always need some kind of challenge and though it has taken a bit of nerve to go out on my own after playing with the group for nearly six years it hasn't been an artistic challenge. Another problem is that I've lost touch with the club scene. There are all these thousands of guitarists and singers floating around and it's a new world to me.'[7]

'He'd always said that when his playing days came to an end we'd retire to the country,' says Heather Jansch. 'He wanted to be a market gardener, that was his dream. Mine was always to breed horses. When we did go to Wales I found myself in this magical land, totally at home. He didn't want to go to Cornwall because that was too busy in the summer and it was still in the folk scene, which he wanted to get away from. He really had had enough – he just didn't want to play any more. He didn't want to go back to Scotland, he didn't fancy Suffolk and the other place where there was a lot of land to be had for a reasonable price was Wales. He was in Paris recording at the time when I was looking for property. He wasn't interested to go and look for himself, which was curious. "Just go and choose a place and we'll go and live there," he said. So I went to the Brecon Beacons and it felt like going home. I bought a place and we moved there without him ever having seen it. He was utterly disinterested as long as it was away from the music business.'

In April 1973, Bert was interviewed for *Sounds* by Jerry Gilbert. Far from hiding in Wales Bert was, it transpired, on the eve of a solo concert tour: 'At present, however, he has very little to talk about,' noted Gilbert. 'Pentangle has gone, the present holds a tour to which he feels largely indifferent and the future is in the hands of the Almighty. He has no plans for anything, a fact that he stressed more than once during the interview. Ask him what John Renbourn is up to these days and he'll mutter, predictably, "You'd better ask John"; ask him why he's playing the London Palladium he gives an evasive "You tell me." It's all a bit of a game interviewing Bert.'[8]

The tour was a half-hearted attempt to push the *Moonshine* album, requested by Reprise and doubtless organised by the inexperienced Myers: 'It's all very vague,' said Bert. 'The record company don't really know what's going on.' Gilbert's interview had taken place in Soho's Capricorn Club and during a discussion on the incongruous possibility of an imminent Jansch concert at the London Palladium, Duffy Power had wandered in. 'Bring all your harps and have a blow,' said Bert. 'I haven't a clue what's going to happen.' That, as Gilbert duly concluded, was the story of Bert's life at that point in time.

The Palladium concert never happened but on 23 April 1973, Bert began his first solo tour in years, at the 'sparsely filled' Birmingham Town Hall. Dennis Detheridge reviewed the show generously for *MM*, although it was clear that Bert was nervous as a performer and far from promoting his new album was relying very largely on old material. He was, of course, 'playing to the converted and his admirers were grateful for the chance to hear pure Jansch for sixty minutes'. Bert had told Gilbert that he had gone back to his earlier albums and relearned what he thought the audiences would like to hear – material that included 'Running From Home', 'Blackwater Side' and 'Angi'. He had recorded three of these old faves, plus the new single, 'Oh My Father', for a BBC radio session a few days before the tour.[9] On the opening date he was joined for three numbers by Danny Thompson on bass, most notably for an improvised crack at Brownie McGhee's 'Key To The Highway'. Bert was not only relearning his repertoire but relearning his trade.

Although there continued to be club dates here and there, Bert became increasingly absent from the music scene and for a while – months rather than the 'two years' it has become in his own memory – did not even touch a guitar. 'I joined the Farmers' Union, the whole bit,' he says. 'Very strange. I think I just wanted a break.' In July he went to the Cambridge Folk Festival simply as a punter, something he would do throughout the seventies. That year's event provided a rare chance to see his old hero Davy Graham in action. Bert's only other noteworthy activities of 1973 were equally nostalgic in nature: he guested on Wizz Jones's *When I Leave Berlin* and on Ralph McTell's *Easy*. Both invitations were perhaps more for old times' sake than for any great want of a Jansch guitar part. There was a danger that he would simply drift away into farming and obscurity and that would be the last the music world would hear of a once great talent.

In the middle of the year the Reprise deal fell apart. 'Warner Brothers' policy shake-up,' says Bert. 'Anything that was dubious or not selling would be scrapped – and that included me and John.' An immediate consequence was the shelving of John's completed solo album. The talked-about solo projects from Jacqui and Danny were also discarded. Bert had offered the label his Paris recordings but no interest had been shown. Rumours of his retirement from live performance began to circulate; in the spring of 1974 a handful of English folk club gigs and European concerts were perceived as a farewell tour in all but name.

Heather, brought up in the country, was used to animals and enjoyed the solitude. During the Pentangle years she had been left to her own devices 'for at least six months a year'. But for Bert, transplanting to an isolated hill farm near Aberystwyth was a change he had not fully thought through. 'The reality of living deep in the country was a shock to him,' says Heather. 'He loathed it, poor sod. Couldn't take it at all. He didn't like milking cows, for sure. He didn't like the Welsh as people. It would have been better if we'd gone to Scotland or even Ireland. And he was bored out of his skull, he'd always be drinking. So he only stayed in Wales for about six months of the first year that we lived there, if that, and then he began to spend more time in London and started playing again. It was quite evident that his music wasn't finished, that he'd got a new lease of life.'

'Believe it or not,' said Bert, referring to that period of his life a couple of years later, 'I can't stand not having a contract. Regardless of whether I'm signed for twenty million years, I still like the security of knowing I have a record contract and that whatever I create I have an ability to present it to the public.'[10] He was still being 'managed' by Roger Myers. Word got back to Tony Stratton Smith, owner of the maverick Charisma label, that the great Bert Jansch was without a recording contract. A fan from the early days, whose own tastes informed his company's A&R policy, 'Strat' became involved immediately and a deal with Myers was duly signed. 'I didn't know quite what was going on at the time,' says Bert. It is unclear precisely what occured next, but either Stratton Smith or Bert or both realised that Myers had to go. The new name in the frame was Ralph McTell's younger brother, Bruce May: 'Ralph wanted me to manage him, but I took on Bert reluctantly,' says Bruce. 'I didn't really feel that I understood him.'

Stratton Smith, experienced in music management himself, very possibly realised that Myers was out of his depth. He would have been aware that

Ralph McTell had recently ended his own relationship with Jo Lustig and was now being handled by Bruce and that Bruce, an Economics graduate who had represented Ralph on the club scene prior to Lustig's involvement, was clearly doing a good job. Tony negotiated an exit deal for Myers. Bert now had a new label, a new manager and a new opportunity to make, if he so wished, the comeback that had so abjectly failed to materialise with *Moonshine*. He also had a marriage that was pulling in precisely the opposite direction.

Tony Stratton Smith was one of the great characters in the music business – generous, caring and passionate about his interests within a business he had been bumbling around in with equal quantities of luck and naivete since 1965. Slipping from a very successful career in sports journalism into the murkier waters of song publishing and artist management, most of Strat's frustrations in the music game had revolved around the workings of record companies.[11] He had made a few calculations, had the necessary contacts and felt that operating as an independent record label – at a time when there were very few at a genuinely national level – was a gamble worth taking. 'This is a gambler's business,' he said, 'this is not a business for bankers or investment people.' His label, Charisma, would be bankrolled entirely by himself and two partners: there would be no banks involved. Setting up shop in the first of several offices all within the bounds of Soho, the first record was released on 10 December 1969.

Strat had estimated that at least ten album releases and around £100,000 in outlay would be needed during the first year to make the venture credible to retailers: in the event, with good fortune on his side, that same period would see fourteen releases and a healthy wholesale return of £117,000. Rarely again would Van Der Graaf Generator enjoy such a welcoming response as they did with their first album for Charisma; never again, after the timely million-plus triumph of their first Charisma single 'Sympathy', would Rare Bird trouble the chroniclers of pop. 'Anything good of its kind, dear boy': that was Strat's maxim, and for a good innings both the public and the pundits would give his musical tastes more benefit than doubt.

Earlier in 1969 Pete Frame, besotted with the romance of Bert's music and lifestyle in the mid-sixties, had followed his own dream and started a magazine. Called *Zigzag*, it was arguably the first publication in Britain to take rock music seriously and was certainly the direct antecedent of the glossy music monthlies of the 1990s. 'An ambitious but ridiculously shoe-string operation, it was never out of financial chaos,' wrote Frame. 'It was one of the great dance-around-the-house-in-wild-abandoned-joy days when Tony Stratton Smith bought us out, assuring us that he was going to sort out all our problems and put us on a sound footing. Strat, bless his heart, was one of the great philanthropic idealists of our age and it soon became plainly obvious that he was no more of a businessman than I was. He ran his record company, Charisma, on a purely whimsical basis and it was only by the grace of God that he ever made a penny. A dreamer, he flew entirely by the seat of his pants, and that part of his body contained therein.'[12]

Strat took over *Zigzag* in 1972 and in April 1974 he bankrolled a lavish fifth birthday party for the magazine at the Roundhouse, featuring one-time Monkee turned country-rock icon Mike Nesmith and his sidekick Red Rhodes. 'Strat got on famously with Nesmith,' says Frame, 'and whisked him down to Crowborough in Sussex, where he had a country retreat. By this time, Bert had been signed to Charisma. Give Strat his due: he was a total shambles by any conventional yardstick, but he had an instinctive and intuitive feel for what was worthy and noble and artistically valuable. For instance, the listening room at Charisma had a great big John Bratby painting on the wall and a desk which had once belonged to Tolkien. There was a framed, handwritten letter from him in the top drawer, confirming that he had written *The Lord Of The Rings* on it. He had a good heart, did Strat, and that's why everyone who worked for him loved the guy. However, having signed Bert, he wasn't at all sure what to do with him. It was all down to finding a sympathetic producer, and the two of them could never come within two miles of agreement. This had been going on for months.'

'In the end things happened really fast,' said Bert. 'All the material that went on the album I had for over a year – Jimmy Page wanted to produce it but couldn't find the time, Bob Johnson turned it down and in fact when I was with Warners I started doing the album with Danny Thompson in Paris. We did eight tracks there. But Warners weren't happy with what we'd done and when I joined Charisma neither were they. Strat didn't want solo stuff so we wrote off £3500 worth of tapes just like that. Strat simply wanted everything connected with Pentangle out, and that included Danny, and I suppose it's true that you can't live in the past.'[13]

A few days after the *Zigzag* event, Strat phoned Bert at Ralph McTell's house in Putney, where he was staying at the time, and invited him down to Crowborough for the weekend. Quality material, in Strat's eyes, was a necessity for success and giving his artists the time and space to come up with the goods was thus paramount. He would often give his acts a few weeks' solitude to get it together in the country at either his own place in Sussex or a farmhouse in Hertfordshire which the label kept for the purpose. 'Having never seen Strat's country residence,' says Frame, 'Bert says, "Yeah, that'll be cool – I'll pop down on Friday evening." From what I recall of conversations with Bert a few weeks later, he got a lift south with John Martyn, who was living in Hastings. They set off from the pub some time in the afternoon, consuming a few drugs to sparkle up the journey, and felt so genial on arrival at John's that they decided to pop round to his local and knock back a few jars over a game of snooker. With about fifteen pence left in his pocket, Bert phoned for a cab to take him to Strat's place – only about thirty-five miles away! After searching all the highways and by-ways of East Sussex for about two hours, they eventually located Strat's gaff, Luxford House, only to find a note pinned to the door, saying, "Bert, we've gone to the pub – please walk in and help yourself to anything you want."

'Having no money to pay the cabbie, Bert invited him in and the two of them were confronted by this enormous banqueting table covered with the debris of a gargantuan meal. They got stuck into a bottle of brandy and were feeling pretty good by the time Strat, Mike Nesmith and sundry chums returned from the pub. Everyone assumed the cabbie was Bert's roadie and kept his glass topped up – until Bert suddenly remembered him and got Strat to stump up the fare, whereupon the guy floated out into the night. Bert was introduced to Nesmith but had absolutely no idea who he was. They chatted, and after more bacchanalia, all straggled off to bed.[14]

'Next morning Bert stumbles down to join Strat, who is halfway through his customary six-course breakfast, when a mobile recording studio suddenly appears outside the window. Strat leaves the table, and before you know it there are microphones and cables all over the place. Not only that, but a film crew arrives and begins to set up. Bert wonders what the fuck's going on and it suddenly dawns on him that the whole shebang has been organised for his benefit! Before he knows what's happening, he's sitting out in the garden cutting a few songs, with ambience mikes strategically positioned to pick up the chirping of the birds. Bert goes along with it for a while. Finally, he erupts: "Look, Tony, I really would prefer to make my album in a real studio!" '

Rarefied as the situation was, six tracks were nonetheless recorded that day,[15] and some of the pastoral ambience exquisitely captured on the opening moments of 'Fresh As A Sweet Sunday Morning'. The song had precisely the aura that Strat had wanted: it was definitively Bert Jansch, enigmatic and angular, and at the same time displayed a very marked break with the sound and style of the Pentangle. It felt like Bert was opening a new chapter but simultaneously reconnecting with his work as a soloist in the sixties – a period and a body of work that had itself been set aside during his time with the Pentangle. Sensual and mysterious, cool and unusual as it was, the placing of 'Fresh As A Sweet Sunday Morning' as track one, side one of the eventual comeback album *LA Turnaround* was a masterstroke: an immediate statement of intent that Bert Jansch was still relevant, valid and artistically unique.[16]

Nesmith and Rhodes had to return to Los Angeles and, fearing a loss of momentum, Bert felt the sessions should continue there as soon as possible. Stratton Smith was all for it and added an inspired touch of his own by enlisting Beatles acolyte Klaus Voorman, whose group Paddy, Klaus & Gibson he had once managed. The richness and smoothness of Voorman's bass playing on the resulting tracks was to prove a wonderful complement to Bert's taut, snapping guitar work, and very possibly the glue that held together the cream of LA's session scene and this most English and unorthodox of guitar players. 'What really amazed me was that all these people knew who I was,' said Bert, 'and I think it frightened them a bit.'[17] Pete Frame later heard that one hired hand 'was so overawed by Bert's virtuosity that he threw up out of sheer panic'.

The method of recording, entirely live with no overdubs as opposed to the piece-by-piece assembly of tracks that had characterised Pentangle sessions, was refreshing. One track per day would be accomplished, all bar two tradititional songs and a Renbourn instrumental being Jansch originals: 'Travelling Man' was a clever amalgam of titles and phrases from well-known folk songs; 'Stone Monkey' was based on a Chinese children's story, later the surreal TV series *Monkey*; 'One For Jo' was a gentle ode of encouragement to Jo Cadman, Bruce May's assistant and wife of Pentangle roadie Bobby Cadman, couched playfully in the language of day-dream and adventure. A sense of poise and maturity was pervasive, spiced by the interplay between the musicians and the acidity of Bert's guitar work. The inclusion of the two exceptional Paris guitar solos, 'Chambertin' and 'Lady Nothing', added balance and provided a subtle link to the style of playing which had given *Rosemary Lane* its brilliance. 'Chambertin' in particular, a taut, dark and almost visibly dextrous baroque-with-swing construction, is possibly the ultimate encapsulation of how Bert Jansch redefined the vernacular of the steel-strung guitar.[18]

Most surprising of all was a re-recording of 'Needle Of Death'. 'I never did like the original recording at the time,' said Bert, not long after his return from California. What had horrified him most when listening to his early albums, for the first time in years, in order to re-learn material for live performance, had been the sound of his voice. His prime concern when recording in the sixties had been the guitar; his work in the mid-seventies would be characterised by a swing to the other extreme, with the pre-sentation of voice and songwriting to the fore. 'I think my songwriting's getting a bit better,' he told the *Melody Maker*. 'It's not so sterile as it was before, not so clean cut. A lot free-er, but then that's only my opinion. A lot of the songs no one's going to understand. But the imagery is there and people can make up their own minds. They just become paintings.'[19]

LA Turnaround was released to a flurry of acclaim in September 1974 and it remains one of Bert's strongest and most accessible. For Colin Irwin at *MM* it was 'not far off being the perfect album'; for Charles Shaar Murray, over at the *NME*, it was 'almost as good as Orson Welles' *War Of The Worlds*'. Bill Henderson at *Sounds* was uneasy at the prominence of steel guitar. Bert, on reflection, would share those feelings. Each of the British weeklies took the opportunity of what was widely perceived as a comeback to run interviews with Bert. It would provide Bert with a platform to draw a line under the Pentangle and to explain his subsequent drift and reappearance, and it would enable the writers to explain to a new generation of readers just who Bert Jansch was. This was virtually ten years after his first album and the world was a different place.

A high-profile tour of British concert venues aimed at promoting the new album and reintroducing Bert as an artist at that level was undertaken during November – December. Bert had hoped to tour with a band comprising album musicians Klaus Voorman and Danny Lane plus English fingerstylist Pete Berryman on lead guitar. It transpired to be a solo tour, with folk-rockers Decameron as support. Modestly attended throughout, it climaxed in a show at London's Theatre Royal. Reviews were respectful rather than ecstatic. Bert, dwarfed on the large stage with only a couple of microphones and a bottle of beer for company, appeared nervous, and the looseness of his intros and endings and a recurring inability to keep his instrument in tune were, while typically Bert, simply inappropriate for a concert professional.

He was, at least, working to a largely prearranged set list for the tour. Starting each night with a newly written song, 'Build Another Band', and following that with the old Pentangle blues 'I've Got A Feeling', a sure favourite with audiences and reviewers, he would continue with half a dozen pieces from *LA Turnaround*. He would follow those with two or three old favourites including the now inevitable 'Angi', a recently-recorded arrangement of 'In The Bleak Midwinter' – an ill-fated stab at the Christmas pop charts[20] – and encore with a blues medley based around 'Key To The Highway'. It was a well-balanced set and Bert was clearly doing his best to adapt to the role of solo concert performer. But he lacked the popular touch of a Ralph McTell or the raging swagger of a Roy Harper. In the past he had succeeded by word-of-mouth, intimate venues, a youthful energy and the off-centre charisma of his personality and passion. Ten years on, and after the interval of being an increasingly anonymous member of a band, a way for Bert to be viewed in the 1970s was still in the process of discovery. 'The commercial success of Pentangle may have diminished some of the man's mystery,' wrote one reviewer, 'but some of the old magic is still there. It emerges only spasmodically now, but when it does it's as potent as ever.'[21]

'The farm's got nothing to do with me,' said Bert, in August 1974. 'It's the wife's farm, I just live there. I just go down to the pub and have a good time with the locals, that's all I do. It's all I've ever done.'[22] Shortly after the comeback tour, around Christmas, Bert returned to the farm and told Heather he wanted to live in London.

'We discussed selling up and moving back,' she says. 'He said that he didn't really want to do that. I said, "What *do* you want to do, then?" "I don't know," he said, "sometimes I think I just want my freedom." So we parted company, sadly but amicably. I don't think either of us felt that it was an irrevocable step, just that something needed to change and we weren't sure what. We'd arrived at a point where we both felt we would achieve more separately than if we stayed together. Neither of us had thought it would end. It's difficult to pinpoint why, but his alcoholism was a part of it. It's very distressing to watch someone destroying themselves when you know that you can't help them, but the only person who could help him was himself. He wasn't ready to stop drinking.'

Bert's priorities were not those of his wife's at the time. He was still unhappy at the situation that had forced his mother to move back to Scotland, with undignified haste, and rely on the hospitality of Bert's sister Mary. As Mary recalls, their mother felt understandably hurt. Bert, having abdicated all responsibility for the move to Heather, was not without guilt. He wanted to make amends, but his wife was on another wavelength: 'Everything was horses,' he says. 'She decided she wanted this extra sixteen acres of ground with this money we had, because she'd sold the house my mother was living in. I said, "Look, you know, the idea was when we're in better shape we'll put her into another house." But no, she wanted this extra land so I split at that point.'

Heather felt very strongly that she did not want her private life aired in public, and given that a child was involved any official split would have made court proceedings inevitable: 'I didn't need any of that,' she says. 'All our financial arrangements were resolved happily between us.' Bert, effectively, left her everything. Heather continued to breed horses and to paint, and she and Bert would not see each other for nearly ten years. Sometime in the early eighties Bert invited Heather to a gig in Somerset: 'I went along full of trepidation,' she says, 'not knowing how I would feel emotionally, and torn between a fear that if he was brilliant I would fall in love all over again, and if the drink had got the better of him and he was awful that would also be incredibly painful. But it was absolutely wonderful and in his true tradition he played a song that he knew only I would recognise for what it was and what it meant and when it was written, and that's typical of the man. It was fantastic that he could still be so good and that I could still feel so good for him. We resumed contact after that.' Heather by then was living in a small village in Devon, fearsomely self-sufficient as a person and herself now acclaimed as an artist in her own field. Although it was by then no more than a formality, Bert and Heather were divorced in 1988.

'There's definitely one small failing that Bert has,' says Bruce May. 'He's the most indelibly heterosexual bloke I've ever known, but he sometimes misses when the woman is in charge. Heather was a very intelligent girl and he's come to acknowledge that. So was Gail Colson. Women like Gail Colson, who could have eaten him for dinner, he regarded as "chicks". She went on to manage Peter Gabriel, had a hugely successful management career. But at that time she was second in command to Tony Stratton Smith.'

'I think Tony had a problem promoting me,' says Bert. 'Personally, I liked him. He was a real character. Lunch was always four hours and you had everything, champagne, whatever. I liked him because he'd sign out-of-the-way people like John Betjeman and I suppose I was just part of that out-of-the-way-ness. I don't think the rest of the company knew what was going on. They were all in Genesis mode, particularly Gail Colson. I was a mystery to her.'

'Bert would come into the office,' remembers Pete Frame, 'and because Strat had put it around that Bert was this great genius everyone would be very deferential to him. But Gail Colson would say, "Well, I've never heard of him. He doesn't mean anything to me." She was very down to earth with him, sent him back into the studio to re-record things, stuff like that. But she liked him.'

Strat's relationship with Gail was a case of 'I sign them, you sell them'. Making Bert a saleable commodity was an unreasonable challenge for anyone at the time: 'We never really got a vibe going together,' she admits. 'But it wasn't the case that I was too busy with Genesis: we gave every artist equal attention. Bert just wasn't commercial. Then again, Genesis weren't exactly commercial and Van Der Graaf Generator certainly weren't commercial! But Bert really divided the company: there were some who raved about him and others who just didn't see it at all. I remember having lunch with him a couple of times and found it really heavy going. I was never Tony's secretary, but the way Bert got on with me he probably thought I was!'

For the first six months of 1975, Bruce May's attention was understandably focused on Ralph McTell. Ralph had reached No. 2 in the UK singles chart in February with 'Streets Of London' and Bruce was frantically trying to build on the breakthrough. As a result of this, Bert spent the first third of the year doing not a great deal beyond drifting between places to stay.[23] One of those he stayed with for a while was singer-songwriter Steve Ashley. Back in 1973, Steve's band Ragged Robin were enjoying a six-week residency at Roy Guest's new venue in Chalk Farm, his third and final club to go by the name of the Howff. As a folk-club organiser in Maidstone during his student days in 1967, Steve had booked Bert and had remained in awe. It was a thrill then to see from the stage of the Howff the great Bert Jansch and Sandy Denny sharing a table and enjoying his performance.

'They came up after and said hello and were very encouraging to us,' says Steve. 'Early in 1975 I met Bert again by chance, at the Half Moon in Putney. It was about two weeks before he went to America to record *Santa Barbara Honeymoon*. I always found him a very friendly, positive sort of character. After the pub we went back to my basement flat in Battersea and Bert said he didn't really have anywhere to stay so I said, "Well, you can stay here," and he did. Next day he went out and bought a big broom and swept out the hall! He never said anything about it, I just came back and it was done.

'I went to one gig he had during that time, somewhere in South London. Gordon Giltrap was doing support. We went on beforehand to one of the London pubs with Bruce May. I was quite anxious because the time was getting on, and we were pottering about having a game of darts. That made me feel uneasy. I was the sort of guy who'd arrive at a gig two hours early, because I couldn't stand the tension of not being there! Bert's got a nice laid-back attitude to what he does but the point was we were drinking a lot, the pub was very attractive, the darts were going on . . . Then he showed me this little game he used to do involving lifting a matchbox up on a packet of cigarettes. I think it was a guitarist's finger exercise – or that's how I rationalised it! Needless to say, we arrived at the gig quite late.

'At the time he was working on a couple of songs, "Build Another Band" and "Lost And Gone". Lovely songs. I had a feeling it was one of those times your life's changing. We sat up late talking one night and the next day he was off to LA. I'd taken his banjo, to be repaired for him, to a guitar maker down in Kent. It's probably still ready for collection. Actually, he left some of his washing behind too and I would occasionally have a few drinks thereafter on the fact that I was wearing Bert Jansch's underpants!'

In April 1975 Bert went back to California for two months to cut his second album for Charisma. It was to be supervised by a man who now called himself Danny Royce Lane and who had only recently been kicked out of

Ralph McTell's road band mid-tour. Somehow, Bruce May had thought this was the right man to put some commercial zing into Bert's music: 'Bert needed a follow-up to *LA Turnaround*,' says Pete Frame, by then bemused to find himself employed as Charisma's A&R man, 'and no one could think of a producer. I wrote to Neil Young, he didn't reply; I wrote to Eric Jacobson, who'd produced the Loving Spoonful and Norman Greenbaum, but he didn't want to do it; I approached Jim Rooney, who later worked with Nanci Griffith, but he didn't want to do it. So almost by default, Bruce got this drummer who'd run off with Nesmith's wife. I couldn't see it.' On reflection, neither can Bert: 'We had this mad drummer as a producer and he was living with Mike Nesmith's ex-wife and kid. He was a nutter. All of them were Christian Scientists and there was a bad case of shingles going through them and no one could do anything to alleviate it. This was all going on at the same time as the album. It was chaos.'

At the time, however, Bert was quite happy to go along with the idea of another record produced by an American, with largely anonymous session players, sugary backing vocalists, whizzing synthesiser, Dixieland jazz ensemble and Jamaican steel drums adding to and occasionally pulverising his delicate songs. 'I've been through a period where I'm not fully convinced about what I've been doing,' he admitted, choosing his words carefully eighteen months later.[24] But the seemingly maverick attitude at work here in Bert's thinking was fuelled more profoundly by his continuing rebound from the Pentangle. 'Towards the end of Pentangle,' he explained to *Sounds'* Joe Robinson, on his return to Britain, 'it got to the point where you were really terrified of playing. The standards were so high and some of the music was so difficult to perform that you were in a real nervous state of shock by the time you actually got onstage. Now I just get on and enjoy myself. I just don't care.'[25]

Bert took the opportunity of being in California to play some low-key gigs, get romantically involved with a strident TV producer called Tisha Fine, to whom the eventual album, *Santa Barbara Honeymoon*, was dedicated, and generally hang out. Cocaine was still a near-mythical substance in Britain but in California's music scene of the mid-seventies it was de rigueur. 'One of my last duties at Charisma,' says Frame, elbowed out in July 1975, 'was to peruse and pass for payment the expenses sheet for the album. It reminded me of the food and drink bill that Prince Hal found in the sleeping Falstaff's pocket.' Lane and his cronies had managed to get through more cocaine than food, drink, tobacco, entertainment and sundries put together.

Never a subscriber to organised religion himself, Bert was baffled by the catch-all nature of Christian Science: 'The basic philosophy is that God will cure everything,' he mused a few months later. 'But I don't understand why they can shove twenty ton of coke down their nostrils at the same time. I've had endless discussions with Nesmith about it but he could always get round it.'[26]

Bert was also surprised, during the California trip, to meet one of his oldest friends, recently retired from the Incredible String Band and another subscriber to esoteric religion: Robin Williamson. 'He showed up at this gig with an entourage,' Bert recounted to MM writer Michael Watts, 'and he's very quiet and mystic with this big fixed smile. All these religions seem to have this thing that you must smile to everyone the first thing you do. So he's got this permanent smile on his face, and eyes which don't actually see anything, and he's trying to speak and he was smiling and floating at the same time. I said, "Why don't you come round to the studio and see what we're doing?" So he came round with his fiddle, his mandolin, his guitar. He got up with his fiddle and tried to do one track, and he played for three hours, but it didn't come together. It cost me about four hundred quid.'[27]

Remarkably, given the decadence of Lane's regime, Santa Barbara Honeymoon came in under budget, at $22,000: cheaper than LA Turnaround and cheaper than some of the Pentangle albums. It would be released in October. In the meantime, Bruce May had formulated some plans to shift Bert's profile up a gear: on 30 June he was to perform a financially-motivated 'reunion' concert with John Renbourn at the Festival Hall, followed immediately (and starting later that night) with a week's residency at Ronnie Scott's jazz club as a solo performer and festival appearances at Cambridge and Montreux a few weeks later. Bert and John's relationship had distinctly cooled of late. They had only seen each other periodically and always in the context of trying to sort out the Pentangle's business affairs. The ex-members would remain in debt to Reprise for years.

Publicity-wise, both the reunion and the twice-nightly Ronnie Scott's performances were successful. All three British weekly music papers gave coverage and Charisma filmed two of the Ronnie Scott's nights for a promo aimed at the BBC's Old Grey Whistle Test, although nothing was ever screened.[28] Performance-wise, however, all was not well. While the brief Bert and John finale to the Festival Hall concert, climaxing in a specially written duet setting of Renbourn's 'Lady Nothing', was judged successful, Renbourn's solo set had been a triumph and Bert's a disaster.

'The contrast with John, at the top of his game, was stark,' remembers one fan, Mike Fox. 'It was a strange gig and I remember the feel of it more than the actual details. It was very clear how far their styles had digressed and there was a sense of partially reconciled antipathy between them. John later confided that he had felt rather snubbed by Bert, that Bert was "doing him a favour" by playing with him. Bert's performance at the Cambridge Folk Festival felt the same – it seemed as if he didn't want to be there.'

While Bert's writing was exploring new avenues at this time, his playing was at its weakest. Some of the new songs abandoned his trademark fingerstyle for simple strumming: perversely, not a playing style Bert was much good at. Again, it was an extreme reaction to his past: 'My guitar might be unusual but in no way am I an out-and-out guitarist,' he told *Sounds* just prior to the Renbourn reunion. 'I have always considered myself primarily a songwriter. It was just my association with people like John Renbourn that put me in that virtuoso bag. He's much more a guitarist than I am.'[29]

When *Santa Barbara Honeymoon* was released in October 1975 it elicited almost palpable gasps of astonishment from the commentators. Judgements ranged from stunned admiration at how Bert was forging ahead to the more exasperated tones of those who felt that, for all its daring, this was simply not Bert Jansch. Angie Errigo, for *NME*, perhaps expressed most clearly what Bert's loyal fans must surely have thought: 'Had it been by someone new I would have dismissed it out of hand as a bore. Because it is Bert Jansch I've played it continuously, trying to find some of the spark that has always made Jansch so special. I cannot believe he was on this album.'

'Some of the songs are among the best I've written. I still stand by them,' says Bert now. Certainly 'Lost And Gone', on oil exploration and the Shetland Isles' ecology, remains a work of rare power, Bert's sombre artistry alone creating the withering emotional force to compel beyond the rants of conventional protest. By way of contrast, an unlikely but sincere cover of 'You Are My Sunshine' and his own 'Baby Blue', lyrically slight, had a freshness and simplicity about them with which Bert was trying to imbue all his songs of the period. Unfortunately, Lane's production overwhelmed anything else that may otherwise have impressed in this way. 'Dance Lady Dance', grafting Dixieland flourishes on to Bert's best efforts at something uptempo, was released as a single and went nowhere. Bert, meanwhile, had gone to live in Putney.

'He was never without a girlfriend,' remembers Bruce May. 'In the period we were working together Bert must have had twelve or fourteen serious, more-than-two-month relationships.[30] He had this strange way of just wobbling from one lady to another. He would always move in with them and it would always fly apart – and you never knew why! Sometimes he'd have a black eye; I'm quite sure they never did. But it would be anybody. There was Tisha Fine in LA, there was Ralph's sister-in-law Astrid, there was a production assistant from the *Old Grey Whistle Test*, then he played a show in Belgium and announced he wasn't coming back, that he'd taken up living with a girl who ran three boutiques – and he must have stayed there for at least three months. He lived with a Danish girl for a while as well. Another was Polly Bolton: a tough girl. So the idea that there was a career or a strategy – how could there be? We were just young men, it was all new to me – bank borrowings, people getting nicked for a having a bit of dope on them, turning up at gigs to find no sound system . . . I mean, Jesus, we were just chasing our tails.'

During the latter half of 1975, Bert locked into a most agreeable way of life based in and around the pubs of Putney, socialising with the 'Putney mafia', a motley crew of folkish musicians who orbited the Half Moon pub, moved in and out of each other's bands and who all seemed to be managed by Bruce May. Bruce's offices were nearby and so too, in a large house by the common, was Bert's new residence. The house itself had featured prominently in a TV ad for Unigate Milk, courtesy of Bert's landlady Caroline whose partner was in advertising, while TV current affairs personality David Dimbleby lived next door and novelist Jilly Cooper up the road. Caroline would host cocktail parties where Bert would be introduced as 'the artist who lives upstairs', while Caroline's bloke grumbled about the hours Bert was keeping. After five months, Bert was asked to find alternative accommodation but not before a Danish TV crew had comprehensively documented the time and place in the documentary *A Man And His Songs*.

A leisurely but compelling English-language film, broadcast only in Denmark, it demonstrates unwittingly both the brilliance and the under-achieving tendencies of its subject: stunning as a solo performer, frustrating as an apparently unambitious man content to plough time and effort into something uncomfortably close to a pub rock band. We see Bert performing a solo concert in Edinburgh, playing darts in the Bricklayer's Arms with Ralph McTell, pottering about in the garden of Caroline's house, and discussing the Pentangle, the Campaign for Real Ale and his lifestyle in general: 'I sit here and play the guitar during the day usually or go out and meet a few friends,' said Bert. 'Putney's like a little village in the middle of London. If I cross the bridge to the other side it's very rare – it's about once a month, unless I'm actually working.'[31]

More than ever, with only odd dates in Europe to concern him, Bert's life was essentially a social drinking scene: 'It was extraordinary,' says Bruce. 'Bert would show up at the Half Moon and toddle off home, leaning sideways to avoid falling off Putney Bridge. I remember once on tour when he was utterly out of his head, walking through this really lovely reception that had been laid on for us – the glass was perpendicular, he was diagonal, but he didn't spill anything, didn't bump into anyone. Other guys, they're crashing into people, throwing up, being obnoxious . . . Bert was never like that. People say "shambolic", and I know the chaotic randomness that he seems to evoke, but to me he's not a shambles. He's a very sinuous, careful, controlled kind of man. And he never, ever complained about anything.'

Bert's soft-spoken, unassuming and easily likeable personality shines through on the documentary, onstage and off. The most affecting performance is 'Blackwater Side' filmed in concert at Edinburgh University. Entertainingly fluffing the intro and later struggling to recall the lyrics, somehow Bert's essence, fallibility and genius are captured in that one piece of single-camera footage. In contrast, three songs from the new band in rehearsal are depressingly mediocre.

'I think he needed a group,' says Bruce, 'I think he wanted to recreate the success he'd had with Pentangle. I thought at the time, "Yeah, fine, if that's what you want to do – but who's gonna pay for it?" They must have played "Curragh Of Kildare" for weeks on end!' The core of the group were Rod Clements on bass, Pick Withers on drums and Mike Piggott on violin. Others would come and go. There would be periodic recording sessions and very few gigs but the rehearsals went on forever: 'I was trying to put a band together and everybody in the whole world seemed to be in it,' Bert recalls, 'all sorts of characters that clashed.' He tried to justify the situation at the time by characterising the personnel flexibility as a conscious alternative to the solidity of the Pentangle era. In truth, 1975 – 76 was a period of aimless floundering. In May 1976, a party of journalists were invited to Croydon's Fairfield Halls to witness the Bert Jansch group, only to find that something had gone pear-shaped and Bert was doing the show solo – a perfunctory set lasting barely an hour – all of which 'caused considerable shrugging of Charisma shoulders'.[32]

One of the most penetrating critiques of Bert's character and status, which still holds currency today, dates from this period. *Melody Maker* writer Michael Watts identified the unique artist behind the shambling domestic circumstances and momentary mediocrity of his music: 'He is among the world's better players of acoustic guitar, and master of a style that perhaps will not survive him. Surprisingly, for one of his contrary reputation, he has a seemingly inexhaustible patience. He is also careful and articulate of speech which, when he's sure of the company he's in, he punctuates with short, sharp laughter. Yet he admits that he's wary of people and that it takes him a long time to accept someone. He barely ever listens to albums, he doesn't go around the clubs and very rarely will he attend a concert, partly because it makes him too nervous he says. He professes himself indifferent to great fame. "It's not necessarily what you're looking for in life, to convince the whole world that you're a genius. Maybe all you're trying to do is earn a

living. If I go in a pub I don't want everyone to know I'm Bert Jansch. I
want to have a quiet game of darts." He has an integrity that seems almost
flinty and old-fashioned in these musical times and towards the end of last
year his life had devolved into a pleasurable routine of Putney alehouses.'[33]

One interruption of the cosy routine was an Australian tour as a soloist,
double headlining with John Martyn and memorable for all the wrong
reasons: 'I was waiting for them in Perth,' says Bruce May. 'There was some
kind of hurricane and they ended up in Melbourne, four or five hours away.
I got a call at 9 a.m. and it was John: "What do you want, the bad news or
the good news?" he said. There was no good news. "I've got a busted lip,
Bert's got a dislocated finger and the road manager's in prison." They'd had a
fight on the plane. Bert had hit John Martyn. I said to Bert the next day,
"Whatever possessed you?" He said, "Well, I knew before the tour was over
John was going to hit me so I thought I'd get mine in first." He's a man not
without courage. Chris, the tour manager, had bought a bottle of Scotch in
an effort to calm things down but it just got worse. Chris took John's bag off
the plane and John for some reason had stuffed a life-jacket into his bag. So
they were stopped as they left and Chris was thrown into prison. By the time
they made it back, having postponed the gig by a day, only John could play.
Later in the tour they were at the Sydney Opera House and it was packed,
principally John's audience. John was reaching the end of his set, going
down a storm, when Bert decided to sweep the stage behind him. He'd
found the janitor's broom. He'd already had a fight with John – what was he
thinking? I bundled him off the stage, got him by the throat – and he was
giving me every kind of grief – but I don't think anybody in the audience
realised it was Bert, and I don't think John ever knew. If it had been allowed
to continue, if John had seen him . . . I was glad to get home in one piece
after that tour. I eventually escaped from John Martyn. Bert and I just drifted
apart.'

Towards the end of 1976, with more than enough tracks for an album in the
can and a Scandinavian tour booked as the first real outing for Bert's infinite
rehearsal band, fiddle player Mike Piggott revealed his dislike of travel. A
replacement was required. Martin Jenkins had been in a band called Dando
Shaft, notable for having worn a Pentangle influence on its sleeve, and
subsequently in Hedgehog Pie. He knew Bert casually from the occasional
shared bill and specifically through a shared roadie, Dave Cooper, and at the
end of 1976 had time on his hands.

'Dave phoned me up and said, "Would you be interested in having a
rehearsal with Bert for a possible tour of Scandinavia?" Of course I was
interested. The rehearsal was at Rod Clements' house in North London and

I came away from it elated. I could fit in fine and it was a tasty little band: guitar, bass, drums and the instruments I play – flute, fiddle, mandocello. We did the Scandinavian tour, three or four weeks, and it was a knock-out trip, really fine concerts and club dates, all in thick snow with a tour bus and seventeen-hour drives between some of the gigs.'

Martin's arrival had the added impact of revitalising the stage material. 'Everywhere on that tour people wanted him to play "Angi",' says Martin, 'but he didn't want to play it. He'd been playing it for years. We did work up another old song, "Running From Home", which I'd sung myself years before in the folk clubs round Coventry. We worked it up as a canon, with me singing first and Bert following a couple of bars after, because he couldn't remember the words.'[34]

With his dextrous style, love of time signature trickery and a distinctive, burbling mandocello sound based on phaser pedals Martin quickly made his mark on the presentation of Bert's music: 'It used to astonish me how many new songs he would come up with,' he says. 'In terms of the arrangement, with Bert's guitar playing it's almost complete in the first place so we didn't really arrange, we just learned the songs. For my part I played to his guitar, catching every little tag that he puts in and trying to remember it all.'

After the Scandinavian tour Rod Clements accepted the offer, too good to turn down, of reunion concerts with his old band Lindisfarne. Then Pick dropped a bombshell. He had been asked to join 'this funny little punk band called Dire Straits': 'We all laughed,' says Martin, 'and then six months later he was recording in the Bahamas, with platinum albums all round the cosmos. So Bert said, "Shall we just carry on as a duo?" ' Bert's period of working with Martin spanned seven years, 1976 – 82. For much of that time they worked as a duo, towards the end of the partnership drafting in other musicians to create a three- or four-piece band known as the Bert Jansch Conundrum.

A Rare Conundrum, having lain on Charisma's shelf for the better part of a year and having inspired the group name in the interim, finally appeared in May 1977 at the height of punk.[35] For all the rehearsing that had gone on with the Rod Clements grouping, Bert had only played a handful of British dates in 1976 – a flurry of solo shows in April, a few band shows in July and a trio of dates at London's Marquee Club in December. Rod, Pick, Martin and even Danny Thompson made their contributions to the shows. 'They were wonderful gigs and had the feel of a comeback,' remembers Mike Fox. The first of the Marquee dates provided an opportunity for Hugh Fielder at *Sounds* to interview his hero – an opportunity offered by a publicist working with Bruce May at the time. The fact that Bert, an artist with a now legendary if over-played antipathy to the press, actually had a publicist at all was an irony not lost on the writer. Bert was clearly happy with the forthcoming album. He was currently more prolific than he had been for a long time, he felt – certainly evidenced by the number of known outtakes from various sessions the previous year – and expressed a liking for the recently split 10CC, a liking for Ralph McTell's song-writing and a disliking for the production on Ralph McTell's records. He was also concerned about the growing abundance of equipment in live and studio situations: 'The more it becomes technology the less it becomes music. There has to be progress but there also has to be a limit. I mean, am I a folk musician or not? There has to be a point where I'm not any more.'

Martin Jenkins would often be surprised, during their time together, at how little Bert seemed to know or want to know about the recording process: he was only concerned with creating the songs. During the early nineties Bert would throw himself at technology, investing in digital multi-track recording gear, computer software, MIDI equipment and suchlike. But until that time, technology was simply a necessary evil and somebody else could deal with it: he was still pursuing the path of an artist. 'I'm still progressing,' he told Fielder. 'There's a lot more to be played and said and heard yet, and there are a lot of new horizons for me.'

A Rare Conundrum was a step removed from the West Coast stodge of *Santa Barbara Honeymoon*, but it was hardly a great leap forward. Featuring some very beautiful if painfully delicate songs that referred to Bert's childhood and early days as a musician, the aura was relaxed to the point of being lightweight and inconsequential. Yet reviews were generous. There was a general sense of relief that Bert was at least making records that sounded 'English' again. Ironically, the one item universally singled out for praise was Bert's handling of the Irish song 'The Curragh Of Kildare', 'discovered' by Christy Moore some years earlier and learned by Bert from the singing of Luke Kelly. Other than that, as Hugh Fielder noted in *Sounds*, 'the themes cover familiar Jansch territory – love songs, reminiscences and tales of homelessness. At times you feel that some of the ground has been covered once too often.'

After the album's release the opportunity arose for Bert and Martin to tour as a trio with Danny Thompson. Danny's period of working with John Martyn had come to an end with the blistering *Live At Leeds* (1975). Martyn's career had reached a momentary impasse and Danny was at a loose end. Bert had written 'Build Another Band', featured on *Santa Barbara Honeymoon*, as an oblique encouragement to Danny. Why not put his money where his mouth was? The new trio toured England and Scotland and had a fine old time, played fantastically well and drank on a monumental scale.

'It can be quite hard,' says Martin, 'so much travelling, so much music. Drinking becomes just a way of getting through the day. You're in the hands of new people every day, and they all want you to boogie with them. People wanted a lot from Bert but it was hard for him to deal with it. Some people are basically outgoing, like Danny Thompson: when Danny stopped drinking it didn't make any difference – he's just as outrageous with or without. For Bert, the drinking helped him deal with everything. It was also quite important just because it was fun. Most of the time when Bert had a few drops with me he could open up enough to just have fun, it seemed to take away some of the troubles which plagued him which I never knew. He was quite private, wouldn't say a lot about his life, never complained, but you knew there were always things that were troubling him. There's so much burning within him. When it comes out, it comes out in his songs.'

By the end of the seventies what remained of the folk scene in Britain was in hock, on the one hand, to guitar-toting comedians like Jasper Carrott and Fred Wedlock, and on the other to hard-line, ear-fingering traditionalists. The folk clubs of Britain had by and large become ale-swilling, chorus-singing, beard-wearing, beer-bellied by-ways of awfulness and irrelevance. With Bert having failed to maintain a solo career as a concert hall artist it was back to the folk clubs if he wanted regular work in Britain. No longer the dazzling stranger of the sixties, or a cultural commentator with any mass constituency like Dylan, Bert was a faded icon who was less than prominent on the current British scene and who could hardly be said to be an 'entertainer': 'People had come to expect performers, particularly folk performers, to entertain them with more than music,' says Martin, 'but that was never a priority with Bert. He's not one for making jokes and gags. Bert's priority was to make music.'

For what would prove to be the final review of a Bert Jansch concert in the British weekly music press, Karl Dallas, nearing the end of his own term as the man from the *Melody Maker*, went along to see Jansch, Jenkins and Thompson at the Queen Elizabeth Hall in September 1977. 'It was a bit like a throwback to the days when we used to sit in the Horseshoe,' he wrote, 'amazed and bemused at the magic being made by the five disparate individuals who fused and became Pentangle, and saw history being made. Except that there was no sense at all of déjà-vu: this was quite obviously 1977, and the music being made was as different from the music of Pentangle as their music was from everything that had gone before.'

Touring Scandinavia as a duo shortly after that performance, Bert and Martin were recorded for Swedish television performing a work in progress that would evolve into one of the greatest works of Bert's career: 'Avocet', then still known by the name of its melodic inspiration, the traditional song

'The Cuckoo'. Bert had been developing the piece onstage from at least the time of the Marquee gigs in December 1976 and musing on it to journalists ever since, often coinciding with an expressed admiration for the classical guitarist Julian Bream: 'I'm still trying to work out what to do with this piece,' he told one writer. 'I'm writing it down more for my own pleasure than anything [but] I don't know yet whether to try and play all the instruments myself or whether I should get other people in.'[36]

'We toured Scandinavia at least twice a year,' says Martin, 'and often went in between for festivals. During one of these tours we were sitting in a restaurant in Copenhagen with Bert's Danish manager Peter Abramson and he said, "Why haven't you recorded this?", to which Bert said, "Because nobody's asked me to." Actually, I think he'd already put it to Charisma and they didn't want it. Peter went off and came back half an hour later and said, "Okay, I've got a fine studio booked for February next year, you can have it for two weeks, you can make the album. I'll give you this much money as an advance, this much in royalties, this much for publishing . . ." Bert said, "Yeah, fine," and we had the whole deal worked out there and then.'

Aside from the epic he had crafted from 'The Cuckoo', Bert had accumulated a number of other instrumentals and Martin had one himself. Danny Thompson was drafted in on bass and production. It was decided to put five short pieces on side two with the magnum opus consuming side one. Every piece would be named after a sea bird or wading bird: 'The Cuckoo' finally emerged on record as 'Avocet':

'Each night we'd take a cassette from the studio back to the hotel and just listen to the day's work,' says Martin. 'It was all written by Bert, all the guitar parts were his and all the melodies that I played on fiddle were basically his suggestions too. When we'd first played it he'd recorded his guitar parts on a little tape machine and then demonstrated over that, on guitar, what he wanted me to play, not for me to copy strictly, but how I wanted within that framework. He also wanted Danny to contribute in his own way. Most of it was mapped out but we had to record it in sections. Bert really had it clear in his head how each piece could flow together with a sense of continuity, in terms of key rather than tempo. I was highly impressed. When I listen to it now I think Bert should have had a better violin player than me because it's really quite a special piece of music. But I'm proud to be on that record.'

Avocet first appeared on Peter Abramson's Ex-Libris label in Denmark in 1978, and was subsequently licensed to Charisma for UK release in February 1979. A charitable interpretation of Charisma's delay would have the label waiting for a gap in the ebb and flow of 'vintage' Jansch from Transatlantic, sold on by Nat Joseph and trading under Geoff Hannington's ownership as Logo. Three volumes entitled *Early Bert*, recycling old albums in distinctly budget-looking guise, had appeared on Transatlantic's XTRA label in August 1976. The legendary *Bert Jansch* would remain on catalogue at full price. A still more tawdry-looking release entitled *Anthology* – a fair selection of material, but lacking any gravitas, information or even the dignity of a sleeve design – appeared in May 1978. It was the shape of things to come.[37]

'I'm not complaining,' said Bert, a couple of years later and with admirable restraint, 'but the Musicians' Union or somebody ought to do something about it. Contracts are contracts, but there ought to be a limit on how many times they can put out the same old tracks under new titles. I'm proud that my first album has continued to be in the catalogue and sell year after year. But to delete an album and then reissue it under a new title, it devalues the new product. In the end, the public begins to think you're not doing anything new.'[38]

Avocet would be the last Bert Jansch album for many years to receive anything like respectable coverage in the music papers. But if Bert was now perceived to be going out of fashion, he was doing so in style. In Britain the new record was hailed as something of a gentle triumph, with reviewers perhaps pleasantly surprised that the once great, more recently meandering, Bert Jansch had once again come up with the goods.

Not least, the album represented a return to almost wholly acoustic music. It was a return all the more striking in being starkly against the grain of the times. Mark Ellen for *NME* felt that, musically, the album was a fulfilment of the promise hinted at in the instrumental work on *LA Turnaround* five years earlier. He was literally correct, for 'Bittern' – complex, edgy, and featuring the trio trading solos in 3/4 time in the exhilarating tradition of the Pentangle at their best – began and ended with a guitar figure straight from 'Chambertin'. Hugh Fielder, in *Sounds*, observed that Bert's guitar style was 'too distinctive to hold many surprises any more but when placed in this setting it blossoms until it becomes positively cosy'. That in itself was something new: this was no easy-listening album but it was eminently *listenable* – something that, to the uncommitted, could not easily be said of every one of its predecessors. For Karl Dallas, in *Folk News*, it was 'quite simply the most splendidly flawless recording Bert has made since *Bert & John* and possibly the finest he has ever produced'. For the unashamedly partisan Dick Gaughan (one of Bert's drinking buddies at the time), writing in *Folk Review*, every track was a winner. Moreover, he felt, readers should listen to the record 'with pleasure, delight, wonder and pride, yes *pride*, because the folk world can say that Bert Jansch started with us, has always stayed close, and will always be part of the folk world'. It was an observation that reflected a strange truth. Bert Jansch had always regarded himself as a folk singer, and yet he had never been a part of the mainstream of the world that was represented now by the folk clubs. He would always remain, to some extent, an outsider. There would be no chance of a sing-along chorus.

During the early summer of 1978 Bert and Martin had toured America with Ralph McTell: 'You keep hearing that the singer-songwriter is dead,' McTell told the *Boston Globe*, 'yet more than eleven hundred people came to hear us play tonight. That's tremendously rewarding.' Socially, the tour was less successful. Bert was by now living in Coventry with Polly Bolton, a zoologist and one-time singer with Martin's old group Dando Shaft. 'I lived with her for about a year,' says Bert, 'I just don't think we suited each other. There were so many incidents – she was so volatile and I couldn't handle it after a while.' Polly had also come on the tour: 'Jesus Christ! That was terrible! Dreadful!' says Ralph McTell. 'Bert was getting pissed all the time and Polly was singing with him and one day she just said, "I've had enough," and went out and got pissed herself to show him what it was like. It was at Princeton University and she came out on to the stage while Bert was playing, completely drunk, and started singing. Bert couldn't go on or wouldn't go on, so Polly continued singing and then Martin played a solo set. I don't think Bert remembers a lot of these things. There's great big blanks in his past.'

However popular British acoustic legends like Ralph and Bert still were in America and Europe during the late seventies, the musical climate was changing. One incident speaks volumes about Bert's ability to remain largely unaware of musical fashion and consequently, in his better moments, to transcend it. Ed Denson, an archetypal Californian hippy, was partner with Stefan Grossman in the Kicking Mule record label. In 1979 Bert became involved with the label and during a tour of the States wound up staying with Denson. As John Renbourn recalls, the story of how Bert influenced the course of punk on the West Coast is the stuff of legend. The connection was Denson's son Bruce: 'In front of poor old Denson's eyes,' says Renbourn, 'the guy develops into this ferocious punk, the head of the Berkeley punk fraternity, and changes his name to "Bruce Loose". These guys are coming into the house and not speaking to Ed and being very unpleasant, but everything changes when Bert arrives. It was the middle of Bert's most horrendous drinking period – he was totally blitzed all the time. Bruce became fascinated, thinking Bert to have the most nihilistic approach to life that he'd ever seen. He'd get the rest of the punk crowd in just to see, following Bert down the streets and into the bars – and Bert never even noticed they were there! I did a radio interview in Berkeley years later and they still speak of him as this Von Daniken type of character: "The Bert"!'

The deal with Kicking Mule was for one album, recorded in London in

1979 and released the following year as *Thirteen Down*. Typical of the label's policy, Stefan Grossman had wanted a solo guitar album with tablature inserts but Bert wanted nothing of the sort. Together with Martin Jenkins, bass and keyboards player Nigel Portman Smith (another of the 'Putney mafia') and drummer Luce Langridge, with Jacqui McShee guesting on one track, Bert delivered an album of songs with a classy, easy-listening sheen. One highlight was 'Sweet Mother Earth', a translation of a song by the Brazilian performer Milton Nasciemento (as recommended by Tony Stratton Smith) and a jagged, punchy complement to the smoothness of the other tracks. But while the presentation was polished, not all the sentiments were as comfortable: 'Where Did My Life Go?', written shortly after her death in April 1978, was a beautiful but desperately poignant song informed by the booze and drugs lifestyle of Sandy Denny, although typically there was no direct reference to its subject. No doubt many listeners, particularly those with an insight into Bert's own lifestyle, believed it to be autobiographical.

A particularly bland track, 'Time And Time', was released in Britain as a single while the album was released with a variety of sleeve designs in Britain, America and Australia.[39] Bert, Martin, Nigel and Luce performed a Danish tour and a few dates in Britain including a BBC Radio 1 *In Concert*, after which Bert, Martin and Nigel toured America. During the tour, as Martin recalls, 'Something happened with the partnership between Stefan Grossman and Ed Densen which I never quite understood. I never got any accounting, never heard anything from them. The deal just vanished.' Later in the year Bert and Martin went to Japan, resulting in an uninspired Japan-only album *Live At La Foret*, recorded by Nippon Columbia with general agreement but without the duo's prior knowledge of where and when.

'I never quite understood why we finished really,' says Martin. 'Bert didn't say anything about it, but that's Bert's way – he finds it difficult to talk about so he just does it. The time we worked together we worked a lot: hundreds and hundreds of gigs. Some of them were fantastic, most of them were fine, and Bert always tried to give the best he could. He had a better audience in Europe than in Britain by that time. But I suppose the work had started to tail off. The last gig we did together was in 1982, but during the summer of 1981 he went to California to make another album, on his own, and we didn't work so much together that year. Maybe by then it had reached its logical conclusion.'[40]

CHAPTER TEN

Heartbreak

'I don't think any of us can be left behind and classified as an old folkie,' said Bert in January 1981. 'Does a young punk in the street have any idea what a folkie is? I don't think anyone's a folk singer these days.'[1] As if to prove the point, Bert, once again without a record deal, accepted an offer from John and Richard Chelew, guitar retailers in Santa Monica, to fly over in June 1981 and cut a solo album in determinedly modern FM radio style. As *Santa Barbara Honeymoon* had done before, the new album was to marry Bert's jagged Celtic artistry with the latest US gloss in the hope of creating something commercially viable. Its name would be *Heartbreak*.

A quartet of session men, including Albert Lee on lead guitar and mandolin, were hired to flesh out a set of songs that were as close as Bert was likely to get to mainstream singer-songwriter territory. A polished revamp of 'Blackwater Side' and the spiky, spacious instrumental 'And Not A Word Was Said' hinted at Bert's unique musical character while cracks at three standards – 'If I Were A Carpenter', 'Heartbreak Hotel' and 'Wild Mountain Thyme' (with Jennifer Warnes on guest vocals) – were punchy and valid. Of the new material, 'Is It Real?' and 'Up To The Stars' had a profundity and restless vigour at odds with the affable langour of *Thirteen Down* and its immediate predecessors. It was a strong album: well performed, well presented (a black and white portrait shot of a resolute, confident looking Bert against an airbrushed backdrop graced the cover) and surely the basis for a career boost.

The album was released in Britain on Logo in February 1982. In April, Bert toured the UK with Albert Lee, Nigel Portman Smith and Luce Langridge, recording a fine BBC Radio 1 *In Concert* and playing Edinburgh's Queen's Hall along the way: 'If the mop-haired maestro looks a bit frayed round the edges, it isn't reflected in his music,' wrote Lindsay Reid in Edinburgh's *Evening News*. 'Looking a bit beefier over the years, this was Bert Jansch on home ground: relaxed, smoking and drinking his way through a set of well over an hour. The magic was still there. He even took time to wish his mum, in the audience, a happy birthday. She's seventy. It's some considerable time since the man was packing the Usher Hall as part of Pentangle but the turnout showed he's not forgotten. The boy did his mum proud.'[2]

This was the last time Bert would tour with a band under his own name. It was nearly ten years since the Pentangle had split and the trajectory of Bert's career, broadly comparable to the careers of its other members, had been essentially downwards ever since. The *Heartbreak* album and tour had been a magnificent effort to say something fresh and bring new listeners on board, but it was simply not happening on any significant scale. By way of both diversion and necessity, Bert had recently acquired a new residence in Putney: Bert Jansch's Guitar Shop, 220 New King's Road.

Bert had stumbled his way into retailing as a pragmatic solution to finding somewhere to live with his partner of recent months, Charlotte Crofton-Sleigh. She had met Bert at a gig shortly after leaving school in 1978, when he was still involved, musically and otherwise, with Polly Bolton. 'Polly used to bring this huge Alsatian to gigs,' says Charlotte, 'and when she wasn't sitting near Bert she'd leave the dog there – like it was a guard dog! It was very funny.' By the time Charlotte and Bert became involved, during 1980, Bert had left Polly and had been staying with first Martin Jenkins in Coventry and then Nigel Portman Smith in Twickenham. The priority for the new couple had not only been to find a good place to live but a solid means of doing so.

'Gigs were sporadic,' says Charlotte. 'There were royalties as well, but not enough to live on. He was earning more from his publishing than from record sales – they were still paying off the advances for one of the Pentangle albums, *Solomon's Seal*. I suppose we were thinking of ways to diversify, really. We found a flat that had an empty shop underneath.[3] My sister made jewellery and we knew somebody else who made pottery or something, so we thought we'd put some of this stuff in the window. We also knew some guitar makers at the time and it grew from there. Bert had a deal with Yamaha and he could maybe give lessons and it all seemed to make sense. We moved into the guitar shop straight after our son Adam was born: November 1981.'

The endorsement deal with Yamaha had been generously arranged for Bert through the influence of Gordon Giltrap, a long-time fan who had recently scaled the UK singles chart with 'Heartsong', an acoustic guitar-led instrumental that displayed traces of the Jansch influence. The deal was more than convenient: aside from a free £2000 guitar (later given to a friend), Yamaha's retainer had provided Bert with the financial credibility necessary to acquire a bank loan and establish his shop, which was to specialise in hand-built instruments. Giltrap had known Bert casually for years but had only recently developed a friendship with his old hero: 'On a personal level, things were pretty grim for me at that time,' says Giltrap, 'and I think Bert and Charlotte took pity on me. I would occasionally stay over and I can even remember taking my father to a pub in the area to meet up with them for a drink. My dad was quite thrilled to meet his son's boyhood hero and, of course, Bert handled it very well in his off-hand, jokey sort of way. I sold a number of surplus instruments via the shop, including the famous John Bailey double-neck which I'd used on my mid-seventies albums. I remember going in one day and Bert was bemoaning the fact that it needed restringing. There were eighteen strings: he said it had taken ages. On checking it out, I wasn't quite sure whether he'd restrung it before or after visiting the pub.'

When Bert's version of 'Heartbreak Hotel' was released as a single in February 1982, he appeared on Capital Radio's *London Tonight* to promote (in typically understated fashion) both that and the shop. Asked why he was not so visible around Britain as he once was and whether he would be on hand at the shop to offer advice to young musicians, Bert's wry response was telling: 'The best advice is, 'Don't do it!'' he said. 'But yeah, I'm there on tap to help out with people's problems.'

'The shop was a struggle,' says Charlotte. 'It was meant to bring in some extra money but in fact what it ended up doing, because we weren't making any money at it and paying commercial rent and rates, was draining the very few resources we had already.' The guitar shop survived just over two years before the bailiffs had their way. But it did achieve something for Bert: after years of playing largely in Europe and America to the neglect of Britain, it put his name quite literally back on the British map. A number of his old friends sought him out there and were happy to give him their business. 'I was sorry it went wrong for him,' says Steve Benbow, by this stage back to playing part-time around the pubs. 'It was a good shop, he had some lovely guitars and I thought he'd be very happy with that situation. Charlotte was very efficient.'

John Harrison, formerly of the Watersons, was another visitor: 'I remember speaking to his lady. "How's business?" I asked. "Oh, we sold a guitar string," she said. "What gauge was it?" I asked, for no particular reason. This guy had come in and said he had to have a 23-gauge string. By pure fluke she didn't have one but said she'd get one in. He came back later on and got his string and she'd asked him what it was for: it was for cutting cheese. So that's how good business was.'

At the same time as Bert had been pottering around as a retailer, a reunion of the Pentangle was under way. Claudio Trotta, an Italian promoter who had regularly booked the John Renbourn Group (featuring both Renbourn and Jacqui McShee), had asked John to canvass the original members on the basis that he would bankroll an album and tour. Rehearsals were now taking place at Jacqui's house in Reigate and at Bert's guitar shop.

'I think everybody was being a bit more enthusiastic about it outwardly than they really were,' says Charlotte. 'Everybody needed the boost at the time, and the money for the Italian tour was quite good, although I think Bert did want to do it for its own sake, not just for the money. But they were a bunch of volatile characters, and ten years down the line they were if anything even more set in their ways: Jacqui had a family by then, Terry was living in Minorca running a restaurant, Danny was as mad as ever, John was thinking about taking a degree in music, and Bert was Bert. Musically, Bert and John had gone in very different directions and that was obvious by then. They didn't *not* get on, but they didn't go out of their way to be with each other, and when they were they were quite formal.'

'When you have a wonderful holiday when you're a child and think you must go back, it isn't the same, is it?' says Jacqui. 'Danny knew this agent in London and Claudio Trotta was pushed aside, which I felt very bad about and so did John. I still squirm when I think I allowed that to happen. The reunion would never have happened if it hadn't been for him, but both John and I are very quiet and if someone else is speaking louder I tend to let them get on with it. Needless to say this other guy put a tour of Italy together which was abysmal.'[4] Emerging from a Pentangle rehearsal in a state of anxiety, Terry Cox had been involved in a road accident and was put in traction at Guildford Hospital. Bert had hoped Terry would play drums on his *Heartbreak* solo tour in April, but that was now out of the question. He would be lucky to fulfil any of the Pentangle dates.

'I don't think Terry's wife wanted the band to re-form at all,' says Bert, 'because they had a nice little life and restaurant in Minorca and all he needed to do was the odd tour with Charles Aznavour. And he was quite happy. To suddenly come back to this chaos of the Pentangle . . . He was nervous all the time, fearing all the old problems would reappear.' At some point Terry rang Jo Lustig of all people, broaching the question of management. Jo's wife and business partner Dee answered the phone and made it clear that she at least would have nothing to do with it. In any case, Jo had tired of musicians and their foibles and was developing a successful new career as a producer of arts documentaries.

The re-formed Pentangle, as an empty-sounding four piece, given Terry's condition, made their debut at Cambridge Folk Festival in July 1982. Filming the whole festival, BBC2 broadcast 'Bruton Town' while BBC Radio 2 aired 'People On The Highway' and 'If I Had A Lover', the *Thirteen Down* track on which Jacqui had guested. 'They weren't the most dynamic act of the festival,' wrote one commentator, 'but Bert Jansch certainly seemed to be enjoying himself among his old mates after all those years in the spotlight on his own.'[5] In December, all five – with Terry in a wheelchair but somehow able to play – completed the tour of Italy. 'Some of it was good, some of it was great,' says Bert of the music, 'but we weren't enjoying the tour and we weren't creative. That to me was the most important thing about Pentangle: absolute creation. This was just resurrecting old stuff and it was painful to have to relearn it. All the old things that would naturally come to the surface did. It would have been easier on everybody if we'd just done the one tour, and then we would have had the chance to have come back in another couple of years and done it again.'

Instead, the group carried on into 1983 and through Danny's agent found themselves touring Australia (a better experience than Italy) and playing some festivals in Germany.[6] By that stage, John Renbourn had enrolled at Dartington College to study music. 'He told me he was going to leave,' says Jacqui. 'I said I would as well, but he said, "No, don't. I'm not going to be working that much, I'm going to be studying, so you should stay with it." I wanted to change the name of the band, but the argument was that Fairport and Steeleye had had loads of personnel changes and had retained the same names, so I went along with it.'[7] Mike Piggott was drafted in as the first replacement in the Pentangle's history. As the band continued through the eighties and well into the nineties as a necessarily part-time concern, it was to prove the first of many departures and arrivals: Danny would be next (after one album), then Terry (after two), then even the replacements would start coming and going. Only Bert and Jacqui would remain constants.

'It just escalated,' says Bert. 'As each member left a new one would appear and I was in the centre of it. I couldn't get out of the situation. I was actually tied to a continually changing band, so that everybody else could get work, basically.' On the one hand it could be argued that over the period of the Pentangle's renewed existence (1982 – 95), and increasingly so towards the end, Bert's obligations as the lynchpin in a band that was perceived to be nostalgic in nature was detrimental to his career. But Bert's solo career had all but run aground and, certainly during the eighties, involvement in a group that was working semi-regularly around Europe and the UK was at least keeping him active. Creatively, there were also opportunities to make recordings under the group's name that were simply not there for him as a soloist. Clearly, the group felt under obligation to record an amount of traditional material, and Jacqui was becoming something of a songwriter herself, but among the five studio albums the group made for Spindrift/ Making Waves, Permanent and the German labels Plane and Hypertension between 1984 and 1993 lurk a small handful of Bert's finest songs.

Best of all was 'The Saturday Movie', a beautifully crafted reflection on

childhood aspirations, which appeared on *In The Round* (1986). So happy
was Bert with the song that he went to see his old friend John Challis, now
working in TV animation, believing that it might work well as a cartoon,
although sadly nothing ever came of this. The escapist sentiments in 'The
Saturday Movie' – playing cowboys and indians, climbing trees, getting
away from real life – were harmless in the context of childhood, but hinted
at the desolation in Bert's own mind at the time. 'Let Me Be', his other
notable contribution to *In The Round*, was a raging, fearful piece of work
denoting a soul in some torment from a God who 'ain't gonna let me get
much older'. The band, now featuring Mike Piggott and Nigel Portman
Smith[8] alongside Bert, Jacqui and Terry, were on the soundest footing they
would achieve in re-formed guise, with a very good record under their belts
and enthusiastic management from Chris Coates, a former road manager for
Ralph McTell. Bert was giving the Pentangle his best shot, but he was doing
so encumbered by a spirit of depression.

'There's an otherness about Bert, like he's not of this earth, like he's
detached,' says Charlotte. 'I always felt very much that he wasn't meant to
deal with the realities of life and the hardnesses. Being from where he comes
from he is very aware of the hardnesses but those were not things that were
in him: he's an artist. He can be quite funny sometimes, when he gets going.
We did have a laugh, it wasn't all dank and depressing. We had some good
times together and I care about him very much, but Bert has always seemed
to me a very blue kind of character.'

Lean times and alcoholism are too easy a summary of Bert Jansch in the
1980s. While those factors were ever-present, even in his darkest hours Bert
was not one to remain idle or to give up creating music or trying to move
forward. Moments of fun peppered the drudge. On one occasion, a Japanese
businessman asked Bert to play the tour guide and take himself and half a
dozen fellow Jansch enthusiasts around Britain: 'He was a millionaire and a
Hawaiian guitar player in some country and western band,' says Bert, 'used
to fly into Nashville and play guitar with all these famous people. So he
made me an offer I couldn't refuse, and it was great fun. They went to
Coventry and met Martin Jenkins, played in Edinburgh folk clubs, met my
sister, my mum . . .'

'I remember arriving home one night, about one in the morning,' says
Maggie Cruickshank, 'to find the lights on and Bert here with all these
Japanese people. My brother had met him in some bar looking for Liz.[9]
Why my brother brought him to my house I don't know, because Liz was
married and living down the road. So we took a pile of drink with us and
went down to Liz's house and there was this succession of bowing. They

were only up in Edinburgh for twenty-four hours but it was such a laugh. In fact, Bert left his bag at Liz's so she had to run up to Waverley Station the next morning.'

Bert went back to his home town for a week-long residency at the Edinburgh Festival during August 1985. Accompanied by Nigel Portman Smith and sharing the billing with piano balladeer Paul Millns, all three decided to work together on each other's material. A very effective piano-led arrangement of 'Is It Real?', broadcast on Radio 4's *Round Midnight*, is the solitary, tantalising glimpse of an experience that the *Evening News's* Alistair Clark concluded 'was all over too quickly'.

Towards the end of 1985 a solo album called *From The Outside* appeared, but only just. Cobbled together from sessions in Denmark and London, with unsympathetic engineers and featuring only guitar and voice, it was Bert's rawest and most cathartic work since *Bert Jansch* twenty years earlier. It slipped out on the tiny Belgian label Konnexion in a pressing of only five hundred copies, and a greater contrast to *Heartbreak* would be hard to imagine. But this time it really was heartbreak. Remixing the album for CD some years later, with a few losses and additions in tracks, Bert added revealing notes on the material. A 'new' track from the original sessions, 'Blackbird In The Morning', a serene love song redolent of James Taylor, was restored to the album and lends a degree of balance. For this was an album adrift on a sea of melancholy, clearly the work of an artist weighed down by the woes of the world. Songs about the nuclear threat, a friend who had died of anorexia, the observed loneliness of old age, the rose-tinted marketing of 'the sixties', and the loss of a loved one all shared space with heart-on-sleeve material that gave vent to his own frustrations.

The abiding message of 'Blues All Around' (lost in the CD transfer) and 'Change The Song' was Bert's desperate search for a way out of what he readily acknowledged in the retrospective notes as 'my depressed and heavy drinking days (gladly no more)'. Yet the songs themselves are classic Jansch, with universal beauty and power. Less potent artistically, but yet more specifically addressing alcoholism, 'Get Out Of My Life' demonstrated at least that Bert was no longer denying his problem. 'Unless you're a really excessive, falling-down drunk it's hard for people to notice,' says Charlotte. 'Bert's drinking was much more a case of get up in the morning, go to the pub, go home and then back to the pub until it closes. He wasn't one for sitting at home all day drinking. It wasn't mad, bingeing drinking as it had been with the Pentangle: it was a lifestyle, so people weren't having conversations with him about it. Also, he had this amazing thing he could do of keeping people away from him. He could be in a crowded room and still sitting on his own, not because he was being nasty to people but because he exuded this thing of "this is my space". But when it came to the crunch, giving up alcohol was a decision he had to make himself.'

Although Charlotte never agreed to marry Bert, she was there for the long haul: in the event, almost to the end of the decade. 'I think one of the things that contributed to our relationship changing,' she says, 'was that when the guitar shop folded and there wasn't much work coming in I had to go out and get a job. I got a job in the film industry and I was becoming quite successful at it, and that was a difficult thing for Bert to deal with. I was maybe more powerful within the relationship than he was comfortable with, because he's very traditional in that way. I was bringing in money, I was quite successful in a career, I was travelling a lot because of that and I don't know how secure he felt. There came a point where I had some decisions to make and he wasn't behind me, and yet I'd always felt that I'd been really strongly behind him in everything. And that changed things for me, to find him being like that.'

Around the end of 1984 Bert had become involved with one Richard Newman, a man with fingers in a number of pies on the London music scene. Known to some of his younger followers as 'the wizard', the character of Newman as described by Loren Auerbach, who worked with him on various schemes and dreams at the time, is typical of the colourful and unlikely personalities who continue to carve themselves niches in the music business. 'Richard was somebody I met when I was eighteen, in 1982,' says Loren. 'I'd just left school and was doing Oxbridge exams – but what I really wanted to do was be a singer and save the world!' Newman was friendly with a number of veteran musicians – among them Cliff Aungier, himself a friend of Bert's at the time – and had booked Michael Klein's Heartbeat Studios for the first of many sessions based on his songs and Loren's singing. Along with Nat Joseph, Richard Newman remains one of the very few people whom Bert actively dislikes, but he was nonetheless a good song-writer and in Loren he had a singer of some character. Bert's role, on what would transpire to be two albums, was ultimately to lend his talent and his name. 'Peter Green was coming to that first recording session,' says Loren. 'Cliff had mentioned this to Bert and Bert had asked if he could come along. He wasn't expecting to do any playing, he just wanted to meet Peter.'

Bert nevertheless did become comprehensively involved in that record, a short but very atmospheric album entitled *After The Long Night*, released in March 1985 on Loren's own label-for-the-purpose Christabel. Bert's name was prominently billed on the front cover. Newman was keen to do a second album. This time, an array of minor legends would be involved: Bert once again, Cliff Aungier, Geoff Bradford and Brian Knight. A handful of other players would fill out the sound, and with Bert's name again flagged on the cover he would also have the opportunity to contribute material: 'Is It Real?', his distinctive arrangements of 'Weeping Willow' and 'Yarrow' and two completely new, if undistinguished, songs, 'Carousel' and 'Give Me Love'. Entitled *Playing The Game*, and released in October 1985, it was a record of very good moments but an occasionally over-egged pudding, lacking the naive charm of its predecessor.

'It was all such a nightmare by then that I find it hard to listen to,' says Loren. 'Richard had been saying, "If Bert's producing it I'm not doing it", and vice-versa from Bert. Richard and Bert always hated each other. But from the moment Bert and I met there was always a bond between us. Bert used to ask me all the time, "What are you doing hanging around with him?" He'd promise a lot and never deliver. That was the problem with Richard in a nutshell. In the end I couldn't bear it any more, but at the time I was young and headstrong and I wouldn't listen to anyone. We put out a thousand albums, they sold, that was the end of that. Richard would never follow things through – he'd jump from project to project, generally revolving around the same group of ageing guitarists.' Bert, for the moment, removed himself from that category and situation. Loren, who had put off university long enough, decided to put some semblance of order into her life with a degree course in English literature.

Open The Door, the first record of the resurrected Pentangle, had done little more than that. By 1986 the group had acquired in Chris Coates a manager with a game plan, and over the next two years everyone would give the all-new Pentangle project their best shot: 'Chris thought he'd got a better chance of getting us played on Radio 2 and doing concerts in arts centres,' says Nigel Portman Smith, 'which was in fact a complete red herring. It wasted a couple years of our careers, really. We were played every morning on *The Jimmy Young Show* and things like that, but it didn't mean we actually sold anything. The people who listen to Radio 2 aren't big buyers of records,[10] and we were playing to half-empty theatres. Chris did his best and it was great to go out on the road and do it, but it just wasn't right.'

Two major tours of Britain were undertaken in February and October 1986. In between, the group went to Europe and America and were well received. 'Surprisingly, the new Pentangle is better than the old,' concluded one reviewer. 'The original band could be inconsistent, reaching elegant beauty one minute and getting too laid-back the next. The new band hits the heights more often, thanks mainly to Piggott [who] gives the band a fire it's seldom had before.'[11] For another commentator, it was Portman Smith who 'has done most to kick Pentangle's sound out of the laid-back lethargy that plagued it before the band split'.[12] Either way, things were moving forward. A number of studio sessions were recorded for late-night BBC Radio 2 programmes,[13] some of them evidence of how good the new line-up of Jansch, McShee, Cox, Piggott and Portman Smith could be on both new and old. Coates's strategy was brave and positive, but ultimately wrong. To compound matters, Making Waves, with whom the new Pentangle had signed a multi-album deal, went bust shortly after *In The Round*'s release. In March 1987 Terry Cox decided to call it quits. 'He'd come to expect his life as a musician would be well looked after,' says Portman Smith. 'Being back on the road with Pentangle, staying in grotty hotels and with Bert boozing so much, it wasn't good enough. Bert was difficult at the best of times. I found it a lot easier because I could get drunk with him, and get closer to him, but Terry didn't drink and Jacqui didn't drink much and I'm sure Bert's condition used to worry them something shocking. His professional reputation was suffering. We were very lucky in finding a couple of agents who'd deal with us. I don't think Bert even today realises how bad his reputation was.'

Given that the Pentangle had positive management and that the other players had a cushioning effect which bolstered his stage performance and got him where he needed to be, the mid-eighties were by no means as bad for Bert professionally as they could have been. A lot of work was put into the group by all involved, Bert included, for very modest financial returns – but at least it was work. As a solo artist, Bert was running out of options: 'Honestly, he would be drunk on stage,' remembers Ralph McTell, 'and you can't do that and continue to get bookings. I've spoken to a lot of agents since then and he's burned a lot of bridges. I think Bert could have been bigger, no doubt about that, and I think he was probably instrumental in preventing that.'

Shortly after Terry Cox left, Mike Piggott did likewise. Gerry Conway, veteran of various British folk-rock groups, had been drafted in as the new drummer; the question of a new lead guitarist was thornier. Bert suggested Peter Kirtley: a friend of a friend, a recent drinking buddy and most conveniently a terrific lead guitar player. Nigel felt that, given their existing repertoire, in the short term a guitarist who could double on fiddle, as Mike Piggott had, was essential. He suggested Rod Clements.

From the time of Rod's original association with Bert in the mid-seventies, some people had felt that Rod's limitations as a musician were outweighed by his attributes as a companion to Bert on the road, a role that should not be dismissed lightly: 'Rod was a strong character,' says Charlotte. 'He cared about Bert and he wasn't somebody who was relying on Bert in the same way that other musicians he knew often were. Rod had his own thing going on with Lindisfarne, and it's more like they were friends. In fact, it was almost as if Rod was not exactly more famous than Bert was, but more successful.'

Lindisfarne were, like the Pentangle, operating during the 1980s as a re-formed part-time concern with full-time aspirations. For the next three years Rod Clements would divide his time between both groups, with one proviso: 'I used to argue with him vehemently about us always being the second choice,' says Portman Smith. But that was how it was. There would be little activity on the Pentangle front until the summer of 1988, but Rod Clements's availability would not be the only reason. Bert Jansch was not a well man.

'I was spending quite a bit of time with Bert and Charlotte at their flat in Redcliffe Square,' says Rod, 'and Bert was spending quite a bit of time in the pub. Even back in the seventies drink used to be a problem for him in terms of gigging. I'd have to phone up promoters and apologise for him occasionally. So I wouldn't say I was shocked, but I was a bit surprised that it had taken over to such an extent. We were rehearsing Pentangle material but I felt that Bert should be doing more than Pentangle. I think, like a lot of people, I'd always felt Bert was a bit diluted in the Pentangle, and at the time I joined they weren't doing very much. Bert seemed to be kicking about at a loose end and spending most of his time in the pub, so I seized the opportunity and asked if we could get a little duo together.'

Rod approached Geoff Heslop, owner of Black Crow, a small record label based in Northumberland, and between them they hatched a scheme to bring Bert back to a level where they believed he would be better off. Geoff agreed to bankroll a Bert & Rod album and in the meantime enticed Bert into a Woody Guthrie tribute project. Also involving Dick Gaughan, Rab Noakes and Rory McLeod and recorded over a convivial three-day session in Newcastle-upon-Tyne during August, *Woody Lives* was released in February 1988. Bert's only vocal, on 'This Land Is Your Land', managed to make Woody's celebratory anthem a world-weary lament.

During that summer of 1987, Bert was also visiting Rod's home in Rothbury, Northumberland, to rehearse material for the prospective duo album. Geoff Heslop had got an agent, Dave Smith, involved, and the unenviable task of assembling Bert's first substantial tour of the UK in years was in progress. Rod was excited by the prospects; Bert was still, curiously, more interested in the Pentangle and was at best acquiescing to the duo project. On Monday, 5 October Bert arrived in Rothbury for the album's final rehearsals: it was to be recorded at Heslop's favoured studio in Newcastle the following week.. 'He really was drinking quite heavily at

this point,' remembers Rod. 'I live about a mile from the village, where the
nearest pub is. Bert would set off at about eleven o'clock in the morning, I
would go and get him at lunchtime, maybe have one with him, and bring
him back to the house to do some playing. Then he'd go down again at six
o'clock and I'd join him later. It was quite difficult to get him to eat very
much.'

'The drinking had got so bad I couldn't lift a glass,' says Bert on reflection.
'I had to look at it for a long time first, and I couldn't talk to anybody unless
I'd had a drink first. And I must have been losing a lot of work. Virginia
McKenna wanted me to play on a film and sent a guy round but the state I
was in . . .'

Rod had organised Bert a gig for the Tuesday at a folk club he was
running nearby. On the Wednesday and Thursday they rehearsed, and then
for the Friday night Dave Smith had organised Bert & Rod a little 'pocket
money' gig at a pub in South Shields: 'Now that night Charlotte and Adam
were coming up on the train,' says Rod, 'which meant Bert wasn't drinking
much. My partner, Marie, met them at the station while we were doing the
gig and we all met up back at my house around midnight. Bert seemed okay,
if a little tired, which I put down to him not having had a drink. We sat
around and had a bottle of wine between us but by the morning of the tenth
Bert wasn't well. He looked like he was in some pain – an awful, pallid
colour, wasn't able to hold himself up right – so we took him down to the
local doctor's surgery. He and Charlotte were in for maybe twenty minutes
then the doctor came out and said, "Can you take him to Ashington
Hospital?" I said, "Yeah, okay, I'll stop off at home and pick up his things."
She said, "No, straightaway." So we drove the twenty miles from Rothbury
to Ashington, all country roads and driving pretty slow because he was in
some pain. I hung around to see if I could be of any use and the next thing I
saw was Bert going past on a trolley with tubes coming out of him.'

Rod went home, returning later to collect Charlotte. They visited Bert
daily for the next week. 'My pancreas had just given in,' says Bert. 'There
was this lady doctor at Ashington who really counselled me through the
whole thing. She had nothing to do with me as a patient but she was a fan. I
never did find out her name.'

In Portman Smith's view, Bert was 'as seriously ill as you can be without
dying'. He was faced with the ultimatum of giving up alcohol or simply
giving up: there and then, he chose the former. 'It was a conscious decision
on his part, and a very courageous and miraculous one,' says Charlotte. 'He
just did it overnight. But then you have something to replace in your life,
and maybe he got a drive back or managed to focus his energies in a way
which started to bring things back to him.'

There can be no doubt that Bert's creativity, reliability, energy, commitment and quality of performance were all rescued dramatically by the
decision to quit boozing, but the road to maximum recovery of health,
artistry and professional credibility was to be no less tortuous than beating
the addiction. It is to Rod Clements's credit that he stood by Bert over the
next few months and (re)organised the touring and recording opportunities
to enable Bert to keep busy. A photo session for the sleeve of Bert & Rod's
projected album took place in November, Bert appearing visibly under the
weather, and between 11 and 16 January 1988, the pair finally threw
themselves into the actual recording. The resulting *Leather Launderette* was
released in March 1988, promoted with sessions for Radio 2's *Folk On Two*
and *Nightride* and an ambitious thirty-one-date UK tour, mostly of folk club
venues, during March and April.

'Dave Smith had a lot of difficulty putting that tour together,' says Rod,
'and it was largely booked on the strength that I would be chaperoning Bert.
But it was a good tour in terms of the audiences we pulled in, because he had
been out of the limelight for a long while. A lot of old fans were curious –
people came out of the woodwork, and the audiences were generally large
and very attentive. But I don't think Bert enjoyed it particularly. It was the
first time he'd done a serious amount of work without drinking and he was
still convalescent. You could count on him getting to the end of a number,
which you couldn't count on before, but he was very quiet. We drove for
hundreds of miles on that tour and he didn't say very much.'

Leather Launderette itself is difficult to assess: jointly credited on the sleeve,
it is best approached as an upbeat, enjoyable but essentially unambitious Rod
Clements record with Bert Jansch guesting prominently. That is not to
denigrate Rod Clements, but to recognise the context in which the album
was made. Bert had little or no new material ready, so Rod contributed and
fronted several rousing country blues covers and pastiches and joined Bert
on a couple of jointly credited instrumentals. For his part, Bert revamped the
now iconic 'Strolling Down The Highway' plus two songs first heard on
From The Outside, an album so pitifully neglected that he was still trying to
salvage something from the wreckage. It was all enthusiastically presented
and arranged-for-duo stuff with Rod on bass and slide guitar. But, for those
concerned with the recovery of Bert's muse, the fragile shoots were to be
found in a wistful arrangement of the traditional 'Bogie's Bonny Belle' and a
beautifully poised, timely revisitation of Alex Campbell's 'Been On The
Road So Long'.

Campbell had died in January 1987, and Bert's re-recording of the song a
year later had resonance with regard to both men: Alex had been beaten by
the road and the lifestyle; Bert had only just made it back from the brink.[14]

His relationship with Charlotte would not be so fortunate: 'We came back
home and things were already difficult between us,' she says. 'We discussed
separation and, in fact, when I brought it up with him a year later he said yes,
he'd already found somewhere else to live. He was the one who went. It was
nearly ten years and really it was no longer going forward. I guess we didn't
love each other any more. He left our flat on Boxing Day 1988 and moved
into a flat in Hammersmith.'

Bert went into Charing Cross Hospital for major arterial surgery in
January 1989, after which he relinquished tobacco. Charlotte looked after
him for a couple of weeks and then moved on. Bert maintains a different
recollection of the split: 'She quit while I was still in hospital. I've no idea
why. I think she'd just had enough of it.' Things could only get better.

'I was very focussed about our son Adam when we split up,' says
Charlotte, 'because I knew Bert had two sons before from previous
relationships whom he'd not kept in touch with very well.[15] Partly it's
difficult for musicians because of the lifestyle, but he's not very outgoing that
way anyway. So for me it was very important that he saw Adam regularly,
and I made sure that happened. He's great with Adam.'

The Pentangle, with Rod Clements on board and Bert hardly firing on all
cylinders, toured Italy, Britain and America during the latter half of 1988 and
recorded So Early In The Spring, an album of largely traditional material, for
the German label Plane. Produced by Nigel Portman Smith, with that
boomy eighties sound one either loves or loathes, it was unsatisfying as folk,
rock, jazz or music of any description bearing the input of Bert Jansch. There
were one or two highlights – 'Lassie Gathering Nuts' was fresh and
imaginative, 'Lucky Black Cat' had a certain swagger – but mostly the
material had already been trampled to death in the folk-rock boom of the
early seventies. 'The Blacksmith' was an old Steeleye Span chestnut and it
was difficult to see 'Bramble Briar', a re-titling of the original Pentangle's
'Bruton Town', as anything other than a crass ploy to avoid giving up
royalties to the owners of the Transatlantic/Heathside copyrights. What,
indeed, had been the point in re-recording it at all? If the band had been
truly fantastic the lack of exciting material might not have seemed so crucial,
but with Bert convalescing, Clements undertaking the role of lead instrumentalist for his first time in any band and Gerry Conway yet to amalgamate
his nail-it-to-the-floor style with the delicate swing of his new employers
this incarnation of the Pentangle could only walk, not fly.

'I wasn't sure of the validity of Pentangle at that time at all,' admits Rod.
'In Germany they seemed to accept the group for what it was, but when we
went to the States it was a different story. People were palpably disappointed
it wasn't the John Renbourn/Danny Thompson line-up. I'm certainly no

John Renbourn and I couldn't play the fiddle like Mike Piggott did, which I realised as soon as they sent me the rehearsal tapes. So I tried to figure out Mike's parts on slide guitar, which I okayed with Bert. It was great experience for me, we felt it was a pretty good band and we liked the album we did – but it was just struggling against the earlier identity.'

Bert and Rod, as a duo, had simply fizzled out: 'To be honest, I ran out of patience with Bert there,' says Rod, 'because he basically wasn't interested. He was interested in Pentangle. The last thing I did with Pentangle was a short tour of Italy. Some work was mooted for the summer of 1990 which I wasn't able to do. I'd already sensed Bert had Peter Kirtley waiting in the wings and said, "Why don't you get Pete?" and that was that. I'd been a fan of Bert's from the sixties, so it just meant so much to be working with him. I feel privileged to have been able to have done so.'

Clements returned to Lindisfarne and Peter Kirtley, who had already been working with Bert on odd dates in 1989 as a duo partner, became the Pentangle's lead guitarist. It was an injection of fresh energy sorely required. A soulful, spiky player from the North East, Kirtley had been a Jansch fan since *Birthday Blues*. He had seen Bert at the Festival Hall concert in 1971 and at Ronnie Scott's in 1975, following his career from afar and more recently socialising with him through mutual friend Ian Vincentini: 'Working with Bert never crossed my mind,' says Kirtley. 'We used to play darts, have a few pints and talk, basically. But I was thrown into it pretty quick. He just said one day, "I'm going to Ireland next week, do you fancy coming?" '

An accomplished, dynamic player capable of great sensitivity and wild bursts of energy, often in the same song, Kirtley had long realised that the key to enhancing Bert's music was first understanding fully how it was constructed and performed: bass lines, melody lines, ornamentation, rhythm and whatever else was going on on that one guitar. 'The thing about Bert's music is that it's already complete,' says Kirtley. 'He can play it by himself or with a band or whatever but other musicians can only orchestrate what's already there. People can copy Bert but they can't write what Bert writes, that's the difference.'

Over in Ireland, a developing circuit of pubs and club venues with an active interest in promoting singer-songwriters and roots music generally would serve Bert well over the coming years of his 'rehabilitation'. Given his status and unblemished reputation there, Bert would enjoy generous TV, radio and press exposure both North and South over the next few years.[16] Similar respect for Bert's status and longevity would begin to develop too among the regional and national media in Britain.

Leather Launderette and *So Early In The Spring* represented the beginning and end of Bert's creative nadir on record. His creative recovery would be a

slow process, entirely down to his own resolution. Any critical or commercial reappraisal was down to external forces: the changing nature of the
media; a new generation of music-minded public willing to salute any
worthy survivors of the punk-era purges; and the advent of the compact
disc, allowing the reissue and rediscovery of now 'classic' recordings. Having
beaten the booze, Bert Jansch had only to re-learn the intangible greatness of
his art. In the meantime, he was single-mindedly pushing forward on the
lonely path between the world of the has-been and that of the icon. In
retrospect, 1989 – 95 were seven years of a career being rescued by stealth
from oblivion.

CHAPTER ELEVEN

Renaissance

For Bert Jansch, on the road to post-alcoholic recovery, the last years of the 1980s were a creative trough. Towards the end of 1989 one new song, 'The Parting', did appear, on *Mastercraftsmen*, a various artists' tribute to luthier Rob Armstrong. The song, a bittersweet reflection on the collapse of his relationship with Charlotte, was Bert's first recording with Peter Kirtley. Signs of a more substantial artistic recovery emerged in November 1990 with two virtually simultaneous releases: *The Ornament Tree*, on the tiny British label Run River; and *Sketches*, on the German label Hypertension.

Sketches, recorded in Hamburg in a single week, was produced by Danny Thompson who also accompanied Bert and Peter alongside a trio of local players. The retrospective focus of the album was not necessarily testament to any lack of ideas on Bert's part – Hypertension had specifically requested oldies revisited. Precisely which oldies was more or less down to Peter, who was amused to find himself 'teaching Bert a few of his tunes'. Given a low-key release in Britain on Temple, even the sleeve was a benign throwback to old times: its designer was Heather Jansch. While the production values reflected something of the budget involved – a thin sound cruelly unfavourable to the re-creation of powerful songs like 'Poison' and 'Oh My Father' – the more delicate material was beautifully executed. 'The Old Routine' (a remake of *From The Outside*'s 'Blues All Around') was a masterpiece, with Peter's moody instrumental 'Afterwards' and Bert's one wholly new offering, 'A Windy Day', more than promising.

In contrast to the cheap and cheerful ambience of *Sketches*, *The Ornament Tree* was a revelation: a fully rounded, beautifully and powerfully realised 'concept' in the manner of *Jack Orion* or *Avocet*. Bert had set out with a very clear idea and had delivered consummately. Reviewing the work in Q, one of a new breed of monthly music magazines that would prove significant to Bert's perception in the 1990s, Ken Hunt put the case for the artist to be regarded no longer as a purely historical figure but as one of contemporary value: '*The Ornament Tree* recaptures the old spirit while the chemistry between Jansch and his accompanists rekindles memories of his finest hours with Jansch sounding in better voice than he has for a long time. *The Ornament Tree* is the stuff we expect of him.' In *Vox*, Martin Townsend was ecstatic: 'The finest folk album of the year? Forget it. This stands as one of the most impressive LPs in any category.'

Bert's fellow musicians included Kirtley, Portman Smith, Steve Tilston and Tilston's partner Maggie Boyle. But more so than any of the previous 'Bert plus group' albums, this one felt determinedly the work of the artist whose name was on the cover. Although Bert has often acknowledged Maggie as a major influence on the album, and as a personal favourite singer next to Anne Briggs, Maggie attributes the vision and execution of the project to Bert alone: 'What was on there was what Bert wanted,' she says. 'There was definitely no chance of duelling whistles on it! Anything too sugary was out the window. Really, all I did was lend him the book where he found most of the songs: Sean O'Boyle's *The Irish Song Tradition*.'

The Ornament Tree reflected Bert's ongoing interest in the London-Irish scene. Aside from his own 'Three Dreamers' (based on a traditional tune) and two 'honorary traditional songs', Hamish Henderson's 'Banks O' Sicily' and Dave Goulder's 'The January Man', the album comprised Scottish and Irish material, faithfully interpreted yet brimming with the understated power and invention of a Jansch performance. The quietly stunning end product belied the problematic process of its creation. 'I did that album track by track and it took over a year,' says Bert. 'I didn't like that approach. It felt like if you'd got a couple of hours free you'd come over and record a track and then go away for a while and completely forget the album. I lost the feel for it, and a lot of things had to be re-recorded because they didn't go well. The studio was on the other side of town. It sometimes took me two hours to get there. But at the same time *Sketches* was done in a week, and it worked. Two different approaches.'

The Run River label had debuted in 1987 with Steve Tilston's *Life By Misadventure* and Maggie's *Reaching Out* (with Bert on guitar). It had been founded by Richard Newman and studio owner Michael Klein but, with the albums in the can awaiting release, Newman disappeared. Fred Underhill, a friend of Steve's with private means and time on his hands, was brought in to rescue the venture. Subsequent releases included *The Grapes Of Life*, the first new album in years from Wizz Jones, featuring a cover of Bert's 'Fresh As A Sweet Sunday Morning', and an eponymous album from John Renbourn's new group Ship Of Fools, an ensemble that included Steve Tilston and Maggie Boyle. Fred Underhill was not especially a Bert Jansch fan, and while the option was there for Bert to have made further recordings for Run River Bert pursued instead the association with Hypertension in Germany.

During the early nineties the Pentangle as a brand name was much in demand from Germany and America, and increasingly from Spain, Belgium, Denmark, Ireland and even the backwaters of Britain. Over the next few years interest in the group as a live act lurched progressively forward, though it was still frustrating for most of those concerned. For Nigel and Gerry, the sidemen, it was clear that the Pentangle was never going to be a genuinely full-time band again (not least because of Bert's increasing solo commitments); as for Peter, he was happier both musically and personally as a duo with Bert. Jacqui was still yearning to record a solo album while Bert was pragmatic enough to express his hopes for the band to become a full-time unit while perhaps realising even then, and certainly with hindsight, that it was holding everyone back from more fulfilling pursuits – himself included.

From a fan's point of view, however, this was another golden era: the Jansch / McShee / Portman Smith / Kirtley / Conway line-up would last almost as long as the original band and was, on a good night, an exhilarating live experience with an identity very much its own. Three albums were recorded before Bert finally called it quits in 1995: the admirable studio albums *Think Of Tomorrow* (1991) and *One More Road* (1993), and the disappointing *Live 1994* (1995). These were the products of a band which had come to terms with its history, its current audience and its creative potential. Mixing styles, from the soft rock of Nigel and Jacqui through Peter's 'heavy soul' to Bert's distinctly individual songwriting and a doff of the cap to the rhythms of world music, these were genuine band albums with everyone bringing something valid to the table. With *Think Of Tomorrow*, recorded for Hypertension over two weeks in Hamburg, it had been remarkable that anything of value had appeared at all.

'It all happened so fast,' says Portman Smith. 'Within two or three weeks of us signing the deal we were in a studio. Bert just brought along a tape of his songs, gave it to us on the aeroplane and said, "Listen to this. Anybody else got anything?" I had a couple of ideas, Jacqui had a couple of ideas – it was a melting pot. Then Bert had a phone call on the Tuesday of the second week saying, "Your tickets are on their way. See you in Milan, Thursday morning." Bert said, "What are you talking about?" It was his Italian agent: he had a tour of Italy. It was a complete shambles. We had to put everything Bert was going to do down on tape there and then. The rest of us tried to change our plane tickets to stay a few days longer, but it was the start of the Gulf War and there was no chance. It was difficult enough to even get into the airport. Gerry was the only one of us who could stay on to do any mixing, which he'd never done before. Gerry still maintains his mix was great. It wasn't!'

Back in London Nigel remixed the tapes, while Kieron Jansch (Bert and Heather's son) designed the sleeve. The album appeared in October 1991, supported by a German tour. A remixed single of the disarmingly funky 'Colour My Paintbook' was also released, if only in Germany. For Bert watchers, there was an assuredness in his playing throughout. In terms of writing, the opening track, 'O'er The Lonely Mountain', was his most compelling piece in ages: a smouldering cry of outrage on environmental issues. Something of a slow-burning, rough-edged epic in concert at the time, particularly as performed on Bert and Peter's duo gigs, the five-minute, air-brushed Pentangle recording was a fair compromise.

There had been US tours for the group during the summers of 1990, '91 and '92, with German tours in the autumns of 1991 and '92. The latter visit was specifically to promote *Anniversary*, an imaginative but controversial compilation from Hypertension drawn from Bert's *Sketches*, a forthcoming Peter Kirtley solo album, the four post-reunion Pentangle albums and seven tracks recorded in Belgium in 1990 at a benefit concert for Derroll Adams. Featuring Bert, Jacqui, John and Danny in a one-off reunion, it was these recordings, licensed in from the concert organisers, which caused the problems. Four of the seven had been previously authorised for release on a multi-artist album of the concert (issued only in Belgium); approval for the use of the other three and, indeed, for the reappearance of any on a· Pentangle album, had not been sought from either John or Danny. They were, justifiably, incensed.

Relations between Bert and John were already at an all-time low. They had toured America in October 1990 as Bert & John, a reunited duo, and did so again, in trio format with Jacqui, in April 1992 as the 'Pentangle founders'. Bert was pragmatic enough to accept the opportunity to tour however it was dressed up. But he was also conscious that such shamelessly retrospective ventures would undermine the current Pentangle, let alone his aspirations as a solo artist. In fairness, John Renbourn did have a place in Bert's recording plans of the time: a *Bert And John II* had been mooted and by 1992 new material, instrumental and vocal, was being jointly rehearsed. Following the US tour in April the idea was dead in the water.

'It was just one of those tours that didn't happen,' said Bert barely a month later. 'Personally, we don't get on well; musically, it left a lot to be desired. The agent over there keeps dreaming up different ways of selling the same old act, basically. This time out it was me, John and Jacqui, next time out it's the [current] band. America won't take chances: I can't get a gig out there with Peter because he's not known. Me and Peter click together onstage. It works, and when it does it really is magic. With John I have to work really hard to arrive at anything that sounds good, however much it's been rehearsed. My timing and John's are two different things – that's the most pleasant way I can put it.'

Soundboard recordings from the tour confirmed how far Bert and John now were from each other as musicians. Jacqui's presence seemed to be the glue holding the act together, musically and otherwise, although with two guitarists of such calibre the performances were never obviously disastrous. A British TV documentary crew led by director Jan Leman had hoped to film the trio in concert at San Francisco's Great American Music Hall, but relationships were fraught and all that could be salvaged was a pre-show set piece with Bert and Jacqui on an empty stage. It was disappointing but hardly essential: Leman had already filmed Bert and John in London, rehearsing at Bert's Hammersmith flat and performing a new instrumental, 'First Light', on a darkened soundstage. Strangely, the catalyst for this work-in-progress filming that became *Acoustic Routes*, a largely nostalgic BBC documentary about Bert Jansch and his sixties' peers, was Bert.

Never one for nostalgia as such, by the late eighties Bert had become concerned that many of the great British acoustic musicians of his era – Davy Graham, Martin Carthy, Roy Harper and the like – were being forgotten and, more to the point, he believed there to be little or no film record of their work. This was a strange concern from someone about whom others could have held, at that time, views of a similar nature. Bert conceived a series of half-hour TV portraits, in which he would be the anchor, interviewing and playing with each episode's guest (which, given Bert's reserved character, was an even stranger concept), and brought on board Jan Leman, a fan and freelance film editor based in Edinburgh. Jan had the contacts and experience to promote the project to broadcasters and, with that in mind, a short pilot film was shot in which Bert performed extracts from 'Angi', 'Running From Home' and 'Needle Of Death', among other personal landmarks, and reminisced about the people and places of that era.

Bert had already, in the late eighties, interviewed on tape Davy Graham and other potential guests of the intended series. He had also discussed his idea with old friend Cliff Aungier, who had then mentioned it to Richard Newman. While Bert was recovering from surgery, he was made aware that Newman was now proceeding with his own version of the concept: a mammoth undertaking involving a prospective series, documentary and all-star album. Danny Thompson became involved and brought in other players through his own influence. As Newman's 'project management' partner Loren Auerbach recalls, it was a 'big scene'.

Loren had been studying for a degree since the Auerbach/Jansch album recordings of 1984–85. Around Christmas 1988 she had, nonetheless, embarked on a new record (never completed) with both Danny Thompson and Bert Jansch among the players. By January 1989 Bert was in hospital and Loren's projected third album had been subsumed into Newman's whole-sale adoption of the folk/blues history bandwagon. In keeping with New-man's track record, only one part of the multi-strand project reached fruition – a video documentary *Living With The Blues*, broadcast on Channel 4 in 1990 and somewhat half-baked in feel.[1]

Three years later, with a premise to explore the contribution made to acoustic guitar music by Bert Jansch and his peers on the British folk scene of the mid-sixties, *Acoustic Routes* made its national broadcast debut on BBC2. It had been a long haul from Bert's initial notion of a series focusing on other players to a one-off film based more obviously around his own story, but it had been a testament to Jansch and Leman's tenacity that such a project had been realised at all. 'I wasn't really in touch with Bert then,' says Loren Auerbach, 'but I remember watching it and thinking, "That's the film Richard wanted to make: Bert's done it and he's done it better."'

Initially commissioned by BBC Scotland as a forty-minute regional programme, the fee-waiving involvement of Billy Connolly as the film's anchor man – linking the performances and ad-libbing Bert's history with humour, affection and the communal pride that comes with reliving one's own part in a movement – allowed for the project's extension to seventy minutes and a network screening.[2] The budget had been desperately small, but the end result had the sheen of class. In one sequence, filmed at 365 High Street, Edinburgh, the old Howff premises, Bert was reunited with Archie Fisher, Hamish Imlach and Anne Briggs; in another, he was teamed up with Al Stewart and Wizz Jones for a trawl around the old haunts in Soho; Davy Graham (refusing to perform with his old rival) is seen playing solo and quaffing cappuccinos at the Troubadour; Ralph McTell explains the music's fragility, Peter Kirtley attests to Bert's influence and Martin Carthy revisits 'Scarborough Fair' under the indignity of a bogus title (neatly avoiding Paul Simon's copyright); Bert plays 'Heartbreak Hotel' one more time with Albert Lee, in California, and meets his original inspiration Brownie McGhee for the first time in nearly thirty years. Brownie had not the first idea who Bert was but he was happy to entertain anyone who had known the blues.

'I was quite proud that I was able to get all those people together,' says Bert, in retrospect.[3] 'But I personally didn't play well during the whole film. I don't know why.' 'Given plenty of airtime on the programme to assert his legend, Jansch did anything but,' wrote David Cavanagh in *Mojo*, another of the new veteran-friendly music monthlies. 'He was reticent, charming and very human.'[4]

Given that the film was necessarily backward looking, it was unfortunate that most of the few 'new' pieces heard in the film (some on its subsequent soundtrack album) were unspectacular. Only 'Paper Houses', glimpsed briefly in rehearsal, gave a hint of Jansch at his best. With the wheels of Jansch grinding slowly, it would be another five years before this one made it on to a record. Nevertheless, this was the first time Bert had appeared on national television in Britain in nearly ten years,[5] and he was doing so in style. It would be difficult to believe that scores of new listeners were coming on board as a result but, certainly, people who had once been fans were being compellingly reminded that their old hero was still out there and was clearly in better shape than he had been in years. Bert's profile, through no contrivance of his own, was creeping up in other ways too: 1993 would provide the foundations to the critical renaissance that would arise so spectacularly in 1995.

In addition to the *Acoustic Routes* soundtrack, licensed for release to the relatively prominent British independent Demon Records, the summer of 1993 saw an avalanche of vintage material appear on CD, through various labels.[6] Very little of Bert's 'classic' work had yet emerged on the new format. Logo/Transatlantic themselves, still under Geoff Hannington's ownership, had issued one underwhelmingly presented Jansch compilation in 1986, with a second set announced but never appearing,[7] while *Rosemary Lane* had been licensed for CD to the German label Line in 1989. It was towards the end of 1992, however, that what has since manifested itself as a relentless flood of endlessly repackaged digital Jansch began in earnest: Stefan Grossman's *Best Of Bert Jansch* compilation appeared on US label Shanachie, alongside a purely instrumental Bert & John set, *After The Dance*, while at the same time in Britain Demon covered similar ground with *The Gardener: Essential Bert Jansch 1965 – 71*. Having successfully tested the water, Demon systematically reissued in full for the first, and not the last, time *Bert Jansch, It Don't Bother Me, Jack Orion, Nicola* and *Birthday Blues*.

A few weeks prior to this torrent of nostalgia, in May 1993, the Pentangle released what would prove to be their final studio album, *One More Road*. With some irony, just as Bert's solo profile was seemingly back on an upwards trajectory, the band had resurfaced with their best album in years, on a British label, Permanent, and with a two-month British tour to support it. However absurd the packaging – Arran sweaters against a backdrop of sky, replicating ducks on a wall – the music inside was a triumph. Everyone was making a contribution – indeed, harking back to the original band's policy, all the tracks were jointly credited – and with the line-up having adapted to each other for three years, the end result was a taut, spring-loaded bundle of energy and a sound that was remarkably fresh and exciting. This time, there were no excuses and none were needed.

Of the tracks that genuinely involved Bert's compositional hand, there were plenty of surprises: 'Hey, Hey Soldier', co-written with Peter, was an incongruously sprightly, and consequently memorable, reflection on the Northern Irish problem; 'Somali' was a rhythmically powerful, African-influenced vehicle for comment on the troubles of another continent; 'Manuel', co-written with Jacqui, was atmospheric and expansive. 'Travel-ling Solo', in some ways the most superficially obvious Jansch song on offer, had in fact been written by Jacqui. Even the traditional material had displayed imagination in their arrangements where once there had been only stodge. Folk-rock was hardly the sound of the times, but somehow the various musical tendencies amongst the final Pentangle's membership had found their balancing point in a convincing update of that very genre – or, alternatively, what an *Irish Times* critic tastefully labelled as 'sophisticated rhythm and blues' – with which they had never, first time around, been associated. 'By dropping the jazz of the Renbourn/Thompson years,' opined Rob Beattie in Q, 'and enfolding the "rosy cheeks and ruby lips" nonsense within impeccable arrangements, there's a real sense here of continuing and enriching the tradition.'

Over the next two years, with both his and the Pentangle's presence in Britain enhanced, Bert would be balancing the demands of two upwardly mobile careers and doing so with increasing difficulty. On at least one occasion, in the summer of 1993 when the group were offered concerts in Sardinia, Bert's commitments as a soloist scuppered the opportunities of the five. 'It was incessant work for me at that time,' he says. 'If I was offered other work outside of the band I had to take it, meaning there was no break for me at all. In the end it was like tossing a coin: it had to be one or the other.'

The one-album deal with Permanent and negotiations with the BBC regarding *Acoustic Routes* had been handled by Deke Arnold, a friend of Charlotte's and agent for Dennis Waterman and other stars of the small screen, who was effectively now acting as Bert's manager. 'He showed me, with Permanent, how to storm into a record company and lay down the rules of what you want out of a contract,' says Bert. 'So he had a go. But, like all managers, he got to a point with me where he didn't know what to do any more.'

Charlotte was still in touch with Bert via their son Adam, whom Bert was seeing on a regular basis. An interview with Edinburgh's *Evening News* from this period, just prior to the Scottish regional broadcast of *Acoustic Routes*, provides a clear insight into how comprehensively he had cleaned up his act from the boozing, self-centred days of the eighties.

'When I'm not on the road, Friday evening is spent at home. I usually have my eleven-year-old son Adam round. I pick him up at school, cook a curry and he stays the night. He's into *Blackadder*, so we watch hours and hours of it on video. Hopefully he'll watch *Acoustic Routes* when it's on. The idea for the programme was one I've had for years and it's great it's finally been made. I wanted to document the various guitar players I've known and who I consider have influenced the music scene. You never see them on the box.

'Travel is a way of life for me. Most of my concerts these days are in Germany or the United States. That's where the money is. Interestingly, although I'm on the move so much, in this country as well, I've never owned a car or learned to drive. In the days when I was drinking it would have been absolutely lethal for me to drive and nowadays, with the number of cars on the road, I don't think I could handle one. Anyway, assuming I'm at home, I'm up on Saturday between 8 a.m. and 9 a.m. Banjo [Bert's dog] wakens me and I take her for a walk in the park. Breakfast is tea and toast. I tend not to eat dairy products as I'm trying to cut down on cholesterol. I gave up smoking a long time ago. At lunchtime Adam and I go to the park and on to McDonalds. If I'm on my own I don't have set times for doing anything, but with Adam I have to sit down and actually plan a meal for the evening. He stays over again on Saturday night and we spend the evening watching videos or he gets his games out.

'I don't play guitar if there's someone here, but if I'm on my own I'll put in an hour or so. I'm always working on something new. Sunday I'm up again at 8 a.m.. I have to get Adam back over to Earl's Court and that takes all morning by the time we potter about in the park. Sometimes we go to the Lyric Theatre, in Hammersmith, where they do live music at lunchtime. Once Adam's home I spend Sunday afternoon working on my computer or playing guitar. In the evening I'll watch a bit of television. Mostly I make a curry but if I'm really lazy I go out for one. Some weekends I'll not be in London at all, of course. I'll either be on tour or up in Edinburgh visiting my sister Mary and various friends. I think I'll eventually retire there, but I don't know when that'll be. I'm one of those people who can't turn down the work. I think I'll be playing till I drop.'[8]

The key facets of Bert's post-alcohol domestic life were evident: his son Adam, his dog Banjo, copious quantities of tea and a predilection for Indian food. There was also a total focussing on his work, aided now by an embracing of modern home-recording and music notation technology.[9]

Bert's conversion from technological luddite to digital self-sufficiency had been a reaction to the indifference he had experienced at the hands of those who had engineered *From The Outside* in the mid-eighties. Never again would he put himself in that situation: he would continue to use studios, when the nature of the work demanded it, but for guitar/vocal work and demos of more elaborate conceptions he would have no reason to leave the flat.

The newly remixed version of *From The Outside* slipped into Britain via Hypertension during 1993's mid-summer flurry of Jansch product. Its re-presenting allowed for the inclusion of two genuinely new tracks, the first to be recorded at home: 'I don't think we should use all the technology that there is in the world to create music,' Bert mused at the time, 'but we should definitely be aware of it. That, I think, is one of the differences between the new band and the old band. In the old days we were quite advanced in putting ideas together but we didn't necessarily keep up with technology. We were left behind.'

Bert appeared as a guest on BBC Radio 1's *Bob Harris Show* in July. It was the first time in over ten years that Bert had appeared on what was then still the nation's favourite station. With *Acoustic Routes*, the Pentangle's *One More Road* and all the reissues there was plenty to talk about. Bert, true to form, was not the most forthcoming of interviewees but agreed with Bob's observation that the music of his early albums had remained largely timeless not least through the very simplicity of the recordings. Be it the sixties or the nineties, a guitar and vocal performance still sounded essentially the same. As the owner of an increasing array of computer technology, music software, DAT machines and sound modules – the nineties equivalent of Bill Leader's Revox – it was a point not lost on Bert: 'I could actually make [an album at home],' he said, 'although I never actually *do* do much recording. I've got all the right gear except the microphones, which I'm slowly getting around to!'[10]

Bert, now being managed by Jeff Beck's guitar technician Andy Roberts, and courtesy of agent Chas Cole, was on the verge of his biggest ever solo tour. Forty-three dates around the UK and Ireland and spanning September – November 1993 were flagged as the 'Thirtieth Anniversary Tour' – thirty years since he had become a professional member of the music business. Andy Roberts's immediate contribution, aimed at profiting from the interest generated by the documentary and the reissues, was the production of some Bert Jansch merchandise for the tour: a souvenir programme and T-shirts.

'It's like everybody else who's had a go at it,' says Bert, 'it's coming in thinking they can do something and that there's a lot of money there. But there never has been a lot of money there: they realise that, they panic and they don't know quite what to do. Andy's a road manager basically, which he's very good at. Mind you, during that time I ended up with one of the weirdest roadies I've ever met – this guy who didn't know anything at all about me or, apparently, music. He was just a weirdo. I remember before the tour coming back to my flat to find two horrible kitchen chairs and three empty beer crates – all things this guy thought we needed on the road and which he'd gone out and pinched from some pub.'

The first half of 1994 saw Bert and the Pentangle alternating short tours or scattered dates around the UK, Denmark and Spain (that season's winner in the 'who's next for a folk revival?' stakes). Chas Cole had organised a series of joint gigs during May for Bert, John Renbourn, Davy Graham and Miller Anderson. Bert, John and Davy would also be among those booked for that year's Cambridge Folk Festival, in July.

Around this time Bert was often bumping into blues/rock guitar hero Rory Gallagher down at the Troubadour which, along with Bunjies, was one of the few original folk venues in London still functioning. Rory, though ill, had been an admirer of Bert's music for years and was keen to involve both Bert and Martin Carthy in a planned acoustic album. He had got as far as sending demos to Bert, hoping to arrange a still more extraordinary collaboration: 'He actually wanted to work with Anne Briggs,' says Bert.[11] 'But she thought he was a pop star and rejected the idea out of hand. I then suggested Maggie Boyle. Maggie lived in Yorkshire and came down to London especially to meet Rory and record the stuff that we'd arranged but he didn't show up. He just drew a blank, couldn't remember having arranged it. I grew disheartened at that point.' Rory died a few months later, in June 1995.

With Demon continuing their CD transfers from Bert and the Pentangle's Transatlantic catalogue, it seemed that the label would be a natural home for his next album proper. Andy Roberts, talking up Bert's potential selling power, was counting on it and a lengthy UK/Irish tour was arranged for Bert spanning October – December 1994 on the assumption that a new album would be ready to accompany it. Through a combination of Andy Roberts's business stance and Demon's caricature perception of Bert's lifestyle, the whole thing went pear-shaped: 'Whatever figure Andy had demanded,' says Bert, 'they'd said, "No way: the deal is ten grand, that's it." And they actually sent round a guy to my house to say, "You're not getting thousands of pounds out of this company to spend on cocaine like you did in the seventies." I was very angry about that. I threw the guy out and obviously the deal fell through.'

Andy Roberts was knocked for six. Bert, however, had been recently

introduced to one Richard Jakubowski, who was running a dance label
called Prima Vera. 'At the time I was well into MIDI recording technology
and there was talk of dance mixes and so on,' says Bert. 'We actually started
work on the album and it was about a quarter of the way through that when
Alan King became involved and Cooking Vinyl took over.'

Alan King is best described as a lovable rogue. Through a combination of his
own personality and the time simply being right for Bert, King's entry into
the picture ushered in, facilitated or perhaps just happily coincided with a
period of time that can be seen as Bert's coming of age as an icon. During the
course of 1995–96, Bert Jansch, finally freeing himself from the Pentangle,
would be hailed repeatedly by the press as a unique figure in British
contemporary music and would be acknowledged amongst a new generation of prominent musicians for his influence, ideas and not least for the
spell-binding quality of his current performances. Alan King, for all the
flannel and dodgy deals, was to provide the platform for Bert to move out of
the folk clubs and into the sun.

Bert had met Alan, running some 'shady gigs' in the East End of London,
through a friend of a friend. 'I was brassic at the time and so I accepted these
gigs,' says Bert. 'Alan himself was actually doing the support. He knew I
didn't have a manager, told me he could do all sorts of wonderful things and
at the time I thought, "Well, why not? Everybody else has had a go at it!" '

Andy Roberts had played all his cards with the Demon deal and gracefully
withdrew to spend more time with Jeff Beck's guitars. With Prima Vera,
Bert at least had an outlet for his new material. Alan King saw it as his task to
up the ante and bring a more appropriate label on board. Bert was less
concerned about securing a new record deal. He had seen it all before:
money was a necessary part of the equation, but huge advances had never
been his prerequisite for creativity. He could once, perhaps, have been a
gardener, imbuing that vocation with the same levels of commitment he had
shown throughout his career as a musician. By this stage in the game there
was no alternative: the creation of music was simply who he was and what
he did.

'The trouble is, with life,' he explained during the Roberts era, 'the more
you settle on one particular thing, then the other things fade on the way, so
that all you are left with is the one. Now I've no other means of actually
earning a living at all other than picking up the guitar. But what I'm happy
with is that whatever I create, a lot of people want to hear it. That makes me
happy. I create, and it just happens to be a guitar I create on. If I'm at home I'm
playing the guitar. It's a continual process. In fact, it's dreadful to go away and
do gigs because I don't play guitar! I don't like to stand on a pedestal or a stage

saying, "Here I am, the greatest player in the world." That's nonsense. To me life doesn't work like that. The record industry works like that.'[12]

During March and April 1995 the Pentangle story staggered to a close on what all involved recognised privately, before a gig had been played, as probably their final tour. Promoting an underwhelming new concert album, *Live 1994* (recorded on a German tour during the autumn of that year), this was a group of people just going through the motions. The brinkmanship and fire apparent onstage during the spring tour of only a year before, and the more adventurous material – 'Light Flight' and 'Train Song' resurrected for the first time – had all dissipated by the time any concerts were taped for the live album.

Peter Kirtley was developing a solo career with his own band and, having moved out to Suffolk, geography alone was a factor in the Jansch and Kirtley duo (neither being drivers) becoming less and less frequent. Gerry Conway was splitting his time between the Pentangle and John Martyn's band and towards the end of 1994 had introduced Jacqui to Martyn's keyboard player Spencer Cozens. The three of them determined to make an album together, which they did the following year. Jointly credited and titled *About Thyme*, it was essentially the solo album Jacqui had long craved. For Bert, the deciding factor in his decision to leave the group – for he wished only to leave it, not destroy it – was the recent development of Jacqui and Gerry's relationship.

'Gerry had virtually taken over the band,' he says. 'With him and Jacqui I was facing up to two people instead of one. But also musically it was going the wrong way for me. I couldn't deal with the metronomic beat any more. Terry Cox always followed what was going on: Gerry can't do that. Sometimes I couldn't physically keep up with him. Also Jacqui, once she's learned something that's it, it never changes. If you want to play something different you can't because it screws up the band. You're playing the same thing every night.'

A handful of German festival dates following the March/April tour were fulfilled by Jacqui fronting the usual group with Alun Davies, former guitarist for Cat Stevens, replacing Bert. It was hardly going out with a bang but at the time those involved were not entirely convinced that Bert was confirmed in his decision: perhaps he just needed a rest? 'Bert has a way of changing his mind,' said Jacqui, later in the year. 'It feels like the end to me at the moment, but it wouldn't surprise me if Bert said that he fancied doing some more gigs. Your guess is as good as mine.'[13] Jacqui, Gerry and Spencer evolved to record and perform together, with Bert's blessing, as Jacqui McShee's Pentangle. The name still lingered, but at last everyone was free.

In June 1995, Bert began a summer residency at a tiny but characterful new London club called the 12 Bar. Located down an alley off Denmark Street, it was one of a number of clubs in that area trying to recapture the spirit of Soho in the sixties. Indeed, the 12 Bar had been started by Phil Phillips: the very man responsible for the Cousins thirty years earlier. Alan King had had a personality clash with Bert's agent Chas Cole, leaving Bert with a Wednesday residency at the 12 Bar, another on Fridays at the Cabbage Patch in Twickenham, and not a great deal else. 'There was nobody booking tours,' says Bert, 'which was why I was doing the 12 Bar every week! It was meant to last one summer but it went on for a year. But it was around this time that I was realising that the gigs were better because I didn't have to be involved with a band or a duo partner. I was in control of it. And because of that I put more effort and concentration into it and my performance improved.'

Not only were Bert's solo gigs of the mid-nineties an exciting experience for long-time fans and for younger followers whose fascination was based on the sixties' recordings, but from the summer of 1993 he had been featuring onstage a quartet of intensely powerful songs that were to form the backbone of his first new collection of original material in ten years: an album that finally appeared, on 28 August 1995, as *When The Circus Comes To Town*.

The new material was quite stunningly equal to, and stylistically reminiscent of, his greatest work of the Transatlantic era. It was as if the intervening quarter century had simply not happened. In another sense, though, it was clearly the work of a individual with a penetrating insight and stoic perspective gained only by years at the coal-face of life: 'Walk Quietly By' observed the breakdown of welfare for the mentally ill; 'Morning Brings Peace Of Mind' praised daybreak itself, with pathos and serene dignity, for release from the nightly troubles of unconscious memory; 'Stealing The Night Away' was less easily penetrable in content but swaggered and teased like a libidinous Delta blues; 'The Lady Doctor From Ashington', a fragile baroque homage to the woman who had counselled Bert through his recovery from alcoholism, was spiritually a lost gem from *Rosemary Lane*. Musically, Bert Jansch was drawing from the well of his past, but he had allowed his muse to gaze at last upon the 1990s. The 1990s were poised to respond in kind.

While Cooking Vinyl was by no means a major label, it had more clout than any company Bert had been associated with in recent years and was enjoying something of a golden era. Bert joined an eclectic roster of artists with cult credibility, including Jackie Leven, Pere Ubu, Ani DiFranco and the Wedding Present. Many of these people were being independently represented by publicist Mick Houghton, whose reputation was founded on working with people broadly 'alternative' in outlook. Happily for Bert,

Houghton was not only Cooking Vinyl's PR of choice but an old fan, a regular at the Horseshoe who had remained an admirer ever since. Houghton's job now was to take the 'was' out of sentences beginning 'Bert Jansch' and to build mainstream awareness. And he knew how to do it.

'I'd say his profile by then was largely non-existent,' says Houghton.[14] 'I thought it was quite strange that there hadn't been any major reappraisal of Bert's career up to that point. He'd basically been neglected. The thing with anyone who could be described as folk or country or anything generic is that unless there's someone actively there to point out to people that you're really an "alternative" act, you're going to get stuck in that ghetto, playing and selling records to the same people. The way the media works, if you've got a long career like Bert has, to some extent it's a career there to be reappraised every third record. And because I was such a huge fan anyway I knew almost without thinking about it which journalists were fans or would be likely to be interested. It wasn't exactly difficult to draw people in.'

Houghton ensured coverage for *When The Circus Comes To Town* in virtually all the national daily and Sunday broadsheets, in addition to the monthly music titles. Over the next four months he used the 12 Bar residency to entice a stream of concert reviews and interview features from publications such as *Q*, London's *Evening Standard*, *Time Out*, *The Guitar Magazine*, *Rock'n'Reel*, *The Scotsman* and *Scotland On Sunday*. Almost overnight, a generation previously oblivious to Bert Jansch became aware that a bona fide 'lost legend' of the sixties – reputedly on a par with Jimi Hendrix, vaguely associated with Bob Dylan, influential on a host of subsequent 'name' players – had a terrific new record out and could be seen playing every Wednesday just round the corner from the Tottenham Court Road tube station. More to the point, he was, by all accounts, one of those rare legends still capable of living up to his reputation.

'With *Circus*, the line we took promotionally was "This is Bert's best album in a decade",' says Houghton. 'It may or may not have been, but most people out there hadn't *heard* a Bert Jansch album in ten years, so it was. The other thing we did was to major on the influence Bert had had on other people, namechecking the obvious examples. Younger, more contemporary musicians were discovering Bert. Certainly, any of the other acts that we were working with at the time and took along to the 12 Bar were all captivated. Performance wise, he was still completely on top of his game.' A mischievous news item planted by Houghton in the *Daily Star* informed pop-pickers that Jarvis Cocker and Noel Gallagher had been among the 'all-star audiences' checking out 'sixties guitar god' Jansch at the club. It may or may not have been true, but the curious came in droves and Bert Jansch was emphatically back in business.

'Sometimes with artists like Bert,' says Houghton, 'you have to make it possible for young people to admit they like him. It has to be cool, and once it is they can acknowledge it. I don't think *Circus* was a truly great Bert Jansch record – I think it was half a truly great Bert Jansch record.' Houghton's view, shared by others who had been attending Bert's shows and keenly awaiting the new record, was that many of the songs had an attack and an immediacy onstage that was less apparent on the record. With retrospect, however, the taut, subdued mood of the album – described in *Mojo* at the time as 'a late-night, candle-lit intoxication' – feels absolutely right. Rather than opting whole-heartedly for the ensemble bluster of *Birthday Blues*, Bert had re-created the dark poise and smouldering energy that had characterised his most enduring work of that era as a purely guitar/ vocal performer. While accompanying musicians were selectively featured – a beautiful string arrangement for 'Morning Brings Peace Of Mind', a soprano sax weaving dreamily through 'Summer Heat', a backing chorus on 'Back Home' – this was very much an album in the stark tradition of Bert's sixties' classics.

Oblique commentaries on modern issues and, of course, on the demons of his own psyche, dominated *Circus*: the title track was, almost impenetrably, a reflection on the crack cocaine epidemic (not to be read as autobiographical); 'Living In The Shadows', a withering metaphor on the UN's role in the Bosnian war, seemingly conducted through television; 'Born With The Blues' tried to explain the other side of fame's coin to those who would covet Bert's celebrity. It was only those songs that strayed away from the solemn 'period' mood, and which were incidentally also the most lyrically obvious – 'Step Back', 'Just A Dream', 'Honey Don't You Understand' and the only cover on offer, Janie Romer's 'No one Around'[15] – that ultimately denied *Circus* the accolade of being a 'truly great Bert Jansch record'. But, at the time, this was a minor detail.

'For too many years, Bert Jansch has been a critical renaissance waiting to happen. In a nutshell, everything that was great and magical about Jansch's work in the sixties is here, present and correct, updated with sparse but thoroughly modern touches,' was my own judgement, in *Mojo*. Other commentators had similar views: 'his best album since the sixties' is an accurate summary of all the major reviews published in Britain. Over in the States, the pundits went further in exploring just how and why this was such a watershed release: 'It may have taken a while,' concluded Chris Nickson in the *Seattle Times*, 'but this is the sound of a man who's finally found peace with himself.' The *New York Press* reviewer cannily observed that while there were no obvious standout tracks '*Circus* does what a Bert Jansch album is supposed to do: it gives you hauntingly romantic songs, played in a

deceptively simple manner that grows more fascinating with each listen.'
Imperfect it may have been, but *Circus* compares with both *Rosemary Lane*
and *LA Turnaround* in having an aura definably its own, and the content to
justify its continuing reputation.

'For all his disdain for the career ritual – amply reflected by the pokiness of
the 12 Bar Club,' explained David Cavanagh, to the hip and happening
readership of *Q*, 'Jansch was once a near superstar. Nobody at the 12 Bar
would mistake Jansch for a superstar now. He is a forbidding-looking,
unkempt man in his early fifties who, while playing, keeps his eyes either
closed or fixed on the fretboard. The songs are introduced in a murmur. He
sits on a wooden chair and sings in a rich, brambled voice. When the gig is
over, he goes home to West London. And every Wednesday he returns to
play at the 12 Bar. He admits he finds certain areas of life difficult and relies
to an extent on sympathetic management. "Being a folk musician, my head's
not geared that way. We could all do with more money, but I'm quite
happy musically. I've got the album almost right – *almost*, not quite – so I'm
heading in the right direction. I suppose I'm a romantic. I like words to be
properly put together. I often spend months on just one line of a song.' "[16]

The creation of Bert's songs up to the point where he feels sufficiently
confident to commit them to record has, in some cases, been a process of
years. The process after recording is to either re-shape them continually
onstage or simply forget them. The recording of *Circus* was, consequently,
the end of the line for most of its songs. By the time *Live At The 12 Bar: An
Authorised Bootleg* was recorded, towards the end of his residency, all but four
of the fourteen *Circus* titles were absent from the set list. Before the end of
the decade it was unusual to hear even that number on a typical Bert Jansch
gig. There were plenty more songs to be written yet.

'I probably only met Bert two or three times,' says Mick Houghton, the man
largely responsible for his critical renaissance. 'I'm not even sure he knew
who I was. The truth was, I was such a fan I was actually a bit in awe of him.
We dealt mainly through Alan King. I guess he was a bit of a wide-boy but
he was good for Bert at that time because he was such an enthusiast. He
created such a good vibe around Bert.'

It would be inappropriate to detail any of King's dodgy deals: at the time
of writing aspects of his legacy are still being delicately resolved. The *Live At
The 12 Bar* album was one fairly harmless King wheeze, a representative,
straight-to-DAT souvenir of a typical Jansch gig, mopping up the otherwise
unreleased cover of Brownie McGhee's 'Trouble In Mind', a staple of Bert's
live repertoire at the time, and introducing one new and as yet untitled
instrumental. Appearing in 1996, it was the second release on King's 'Jansch

Records'. The first, the previous year, had been a CD salvaging of the long-lost *Moonshine*. One final triumph for Alan King's ducking-and-diving regime was the netting of three live television spots. Two of these, on Sky TV's *Selina Scott Show* and the Welsh language channel S4C, were of little consequence; the third, on BBC2's *Later With Jools Holland*, was more like it.

As an increasingly credible name living within easy reach of the show's studio, Bert had actually been on the 'subs' bench' for this flagship live music series for a few months before finally appearing, on 15 June 1996, alongside ZZ Top, Nigel Kennedy, Altan and others. Irish traditional band Altan were promoting *Blackwater*, an album featuring their version of 'Blackwater Side', a song Bert was synonymous with. The show's producer, Mark Cooper, felt a duet was appropriate – in the event, a Bert cameo in Altan's arrangement. More representative was the 'difficult' title track of *Circus*, performed with presenter Jools Holland on piano. There were more accessible tracks on the album but, at the very least, on this, his first appearance on national television since *Acoustic Routes*, Bert's enigma remained intact. Meanwhile, Alan King's house-on-sand management edifice was in the process of falling apart.

Bert had finally realised that Arthur Daley was a television character and anyone carrying on like him in real life was in danger of causing long-term disaster for all concerned. He approached Cooking Vinyl, who suggested a number of options including Artistic Upstarts, an Edinburgh-based operation fronted by Andrew Hunter.[17] Within six months of agreeing to take Bert on, Hunter employed Kresanna Aigner with specific responsibility for their new client's tour management. 'As I understand it,' says Kresanna, 'Cooking Vinyl came to Andrew and said, "Help! We have an artist who's just been through the mill with an atrocious manager. We're trying to relaunch him and we need someone to deal with the touring, sort out the contracts and so on." So Andrew inherited this mess. What he attempted to do was to sift through a lot of contractual stuff, where people maybe hadn't paid Bert royalties for given periods or hadn't raised royalty percentages when they should have, various scandals like that. And he only ever got to the tip of that iceberg during the whole time we worked with Bert.'

What Andrew Hunter sought to redress immediately was the touring situation, which had trickled on without focus for nearly two years. The first thing Andrew needed to do was find a good agent – any agent. After various refusals (Bert's reputation with alcohol died hard) the burden was eventually laid at the door of another Edinburgh man, John Stoneyport – 'totally the right person' in Kresanna's view. 'He understands Bert, he's from the same era, he's got similar artists like Dick Gaughan on his roster. Plus Bert's also Scottish, which people forget.'

Slightly predating the advent of Andrew Hunter's management, which was to focus on repairing Bert's touring situation, Bert had decided to help that very cause by removing himself, after a year's worth of Wednesday nights, from the 12 Bar. It had been a curious little castle in which he had been king, but the musicians around him on that scene were arguably looking to Bert – owner of a celebrated if somewhat rudderless career at the time – to help them get their own acts together. Bert had happily helped out a number of lesser-known musicians over the previous few years – Loren Auerbach, Maggie Boyle, Janie Romer, David Hughes, Bobby Barton and Jenny Beeching among them – on recordings and/or in providing opportunities to join him onstage or play as special guests at his shows. During the 12 Bar era Bert was now regularly in the company of a whole host of people trying to make their way in the music business, many of whom were enjoying the benefits of his generous spirit. A number of those associated with Bert during the nineties, including his time at the 12 Bar, could be viewed as coat-tailing opportunists. But Bert was never one to pre-judge character: 'I have faith in people,' he told one questioner at the time. 'I still defend my right to accept somebody as they are. I've always stood by that. I think that's possibly why I've never actually made it in the music biz.'[18]

During the latter half of 1996, Bert saw through various concert and festival commitments arranged largely prior to his change of management: a summer club and festival tour of the UK (ironically, his most cohesive since Alan King had dismissed Chas Cole from the team), three festivals in Canada and a foray through Hong Kong and Australasia, where Cooking Vinyl had licensed *Circus* to Festival Records. The Australian press were more than happy to make Bert's 'renaissance', a term now commonplace in Jansch publicity, global. But the real fruits of Hunter's new management policy were revealed in February 1997 with Bert's first substantial solo tour of Europe in a long time: twenty-three dates covering Switzerland, Germany, Denmark, Norway and a lot of miles in between. Kresanna Aigner, vivacious, efficient and raring to go, was Bert's driver and organiser.

'I knew nothing of Bert beforehand,' she admits. 'All the fans, the superstardom – which obviously unravelled as the tour went on. I remember somebody showing up in Sweden with every single album Bert had ever done, wanting Bert to sign every one! I was gobsmacked – I just had no idea what a legend he was. The tour itself was touch and go in places, a little on the depressing side. He would do everything from a really terrible gig with six people to a handful of good concerts with two or three hundred. It was a time when gigs in Germany were getting difficult for a lot of people. There were new tax nightmares for touring artists and the audiences were going down. We then did Denmark, which Bert was looking forward to. But it was a first-year relationship with a new agent and again the gigs were mixed. Bert just felt, "Well, I know I need to tour but I'm too old for this palaver."

'We were on the road for four or five weeks and it was ten-hour drives a day to get to most of the gigs. He had also had a hernia operation a week or two before the tour so it was really hard going for him. I think what kept it okay was my enthusiasm, and I think Bert enjoyed that. He'd had never had a woman tour manager who wasn't a wife or girlfriend and it was also my first trip to Europe, so it was a novel experience at least. I was all very organised and had researched every route, with maps and notes to hand, to which Bert would be saying, "Ah, just follow the sun, it'll be up here somewhere . . ." And actually I can see now that he's right: when you've toured for a while you can go to a city and very quickly get a sense of where the gig is. He's a very serious, focussed person offstage: he doesn't say very much but he takes it all in, the scenery, the people he's with, passers-by. When we came back to London we went down to the 12 Bar to have a drink and a lot of his friends there said it was the happiest they'd seen him coming off a tour.'

In April Bert began a UK tour, the first to be organised by John Stoneyport. Again, Kresanna was road managing, with sax player Mark Ramsden as special guest and prospective biographer. Organising a biography had been another of Hunter's priorities and Ramsden was game to try: 'I don't know why anybody ever thought he should write the book,' says Kresanna. 'I think he just wanted to hear the "sex, drugs and rock'n'roll" stories, but it was quite frustrating for him because there's big chunks of his life that Bert simply can't remember. But what I noticed at a lot of the gigs were fathers, the initial fans thirty years ago, coming along with their sons and daughters and a whole new generation discovering him. I think in 1997 he started to realise his age, started thinking a bit more about his past.'

In August Bert played the Edinburgh Book Festival; in September he toured Ireland; in October he returned to Australia, building on the groundwork of the previous tour and recording some dates, with local bass and percussion players, on digital multi-track. There were more UK dates as soon as he returned and in November he was off on a tour of the States, including a couple of shows with Archie Fisher. In Hunter's view, if Bert was going to be able to pick and choose 'quality gigs', where the masses would come to him, he first had to go to the masses: to tour relentlessly and re-establish his name in the regions. Bert himself, while admitting to writing 'with a younger audience in mind than the one that actually comes to the gigs', had a very clear idea of just who his audience was: 'The thirties generation might have heard of me but not enough to draw them out, and also they've got their babysitters. It's the generation my age and slightly behind me – their children are grown up and they've got nothing to do, they see a name in the paper they used to go and see and they come out. Sometimes they bring their children along.'[19]

In the middle of all this touring Bert had retreated to Lochranza, a little village on the Isle of Arran off Scotland, to record the basic tracks for his next album. Tam Kenny and Vicki Hudson, proprietors of an art gallery and guest house in the village – converted from an old chapel – had been fans of Bert's for years and had recently been organising tours for himself and others in the Highlands and Islands region. The ambience of the old church, and a van-load of portable recording gear, would provide Bert with all he needed to deliver what the commentators saw as the all-important follow-up to *Circus*. Jay Burnett, engineer on *Circus*, went along as producer. During the course of the intensive two-week sessions another old friend was in attendance: Loren Auerbach.

Loren had lost touch with Bert during the early nineties, but a friend had persuaded her to attend one of his gigs at the end of 1994: 'I was a bit nervous but, as ever, he was pleased to see me, gave me his phone number and we got back in touch. When we went up to Arran we were just friends, and we were more than friends when we came back. I think I always knew that he was interested in more than friendship but I didn't want our friendship to be spoiled so I pretended it wasn't happening – in that kind of naive way that you do. Right from the start we'd always clicked in some strange way. From Bert's point of view, he never pushed for anything more than friendship because he told me later he'd rather have had me in his life as a friend than try and push for something more and end up with nothing. It's funny, during the 12 Bar time I was actually involved with this other guy, but I'd be going to the club practically every Wednesday, watching Bert, thinking, "This is where I want to be." '[20]

Aside from the developments in his private life, Bert returned from Arran excited at the quality and feel of the recorded work. It had been two years since *Circus* but, away from live performances, he had been far from idle: 'I literally spend all of my waking time writing songs,' he told one questioner in the intervening period. 'There's no point in the day when I'm distracted doing other things. If I'm on a bus I'll be thinking of writing a song. I often get on the wrong buses.'[21] This was still only part of the equation: Bert had upgraded his home studio and, partly as a way of learning how it all worked, had been devoting a great deal of time and energy to producing other people. First in line were the Magic Bow, a couple of homeless buskers and their dog from Huddersfield, and then more prolonged work on full-scale albums for 12 Bar associates Dave Sutherland and Johnny Hodge.[22] Work on his own album was having to progress in parallel.

Contributions from a number of other musicians (including old friend Pick Withers on drums) were recorded at Boundary Row Studios in London. To Bert's mind the album was ready to go well before the end of the year, but Martin Goldschmidt, MD at Cooking Vinyl, had become obsessed with trying to graft on some of the rock celebrities who had been name-dropping Bert in the wake of *Circus*. Bert was not necessarily against the idea of working with the likes of Jimmy Page or whoever else but he was distinctly uncomfortable with Cooking Vinyl ringing round such people and creating an artificial situation. He also believed that Martin Goldschmidt had not actually listened to any of the demos that had been sent in of prospective tracks for the new album. If he had, Bert felt, he would have realised that this was not a record crying out for loud guitars. *Toy Balloon* finally escaped, *sans* superstars, on 30 March 1998. 'They'd been hanging around for Jimmy Page for about six months,' says Bert, 'and when they didn't get him they just lost interest. And because it had dragged on so much, I lost interest.' Things were beginning to unravel again.

During December 1997 Andrew Hunter had taken a month-long sabbatical, and when he came back he announced that he was leaving music manage-ment. 'It was all up in the air,' remembers Kresanna Aigner. 'Bert was wondering if he'd keep me on, and I was wondering what I was going to do. I was proposing to him that he did keep me on, but I think Bert really needed someone with more experience of contract situations.' Bert con-tinued with Kresanna as caretaker-manager during the first quarter of 1998, in which time he completed a five-week tour of Australia. But, guided particularly by Loren's businesslike zeal, a change in management was now regarded as the way forward. Privately, it was already apparent to Bert that it was time to remove himself from Cooking Vinyl: on his terms.

Toy Balloon, the second instalment of a three-album deal with the label, received a respectful if muted response. Mick Houghton, once again handling promotion, was no longer sure who was managing Bert and, having played the 'career reappraisal' card last time around, saw nothing viable in the way of a press angle. 'One problem was the delay,' says Houghton, 'but also it was pretty much *Circus* part two. Other than Bert Jansch making another record, there was no story. If nothing else, he needed to do a prestigious concert at somewhere like the Festival Hall. The press need those things to keep writing about someone. They're not going to write about you if your London gig is some community centre in Crouch End. The idea of bringing in celebrities was worth pursuing – Cooking Vinyl were holding out for that – but, without having direct access to Bert at the time, I sense now that it wasn't something he wanted to do.'

What Bert had done was create an album of which at least half the tracks were on a par with the best work on *Circus*: between them, indeed, was one truly stunning record. *Toy Balloon*'s mood was less of a piece than its predecessor, moving between the monochrome guitar/vocal ambience of that album and almost incongruously upbeat R&B/soul workouts with bass, drums, and sax and more reminiscent of the Blues Brothers than the alternative rock of Martin Goldschmidt's hopes. 'Sweet Talking Lady', Bert's funky ode to his guitar, had been the track earmarked for Jimmy Page to embellish. When it became clear that Page's diary was always full, Bert invited Charlotte's new partner, and James Brown's sax man, Pee Wee Ellis to do his thing on it instead.

At least half the material on *Toy Balloon* had been written subsequent to *Circus*. But few of the new album's songs had been featured regularly, prior to release, in Bert's live shows: 'Bett's Dance' had been aired before, as an untitled encore on *Live At The 12 Bar*; 'Born And Bred In Old Ireland' had previously been recorded for, but discarded from, *Circus*; while 'Paper Houses', a gentle reflection on homelessness in Edinburgh, had been a masterpiece in waiting since the Bert & John US tour of 1992. Of the more recent songs, the breathtakingly beautiful title track recaptured the poignancy of his *Rosemary Lane* lullaby 'Tell Me What Is True Love?'.

This was an album only superficially similar to *When The Circus Comes To Town* but, from Mick Houghton's perspective, not sufficiently different to warrant a further burst of attention. Nevertheless, for those who had followed Bert's career from the start there were subtle signs that he was indeed, as Kresanna Aigner had felt, beginning to reflect upon on his own history. Two tracks into the new album, 'She Moved Through The Fair' was the most spectacular example of Bert's tendency to let material gestate over a period of years. This was a song dating right the way back to Len Partridge, Bert's mentor at the dawn of the sixties, to whom Bert would attribute its learning in concert. 'You wouldn't classify it as a right old laugh,' noted one reviewer, 'but it's a strong reminder of his skill.'[23]

With a similarly retrospective flourish, the album's opening track was an awesome and quite unexpected reading of Jackson C. Frank's 'lost' masterpiece '(My Name Is) Carnival'. Frank had recently been 'rediscovered', crippled and living in welfare institutions in upstate New York. Through the intervention of well-wishers his one album, 1965's *Jackson C. Frank*, had been reissued on CD in 1996 as *Blues Run The Game*. Rarely a listener to recorded music, Bert had long treasured his vinyl copy. For *Toy Balloon* he had crafted a surely definitive arrangement, adding yet more *film noir* profundity to an already portentous original, of a song rich in timeless metaphor which had, remarkably, never been covered on record before. In possibly his final interview,[24] Jackson himself had expressed surprise that 'Carnival' had been neglected in this way. He died within a year of *Toy Balloon*'s release, and it is not known if he ever heard his old friend's spell-binding retrieval of that very gauntlet. Blues, for Jackson Frank, Bert Jansch and all the Soho brotherhood, would always run the game. He had left behind a dark hymn to those who would play their cards in the industry of music:

> *I see your face in every place I'll be going*
> *I read your words like black, hungry birds read every sowing*
> *Rise and fall, spin and call*
> *My name is Carnival*

> *Sad music in the night seems a string of light out of chorus*
> *Voices you might hear appear and disappear in the forest*
> *Short and tall, come throw the ball*
> *My name is Carnival*

> *Here there is no law but the arcade's penny claw, hanging empty*
> *The painted, laughing smile and the turning of the stile – do not envy*
> *And the small can steal the ball*
> *To touch the face*
> *Of Carnival*

There comes a point for every artist where the balance changes: a point where the public no longer want or expect any further development, but rather an endless re-presenting of what is already fondly familiar to them. Some artists accept the situation and become unashamedly purveyors of nostalgia, doing so with either dignity or caricature; others wrestle with the tide, refusing to acknowledge that people move on, and often within a cruelly short passage of time.

By the time he reached 1995 and delivered his first wholly new album of the decade, Bert Jansch had been determinedly following and honouring his muse for thirty-five years. His style of writing, playing and performing, even his lyrical vocabulary, had changed essentially not one iota from the time his first album had dazzled and astounded in 1965. Whether through dogged determination or inherent inability to stray too far from what came naturally, Bert Jansch had been doing the same thing for years and the wheels of the music world had revolved to face him once again. He may never have been a household name but he had outlasted, creatively and professionally, many who were and had done so with credibility intact through long years of critical and public indifference and personal upheaval. He had traversed the sixties all but unaware of the Beatles and by the same token had survived, in blissful ignorance, any number of subsequent trends in music, emerging in the mid-nineties into the glare of a whole new generation of commentators, musicians and music-literate public. People were now at the very least deferential towards his unique status in British music history: an influence, an innovator, an enigma, perhaps even a genius, a man of few words, deep principles and unassailable integrity – a stylist as singular and as instantly recognisable as icons like Johnny Cash, Jimi Hendrix and John Coltrane.

He will continue, no doubt, to write songs which are occasionally brilliant and occasionally so-so; to make records which, at best, dazzle and surprise even hardened admirers or, at worst, do nothing to diminish his status; to confuse Neil Young with Neil Diamond, and to fail to see how he could possibly be an influence on either; to view Clive Palmer as a genius; to gravitate tantalisingly close to, and yet perennially miss, those periodic opportunities truly to ascend the ladder of popular success. He will continually play down 'the legendary Bert Jansch' and yet he will continue to be, without doubt, the legendary Bert Jansch.

POSTSCRIPT

'I thought it was a great scene,' says Donovan, 'to be able to go there to Les Cousins, stay up all night and then have breakfast in the Greek Café down in Soho. So I'm sitting there talking at six in the morning and all the deadbeats are there, all the bums, and then running into the street singers who you might call the real folk singers singing to the cinema lines: "'Allo Bert, 'ow's it going? Bit cold, innit?" So the busking, the strippers, the students, the poets, the painters, the folk singers, the blues singers – it was a golden age. It couldn't last forever but what does last forever is the music, and I can't say enough about Bert's new music. I'd heard all these horror stories where he'd got ill and nearly died and then when I heard the music, the resilience . . . It just blew me away.

'But the power of all this is extraordinary. There was a young man at a gallery opening in Dublin, he comes up to me and says, "Hey, Donovan, I'm just beginning to play guitar, have you got any advice?" And the first thing that comes into my head is, "Have you heard of Bert Jansch?" Now, I knew that I would start him down a road. He didn't know who Bert Jansch was but I said, "He's a guy that we all learned from. If you play a little bit you'll play more just listening to it." And his eyes lit up as if he'd heard Bert. He got this "high" off me and I thought, "My God, it doesn't matter that we're in our fifties, if we're remembered as teachers as well as guitar pickers . . ." He took out a pencil and said, "How'd you spell it?" And off he went. Maybe he didn't get it or maybe he got it and his life changed. It's not just your guitar life changes, I think your life changes if you're exposed to a certain book, a certain artist, a certain film — and to be exposed to Bert Jansch can change your life. There should be a warning on the label!'

Epilogue

In April 1998, Bert Jansch came to Ireland. Half a dozen dates North and South were by now an annual fixture. This time around he was including two dates in the North: a Saturday night at Downpatrick Folk Club and the following night upstairs at Morrison's Bar in the centre of Belfast. His driver and promoter for the Northern gigs, as usual, was the long-suffering Nigel Martyn, a man of both supreme musical taste and extraordinary bad luck. A few weeks earlier Nigel had promoted an Ulster Hall concert by an international rap ensemble, then currently No.1 in the UK charts, and still managed to lose his shirt. Promoting Bert, it had always been a case of love before money. Upwards of a hundred punters on the door allowed all concerned to cover the costs, make a healthy profit and enjoy a great night of music from one of the masters. These days, with Bert's legendary status assured, even Nigel could always count on those goals being met.

After the Downpatrick gig, with Nigel still having a good time drowning his sorrows in pleasant company, I offered to drive Bert up to Belfast. 'By the way,' said Bert, at one point along the dark and winding highway, 'would you consider finishing the book?' I was shocked and stunned. If there had, at that juncture, been a road sign announcing 'Wrong Way: Next Left', I would quite possibly have taken it. This was a man who seemingly never even reads his own reviews, and though never standing in the way of my earlier efforts at writing a book he had certainly never displayed any active interest in it. For myself, the passing of several years and the consequent replacement of naive enthusiasm with greater knowledge and insight had not made the subject of a Bert Jansch biography less daunting: quite the opposite. I could not imagine what had suddenly made it seem like a good idea to Bert. I still don't know the answer to that one.

I reviewed his show the following night, leavened by the thrill of hearing no fewer than five new songs, and promised to give the matter some thought. It would be a major undertaking, not only professionally but personally. We agreed to meet in August during the Edinburgh Festival, conduct some interviews and review any progress with publishers. Where previously, in the early nineties, no one had been interested, several publishing houses were now responding positively. In November, a deal was signed with David Reynolds of Bloomsbury Publishing, over lunch in an agreeable restaurant two doors down from the old Cousins premises in Greek Street. Reynolds had been a Cousins regular himself in those days. It felt right.

Bert continued to go about his business: he was available and willing to do whatever was necessary to assist with the project. My own conviction was that the best way to proceed was to work on in seclusion with an already towering collection of researched and accumulated material relating to both Bert and his peers. It had taken the middle months of 1998 just to catalogue the stuff in preparation. Local vendors of box files and envelope folders had had a field day.

Back in May 1998, Bert had negotiated himself out of his contractual association with Cooking Vinyl, unhappy with aspects of their operation and with the company's attitude towards him as an artist over the past year. The lingering management association with Kresanna Aigner had been amicably concluded and a new manager by the name of Brian Hallin – a 'safe pair of hands', unlikely to push Bert into any visionary schemes, wide-boy transactions or relentlessly ambitious touring strategies – was welcomed to the fold. In December 1998 another new name on the scene, Matthew Quinn, asked for a meeting with Brian and myself in London. He wanted to make a documentary on Bert, and to someone already experiencing the malaise and terror of standing upon the foothills of such an Everest, in print form, Matt's enthusiasm was most refreshing. He had, he explained, recently been the best man at a friend's wedding. That friend was a Bert Jansch fan and Matt, blissfully unaware of the awe factor, had simply tracked Bert down and asked if he'd play at the wedding. He had said yes.

Three months later, in March 1999, it was my turn to get married. My fiancée Heather, who had first met and indeed first heard Bert that night in Downpatrick, had suggested I ask Bert to play. It was a preposterous idea: the wedding was set to take place in a particularly inaccessible corner of Donegal, Bert was a living legend with surely better things to do, we could at best cover his expenses but – well, he could only say no. He didn't: he said yes. The fact that Bert Jansch would willingly make such a gesture says a great deal about his character and at least partly explains why both Matt and I have invested time, money and effort on documenting the life and work of this extraordinary individual.

Matt began filming in May 1999, and in August we all convened at Bert's now annual concert at the Edinburgh Book Festival. Matt and Darren, his partner in the documentary project, would spend their trip dashing around Scotland interviewing various 'Chapter Three' people – Dolina Mac-Lennan, Owen Hand, Len Partridge – and filming Bert's gig. Heather and I were simply enjoying a holiday that just happened to coincide, as most of our holidays seem to do, with a Bert Jansch concert nearby. On this occasion, Bert debuted in public 'Caledonia Forever Free', a song he had demoed long before and was then considering as the title track of his next album. It was, he confided to the four or five hundred present, still a psychological hurdle to perform a song in public for the first time.

Between May and October that year, Matt filmed several gigs around the country, interviewed on camera many of those whose tributes and recollections appear in this book, and others besides, and enjoyed Bert's co-operation in a number of specially staged sequences. Bert had agreed to perform three of his most archetypal songs – 'Morning Brings Peace Of Mind', 'Fresh As A Sweet Sunday Morning' and the immortal if rarely aired 'Reynardine' – several times over in the controlled environment of an empty Cecil Sharp House. He had also participated in genuinely spontaneous duets with two celebrity admirers he had never previously met, Bernard Butler and Kelly Joe Phelps.

If Bernard and Kelly Joe were nervous of playing with Bert, they were not alone in that feeling: 'I'm actually terrified of those kind of situations,' says Bert, on reflection, 'but I'm proud that I played with Bernard and Kelly Joe. If I met Jimmy Page now and tried to play something with him there'd be nothing worthwhile happening. Here, something came out that was new, that hadn't been there before – and this was us meeting for the first time.'

In April 1999, in partnership with Loren, Bert finally acquired a new and more home-like flat, down a leafy lane in Kilburn in North London. In June they were engaged. While Bert continued the business of writing and recording songs for his next album, and Loren continued to juggle various writing and teaching obligations of her own, the complex wheels of organisation began turning for what was to to be a lavish long-weekend wedding celebration on the Isle of Arran, culminating with the ceremony itself on 1 November.

Many of Loren's extended family had flown in from South Africa, yet it was probably Bert's family who were more surprised at being in the same place at the same time. Along with sister Mary and her family, and his own son Adam, Bert's elusive brother Charlie had also accepted the invitation. It was only the second time he'd seen Bert in thirty years and thus politely he concluded that he would be of little use to a biographer. From the music world, Gordon Giltrap, Maggie Boyle, Johnny 'Guitar' Hodge and Bert's agent John Stoneyport were there (Ralph McTell, Jacqui McShee and Dick Gaughan all had prior commitments, while Anne Briggs was remaining elusive); from the Howff days, there was only his thus-far mysterious friend 'Wee Jimmy'. Matthew Quinn and I had both been invited, somewhat unnerved by Bert's prior suggestion that this time it would be us who would have to play. Was he serious? It transpired that he was.

'Sometimes it irritates me,' Bert told an interviewer from the *Evening Standard* in 1995, 'people saying, 'If you hadn't done *that* then *this* would have happened. It's a strange thing: it doesn't bother me personally [thinking of what might have been], but it does seem to bother a lot of other people on my behalf.'

There are a fair number of people 'around' Bert in a semi-detached sort of way – old friends, admirers, other musicians and people in the media – who are all united by a strange sense of aspiration on his behalf. It is perhaps there not only because he is such a hero to all of us, but because he seems entirely disinterested in playing the music business game and remains thus desperately exposed to being torn apart at regular intervals by the sharks in that treacherous sea. From my own perspective as one of those vaguely orbiting Bert over the past few years, I could recount several examples of where I believe wrong career decisions were made, business and musical associations made with dubious individuals, and opportunities missed. To those of us in this virtual Bert Jansch solar system, the shrugging of shoulders is a regular occurance. He has done it his way, and he shall continue to do so.

Towards the end of the writing process, in late November 1999, Matthew Quinn secured a broadcast slot with Channel 4, for June 2000, timed to coincide with the publication of this book and the release of *Crimson Moon*, Bert's first album for Castle Communications, current owners of the Transatlantic catalogue. For Bert, the decision to sign with Castle was a pragmatic one – at least now the flood of reissues may conceivably be contained or controlled. He is arguably now producing his best work since those Transatlantic recordings which first brought him to prominence in the sixties, and he will hopefully continue to do so for a long time to come.

At the time of writing, various projects were in progress or in planning that will hopefully bring his work to the attention of a wider audience. Following the release of *Crimson Moon*, Castle have scheduled a double CD Jansch anthology, reining in material from several labels, much of it not previously or only obscurely available on CD. Significantly, this will be the first Jansch compilation to cover his whole career and will be the ideal introduction for newcomers. A systematic series of individual album reissues is planned for 2001, likely to utilise better quality masters than have previously been available and to include the handful of Transatlantic-era outtakes known to exist in private hands. A box set is also tentatively planned. While a smattering of worthy unreleased material does exist from most periods of Bert's career, it would benefit the project greatly if anyone in possession of quality amateur or off-air recordings of Jansch from the sixties and seventies would make themselves known to the author or to Castle Communications. Two tribute projects will also have appeared around the time of this book's publication: Gordon Giltrap's *Janschology* EP, in May 2000; and, in August, a various artists set on Market Square Records entitled *Letters To Bert*, a sincere and splendid collection of Bert's peers, associates and more recent admirers ending in style the age-long dearth of Jansch covers on record.

For the longer-term, Bert has an inclination to do less touring; has an idea to construct a guitar course, for sale over the internet; and has a plan to document his music in a book, in printed notation form. Asked to choose a favourite from his own recordings he says this: '*Avocet* and possibly one or two tracks on *Rosemary Lane*. But there's always one track on every album. People don't realise that I've a set idea for each album and if it hasn't worked out that way I'll reject that album. *Toy Balloon* started off great, fantastic. But the finished album, I couldn't listen to it.' Far from wallowing in it, he remains slightly uncomfortable about the increasing quantity of celebrity musicians who cite his influence: 'I don't pay much attention to it. It does bug me a little in that with interviewers the first questions will be Jimmy Page, Neil Young – and the list goes on from there! But it's all part of being in the music business. It's like being a bricklayer. If it's the only thing you know how to do, you have to be in the building trade to do it.'

It is my sincere hope that this book, Matthew Quinn's documentary and the various other projects mentioned above will go some way towards encouraging a fuller appreciation of the man and his music, loyally beloved of many and perhaps now entering an era in which he may be discovered and cherished by many more.

Notes

CHAPTER ONE

1. There are, for example, only five bearers of the Jansch name in the current Austrian telephone directory – one of them named Herbert.
2. Margaret was granted a divorce from Herbert Jansch in 1954.
3. *Disc*, 18/4/70. Even in the mid-seventies, when songs about the experience had worked themselves out of his system and when he had been a modestly well-known figure within Britain for some time, and regularly visible on television during the Pentangle years, 1968 – 72, Bert could still claim to feel 'bitterly disappointed' that his father had never bothered to get in touch.
4. *Ptolomaic Terrascope*, 7/97.
5. 'The Saturday Movie', *In The Round*, 1986.
6. *NME*, 21/5/77.
7. As note 3.
8. Quotes combined from: *Zigzag*, 9/74; *Frets*, 3/80; *Dirty Linen*, 10/90; *Ptolomaic Terrascope*, 7/97. Bert has told this sory several times, with slight variation in detail – principally, on how old he was when trying to build guitars. Various ages between seven and fifteen have been given, but the inspiration of Lonnie Donegan would place this activity most likely between 1956 and 1958.
9. *Guitarist*, 3/95.
10. 'When I Get Home', *Reflection*, 1971.
11. *Zigzag*, 9/74.
12. As note 3.

CHAPTER TWO

1. *Guinness Encyclopedia Of Popular Music* (Concise Edition, 1993)
2. As note 1.
3. *Alexis Korner: The Biography*, Harry Shapiro (Bloomsbury, 1996). Although the British Musicians' Union employed a ban on American musicians working in Britain between 1935 and 1956, in response to a similar ban on British players in America, blues artists were nevertheless able to slip through the net by applying for work permits as 'entertainers' rather than 'musicians'. On the subject of Broonzy's anti-racist commitment, several national newspapers in the UK reported on 22/1/99 the bizarre instance of racism engendered by the regular and well-intentioned singing of his song 'Black, Brown and White' in a school assembly in Bury. The

irony of the chorus, *'If you're white you're alright / If you're brown stick around / If you're black get back, get back, get back'*, was clearly not appreciated as the heads of those assembled regularly turned to the only black pupil in the school.

4. *Acoustic Routes*, BBC Scotland 25/1/93.
5. *The Story Of The Blues*, Paul Oliver, 1969 (Updated Edition, Pimlico 1997).
6. As note 5.
7. *Skiffle: The Story Of Folk-Song With A Jazz Beat* by Brian Bird was published in 1958. Forty years later, the skiffle buff's bookshelf trebled in weight with an anecdotal compendium from Chas McDevitt *Skiffle: The Definitive Inside Story* (Robson, 1997) and an academic analysis from Mike Dewe *The Skiffle Craze* (Planet, 1998).
8. 'The first king of Britpop', Neil Spencer, The *Observer*, 10/1/99.
9. Mike Dewe, in *The Skiffle Craze*, concludes that there is no evidence for the word 'skiffle' being used to describe a form of music as such, or being part of any group's name, before the war. Rather, it was one of many euphemisms to describe a house-rent party. He also mentions the tantalising story of one Bill Skiffle, a poor black man particularly known for such events. Karl Dallas points out that Alan Lomax wrote an interesting piece for *MM* in the fifties 'relating skiffle to the minstrel shows of Victorian times, pointing out that though black influenced (like the minstrels) it was in fact very English (like Morris dancing and the sea shanty, both black influenced English movements). This is relevant in considering Lonnie Donegan's later career in panto (another black import) and cabaret.' On a similar theme, Mike Dewe makes the observation that while the 'original' American skiffle was largely instrumental and piano based, its British counterpart was guitar based and largely vocal.
10. Adapted from the uncredited sleeve note to Brownie & Sonny's *At The Bunkhouse*, 1965. Much of the preceding biographical material on the pair also derives from this source, which seems more reliable than contradictory information on McGhee in the *Guinness Encyclopedia*.
11. *The Skiffle Craze*, Mike Dewe (Planet, 1998). In the preface to this comprehensive and authoritative account of the movement's rise and fall, Dewe notes that from conversations with Chris Barber himself 'there seems to be a query as to Lonnie Donegan's involvement with his band prior to 1952'. Other evidence appears to contradict this recollection.
12. As note 1. Ken Colyer, in his autobiography *When Dreams Are In The Dust* (Ryarsh, Kent, Milbury 1989), recounts how he acquired a collection of Leadbelly 78s in New York and a guitar in Canada during 1947. These are emphasised by Mike Dewe as possibly crucial events in the skiffle story, although both he and Shapiro mention the curious case of the Original London Blue Blowers, a seemingly unrecorded 1945 – 48 British 'spasm' band – 'spasm' being a variation on skiffle based around kazoos and exemplified during skiffle's boom years by Russell Quaye's City Ramblers. The OLBB resurfaced on the 1957 bandwagon as the Bill Bailey Skiffle Group.
13. As note 11.
14. As note 8. Karl Dallas recalls that 'Rock Island Line' got its first airplay on the BBC's Sunday morning Christopher Stone show: 'Jeff Smith of *MM* told me that when the song came on he immediately slapped on his tape recorder – which most of us had in readiness at all times because "folk" snippets on air were so few and far between –

and was quite irritated later to find that it was not in fact a "genuine" black artist singing, but a cockney cowboy from Glasgow.'

15. *Dirty Linen*, 10/90.

16. As note 8. It is fair to say that of all the skifflers Donegan had always employed the widest repertoire, adapting material by white folk and country artists including Woody Guthrie, the Carter Family and Hank Williams into his act.

17. 'A Raver's Guide To Soho', John Platt, *Comstock Lode*, c.1979. Some of this material was later included in his *London's Rock Routes* (Fourth Estate, 1985).

18. *The People*, 6/10/57. Sourced from 'English Folk Revival: The Early Years', Colin Irwin, *Southern Rag* No.19, Jan–March 1984.

19. Emblematic of the period, the 2 i's was a coffee bar with a smoother, hipper agenda (daddy-o). It opened its doors in 1955, catering for sharply dressed suburban kids and became in no time at all the prime source of all those clean-cut British 'rock'n'roll' crooners – Tommy Steele, Terry Dene, Cliff Richard et al. – who littered the stages of producer Jack Good's throwaway pop TV programmes for the next few years: 'It was the first and most successful purely teenage meeting place,' notes Platt, 'complete with juke box. When skiffle started Tommy Steele worked there, promptly got discovered and they were made.' The first mention of Bunjies operating as a music venue was in February 1962 when Colin Wilkie and Malcolm Price started a folk club on the premises. Unlike other Soho venues, it rarely advertised in *MM* and thrived on word-of-mouth. Back in the fifties, with some poetic justice Chas McDevitt – who had enjoyed a 250,000-seller hit with veteran songster Elizabeth Cotten's 'Freight Train', unscrupulously claiming the authorship himself – ploughed his royalties into a Soho coffee bar of that name, modelling it on the 2 i's, aiming it squarely at the beat crowd and failing to fool anyone. Cotten had been employed as a nanny to the Seeger family in America, and Peggy had helped her to copyright the song although, as Steve Benbow suggests, 'I don't suppose she wrote it either. It's the same chord sequence as "Railroad Bill" . . .' With some assistance from her Brit-folk pals, Cotten sued MacDevitt and his singer Nancy Whiskey in 1960. MacDevitt maintains in his 1997 book *Skiffle* that the problem was amicably settled out of court but Whiskey was fed up with the whole affair and successfully disappeared until 1998's 'Roots Of British Rock' skiffle revival show at the Royal Albert Hall. She sang 'Freight Train'.

20. The Skiffle Cellar opened during 1957, although Quaye's City Ramblers had been active since 1954, playing often at the Princess Louise during 1956. Also on Greek Street was John Hasted's 44 Skiffle Club. The John Hasted Skiffle & Folksong Group, as they were known, included future soloists Redd Sullivan and Shirley Collins. Their repertoire, reflecting Hasted's keen hope for a full-scale folk revival, included British songs alongside the standard American fare. Karl Dallas points out that Hasted was 'a very influential figure in his time, doing more to spread the gospel of folk outside of London than anyone else'. Hasted was then a doctor of physics at University College, later a professor at Birkbeck. Dallas met him through Russell Quaye's first vocalist, Hylda Sims, whom he had met at a Young Communist League social. 'Since I am virtually musically illiterate,' says Dallas, 'I used to sing him my new songs over the phone from my newspaper office in Fleet Street to his physics lab at University College and he would note them down to appear in *Sing*.' Hasted married in the early sixties and his wife persuaded him to 'give up' folk.

21. Benbow himself has never given the matter much thought: 'What about Elton Hayes?' he suggests. 'He was Alan A'Dale in the *Robin Hood* TV series. He was accompanying English folk songs on guitar when I was at school. A very good guitarist. I used to listen to him on *Children's Hour . . .*' Regarding Elton Hayes, Karl Dallas believes he accompanied a 'proper' traditional singer, Bob Arnold, on a couple of HMV 78s. Arnold subsequently enjoyed fame in that everyday story of country folk, *The Archers*, on BBC Radio 4.

22. *Barrack Room Ballads*, Topic 1958.

23. *Journeyman: An Autobiography*, Ewan MacColl, Sidgwick & Jackson 1990. Subsequent MacColl quotes this chapter are from this source unless otherwise credited.

24. None of Benbow's recordings are currently available on CD. I'm indebted to John Beecher at Rollercoaster Records for providing a copy of an as yet unreleased 1958 live tape – an intoxicating melange of folk, jazz, cabaret and calypso.

25. 'Cynic's Progress', Maggie Holland, *Folk Roots* 10/90.

26. As note 25.

27. As note 25. Bentley and Craig were two Croydon youths who were charged with shooting a policeman during a robbery in 1951. Derek Bentley was executed for the crime but there was widespread public controversy at the time, believing Craig (too young to be hanged) to be solely responsible.

28. 'Wizz Jones At 50', interview probably from *The Cornishman*, 89.

29. As note 3.

30. 'The singer and the audience', Ewan MacColl, *Folk Music*, 11/63.

31. From its embryonic beginnings in 1951, Hamish Henderson was a founder and guiding light of the School of Scottish Studies and as a field-recordist and folksong collector, the Scottish equivalent and peer of the Lomaxes in America, Seamus Ennis for Radio Telefis Eirean in Ireland, Peter Kennedy for the English Folk Dance & Song Society and the BBC and Bert Lloyd for Topic and the BBC in England. In his foreword to Ailee Munro's *The Democratic Muse: Folk Music Revival In Scotland* (Scottish Cultural Press, 2nd Edition, 1996), Henderson cites Lomax's first visit to Britain as 'the inception of the present "folk revival" – as far as Scotland is concerned'. In 1951, Henderson toured Scotland as a guide for Lomax, recording 'source singers' for Columbia Records' *World Albums of Folk and Primitive Music* series and, on the side, for the new and bare shelves of the School of Scottish Studies – at that stage residing in a dusty corner of the Phonetics Department at Edinburgh University. Henderson specifically recalls Ewan MacColl, whom he knew through the 'fringe' folksong events around the early Edinburgh Festivals, as his introduction to Lomax. MacColl, in his autobiography, implies 1954 was the date of his first encounter with Lomax. I view Henderson's account as the most plausible. To digress slightly, Lomax – a tireless, inspirational and ebullient fellow by all accounts – was the instigator of the first meeting between Ewan MacColl and Bert Lloyd, circa 1954. Both men knew each other by reputation – and let us remember that the folk scene of the early fifties did not offer succour to those wishing to lose themselves in a crowd – but only in Britain, felt Lomax, would neither consider the prospect of introducing themselves.

32. *Folk News*, No.16 1978. Letter from Dominic Behan to the editor. Karl Dallas now notes that 'Dom is being a bit (typically) malicious here. Ewan's Theatre Royal

concerts (at which I and my then wife Betty sang) were 'benefits' for Theatre Workshop so, far from getting a loan from TW the boot was on the other foot.'

33. Winter fell out permanently with MacColl in 1961, after publishing a damning critique of his Singers Club in *Sing*, but Dallas maintained something of an off/on relationship: 'Because I was close to Ewan, though often quarrelled with him,' he says, 'people seemed to think I necessarily adopted all his various "lines" – which changed as often as a Communist Party line, I always felt – and that I was therefore guilty by association.' MacColl's prestige and formidable persona gave him an ability to grant or deny people status and to some extent this made him a natural fall-guy for those wishing to explain away their lack of success. In those days Steve Benbow was rarely off the airwaves but rarely in the papers. He certainly fostered the suspicion that one effect of MacColl's perceived influence was an implicit disdain of his activities. 'My impression,' notes Dallas, 'was that Steve disdained a lot of *us*.'

34. Dallas wrote for the *MM* from 1957 to 1981, predating Eric Winter at the paper – with a piece on the folk roots of skiffle in July 1957 – although Winter was a more regular contributor during the earlier years. Dallas also wrote on the subject of folk music for numerous other publications – from specialist titles including *Folk Music*, a mid-sixties journal which he edited, and broadsheet newspapers including *The Times* and the *Daily Worker/Morning Star*. Two people wrote the *Melody Maker*'s Focus On Folk column between Winter's departure in October 1963 and Dallas's arrival in mid-'65. One was Jeff Smith and, with some irony given his *MM*-vs-Benbow conspiracy theories, the other was Steve Benbow. Between 1977 and 1979 Dallas edited and published *Folk News*, a substantial folk music monthly broadsheet which allowed plenty of space for exhaustive career retrospectives on long-standing figures like Martin Carthy and Alex Campbell. With the demise of *Folk News*, he reverted to A4 glossy format with the short-lived *Acoustic Music* in 1980 following which, and aside from a biography of Pink Floyd, he has written largely on Information Technology. His vast and always illuminating knowledge on folk music and its performers still crops up in occasional sleeve notes, obituaries for *The Independent* and articles on the internet. In 1984, after fifty years of atheism, he converted to Christianity. 'I still think of myself as a communist, though I joined the Labour Party after the Communist Party of Great Britain was destroyed.' He maintains with some vigour that the infamous 'Skiffle Won't Die' headline of that debut piece for the *MM* was not his idea.

35. Six of the *Radio Ballads* appeared on Decca between 1965 and 1972, in similar form to the original broadcasts. All eight became available on Topic in 1999.

36. Mike Dewe refers to a sell-out 'Ballads & Blues' concert at the Royal Festival Hall in July 1954. The concert ranged across folk, jazz and an early form of skiffle courtesy of Ken Colyer's group. Other artists included Bert Lloyd, Ewan MacColl, Isla Cameron and various traditional Irish musicians. As a diarist in *Jazz Journal* noted: 'A more unlikely collection of participants never graced the Festival Hall.'

37. As note 30. Specifically, MacColl's justification here refers to his second and more notorious platform, the Singers Club, inaugurated in June 1961.

38. 'I wasn't really true to any particular kind of music in those days,' Moore continues. 'I was just happy to go to a town, go to the folk club, sing whatever was needed, get a few bob, party through the night and head to the next town. It was a brilliant lifestyle.'

39. The timescale of the Nixon/MacColl divergence is complex, but summer 1959 seems likeliest. There may have been a period when MacColl continued operating as the Ballads & Blues at the Horseshoe Hotel in Tottenham Court Road (ironically perhaps, the very place where Bert Jansch would host his own club in 1967). Overlapping the Nixon/MacColl situation, and further complicating the lineage, the MacColl disciple Bruce Dunnet started his own club Folksong Unlimited with a group of regulars drawn from MacColl's circle: Dominic Behan, Stan Kelly, Shirley Collins, Isobel Sutherland and others. There is a suggestion that this club also had its premises for a time at the Princess Louise.

40. 'Celtic person makes SR cover – shock, horror!', *Southern Rag* No.16, April-June 1983. Shortly afterwards, Andy purchased a copy of Harry Smith's legendary *Anthology Of American Folk Music* which provided the enlightening bridge between dustbowl balladry and traditional music.

41. As note 40. Irvine also recorded performances by both Jack Elliott and Derroll Adams at the Ballads & Blues on a borrowed tape machine during September 1959.

42. 'Like many extroverts,' notes Karl Dallas, 'Ewan was actually quite shy and never spoke to anyone he didn't know, unless someone else introduced him or spoke to him of them. He couldn't make small talk.'

43. Noel Harrison has two claims to fame: being the son of actor Rex Harrison and scoring a sole hit in 1969 with 'Windmills Of Your Mind' from *The Thomas Crown Affair*. One of those classic examples of a memorable song whose singer nobody quite recalls. Long John Baldry fared, arguably, rather better with his contemporaneous bid for MOR mythology 'Let The Heartaches Begin'. Baldry's problem was not so much the name-recognition thing as the fact that he had three *further* hits that nobody recalls. On the subject of Ewan's non-folk repertoire, Karl Dallas notes that he 'had a fine stock of music-hall and thirties pop songs which he never sang in public. I remember turning up for a demo wearing a particularly fine Herbert Johnson (of Bond Street) velour wide-brimmed trilby, and Ewan launched into a full-scale version of Harry Champion's "Where Did You Get That 'At" in a strange amalgam of the Cockney original and his own Scots-Salford dialect. Then he always was a fine mimic.'

44. While Irvine is certain of seeing Peggy there while Baldry performed his English blues, his memory is less certain in placing MacColl at precisely the same place and time. Nevertheless, Peggy herself explained on BBC Radio 2's *As I Roved Out: A Century Of Folk Music* in 1999, that it was through 'discussing' material with Baldry at the B&B that led to MacColl's subsequent policy of performers singing only the songs of their own tradition.

45. Part of this quote from 'The Carthy Tapes', Karl Dallas, *Folk News,* July 1978; part from an interview with the author. 'The Witches Cauldron' was the most fondly recalled Hampstead coffee-bar, but it didn't open to music until September 1961. Opening acts: Martin Carthy and Redd Sullivan. By the mid-sixties the Three Horseshoes, in Hampstead, was one of the more significant London folk clubs outside of the centre.

46. *Robin Hall Remembered*, BBC Scotland 31/12/98. Subsequent Macgregor quotes are also from this broadcast.

47. 'Carthy's Commitment', *Southern Rag* No.24, April-June 1985.

48. 'The Carthy Era', Sarah Coxson, *Folk Roots*, November 1987.

49. 'The Carthy Tapes', Karl Dallas, *Folk News,* July 1978.

CHAPTER THREE

1. 'Reflections by Roy Guest', *Folk Scene*, November 1964.
2. Sleeve notes to *Love Songs & Lullabies* (1964) by Roy Guest and Kate Lucy.
3. 'Guest Nights', Karl Dallas, *MM* 28/10/72.
4. As note 1.
5. As note 1.
6. As note 1.
7. *Journeyman: An Autobiography*, Ewan MacColl (Sidgwick & Jackson, 1990). Unless otherwise credited, all further MacColl quotes in this chapter are from this source.
8. Perambulatory names were clearly in vogue. During 1956 Alan Lomax had persuaded Granada TV in Manchester to commission a series of programmes of international folk singing called *The Ramblers*, featuring an especially assembled group of the same name. The group needed a five-string banjo player for Appalachian repertoire and Lomax brought over Peggy Seeger, then in Denmark, for the purpose. It would be Ewan and Peggy's first encounter. In Glasgow, from 1959, Ray & Archie Fisher performed with fiddler Bobby Campbell as the Wayfarers. Dave & Toni Arthur, latterday stalwarts of English traditional song and children's television, would begin their career in 1962 on *Thank Your Lucky Stars* as the Strollers – Britain's answer to Nina & Frederick. Britain, unfortunately, had not asked that particular question.
9. As note 3. The *Scots Dictionary*, more politely, defines a howff as 'a place of resort or concourse; haunt; a much frequented tavern; an abode, residence; a shelter'.
10. *Dirty Linen*, 10/90. Bert left Leith Academy early in 1960. His gardening sojourn lasted at least until August 1960. It was during this gardening period that he discovered guitar lessons at the Howff.
11. 'Liver Archie', Ewan McVicar, *Folk Roots* 8/87.
12. Part of this quote from *Folk Roots* 8/87, part from the outtakes of BBC Scotland's *Acoustic Routes*, 25/1/93. MacColl and cohorts performed two or three such 'Ballads & Blues' evenings in Glasgow during the late fifties, at the Iona Community Centre in Clyde Street.
13. *Zigzag*, 9/74.
14. *Cod Liver Oil And The Orange Juice: Reminiscences Of A Fat Folk Singer*, Hamish Imlach & Ewan McVicar (Mainstream Publishing, 1992). Unless otherwise credited, and bar one or two from an interview with the author, all further Imlach quotes in this chapter are from this source.
15. 'Talking Army Blues', a satire on British national service, was written by another 'Broomhill Bum' Ewan McVicar. As McVicar notes in his memoir *One Singer One Song* (Glasgow City Libraries, 1990), released on Top Rank it was a national hit single in every chart of the day bar the one used by the trade publication *Record Retailer*. This chart, from March 1960, is the one favoured by the *Guinness Book Of British Hit Singles*. 'Messin' About On The River', from the pen of TV themes supremo Tony Hatch, has been similarly excised from chart posterity. The Reivers were brought together by Norman Buchan as residents for *Jigtime*, performing exclusively Scottish traditional songs. McVicar notes that the group 'had much success in the late fifties, making recordings, appearing in concerts, performing for the intervals at barn dances and even touring dance halls in Scotland. Younger

singers in Glasgow were busy performing wherever they could corral an audience – social clubs, talent competitions, bingo halls and especially clubs for the elderly.'

16. The Broomhill Bums were chuffed to discover, from Cisco Houston, that Woody Guthrie had spent time in Glasgow during his days in the US Navy. The American influence was an enduring inspiration in Scotland. Ailee Munro quotes the late Josh MacRae from an interview in 1976 suggesting quite profoundly that 'there's more in common between a Celt and a cowboy than between a Celt and an Englishman'.

17. Outtakes from *Acoustic Routes*, BBC Scotland 25/1/93.

18. As note 17. Unless otherwise credited, all further Fisher quotes this chapter are from this source.

19. As note 17.

20. *Acoustic Routes*, BBC Scotland 25/1/93.

21. As note 17. It seems that Sonny & Brownie toured Britain in 1959 between 11 September and 14 October. The tour included two English concerts with the Weavers and Jack Elliott but the Glasgow show with Barber must have been a one-off – there were no other shows with Barber mentioned in *MM*, although the duo did record with his band during this trip. As the Barber group left for America around 24 September, that leaves a two-week period for both the Glasgow concert and recordings to have taken place. I am indebted to Richard Johnson for this information.

22. *One Singer One Song*, Ewan McVicar (Glasgow City Libraries, 1990).

23. As note 20. Putting a date on Sonny & Brownie's visit to Edinburgh in 1960 has proved extraordinarily difficult. The *Melody Maker* mentioned in some form, either before or after, many of their dates during previous visits in 1958 and 1959. But there is only one tantalising *MM* reference during the entirety of 1960: a report in April about a British tour scheduled for October. There are no further mentions. It is known that the duo were in New York on October 26. I am indebted to both Richard Johnson and Pete Frame – and blues experts including Trevor Hodgett, Chris Smith, Val Wilmer and Spencer Leigh – for their efforts in trying to pin this thing down. Nevertheless, the weight of circumstantial evidence is overwhelming and I am personally in no doubt that Sonny & Brownie did appear at the Usher Hall, Edinburgh during the latter part of 1960, and subsequently at the Howff – probably between August and October. An October date is tempting as Maggie Cruickshank, a Howff devotee, remembers her sister and brother (but not herself) seeing them there. Maggie sat her finals in October 1960. Remarkably, Len Partridge actually recorded the session, which is splendid, but neglected to record the date. His memory favours early 1961: 'We recorded that night in its entirety with their permission. Well, that's not entirely true. They discovered it halfway through and said, "What's this mic doing here?" You can't hide a bloody Ferrograph! But it was fine.' Unfortunately, Sonny & Brownie did not tour Britain in 1961 until September–October.

24. *Ptolomaic Terrascope*, 7/97.

25. *The Story Of The Blues*, Paul Oliver (revised edition, Pimlico, 1997).

26. As note 20.

27. 'Uncle Wattie was a sweetheart,' says Maggie. 'He did a night in the Crown for a while, and also ran a club down Victoria Street called the Place. Liz and I were home from Canada on holiday [c. 1966] and we had this party. And among the

people Barbara Dickson arrived. My father came through saying, "Come and hear this guy, he's the most wonderful player" – and this is Wattie. Somehow Barbara was left in the living room listening to Wattie with my mother and father and we'd all retreated to the other room with the big boys. No wonder Barbara doesn't speak to us now.'

28. *Sounds*, 9/1/71. Intriguingly, Owen Hand retains the original writing of an otherwise unknown Bert Jansch song called 'John Keith' from this period: 'I reminded Bert of the song once and he became a bit huffed, thinking I was putting him down,' says Owen. 'This was not my intention as it's not as bad a song as Bert remembers but I think it was the first song he ever wrote and it embarrasses him.'

29. The shop in question may or may not have been a greengrocer's.

30. I am indebted to Geoff Harden for access to his extraordinary collection of live recordings from the St Andrews club. Check out the 1966 Davy Graham concert from this source, on Rollercoaster Records.

31. The writing credits for 'Hey Joe' are a complex issue. Currently claimed in terms of arrangement by Tim Rose, it was nevertheless recognisable to Len Partridge in its 1966 Jimi Hendrix version as the song he had helped write with Bill Roberts in Edinburgh ten years earlier. There was a coffee bar in Old Fishmarket Close called Bunjies, named after the London premises of the same name. Around 1956, shortly after Len had acquired his twelve-string guitar, a friend of Len's discovered the place and reported the presence of an American playing there, also with a twelve-string. 'So there was this guy, dressed in black from, I think, Knoxville, Tennessee,' says Len, 'and we ended up, of course, two like minds with two twelve-strings, at a time when there are only two others you know of in the world! We played quite a lot together but only at Bunjies or the odd party, because there was nowhere else to play. And one of the things which came out of that period was "Hey Joe". I can't claim credit for it – that really does have to go to Bill Roberts. Don't even ask me now what bits were added by me because I can't tell you, it just evolved, it was one of those things you chucked around. This is the thing: if somebody asked me how many songs I'd written I'd find it very difficult to come up with more than two or three titles and yet there must have been lots that just happened and were soon discarded. You never thought about it. We weren't professional – or we certainly didn't have any bloody foresight. Luckily, when Bill Roberts went back to the States he at some point must have copyrighted it. Bill wasn't credited on the original Hendrix release but his name did appear later. It's one of those things which some people have said, "Do you not feel a bit miffed about that?" But I don't think I've anything to feel miffed about.'

32. As note 13.

33. The anti-Polaris demonstrations began in 1961. In 1963 a record entitled *Ding Dong Dollar*, encompassing many of Blythman's satirical songs set to the tunes of Glasgow street songs, came out on the US label Folkways. Purportedly, no UK company would touch it. Hamish Imlach's recordings for the project, with JFK as the target of his ire, were scrapped as the President had just attained sainthood in Dallas.

34. Gordon McCulloch, *Folk News*, 12/79. Although not contemporary with the events of this chapter, the extract used encapsulates what I have found to be a widely held view of MacColl's performance style regardless of era.

35. Aside from those already mentioned, 1961 folk clubs in Greater London included

the following: on Mondays, a new blues night with Gerry Loughran and Cliff Aungier at the King & Queen in Soho; on Wednesdays, Derek Serjeant's new and destined to be long-enduring enterprise at the Oak Hotel in Surbiton; on Thursdays, the Star & Garter in Bromley; on Fridays, the King's Arms in Putney, the Rose & Crown in Wimbledon or the White Hart in Southall; on Saturdays the old faithfuls, the Ballads & Blues (now at Carlisle Street, Soho) with Steve Benbow as resident, Martin Carthy at the Troubadour, and a regular club at the Cellar in Cecil Sharp House; on Sundays, should one not fancy an evening in the company of Ewan MacColl, there was always the Robin Hood in Potters Bar, Les Faux Hiboux (the Mad Owls) in Streatham or a club boasting the residency of Alex Campbell at the Community Centre in Richmond.

36. Seeger at the Albert Hall was a triumph, but not everyone was jumping with self-congratulatory joy. Andy Irvine for one: 'He came out with an axe and sang a wood-chopping song at the beginning. I thought, "Fuck this". It was bad.' That very theatricality was what had delighted others. 'Andy would have seen Pete chopping a log onstage,' says Martin Carthy, 'with this huge chip of wood flying about forty feet up in the air, and singing a song at the same time. I didn't know Andy in those days, but to me it was amazingly impressive.'

37. Spinners member Tony, interviewed in *Folk News*, 9/77, recalled their club thus: 'We set a policy at the beginning, with three aims. The first was to get people singing songs, folk songs if possible; the second was to learn all we could about traditional music; and the third was to tell the people in our club what we learned. That was the credo of our club and we've fairly well stuck to that.' At the height of their light entertainment popularity, the group were still running their Liverpool club with great success. Deferential to the EFDSS and Ewan MacColl, when the Singers Club began the group also sought advice on club organising from Bruce Dunnet.

38. Fife is a populous corner of Scotland to the immediate north of Edinburgh. Including the Fife clubs at St Andrews, Dunfermline and Kirkaldy, the Edinburgh venues, the clubs in Dundee and Perth (just beyond Fife to the north) and in Bo'ness (in the West Lothian region that surrounds Edinburgh on its landward side to the south), this represented quite a circuit. No club was more than fifty miles' drive from any of the others.

39. 'High Street Howff', Jeremy Bruce-Watt, unidentified Edinburgh newspaper, circa 1990s.

40. As note 17.

41. At least some of Martha Schlamme's incredible coverage, and consequently the lure of profit that led to the demise of the Howff, must lie at the door of Magnus Magnusson. Yes, that one. Magnus was part of the Howff circle at the time, worked in journalism and had something of a crush on Martha Schlamme. Outrageously prolonged coverage ensued. Evidently, he started and couldn't quite finish.

42. Waverley Records may not have been quite the 'house label' Roy was suggesting, but Bryce Lane was certainly tapping into the Howff's reservoir of talent. A record of Archie Fisher was issued on the label before March 1963, while three Edinburgh-centric compilations appeared during 1964 and '65: *Hoot'nanny Show Vols 1 & 2* – including Ray Fisher and others featured in the BBC TV show of that name, broadcast as one series during 1964 live from Edinburgh. Roy Guest was the

presenter and possibly also appears on the records. The other release was *Folk Festival: Festival Folk* in 1965. Catalogue numbers suggest over thirty records were released on the label up to this point. Len believes both Craig Hall Studios and Waverley Records were eventually subsumed by EMI, although the studio and all trace of Bryce Lane had disappeared by the late seventies.

43. As note 3.
44. As note 1.

CHAPTER FOUR

1. 'Three Dreamers', first released on the Danish version of *A Rare Conundrum* (1977), later re-recorded for *The Ornament Tree* (1991). A Rare Conundrum contained a number of songs concerning Bert's youth: 'One To A Hundred' is about the death of a childhood friend; 'Three Chord Trick' contains oblique references to Jill Doyle and the Howff; 'Daybreak' is about the all-nighters at Les Cousins in the mid-sixties. 'Three Dreamers' is, of course, a reflection on himself, Clive and Robin living together in Edinburgh at the beginning of all their careers. The archway and courtyard, at 9-15 West Nicolson Street, are still there.
2. *Dirty Linen*, 10/90.
3. *Ptolomaic Terrascope* 7/97 and *Beat Instrumental* 8/77 (quotes combined). attributed to Karl Dallas's invention.
4. 'Folk Routines', Ken Hunt, *Folk Roots* 5/97.
5. As note 4.
6. As note 4.
7. Outtakes to *Acoustic Routes*, BBC Scotland 25/1/93.
8. Davy's invention of DADGAD can only be dated by reference to the date of his first recording with the tuning. Recorded with a live audience in a Decca studio on July 3 1963, Davy's arrangement of the Irish tune 'She Moved Thro' The Fair' was a ground-breaking moment. It was released on *From A London Hootenanny*, an EP shared with the Thameside Four, on 27 September 1963. Davy performed it on ABC TV's *Hullaballoo*, tele-recorded around June/July 1963. Martin Carthy recalls Davy introducing the tune at the Troubadour two weeks before the EP recording. He had visited Tangier in 1961 and had developed the tuning in response to the demands of re-creating Moroccan music on guitar.
9. As note 4.
10. As note 7.
11. *Midnight Man: The Davy Graham Fanzine*, No.1, July 1999.
12. *Cod Liver Oil and The Orange Juice*, Hamish Imlach & Ewan McVicar (Mainstream Publishing, 1992).
13. *MM*, 17/1/76. Traditional songs from Clive's repertoire in this era continue to slip into Bert's, e.g. 'Rosemary Lane' (*Rosemary Lane*, 1971), 'The Lily Of The West' (*One More Road*, 1993).
14. *Zigzag*, 9/74.
15. 'The Loneliness Of The Long Distance Folk Singer', Ken Hunt, *Swing 51*, No. 13, 1989.
16. Robin's early performing career is difficult to reconstruct. 'I worked vaguely with Archie, off and on, playing whistle, around the clubs in Fife and Glasgow and

Southern Scotland,' he says. Robin and Clive worked the same clubs as a duo and also around the North of England for what Robin recalls as 'a year or two'. Robin also toured, as a fiddler, with bluegrass man Tom Paley around the working men's clubs of Northern England and appeared on fiddle with Hamish Imlach and Josh MacRae, standing in for Bobby Campbell, on the Emmetones' one and only live performance, in Glasgow. Somebody had offered Hamish £50 for the pleasure and it was unrefusable. There are live recordings of Robin and Clive in Edinburgh, August 1963, and in St Andrews, November 1964. Robin was also recorded in splendid partnership with Owen Hand at the St Andrews club in October 1963. Joe Boyd, responsible for the Incredible String Band's recording career, believes he first heard them play in an Edinburgh pub (most likely the Crown Bar) circa March 1965. However, as Dolina MacLennan recalls: 'Bill Leader and Eric Winter sent him up to stay with me and my husband in Edinburgh and we took him to hear the boys. I remember the day he came because it was his birthday and we made a cake!' Joe Boyd's birthday is 5 August. In November 1965, Joe Boyd opened the London office of US record label Elektra. Around February 1966 he visited Clive's new club, the celebrated Clive's Incredible Folk Club, in Sauchiehall Street, Glasgow – stopping to take directions from Hamish Imlach. The ISB's first album was recorded that summer.

17. *Edinburgh Nights*, BBC2 19/8/92.
18. Thirty songs from Bert Jansch performances recorded in Glasgow during the early sixties are available as *Young Man Blues: Live In Glasgow 1962-64* (Ace, 1998). Since that package was assembled, at the very beginning of the process of writing this book and with a tight deadline for sleeve notes, it has been possible to re-examine the chronological jigsaw and the hazy recollections of relevant parties and to conclude that the fifty-six remaining tracks represent the vestiges of, almost certainly, four separate gigs. From sonic evidence, only four tracks – 'Come Back Baby', 'I Am Lonely', 'Tic-Tocative' and 'Blues Run The Game' (all featured on the CD) – survive from one of these four gigs. Other evidence suggests that this gig remnant must date from late 1965: Bert strongly believes that 'I Am Lonely' and 'Tic-Tocative' were written during the latter half of 1965 while Jackson Frank, author of 'Blues Run The Game' (not available on record until December 1965), was not in Britain until April 1965. Bert would most likely have learned the song from its author. Unfortunately, reasons of space preclude a more rigorous examination of the Glasgow tapes.
19. As note 14.
20. 'McClelland's own hang out was a club in Glasgow called the Cell,' says Challis. 'I went to Glasgow that time myself because we'd discovered all the people supplying dope in Edinburgh were getting it from Glasgow so we thought, "Well, cut out the middle man" – although that also cut out the fun of it. These were the days when nobody did it for profit, you did it because it was a whole new world that was opening up.' During his Edinburgh days Bert and his friend 'Wee Jimmy' would often visit the Cell for late-night jazz sessions.
21. Blass remembers Bert's companion on this occasion as a girl.
22. As note 14.
23. 'Cynic's Progress', Maggie Holland, *Folk Roots*, 10/90.
24. As note 14.

25. Foreword by Peggy Seeger to *The Peggy Seeger Songbook*, ed. Irene Scott (Oak Publications, 1998).

26. *Folk News*, 6/78. All further Alex Campbell quotes are from this source.

27. *Folk News*, 10/78.

28. *Folk News*, 12/78. As Sutton also noted: 'If a fair history of the folk revival ever gets written, no doubt the author will draw gratefully upon Behan's testimony, but I hope that he will consult other sources as well.' Indeed.

29. Bert first recorded 'Been On The Road So Long' on *It Don't Bother* Me (1965). It later appeared on *Leather Launderette* (1988), issued a year after Alex Campbell had died. A third performance was used as commentary on Bert's own career in the BBC documentary *Acoustic Routes* (1993).

30. Back in London around 1959, Alex also began busking with blues shouter Redd Sullivan. Another singer called Marion Grey became involved and then Long John Baldry, still at school at the time, asked to tag along. 'When I went back to Paris,' said Alex, 'John left school and joined the group. Then, I think, Wally Whyton joined, Martin Carthy joined, Davy Graham, the lot. But that group started off with Redd and me, that was the original Thamesiders.' Aside from his own testimony, Alex Campbell's role in starting off the embryonic folk revival's quintessential equivalent to the Yardbirds – every guitarist a legend of tomorrow – is obscure. He was at best the Anthony Topham of the group (the bloke before Eric Clapton, whom nobody much remembers). Later standardising the name to the Thameside Four, the group's 'classic' line-up was centred around Marion Grey, Pete Maynard and Redd Sullivan. Long John, Wally Whyton and possibly Martin Winsor (manager of the Gyre & Gimble coffee bar and later an inseparable sidekick to Sullivan) passed through the ranks before Martin Carthy was recommended in 1961 by Jenny Barton, manager of the Troubadour where Carthy was now enjoying what was to become a lengthy residency. Never a major influence on anything much, they were nevertheless one of the earliest folk groups and a popular act at the time: 'What we did was a mixture,' says Carthy, 'a lot of blues, a few simple jazz standards, gospel, English stuff, sea shanties, the occasional bit of music hall. It was an enormously wide repertoire.' Forty years on, the group's claim to fame is occupying the other side of *From A London Hootenanny*, the 1963 EP shared with Davy Graham.

31. As note 12.

32. As note 15.

33. 'Two Festivals – Part 1', *Folk Review*, 5/77. The precise role of co-credited BBC producer Charles Parker in MacColl's *Radio Ballads* series is controversial. MacColl believed that from being initially sceptical, Parker later basked in an inferred ownership of the project's concept and execution. All subsequent Ian Campbell quotes are from this source.

34. Robin also recalls, perhaps coincidentally, perhaps not, his own first professional engagement being at the Rotherham club.

35. From Frank Coia's perspective Dick Gaughan later did with traditional music what Bert had done with the blues. Gaughan, today recognised as a flag bearer for Scottish traditional song, exquisite guitar playing and stalwart champion of the socialist values espoused by many of the early Scottish revivalists, was brought up in Edinburgh like Bert: 'By the time I started going round the clubs he was gone,' says Dick. 'It would have been 1966 and he was in London by then. The influences

that I had then were people like Bert and Archie Fisher and Hamish Imlach, but I suppose it was secondhand by the time it got to me. I first ran into him in Sussex in 1972, but I'd already heard everything he'd ever done. He's always had this status of being a legend – I'm sure Bert was *born* a legend! He's always had this kind of "aura" about him. He's never exploited it or been particularly conscious of it himself, I think, but it's always been there. He revolutionised the guitar. He influenced everybody – his playing, directly or indirectly, influenced everybody. I don't think anybody has ever been revered as much as he is.'

CHAPTER FIVE

1. *Disc & Music Echo*, 19/12/70.
2. It would be wonderfully convenient to believe that Bert, Robin and Anne met up at the home of their mutual friend David Blass. Almost certainly Blass was the connection, although Bert is adamant that he and Robin found their own place to stay in the Earl's Court area. Blass's recollection of meeting Anne in Edinburgh is intriguing: it has to be subsequent to the Centre 42 events in August and September 1962, but why, having been offered a job in London by Centre 42, was she in Edinburgh at all? Anne had met Gill Cook, an assistant at Collet's record shop, on the Centre 42 tour and Anne would often thereafter stay with Gill at her flat off Gray's Inn Road. Conceivably, Blass met Anne in Edinburgh not in 1962 but in 1963, when she was living in the city with one Gary Field, whom Blass also remembers. The problems then are these: (a) who introduced Anne and Bert to each other in the Earl's Court area during the early weeks of 1963? (b) why did Gill Cook not meet Bert, by whom she later had a child, until much later in the year?
3. *Acoustic Music*, 9/80.
4. *Acoustic Routes* pilot film, 1990. Jenny's policy was to pay everyone the same, with the unassailable argument that 'they all did the same amount of work'.
5. Current Dylanology has it that Bob played the following dates while in Britain for the TV play: Dec 21 1962, King & Queen; Dec 22, Singers Club; Dec 29, Troubadour; Jan 12 1963, Troubadour. Dunnet's recollection, which must apply to this visit by virtue of his venue identification (the Pindar of Wakefield hosted the Singer's Club from October 1962 to September 1963), adds a Roundhouse visit to the list. The Singers Club met, at this time, on Saturdays and Sundays: 22 December was a Thursday, but Christmas may have been a factor. Brian Shuel was also at the King & Queen the previous night, where he took some shots of Martin Carthy. His project at the time was to capture the atmosphere of the clubs themselves – it was purely incidental that Dylan or anyone else of note happened to be there.
6. 'I loved the way he sang,' says Robin, of Joe Heaney. 'It was a particularly lyrical and embroidered style. A mixture of him and Indian music was the main inspiration in my approach to my own style of singing.' *Swing 51*, No. 13, 1989.
7. 'Anne Briggs', Ken Hunt, *Swing 51*, No. 13, 1989.
8. 'The Loneliness Of The Long Distance Folk Singer', Ken Hunt, *Swing 51*, No. 13, 1989. 'Most of the blokes who ran into Anne fell madly in love with her,' says John Challis, 'a stunningly beautiful woman with a stunningly beautiful voice. Even her feet were beautiful – she never wore shoes unless she had to.'
9. 'The Bill Leader Tapes', Karl Dallas, *Folk News*, March 1979.

10. Stan Kelly was a gifted mathematician, author of such latterly well-known vignettes as 'Oh, You Are A Mucky Kid', 'In My Liverpool Home' and 'The Leaving Of Liverpool' and was also a working-class Scouser with four kids: something of a novelty in Cambridge. Wherever he went on the early folk scene his humour was a welcome relief from the dogma.

11. Part of this quote as note 9, part from an interview with the author.

12. Nathan Joseph: Foreword to *The Transatlantic Story*, 4CD set, Castle Communications, 1998.

13. George Martin made three Parlophone singles with Benbow. With the advent of the Beatles' success, his priorities were elsewhere and Benbow was passed on to a less sympathetic producer, engendering a transfer to Decca. Decca: the people who had turned down the Beatles and the people who would, by way of small compensation, enjoy modest success with Val Doonican. But not with Benbow. As regards Malcolm Nixon, he had virtually run Alex Campbell into the ground the previous year, with no strategic benefit to Campbell's career. Nixon would eventually declare himself bankrupt and, according to Gill Cook, get taken under the wing of Bruce Dunnet – a much cannier operator.

14. Courtesy of Ken Hunt, from an interview conducted in April 1992.

15. *Zigzag*, 9/74.

16. 'Two Festivals' Part 2, Ian Campbell, *Folk Review*, 6/77. All further Campbell quotes are from this source unless otherwise credited.

17. As note 15. A certain Eric, one of Bert's guitar students from the Glasgow Folk Centre, met up with Bert and Lynda in Morocco. Robin Williamson later travelled there himself, around 1966.

18. Sue Thompson: 'Dave had independent money from some invention of his father's or something, and so he never had to do any work. In a situation like that it becomes all too easy to become a dilettante – in Dave's case to get an expensive camera, take up photography for a while and then pick up something else. Bert was the opposite – I don't think he ever had any money!'

19. Bert's version of this incident is less colourful: he had, he believes, stumbled in on Mr Hand and the woman from the Chinese restaurant enjoying rather more than a bottle of whisky.

20. Like John Challis, Pete Townshend was already familiar with the work of some of the people who had influenced Bert. The local record shop, otherwise rather conservative, stocked Leadbelly, Broonzy and Sonny Terry & Brownie McGhee. These were consequently amongst the earliest records Townshend bought, but both he and Challis had already been exposed to the exotic record collection of a couple of American friends at the college. Tom Wright and Cam Bruce were studying photography. In Pete's eyes, Tom was 'a glamorous figure', chased by girls, abundant with grass – perhaps too abundant. The police clamped down and a swift deportation order was applied, with the effect of a vast collection of prime US vinyl suddenly adrift. Records by Jimmy Reed, John Lee Hooker, Ray Charles, Lightning Hopkins, Jimmy Smith, Sonny Boy Williamson, Howling Wolf, even some Joan Baez and all sorts of other goodies on the Chess and Imperial labels – none commercially available in Britain at the time – were looking for a home. They didn't have to look very far. Some of the collection was sold to David Blass; the bulk of it passed on long-term loan to Pete Townshend. It would provide both the

knowledge and impetus for Pete to build up a collection of his own. Similar to David Blass, who enjoyed private means, Townshend was becoming relatively well-off within his peer group, albeit working long and hard for the privilege. His 'school band' the Detours had landed themselves on the books of a professional agency in November '62 and were soon accumulating lucrative residencies, corporate socials and wedding gigs. His family were not wealthy but, by the time he met Bert, Pete was sharing a fine apartment with a friend, the rent easily covered by a student grant, and making phenomenal money with his band. From November '62 well into 1964, the Detours were playing four or five shows a week at upwards of £12 a night. At the same time Pete was trying to get himself a degree. 'I did go to my course leader and discuss the problem,' says Townshend. 'He was saying, "You'd be very good at graphics, you could be a good painter, what do you want to do?" At that time I was a bit whacko – I was talking about installation scuptures, auto-destructive art, all kinds of weird things. "The distraction is, I've got this little group," I said, and he replied, "Well, how much do you make in this little group?" "Oh, about £30 a week." "Leave!" '

21. Anne played an unadvertised gig with Lou Killen at the Troubadour soon after she had arrived in London, around April 1964. Killen was, or had been, romantically involved with traditional singer Frankie Armstrong around this time. Anne's next advertised gig was 31 July at the Broadside club at the Black Horse, with Alex Campbell.

22. Owen married his current wife Ruth in 1965. In 1966, after Owen had spent time as a professional folksinger in London, they were back living in Edinburgh: 'On one occasion,' continues Owen, 'when Bert was coming to visit Ruth and I in Edinburgh he saw Field in the railway station and ran away from him. The following day we had the drug squad round with warrants to search the premises and the persons of Bert and myself. No one knew that Bert was in town except the three of us, and of course Gary Field. I later challenged Field on this matter but he swore he had no involvement. Soon after this he was dead and I shed not one tear.'

23. Gill Cook believes that Bill Leader had actively brought Bert down to London after the *Edinburgh Folk Festival* sessions with a view to making a record. Given that Bill had made similar overtures to Owen Hand this seems plausible but neither Bill nor Bert recalls this: it seems the recording of *Bert Jansch* was largely ad hoc, as described.

24. Quote sourced from *Touched By The Hand Of Bob*, Dave Henderson, The Black Book Company, 1999. Like Briggs, Joan Baez was (from her career-making appearance at the first Newport Folk Festival in 1959 to the point in 1963 when she met Dylan and began covering his songs) exclusively a singer of traditional songs, and from the more mournful end of the genre at that. However, by 1963 Baez had released four albums and appeared on the cover of *Time* magazine, which is where any superficial comparison to Anne Briggs must be jettisoned as an attractive but unsustainable idea.

25. Released in 1963, *Hootenanny In London* had been coordinated by Wally Whyton who was reportedly as 'embarrassed as hell' to find Briggs, who had simply been in the audience during the recording, prominently featured on the sleeve. Martin Carthy, yet to make a proper solo recording, was among those actually on the record: 'No point in trying to hide it,' he says. 'It was dreadful.' It could always have been worse: the working title had been *Surfin' Hootenanny*.

26. 'The Spinners Tapes', Karl Dallas, *Folk News*, 9/77. Further Spinners quotes are also from this source.

27. In mid-1964 the Spinners went further down the road of light entertainment with a thirteen-week series for BBC Manchester called *Dance and Skylark* (during which they turned fully professional) wherein they were persuaded to perform with trained animals and sing sea-shanties from the deck of a ship wearing sou'westers. As long as the music retained some integrity, they felt, the tom-foolery that went along with it was fine. Occasionally, the demands of Light Entertainment were hard to swallow – a parody of 'The Desert Song' involving a dance routine in pin-striped suits is recalled – but the group knew the pros and cons of their medium and how far they could stretch it: 'We had an unaccompanied British ballad on TV in 1964, you know,' said Tony. 'This is what people forget.' The ballad in question was 'Henry Martin', later recorded by Bert Jansch.

28. 'Two Festivals' Part 1, Ian Campbell, *Folk Review*, 5/77. There were thirteen episodes of *Hullaballoo* in all: two series, taped in June 1963 and circa April 1964. Remarkably, all survive.

29. A second series of *The Hoot'nanny Show*, announced for autumn 1964, was never broadcast but was superseded in October 1964 by a new show, *Singalong*, also recorded in Edinburgh, with TV veterans Martin Carthy and Nadia Cattouse resident. Many people recall *The Hoot'nanny Show*'s producer W. Gordon Smith using it as a vehicle to feature his protégés the Corries, who went on to enjoy many more years of tartan TV celebrity in the manner of Hall & Macgregor. Surprisingly few recall Roy Guest's involvement.

30. It would appear that Roy had initially been on the Davidson Agency's books as an artist before proving himself, by virtue of his massively attended 'Brighton Hootenanny' in June 1964, as a promoter whose golden touch was within a field outside of the agency's previous experience. An *MM* piece by Ray Coleman in February 1964 had reported the Davidson Agency's recent conference with delegates from student unions around Britain. A spokesperson noted that 'the delegates did not go so far as to say that the next pop music rage would be folk, but they are certainly moving towards that music more than anything. It would seem folk is the coming thing.'

31. Gill Cook believes the hotel session was the result of Owen, Bert, herself and Marian McKenzie (of Owen's Three City Four group) leaving a Soho folk club at 2 a.m. and stumbling into Gary Davis and Otis Spann in D'Arblay Street 'looking for some action'.

32. 'A Raver's Guide To Soho', John Platt, *Comstock Lode* c.1979.

33. 'The Alex Campbell Tapes', Karl Dallas, *Folk News*, 6/78.

34. *Acoustic Routes* pilot film, 1990. The pub was Finches, later homaged in a Jansch composition.

35. Enhancing his theory, Townshend also believed, wrongly, that one of the previous tenants of 19 King's Avenue had been a convicted heroin dealer. Regarding Bert's appearance, as John Challis notes: 'I remember Bert coming to London and being very broke and wearing a suit that someone had bought him, the idea being that he had to look respectable to make a career in London! He got very embarrassed about wearing this suit. I'd just bought myself a new pair of Levis so I gave him the old pair. They were pretty well worn out but Bert was glad to get them.'

36. Part of this quote as note 32. Bert has subsequently denied or forgotten seeing an actual gig, as opposed to rehearsals, by The Who. Mid '64 was nevertheless the period where Pete was perfecting his guitar-smashing routine, having begun it by inadvertently poking his guitar through the low roof at the Railway Hotel, Harrow.

37. Bert would already have been aware of the Mingus tune 'Better Git It In Your Soul' (spelt variously) from its inclusion on the 1959 CBS live album *Mingus Ah-Um* – a favourite among the Edinburgh set. Another version appeared on the 1964 Impulse album *Mingus Mingus Mingus Mingus Mingus*, while a third (renamed 'Wednesday Night Prayer Meeting') was on *Blues and Roots* (1959). The EP in question was in the Philips *Jazz Gallery* series, released in 1960 and featuring the *Mingus Ah-Um* version. Pete would not have been aware that Bert already knew the tune. The matter is intriguing as both Jansch and Davy Graham would go on to record versions of the tune in late '64, both released on albums in 1965. Bert maintains that his version, effectively rewritten and consequently retitled 'Veronica', comes directly from Davy Graham's arrangement. As the Coia recordings seem to suggest, Bert was playing a version of this before either artist had recorded it. Davy Graham confirms that he was indeed playing his ground-breaking arrangement of the tune 'a number of years' before it appeared on his *Folk, Blues & Beyond* (1965) LP. The problem, then, is how did Bert hear it? He didn't witness Graham playing anything until autumn 1964 but may conceivably have heard Davy's arrangement on an amateur recording of the guitarist made in London in 1961 by Len Partridge. He had, after all, worked out 'Angi' by similar means. Entirely incidental to this, around 1961/62 Davy and a friend ran a somewhat bohemian café in Forest Hill, London. Its name, of course, was 'Café Mingus'.

38. One of the High Numbers' Railway gigs, in August, was advertised in *Melody Maker*'s Folk Forum. Surely some mistake . . .

39. Partly from *Leader's Tapes* (BBC Radio 2, 1998), partly as note 9.

40. Bert also recalls staying with songwriter Paul McNeil – almost certainly during the summer/autumn of 1964. Never a major name, McNeil had been co-billed with Bert on his 17 March 1964 Troubadour show, where Bert recalls him being a resident. At that time McNeil, Carthy and Paul Simon all lived near each other in Swiss Cottage and comprised, from Bert's perspective, something of a clique. McNeil later partnered Linda Peters on record.

41. Two guitars were used on Bert's first album: one for accompanying vocal pieces, one for instrumentals. One had been borrowed from Sandy Darlington, of the duo Sandy & Jeannie, who lived nearby to Bill Leader, the other was owned by Les Bridger. Bert became flatmates with Les circa October/November 1964 and wound up purloining Les's guitar to the extent of paying its h.p. instalments.

42. This is conjecture: Bert distinctly recalls meeting Davy and Shirley at Leader's flat and believes them to have been recording there in parallel with his own sessions. Graham was living nearby: 'He'd be walking round like a young retired colonel,' says Leader, 'brisk walk, short hair cut, which was out of keeping at that time and very out of keeping with the sort of idea you had of him as well'. Davy himself recalls only the Decca sessions for *Folk Roots, New Routes*. Either way, Bert first saw Davy playing during this time and at Bill Leader's flat.

43. *Penguin Encyclopedia Of Popular Music* (2nd Edition), ed. Donald Clark (Penguin, 1998).

44. 'Roots Of Renbourn', Maggie Holland, *Folk Roots* 4/93.
45. *MM*, 17/1/76.

CHAPTER SIX

1. *Zigzag*, 9/74.
2. From January 1965 Gill Cook partnered Roy Guest in running a club at Cecil Sharp House, where Roy had just taken the job of EFDSS agent. Gill, however, found Roy 'rather slippery' and the association was brief.
3. The recording period is debatable. Bert has variously suggested it was 'two or three sessions' or a case of 'every month or two I'd lay down a song until we got enough to fill an album'. The truth is somewhere in between. I estimate it to span September 1964 to January 1965. Bill Leader had previously, at his flat, recorded contemporary songwriter Paul Simon, on 23 April 1964. Topic turned the recordings down, they were never offered to Transatlantic and they have never surfaced since.
4. *Sounds*, 9/1/71. Roughly half the material on his first album is glimpsed on the Glasgow live recordings of 1962-65, recorded largely prior to *Bert Jansch*'s release.
5. 150,000 is the last figure quoted anywhere regarding the sales of *Bert Jansch*. The record has been repackaged several times, on both vinyl and CD, but its influence remains greater than its relatively modest sales may suggest. The figure of £100 for the album's rights has become legendary but Bruce May, who managed Bert in the seventies, saw the contract then and was amazed to find that Nat, a stickler in matters of business, had deducted £10 for something or other. Bert received £90.
6. Davy Graham's project with Shirley Collins racked up at least thirteen performances between July 1964 and 30 May 1965 – some club dates but mostly concerts, concluding at the New Lyric Theatre with the New Jazz Orchestra. Shirley, a mother of two young children at the time and already pursuing a heavy schedule as a solo singer, had had enough: 'It was really masterminded by my then husband, John Marshall,' she told *Folk Roots*. 'I didn't think it was ever quite right, but I think it was a brave experiment. It became very difficult working with Davy because he was talented but moody, and a late train-catcher. It was a really interesting episode of my life but when John wanted to push it a bit further, into working with a jazz orchestra, I opted out.'
7. 'Folk Routines', Ken Hunt, *Folk Roots*, 5/97.
8. 'In the eye of the hurricane', Jas Obrecht, *Guitar Player*, 3/92. 'The first record that he made,' continued Young, 'great record. I was particularly impressed by "The Needle Of Death". This guy was just so good. Years later I wrote "Ambulance Blues" for *On The Beach*, and I picked up the melody from his record – the guitar part, exactly – without realising. Years later someone mentioned it to me and sure enough, it's almost like a note for note cop of his thing. I did meet him once when I went to England in the early seventies and got together with Pentangle. But I had a big limo and everything, because I didn't know where I was going, and they kind of had an attitude about me, like I was a pop superstar and kind of a dickhead.'
9. Pete Frame's vocation began with founding the pioneer music magazine *Zigzag* and the 'Rock Family Trees' for which he is still best known. Part of this quote, like others below, is from an interview with the author, part from Frame's detailed memoir 'Catching Dreams From The Clouds', *Zigzag Wanderer*, No.5 1999.

10. *MM*, 6/2/65.
11. 'Donovan: heading for fame or misfortune', Bob Dawbarn, *MM* 20/2/65.
12. Dorris Henderson has often cited her arrival in London as being early 1965 but in *MM*, 14/11/64 she was 'currently taking London by storm'. The following week she is mentioned as resident at the Roundhouse. She has also said that her second gig was at the Student Prince. Not so. Dorris was indeed at its opening night, along with Alex Campbell, but the venue only opened on 2/1/65.
13. 'Roots Of Renbourn', Maggie Holland, *Folk Roots*, 4/93. Davy Graham played with the second version of John Mayall's Bluesbreakers for about three months, subsequent to his 1961 – 62 association with Alexis Korner. Unlike Korner, blues-purist Mayall was only ever advertised once at a folk venue, the Troubadour, 22 June 1963, with Martin Carthy.
14. Between October 1964 and March 1965 Anne had fourteen advertised gigs in the London area: five were with Bert.
15. When Bert came to record 'Go Your Way', on *Nicola* (1967), he wrote an extra verse for it, giving the song a sense of despair missing from Anne's more poignant reading on *Anne Briggs* (1971): 'I never sang it because I never felt easy about that particular verse,' says Anne. 'There was always angst in Bert's life and I think that came through. I don't think I suffered angst at all.'
16. 'Davy Graham, acoustic pioneer', *MM*, 18/7/70.
17. Part of this quote from *Dirty Linen* 10/90, part from an interview with the author.
18. The only occasion Bert and Anne performed together was for the BBC doc-umentary *Acoustic Routes*, filmed at the old Howff building in Edinburgh, March 1992. They played 'Go Your Way' and 'Blackwater Side'.
19. *Journeyman: An Autobiography*, Ewan MacColl (Sidgwick & Jackson, 1990). Unless otherwise noted all further MacColl quotes in this chapter are from this source.
20. *As Far As The Eye Can Sing: An Autobiography*, Frankie Armstrong with Jenny Pearson (The Women's Press, 1992). As the group continued, Armstrong notes that: 'Ewan's incapacity to brook criticism became increasingly evident and those members who would voice criticisms on behalf of the group would often be verbally annihilated by his articulate, mind-blitzing self-defence. He could always produce half a dozen authorities to justify any action he took.'
21. Noted down by Richard Lewis, Bert's 19/3/65 set was: 'Key To The Highway / Rockin' Chair Blues / One Day Old / Come Back Baby / John Henry'.
22. There is an element of conjecture here. Anne cannot recall exactly why the co-writing with Bert at Gill's flat stopped suddenly but feels that one of them must have gone off travelling. The evidence points at Anne, who is known to have been involved with Koerner for a while. Koerner's first UK gig – at yet another club run by Les Bridger – was 14 March 1965. There are suggestions that Anne may not have turned up for some advertised London shows in February and March, with none advertised for April. But she was certainly present again for a show with the Dubliners on 7 May, leading indirectly to her long-term involvement with Irish musician Johnny Moynihan.
23. Bruce Dunnet: 'When I came to London in 1945 I worked for Central Books, a communist bookshop, for fifteen months. I then had twenty-six jobs in twelve years because I wouldn't keep my mouth shut. I was in the Clerical and Administrative Union and I always complained if conditions were bad. And time after time I was

sacked. After that I was a book-keeper, office administrator, commercial consultant, managing director in the "Swinging Sixties" of Quorum, with Ossie Clark and Alice Pollock, the way-out designers.'

24. Also on the bill were Jo Ann Kelly and future Groundhog Tony McPhee. Renbourn's name was misspelt. This deserves attention: Bert's surname causes very occasional problems – Jantz, Jones, Jansom, etc – for people advertising his presence somewhere. But, inexplicably, Renbourn's surname routinely turns otherwise literate people into blancmanges. More often than not there is an 'e' on the end. Other variations that appeared in print during the sixties include Wrenbourn, Ranbone, Stenbourn, Reinbourn and Rendell. Is it really so difficult?

25. The context may be wrong – Townshend was never involved in running folk clubs – but I don't doubt the essential elements of the incident occurred. Indeed, it seems to have become something of an urban myth: one correspondant was told by a third party that the tale involved the organiser of the Troubadour waking Bert up somewhere and asking him to do a gig at short notice for a pound. Bert rummaged in his pocket, found a pound note and replied, 'No thanks, I've already got one.'

26. The Swiss Cottage club was to close in a few weeks with memberships transfering to the new club. Unlike his residency at the Scot's Hoose, Bert's involvement at the Marquis appears to have been relatively short-term.

27. 'My Donal' entered Bert's repertoire in 1998.

28. The 'Angi' composer credit on Jansch reissues changed during the 1990s to reflect this. Bert has always been incredulous that subsequent versions of 'Angi', including Paul Simon's, are based on his arrangement 'mistakes and all'. Incidentally, that well-known guitar hero Gill Cook recalls teaching Bert's middle eight to Simon.

29. The *MM* described the party, on around 18/19 March 1968, as being a 'six-hour jam' involving Paul Simon, Jansch, Renbourn, Davy Graham and Roy Harper. 'Everybody on the folk scene showed up for it,' says Bert. 'It was a good party. I think that night we ran 'em out of champagne, if I remember right – and I had a gig to go to!'

30. *Guitarist*, 4/99.

31. Quotes sourced from various interviews in *MM* spanning February 1965 to May 1966.

32. 'Focus On MacColl', Karl Dallas, *MM*, 18/9/65. 'Bob was being touted as the heir to Woody Guthrie,' says Martin Carthy, 'but he didn't do that thing which Woody did, and which Ewan & Peggy did in their writing, which was name names and point fingers. Ewan had a problem with that.'

33. 'The Great Dylan Row', *MM*, 2/10/65.

34. *MM*, 19/2/66.

35. As note 13.

36. Les Bridger and Jo Ann Kelly were the featured artists on the Cousins opening night, when it secured eighty memberships, but they were never its residents. Of the established artists who did not perform at the Cousins during its heyday, Martin Carthy is the most notable: 'I was working round the country,' he says. 'And I probably thought of myself as being different from the Cousins people because I was never a blues person. I did love Bert and John, and I loved playing the guitar but I was never terribly interested in that guitar-centric stuff.' Carthy was never convinced about the artistic rewards of the 'all-nighter' although he did play one at the

Student Prince. Of those who did perform at the Cousins, many were never advertised or were regulars long before earning the accolade of an ad. Bert first performed there, in an unadvertised floor spot, on 7/5/65. The following chronology of some key artists' first *advertised* appearances at the venue may be of interest:

    Fri. 16/4/65   club opens
    Fri. 14/5/65   Dorris Henderson & John Renbourn
    Thur. 10/6/65   Bert Jansch
    Sat. 12/6/65   Paul Simon
    Sat. 3/7/65   Al Stewart
    Sat. 10/7/65   Long John Baldry
    Fri. 6/8/65   Young Tradition
    Tue. 5/10/65   Roy Harper
    Fri. 13/5/66   Sandy Denny
    Sun. 22/5/66   Incredible String Band
    Sat. 13/8/66   John Renbourn & Jacqui McShee
    Fri. 9/9/66   Dave & Toni Arthur

37. 'Roy Harper: One-man Rock'n'Roll Band', Karl Dallas, *Acoustic Music*, 7/80.

38. I am not personally aware of a single photograph of any artist taken at the Cousins during 1965 – 1966. It can be glimpsed in two surviving TV films: *Meeting Point*, a 1965 BBC documentary on Soho which included brief clips of Al Stewart and, uniquely, of Jackson Frank in performance; and *Folksingers In London*, a short Danish documentary on the music and lifestyle of the new breed of guitar/vocalists. John Renbourn and the otherwise obscure American Marc Sullivan are filmed at the Cousins. Extracts from the former appear in the 1992 Jansch BBC documentary *Acoustic Routes*, while part of the latter can be seen (miscredited to 1965) in the 1995 John Renbourn video release *Rare Performances*.

39. As note 37.

40. Of all the Soho rivals to Cousins only the Scot's Hoose, a complementary rather than rival establishment, would last the course. A little out of the way, both the Mercury Theatre in Notting Hill Gate and the Centre in Balham opened within weeks either side of the Cousins. Both were booking the very best acts, in contrast to the Cousins' early weeks which were remarkable in featuring guest artists who were even at the time complete unknowns, with no other claim on posterity. The Mercury Theatre club would continue for several months to run popular, varied midweek sessions featuring the likes of Andy Irvine and Peter Bellamy, but it never attempted to rival the Cousins. The Centre, however, was a licensed premises, and claimed to be open seven nights a week. As early as May 1964, Bill Leader had announced that he was planning an all-week licensed folk 'night club'. It was an idea he never saw through, but it was still the holy grail of the folk club world. Was it not now, in 1965, within grasp? One cannot be absolute, but it seems the Centre's claim was disingenuous – probably a public house that dabbled briefly in folk music, but certainly not a venue with a lasting presence. Other venues were similarly rash in their announcements and short-lived in their lifespan. In September 1965, the London Folk Music Centre opened at 38 Goodge Street, in Soho. It announced its hours as 6.30 to midnight, six nights a week, and all day at weekends. Recalling Roy Guest's short-lived plans for the Howff, it would feature a tape library and coffee shop alongside live performances, but it is not an institution that endured long

enough to be ingrained in many memories. Launching in October at 22 D'Arblay Street, Soho, Leduce billed itself as 'London's only contemporary folk club' – dedicated to singer-songwriters. Its opening bill was strong – Paul Simon, Jackson Frank and Sandy Denny – and it would regularly feature Al Stewart thereafter. But, again, this is not a club at all widely remembered. Likewise the Excelsior Club, which opened in Charing Cross Road in March 1966 with a similarly contemporary agenda.

41. When the trad jazz boom took off in the mid-fifties the all-nighter concept was repeated on an annual basis at Alexandra Palace. The only places in London still flying the flag for the all-nighter immediately prior to the folk venues of 1965 were the Flamingo – an intense, amphetamine-fuelled R&B/jazz scene popular with black American servicemen from which Georgie Fame emerged – and the Roaring Twenties, a similarly appealing mod venue. There were also, at the other extreme, the Irish pubs: 'It was always a "friends of friends" situation,' says Bert. 'You could always go there for a drink at any time of the night.'

42. *Zigzag*, 9/74 and *Comstock Lode* c.1979. Quotes combined. On the subject of Andy Matthews, opinions differ as to how important he actually was in the Cousins' success. To a degree it was 'right place, right time'. His is the name most associated with running the Cousins although the otherwise little-remembered Phil Phillips was certainly the man in charge up to at least January 1966. To Duffy Power, Andy was a 'spoilt brat who smoked too much dope' and for whom the Cousins was a plaything; to Roy Harper, on the other hand, 'Andy was pivotal in all of it and nobody has given him enough credit.' From Bert's point of view: 'Andy was the first guy I knew who took notice of the Beatles. He'd say, "You gotta listen to this" and he'd play whatever it was. "Er, right, so who is it then?" To me it was just another pop band, I couldn't tell any difference. I much preferred the Rolling Stones anyway.'

43. As note 13.

44. *The Al Stewart Story*, BBC Radio 2, 7/99.

45. 'Al Stewart: Platinum Bard', Ian Anderson, *Southern Rag* No. 22, October/December 1984.

46. As note 1. Bert has continued to keep 'Blues Run The Game' in his own repertoire and added a second, 'My Name Is Carnival', just prior to its author's death in the late nineties.

47. 'Frank . . . and the once young king', an open letter to Karl Dallas/*Folk News* in 1978. Unless otherwise credited all subsequent Jackson Frank quotes are from this source.

48. *NME*, 24/8/74.

49. Andy Irvine left Dublin in early '65, coming to London with some friends and intending to make money and move on to Israel. 'I got a job in the gasworks at Wandsworth, shift work, which I stuck for about four months. Two of the shifts were useless to my social life. I was waiting with bated breath for the third one, which went from six till two. And the very first day I got off at two o'clock I went to the Troubadour with Annie Briggs [possibly 7 February 1965, when Anne had a gig there] and of course we ended up slaughtered drunk, sleeping on somebody's floor. I got in four hours late the next day and realised then that there was absolutely no shift that would allow for the kind of lifestyle I wanted.' Andy soon left the gasworks

and touted for BBC radio drama jobs, which, with the support of his girlfriend Muriel, made things a whole lot more convenient. 'I couldn't have existed without her. She kept me going for years.' Eventually, gigs simply took over from the BBC work. On a trip over to Britain the previous year, and through Anne Briggs, Andy had ended up at a Bert Jansch gig in Leicester: 'The next time I met Bert,' says Andy, 'he was introducing me onstage as being from Leicester! I got his first album pretty much as soon as it came out. It wasn't quite my kind of music but he was one of the good guys.'

50. As note 1.

51. 'The House Of Jansch', an encoded résumé of the situation, appeared on Donovan's *Mellow Yellow* (1967). An earlier 'tribute', 'Bert's Blues', was included on *Sunshine Superman* (1966). 'Do You Hear Me Now?', a first album Jansch composition, appeared as the B-side of Don's third single 'Universal Soldier' in September 1965. In 1968, Don coralled his hero into a studio with producer Mickey Most where he was recording the US-only LP *Hurdy Gurdy Man*. Bert plays uncredited but highly distinctive guitar on one track, 'Tangier'. Pop supremo Mickey Most had no idea who Bert was and was apparently baffled by the whole business. Even less known, and no doubt impossible to find, Roy Harper's 'Pretty Baby' (the non-album B-side to his first fingle, released in March 1966) is also a tribute to Bert.

52. The titles of various Duffy Power B-sides from this period seem in retrospect remarkably pertinent: 'What Now?', 'If I Get Lucky Someday', 'Woman Made Trouble', 'Tired, Broke And Busted', 'Where Am I?' . . . Duffy is perhaps best remembered from this period as being only the second person, after Kenny Lynch, to cover a Beatles song, 'I Saw Her Standing There' – purportedly written especially for him.

53. A US single, a UK single, a French EP and two tracks on a compilation were Duffy Power's only releases between 1965 and 1971. In 1971, Transatlantic issued *Innovations*, a stunning LP collecting some mid-sixties recordings with Danny Thompson, Terry Cox, John McLaughlin and others. Those recordings and other group work from the same period are now on CD as *Little Boy Blue* and *Just Stay Blue*. An acoustic folk/blues album recorded for ex-Donovan manager Peter Eden in 1969, eventually trickling out in 1973, is also available on CD as *Blues Power*. A hugely under-rated artist.

54. Alexis had recorded *Red Hot From Alex* for Transatlantic in 1964, the first of what was announced as a four-album deal. *Sky High,* his 1965 LP with Duffy, came out on the tiny Spot label. I have no idea what happened to the Transatlantic connection. At one point, Alexis asked Roy Harper to form a group with him. Roy declined.

55. Of all the Cousins irregulars, Roy Harper was to prove especially adept at polarising opinion: 'I remember Roy onstage one night being just awful and so pompous in the way only Roy can be,' says Ian Anderson. 'There was a ceiling fan and one night he decided this was interfering with the ambience of his performance and he shouted a command at someone, "Please turn the fan off!" and this voice comes back "I shouldn't do that if I were you Roy, it's the only one you've got in here." It could be a cruel place, the Cousins.'

56. Regarding benefit concerts: 'I did one once I think, for the Labour Party,' mused Bert, 'something to do with miners. I didn't know if it was a good thing or not at the time but Ralph McTell had told me I ought to do it.'

57. *Folksingers In London*, DR 15/7/67.

58. Finishing his postgrad at the end of 1966, Challis was offered two jobs in the course of the week: one with the Savoy Brown Blues Band, the other in TV animation. 'I was all of twenty-three but I was beginning to feel a bit burned out so I went for what I thought was the safe option: the animation. And towards the end of that year *Yellow Submarine* started and I had two years of solid work.' During the 1970s Savoy Brown became Foghat and blazed a hard-living, stadium-filling trail across America while Challis, never entirely sure he had made the right decision, worked on the children's TV classic *Roobarb*. He still sneaks out of an evening to play piano in bars. And am I alone in suggesting that posterity has perhaps been kinder to *Roobarb* than it has to Foghat?

CHAPTER SEVEN

1. Bert would only perform at Les Cousins on twelve occasions during 1966, a long way short of his presence there the previous year.

2. After a year of litigation, Donovan made a triumphal return to the UK Top 10 with 'Sunshine Superman' in December 1966, a song that had been a US hit months before. He subsequently pursued a very successful pop career but retains an affinity with his Cousins peers: 'Donovan's a talented guy,' says Roy Harper. 'He has his own place among us on merit.'

3. *MM*, 28/8/65.

4. *Isis*, 2/2/66.

5. Combined from: *Sounds*, 21/4/71; NME, 21/4/73; *Trouser Press*, 9/77.

6. During 1965 there were folk-friendly variety programmes like ITV's *Eamonn Andrews Show* and BBC's *Val Doonican Show*; there had been the children's shows *Gadzooks! It's All Happening* (BBC), on which Renbourn and Dorris Henderson had featured, and *Five O'Clock Club* (Rediffusion), putting pounds in the pockets of Wally Whyton and Alexis Korner. Rediffusion had also launched a dedicated folk show for grown-ups, *Heartsong*, to which the BBC responded with *Tonight In Person*. Out in the regions George Melly was fronting *My Kind Of Folk* for Southern TV, Ulster TV had *Swinging Folk*, TWW had *Folk In The West*, while Grampian TV had won the Italia Prize with their documentary *An Impression Of Love*, featuring Ewan MacColl & Peggy Seeger. In May 1966 there had been a national broadcast for *Travelling For A Living*: a gritty, incisive documentary on the music and lifestyle of the Watersons, with cameos from Roy Guest, Bill Leader, Lou Killen and Anne Briggs. Briggs was also enjoying a residency on a regional talk show in the West Country, title unknown. Regarding Bert's appearance on *Hallelujah!*, it has not survived.

7. The other two US albums were *Stepping Stones* in 1969 (*Bert And John* plus two vocal tracks from *It Don't Bother Me*) and a similarly enhanced version of *Jack Orion* in 1970.

8. *MM*, 16/7/66.

9. *MM*, 15/10/66.

10. The tracks unknown to me were notated as: 'Little Maggie', 'Ten', 'Inside Your Mind', 'Neurotic Woman' and 'Whisky Man'. It is unlikely that 'Whisky Man' is the John Entwistle song of that name.

11. The *Nicola* tracks played at Birmingham were: 'A Little Sweet Sunshine', 'Life Depends On Love', 'Weeping Willow', 'Woe Is Love My Dear' and three others that were recorded during the *Nicola* sessions but not included on that album. Two of the three, 'In This Game' and 'Dissatisfied Blues', would later surface on the *Box Of Love* compilation (1972). The third, 'Train Song', would be re-recorded for the Pentangle LP *Basket Of Light* (1969).

12. 'Thyme Honoured', John Tobler, *Folk Roots* 10/95. Chris Ayliffe subsequently cameoed in the Pentangle story with a splendid sleeve design for *Solomon's Seal* (1972).

13. 'The Roots Of Renbourn', Maggie Holland, *Folk Roots*, 4/93.

14. Partly from an interview with John Reed, *Record Collector*, 1/95.

15. *Hokey Pokey*, 1/88.

16. A stunning radio broadcast by the Danny Thompson Trio was released as *Live 1967* in 1999. Although Danny talked about making a record proper as late as November 1968, the Pentangle took off and the Trio was shelved.

17. As note 12.

18. As note 15.

19. Renbourn had included a tune called 'Judy', for Judy Hill, on his first album. Hence Bert's use of Judy, Nicola Cross's middle name.

20. *Sounds*, 9/1/71.

21. Inspiration from children's stories and from children generally would become a regular theme in Bert's writing: 'You always find that you can let your imagination really go with kids' books,' says Bert. Aside from Kenneth Grahame, Bert had also by this stage absorbed the work of Mervyn Peake and JRR Tolkien: 'I don't know if they influenced me. I suppose they must have.'

22. 'There was a Jewish over-forties club upstairs,' says Jacqui, 'and every time I sang an unaccompanied song they'd start into "Hava Nagila" with all the feet-stamping. They're the sort of memories that stick out.'

23. The one-phrase review, by Chris Welch for *MM*, was based on a secondhand opinion. Welch had not personally seen the band. Bouchant's death became the oblique subject of the Pentangle's first single, 'Travelling Song', released in May 1968.

24. For all his reservations, Nat had supplied sound equipment for the Horseshoe, arranged the Windsor booking and was arranging a November college tour for the group. He had also allowed Bert to have some of his compositions on *Nicola* published under 'The Pentangle Ltd.' (Strangely, publishing for the group's early recordings went through Gold Disc/Carlin. Later work was published by the group's own company Swiggeroux). Recording sessions for the first group album, necessarily for Transatlantic, were announced to the press as beginning in August 1967, but were presumably abortive. The recordings which comprised their eventual debut *The Pentangle* were made in February 1968.

25. Around May/June 1967 Danish TV had filmed Bert and John in London. The pair are glimpsed at St Edmund's Terrace writing/rehearsing the Pentangle instrumental 'Bells'. Bert is later interviewed. The resulting programme *Folksangere – i London*, also featuring Martin Carthy & Dave Swarbrick, was broadcast in Denmark on 15/7/67. While the Pentangle were in Denmark in August they performed a concert for Danish radio with Carthy & Swarbrick. There is also compelling circumstantial

evidence of a Danish TV concert. One fan, Lars Fromholt, even recalls the songs performed, including Bert solo on 'Nottamun Town', Bert & John with 'Orlando' and a unique occurrence of the group performing Bert's 'Poison'. Unfortunately neither of the possible broadcasters, DR and NDR, can trace the programme. The first time the group categorically appeared on TV was in May 1968. Of their many broadcasts thereafter, there are no (further) known occurances of Bert performing solo.

26. *Comstock Lode*, c.1979.
27. Alexis Korner had brought Hendrix down to the Cousins on 5 October 1966. Bert was elsewhere at the time.
28. Jimi's soundcheck was being filmed and the one-chord routine was possibly for effect. As Bert noted in *Mojo*, 10/95: 'He came on a while after that and did a proper soundcheck. It was dramatic to watch him in an empty hall. I shook his hand and I'm very proud that I did.' The concert was an awareness-raiser for 'International Liberal Year', with British Liberal Party leader Jeremy Thorpe in attendance. Thorpe had photos taken posing with Hendrix. But not with Bert.
29. Neil Young: *Guitar Player*, 3/92. Jimmy Page: *Trouser Press*, 9/77.
30. Bert turned up ill at the Manchester show on 9 February 1968. Carthy & Swarbrick, in the audience, deputised on borrowed instruments.
31. *Daily Telegraph*, 1/7/99.

CHAPTER EIGHT

1. Danny and Terry had got their feet on the property ladder not through the Pentangle but through their involvement, as Alexis Korner's group, on the lucrative 1965-66 children's TV show *Five O'Clock Club*. Terry's wife opened a restaurant in Minorca. Towards the end of the Pentangle era John split with Judy and moved deep into the Devon undergrowth, with fiddler Sue Draheim, hence the title of his 1973 solo LP, *The Hermit*.
2. *Zigzag*, 11/69.
3. *Birthday Blues* was released on 17/1/69. Bert, with Danny, recorded a BBC *Night Ride* session on 11/12/68 featuring three *Birthday Blues* tracks ('Tree Song', 'I Got A Woman' and 'Birthday Blues') alongside an otherwise unrecorded Jansch crack at the traditional song 'Thames Lighterman', the rarely performed *Sweet Child* track 'I Loved A Lass' and the Danny Thompson solo 'Haitian Fight Song'. On 25/1/69 Bert appeared solo on *Country Meets Folk*, broadcast live from the Playhouse Theatre. He performed two songs from the new album, 'I Am Lonely' and 'Come Sing Me A Happy Song', along with 'Come Back Baby'. Additionally, the Pentangle were given their own BBC Radio 1 series of four half-hour shows, first broadcast during December 1969/January 1970. The shows were to feature the group members showcasing their talents in various combinations, doubtless including solo performances. The shows appear not to have survived.
4. As note 2.
5. *Disc*, 18/4/70.
6. 'Light Flight' was a UK No. 43 in February 1970, allowing the Pentangle their one and only appearance on *Top Of The Pops*. Seemingly released simultaneously to *Basket Of Light* in October 1969, with *Take Three Girls* (the BBC series it themed)

beginning in November, it is unclear to me why the single took so long to attain a chart placing and why the album did so much better (a UK No. 5 in November 1969) and in less time. One may only conclude that Transatlantic really were appalling, as Nat Joseph suggests, at promoting singles and/or that the Pentangle audience were essentially album buyers.

7. *MM*, 30/5/70.
8. The Festival Hall concert of 30 July 1971 was Bert's only real opportunity to perform the *Rosemary Lane* material at the time. A BBC Radio session recorded two weeks before the concert included three songs from the album: 'Bird Song', 'Nobody's Bar' and 'Tell Me What Is True Love?' (plus the traditional songs 'Twa Corbies' and 'Omie Wise'). 'Reynardine' was seemingly the only album track to have a long stage-life, featuring on the final Pentangle tour in 1972 and on solo gigs in 1973. During the 1990s Bert occasionally performed 'Rosemary Lane' and 'Tell Me What Is True Love?', and in 1999 'Reynardine' was dusted off for two weddings (one of them mine) and the Channel 4 documentary film *Dream Weaver*. The wedding? It was legendary.
9. *Disc,* 18/4/70.
10. *Sounds*, 16/1/71. Bert was persuaded to return to America for a four week Pentangle tour spanning November – December 1971.
11. As one of the popular highlights of the Pentangle's career, John's tale of a doomed sailor has become the perennial harbinger of disappointment to elements of Bert's concert audience. He didn't sing it then, he doesn't do so now.
12. Jo Lustig's managerial interests expanded markedly in 1971. He had already been handling Ralph McTell since mid-1970. In February 1971, the Pentangle reluctantly re-signed with him. In May 1971, he agreed to manage Gillian McPherson, a young singer/songwriter from Belfast. Danny Thompson would produce her first album. In September 1971, he signed the Dransfields (brothers Robin and Barry) although by the end of the year the brothers had split – publicly denying this was caused by Lustig's punishing tour schedules. By December, following the departures of Ashley Hutchings and Martin Carthy, Jo had signed up folk-rockers Steeleye Span and would soon be overseeing their most lucrative and successful period. By February 1972 he was also representing former Beatles' protégée Mary Hopkin.
13. *Disc,* 24/7/71. As session men, both Danny and Terry enjoyed numerous other outlets during the Pentangle era. In 1971, for example, Terry worked with David Bowie, John Williams and the Stanley Myers Orchestra; while Danny appeared on at least a dozen albums.
14. In 1971 Richard Robinson, MD of CBS, believed folk was the coming thing. Not knowing anything about it, he assumed that Jo Lustig could come up with the names. Jo knew nothing about music but knew some people who did: John Renbourn recommended his old mentor Wizz Jones, Ralph McTell championed Clive Palmer's new band, while Bert suggested Anne Briggs. An act from Northern Ireland called Therapy were also in the frame. They were all brought under Lustig's management and all made horrendously unsuccessful records.
15. Anne Briggs would continue performing until spring 1973, a short club tour of Belgium comprising probably her last engagements. A third album was recorded, again for Jo Lustig, though at Anne's insistence this was not released at the time. Featuring both traditional and original material, it was recorded with an electric

band led by Steve Ashley and eventually surfaced, with Anne's approval, as *Sing A Song For You* in 1997. But back in '73, pregnant for the second time and increasingly disillusioned with her own music and the nature of the music business, she moved to Caithness with her new family and slipped quietly away.

16. Unfortunately, Bert's performance from *Once More With Felix* is believed lost. I've not managed to confirm the date of this appearance although autumn 1971 seems likeliest.

17. 'I got my cab licence in 1972,' says Benbow. 'When I started cabbing I was still doing a few broadcasts – used to park the cab in the rank, go and do the gig then back in the cab and off to work. Terrific!'

18. *Comstock Lode*, c.1979. When Bert lived in Ticehurst it was 'just up the road' from Gerry Rafferty, himself a Transatlantic recording artist, whose wife was friendly with Heather. Bert would often end up on the train with Gerry, whose ambition was reminiscent of Paul Simon's: 'I have to say,' says Bert, 'he's one of the most boring characters I've ever met. Used to drone on and on about how he was going to make it.' And also like Simon, he did.

19. Milltown Malbay now hosts the annual 'Willie Clancy week' – a summer tuition school and jamboree for trad buffs and revellers.

29. Several years earlier Christy Moore had worked in Milltown Malbay for a couple of months and would often go to the same pub, Hennessey's, to hear Willie Clancy: 'Money would not have changed hands,' he recalls. 'Willie was a carpenter who loved to play music. I don't know if he ever did any "gigs" in his life.' The one record that would confirm the existence of a commercial context to allow for this 'revival' of Irish music – or, perhaps more accurately, to allow for the development of an Irish folk scene where money would finally start changing hands – was Christy Moore's *Prosperous* (1972). Having effectively served his apprenticeship on the English club scene since 1966, Moore had returned to Ireland in 1970 with repertoire and ideas and as a master of the performer's craft. Accompanied by a band of now legendary musicians, among them Andy Irvine, Moore was recorded for Bill Leader's own label Trailer. The resulting album, *Prosperous*, was initially released only in Britain but demand began to grow in Ireland. As Mark Prendergast notes in *Irish Rock* (O'Brien, 1986), though it was not a fusion of folk and rock as such, it was progressive in spirit: 'It had a spontaneity, a certain youthful exuberance and enough original ideas on presentation to make people realise that Irish traditional music had to change. The time was right to give the dusty native Irish scene a taste of what was happening in the UK.' The Pentangle did perform a handful of concerts in Belfast and Dublin, but the influence of Bert, John and/or the group was largely via recordings. They had been heard by many of the people who would go on to play key roles in Irish music's renaissance: Rory Gallagher; Johnny Fean, guitarist with Horslips (1972+); the future members of Clannad (1970+); and Michael O'Domhnaill of Skara Brae (1970-71), subsequently of the extremely influential Bothy Band (1975-78). Discovering it in 1970 from information on the back of a Bert Jansch record, O'Domhnaill appears to have been the source for the DADGAD tuning entering Irish music, wherein it is now used by virtually all accompanists of the instrumental tradition.

21. Not having seen the contract, I can't clarify what small print or unfulfilled condition on the part of the Pentangle had allowed Nat to cease royalty payments. Indeed,

Nat has told me that his recollection is that Jo's lawyers may have actually provided the final draft of the document. I don't doubt that Nat was entirely within his rights.

22. In a nutshell, Transatlantic's own fortunes declined after 1971. There were still periodic successes but a move from Marylebone Lane to more ostentatious offices in Marylebone High Street around this time drew a symbolic line under the label's modest but consistent triumphs as a folk-based operation. A series of singularly unsuccessful progressive rock bands were signed while the label endlessly recycled its back catalogue, often on the back of its ex-artists' subsequent successes, and continued to act as UK/European distributor to fifteen other labels. The distribution aspect was lucrative on balance but engendered short-term cash flow problems. Seeking new capital, Nat sold seventy-five per cent of the label to Granada in 1975 but the deal was not as successful as had been hoped. In 1978 Transatlantic was sold, largely as a catalogue resource, to Logo Records run by Geoff Hannington. Nat became a financier of theatre projects. In the 1990s, Hannington sold Transatlantic to Castle Communications. Castle's 1998 box set *The Transatlantic Story* is recommended.

23. Bud Scoppa, *Rolling Stone,* 18/1/73.

24. 'The Toe-Rags' was one alternative name bandied around at the time, undoubtedly by Danny and most likely in jest. One hopes.

CHAPTER NINE

1. Renbourn's album was delivered to Warners in the midst of an in-house reshuffle. It was never released at the time but surfaced on Demon in 1996 as *Lost Sessions.*

2. *NME,* 18/10/75.

3. Dannie Richmond was in Britain to record with Jon Mark. Danny Thompson was also involved in that project and persuaded Richmond, against the drummer's instinct, to play on *Moonshine*: 'He loved it,' said Thompson. 'When he finished he said, "Hey man, I knew you was going to lay some heavy shit on me. When I get back to the States I'm going to play this 'English folk music' to everybody." ' [*Hokey Pokey,* 1/88]

4. *MM,* 17/1/76.

5. John and Jacqui continued as a duo, recording BBC radio sessions together in May and July 1973. The John Renbourn Group, featuring Jacqui, was formed in 1974 and extended to the Pentangle reunion of 1982. John would also record solo instrumental albums during this period, beginning with *The Hermit* in 1973. 'I'd discovered that a whole cult of fingerstyle guitar had grown up in France since I'd been on the road with Pentangle,' says John. 'I'd put out a book of instrumental guitar pieces and these tunes were being played all over France, so when I started playing there I was a hero. At least 50 per cent of the stuff in those tunes had been improvised but I felt so pleased that these people were taking so much time to play my stuff note for note that I thought I might as well give them something a little more systemized to play.' Hence, John's future as an guitar instrumentalist was secured. Danny would spend the next couple of years touring and recording with John Martyn. Perhaps surpisingly, his session work in the seventies was less prolific than it had been during the Pentangle era. John, Jacqui and Danny would all periodically reappear in live and/or recording contexts within Bert's career during the ten years between the Pentangle split and reunion.

6. It seems likely that Bert and Danny stayed on for the recordings while the others returned to Britain. George Chatelain, a French singer, was a fan of Bert's who owned a studio. Bert recalls any recordings as a fun thing rather than an album project as Dallas's piece suggested. Nevertheless, eight songs and instrumentals intended as Bert's next album (1974) were recorded in Paris during this trip or very shortly after. Produced by Danny and featuring just himself and Bert, only three of these recordings actually surfaced: two on *LA Turnaround* (1974) and one on *A Rare Conundrum* (1977).

7. *MM*, 31/3/73.

8. *Sounds*, 21/4/73.

9. *The Sequence*, BBC Radio 1, broadcast 11/5/73.

10. As note 4.

11. Prior to founding Charisma, Strat had managed Paddy, Klaus and Gibson, Beryl Marsden, the Creation, the Bonzo Dog Band and the Nice.

12. Charisma memoir, Pete Frame, *Rosemary Lane* No.2, 1993. Most Frame quotes in this chapter are from this source.

13. *Sounds*, 19/10/74.

14. As Frame also notes: 'Bert was probably too pissed to notice any ghosts, but the place was said to be haunted. A couple of years earlier, two of Strat's trusted aides – Glen Colson and producer John Anthony – had been sitting there listening to a Van Der Graaf Generator album, when Glen heard a noise and turned round in time to see this old boy disappear into a painting. I put it down to drugs, myself, but they both swear it's true. The house had belonged to some old codger called Sir Hugh Beevor, who had actually died in the front room. Strat only paid £20 a week rent for it – and turned down an invitation to buy it for forty grand. It had nine bedrooms and acres of land. It must be worth a fortune now.'

15. Two tracks were recorded in the garden, four indoors.

16. A thirteen-minute promotional film emerged from the Luxford session, including 'Fresh As A Sweet Sunday Morning' and three other tracks alongside *cinema vérité* of Nesmith, Jansch and Rhodes rehearsing, playing some arcane version of billiards, pottering about in the garden and eating lunch. Every so often, in rehearsal, the two Americans would ask was this where the turnaround was – muso vernacular for a verse into chorus chord change. 'No,' Bert mumbles, with a hint of exasperation, 'you just keep playing the tune . . .' A more elaborate promotional film of Bert 'tarted up' had already been shot, with a view to promoting him to college bookers. A preview screening was held around February/March 1974: Strat was delighted but Bruce May felt it was the wrong way to go and the project was shelved. The film-maker was probably one Gordeon Troiler, erstwhile manager of Van Der Graaf Generator, whom Strat often commissioned for such projects, including an early Genesis promo. During 1974 Troiler's company hit the wall and his assets disappeared. Gail Colson has been unable to trace the Genesis film to this day – what hope, then, for 'Bert Jansch: The Movie'?

17. As note 13.

18. Even Jansch was reluctant to repeat the track live. It was attempted at least once on his November 1974 UK tour and around the same time he was asked to perform it on a UK TV show, of unremembered title. A pre-recorded show, Bert recalls he took two attempts to get it right. It has yet to reappear in his repertoire. Gordon

Giltrap bravely attempted the tune at Bert's wedding to Loren Auerbach in November 1999, and subsequently recorded it for his May 2000 tribute EP *Janschology*.

19. *MM*, 29/6/74.

20. Ralph McTell had convinced Bert the old hymn suited his style, while Bruce had convinced Strat it was going to be a Christmas smash. Featuring vocal group Prelude (fresh from hit single success with 'After The Goldrush') and Lindisfarne's Rod Clements on bass, Bert constructed a beautiful arrangement but sang only two verses – all that Ralph could remember. Pete Frame was at the session: 'After it was finished, Ralph uncorked a very good bottle of Chambertin (what else?) and we toasted the record's success. Ha! Optimistic fools! Strat hired this whizz-bang independent plugger to procure airplay – but after we played the record to him once, we never saw him again. I guess he didn't have too much faith in it.' During the same session, with the same personnel, Ralph recorded a new version of an old song of his, 'Streets Of London', also to release as a single. One of the two was destined for huge success. Ironically, Bert's recording has earned him the most individual mechanical royalties of his career by stealth: by subsequently appearing on the *Best Christmas Album In The World Ever* CD.

21. Allan Jones, *MM* 16/11/74. The Theatre Royal concert, to a three-quarters-full auditorium speckled with celebrity musicians, was covered by all three weeklies.

22. *NME*, 24/8/74. A longer than published quote, courtesy of the interviewer.

23. Bert played three or four dates with Ralph in Scandinavia around January/February 1975, and it was probably on this trip that the TV special *Four Guitars* was filmed (broadcast in Denmark in June 1975). Bert and Ralph joined Stefan Grossman and Dutch fusion wizard Jan Akkerman for an amiable round of tune trading in front of a small audience. Bert, characteristically dishevelled and almost as relaxed as Akkerman, turned in his Christmas flop, two tracks from *LA Turnaround*, a duet on 'Moonshine' with Ralph and a jam with all present on 'Come Back Baby'. Never broadcast in Britain, stills from the show rather bizarrely cropped up in a number of British music papers thereafter.

24. *Sounds*, 8/1/77.

25. *Sounds*, 28/6/75.

26. *MM*, 17/1/76.

27. As note 25.

28. My information on the Charisma/Jansch filmings is incomplete but Jansch film was apparently shot on 1/7/75 and 4/7/75: both dates during the Ronnie Scott's residency. There is also something referred to as a 'Whistle Test film' in Charisma's written archives. Record company promos were often shown on the *OGWT*, but there is no mention of a Jansch broadcast in the (admittedly incomplete) BBC archive of *OGWT*s.

29. As note 25.

30. Bert feels certain that Bruce's figure is an exaggeration.

31. *A Man And His Songs*, DR 14/4/76.

32. As note 24.

33. As note 26.

34. The canon version of 'Running From Home' is most easily available on Bert's *BBC Radio 1 Live In Concert* (1993). Also on this Scandinavian tour, Bert featured

'Moonshine' and 'Blackwater Side' as extended duets involving himself on guitar and Pick on drums with brushes. An unusual combination that was sadly never represented on record.

35. *A Rare Conundrum* appeared in Denmark on Peter Abramson's Ex-Libris label with three tracks otherwise unavailable: 'Three Dreamers' continued the nostalgic theme; 'Dragonfly' was a beautiful, near-mystic evocation of that creature left over from 1974; 'Candyman' was a cod-reggae interpretation of the old Gary Davis blues. Abramson also, around this time, roped Bert and Martin into playing on a track on another Ex-Libris album, by Danish singer Erik Grip. The track provides a rare example of Bert playing a lead guitar line.

36. *Beat Instrumental*, 8/77.

37. Aside from Transatlantic's incessant re-usage of Jansch and Pentangle material on their own compilations they had also already licensed material to bargain-bucket labels. Under Geoff Hannington, Transatlantic would continue the process well into the nineties, when the catalogue was bought by Castle Communications. By that stage, the compact disc had arrived and the compilation party had only just begun.

38. *MM*, 10/1/81. The last Jansch interview in any of the British music weeklies.

39. The American sleeve in particular was a travesty. The CD version released on Ace in 1998 uses the British design – photos of Bert and the boys playing darts in a pub.

40. After eighteen years together, Martin's wife suddenly decided she'd had enough: he was to give up music and get a job in a Coventry car factory or she was leaving. She left, and Martin's luck temporarily expired: 'All in one period I broke my leg, got banned from driving, got thrown out of my house and came to the end of my job with Bert.' Martin formed a band with some old friends and started 'a dynamic, outrageous club in a really ferocious pub in Coventry' and started figuring out his next move. Within two years he was in a popular all-acoustic group called Whippersnapper, fronted by fiddler Dave Swarbrick. 'I still see Bert from time to time if he's playing locally, or pop in to see him in London and he'll play me a bit of what he's up to. I learnt a lot from Bert – being on the road, booking travel, dealing with pressure and playing in better places I'd ever played before. And also from Bert's writing, the way he puts words together – sometimes they're a bit flowery but they're beautiful. It gives you the courage to write without fear and to have the courage to deliver it to people with sincerity.'

CHAPTER TEN

1. *MM*, 10/1/81.
2. Lindsay Reid; combined from *Evening News*, 27/4/82 and 3/7/82.
3. Bert and Charlotte originally moved into 33 Felsham Road but quickly transferred to the New King's Road address and opened the guitar shop. Towards the end of the guitar shop, in late '84 and in danger of being evicted by bailiffs, they acquired a flat in Redcliffe Square.
4. Combined from 'Thyme Honoured', John Tobler, *Folk Roots*, 10/95 and 'Roots Of Renbourn', Maggie Holland, *Folk Roots*, 4/93.
5. Colin Irwin in *Thirty Years Of The Cambridge Folk Festival*, Ed. Dave Laing & Richard Newman (Music Maker Books, 1994).

6. Remarkably, the group had never previously performed in either Germany or Italy. They had toured Australasia in 1972.

7. 'Thyme Honoured', John Tobler, *Folk Roots*, 10/95.

8. Bert had been keen to involve Portman Smith as a sixth member, on keyboards, in the 1982 line-up but the others had not been convinced. Bert and Nigel's relationship had cooled briefly in 1981 when Nigel opted for a lucrative European tour with Eric Burdon, obliging Bert to call on Rod Clements to help out on some Conundrum UK dates. Around the time of the Pentangle reunion, however, Bert and Nigel had worked together on the theme and incidental music for the David Bellamy TV nature series *You Can't See the Wood*. A handful of jointly composed songs have also appeared on latterday Jansch and Pentangle records.

9. Bert had kept in touch with Liz Cruickshank throughout the sixties, with Liz spending a few weeks in Bert's company on holidays in London during 1965 and 1967. She had married in 1971 but was still something of an inspiration. 'Change The Song', on *From The Outside* (1985) had been created from a traditional tune Liz had taught Bert during Howff days. Indeed, the title track of that album was basically an instrumental take on another simple folk song from those times, 'Oh Dear Me'.

10. Portman Smith made these comments about Radio 2 in 1992. One suspects the subsequent repositioning of the station has resulted in a more proactive audience.

11. Brett Milano, *Boston Globe*, 23/7/86.

12. Alan Rawlinson, *Folk Roots*, 12/86. Rawlinson could also applaud Bert's version of Snooks Eaglin's 'One Scotch, One Bourbon, One Beer', with Bert 'looking and sounding as though he had thoroughly researched the subject'. A suitably slurred but compelling reading of the song had appeared as Bert's contribution to the CBS charity album *Just Guitars* in 1984, recorded at a multi-artist concert organised by Ralph McTell. McTell was as supportive as he could be of Bert during this period, going so far as to record simplified demo arrangements of Bert's songs in an effort to convince other artists that they were indeed coverable. Eddi Reader was at one point interested in recording 'Is It Real?' while Mary Hopkin (with whom Bert performed on occasion at the Half Moon) talked about recording 'Ask Your Daddy'. Neither appeared.

13. The Pentangle Radio 2 sessions of the Chris Coates management era were: *Nightride*, 86, *Folk On Two*, 12/86 and *Nightride* 87. There was also a Radio 2 Pentangle concert broadcast from the Queen Elizabeth Hall on 17/9/88.

14. 'As time went on, Alex wanted to get out of the folk scene but could see no way of doing so,' says Brian Shuel, recalling Campbell's view even during the sixties. 'Though he performed brilliantly, he was completely fed up, and indeed ill, with the endless grind of cheap travel, smoky clubs, booze, partying, sleeping on the floors of grotty smoke-filled pads and being ripped off by the hopeless "organisers" who infested the scene. However, he could see no realistic way of making an alternative living. Of course, he did like his drink and enjoyed performing but he knew the life would destroy him in the end, and it did.'

'Alex and I did a gig together at the Marquee once,' says Roy Harper, 'and we were chatting afterwards. He looked at me with a kind of knowing smile and said, "Ah, ye young whippersnappers, ye'll be the death o' me." It was like he was saying, "Okay, you're here now, you're taking the reins, so get on with it'. He was a lovely guy. He could relate to his own generation and to mine and I've never forgotten that.'

15. Charlotte had never had a problem with Bert's previous relationships and children: 'I met Gill and liked Gill very much; Heather and I got on quite well; I also met Judy. I've always found that when you meet a woman who's been before with a man that you're with there's things you can share like, "Oh, he always throws his socks on the floor" or something! We understood each other.'

16. Bert appeared a number of times on the late-night magazine show *Nighthawks* on Irish TV during the late eighties and early nineties. He also appeared, with Peter Kirtley, performing 'Heartbreak Hotel' on BBC Northern Ireland's *Anderson On The Box* in November 1992. A scheduled appearance on Ulster TV's *Kelly* in April 1998 was apparently cancelled at the eleventh hour when the producer actually listened to Bert's latest album. To my knowledge, Bert's only other TV appearance of the late eighties was direct from Denmark's Skagen Festival in June 1988. Regrettably, the station (DR) did not archive the live broadcast.

CHAPTER ELEVEN

1. The central premise to *Living With The Blues* was that Cyril Davies was the first great British bluesman – a tradition subsequently that reached its apogee with Peter Green. Unfortunately, Newman had acquired no footage of either artist to back up this view but had instead assembled a loose collection of veteran British blues players – seemingly, whoever was handy – who are seen performing and/or swapping anecdotes about the sixties.

2. *Acoustic Routes* was premiered at the Edinburgh Film Festival, August 1992, broadcast in Scotland on 25/1/93 and nationally on 12/4/93. It was also shown, with British Council sponsorship, at the Sofia Musicfest in Bulgaria and at film festivals in Vienna and Leipzig, during 1993 – 94. It was shown again at Sofia in June 1998, with Bert also performing live at the event.

3. Jimmy Page, Neil Young and Robin Williamson were all scheduled to appear in *Acoustic Routes*: Robin was missed through being marooned in LA during the riots; a vague arrangement to meet Neil unravelled; Jimmy Page failed to make two appointments.

4. David Cavanagh, *Mojo,* 1/94.

5. Bert had appeared on BBC's *Russell Harty* in 1984, jamming on 'Angi' with Ralph McTell and classical virtuoso John Williams, in support of the *Just Guitars* charity project.

6. The summer 1993 vintage Jansch CDs were: *Bert Jansch + Jack Orion* (Demon*);* BBC *Radio 1 In Concert* (Windsong), *Three Chord Trick* (Virgin) and *From The Outside* (Hypertension), remixed and annotated by Bert himself.

7. The 1986 Transatlantic Jansch CD was *The Essential Collection Volume 1: Strolling Down The Highway.* Track details for *The Essential Collection Volume 2: Blackwater Side* appeared in trade directories, as did information on a 4 CD boxed set linking the Jansch compilation with individually issued Pentangle and Renbourn titles, but neither the boxed set nor the Jansch Vol.22 appeared.

8. *Evening News,* 20/12/92.

9. In the early '90s, Bert's recording and musical support gear included: an Atari

SM124 computer with C-Lab notation software; a Panasonic SV-3700 DAT deck and Casio DA-R100 portable DAT (for recording gigs with Peter – a live album aspiration that was realised); an Alesis Microverb III 16-bit Digital Reverb/Delay; a Roland U-220 Sound Module; and a Roland GR-50 Guitar Synth. At the time of writing the key components of Bert's home studio include: G4 PowerMac, Logic Audio Software, Roland G50 Guitar Synth, Roland U220 Sound Module, Korg 707 keyboard, Korg X5D keyboard, Yamaha MU10 Sound Module, Yamaha 02R Digital Mixing Desk, Mark Of The Unicorn MTPAV Synchronizer and Korg 12-12 1/0 Sound Card. During the early '90s he used a Peavey Profex unit onstage to enhance his guitar sound, before switching to Yamaha pedalboard and currently a Linefix Pod. It remains intriguing that, for all that, he continues to favour guitars with difficult action and not especially bright strings. Current stage guitar is a Yamaha LL/11E.

10. *Bob Harris Show*, BBC Radio 1, 14/7/93.

11. Anne, having slipped out of music in 1973, was living in Lincolnshire at the time. Encouraged by Martin Carthy & Dave Swarbrick, she had made a brief return to live performance around 1990 – 92, effectively culminating in her appearance with Bert in *Acoustic Routes* filmed in March 1992. Rory may have seen her performing at The Troubadour or on the film.

12. *Guitarist*, 3/95. [interview conducted in 4/94]

13. 'Thyme Honoured', John Tobler, *Folk Roots*, 10/95.

14. I authored Bert Jansch/Pentangle features in a number of publications during late 1993/early 1994 (*Folk Roots*, *Record Collector*, *Replay* and *Acoustic Guitar*) and reviewed concerts for both *Mojo* and *The Irish Times*. Additionally, there were certainly concert and record reviews in publications at this level and above from several other writers during this same period. Mick Houghton did an exceptional job with the intensity of the publicity surrounding *Circus*, but the notion that Bert hadn't been written about in ten years is somewhat exaggerated.

15. Janie Romer was the wife of studio engineer Jay Burnett, who worked on the remix of *From The Outside* (1993), engineered *Circus* (1995) and produced *Toy Balloon* (1998). During 1993 Bert had featured Janie as a guest at odd shows of his own. She contributed backing vocals to both *Circus* and *Toy Balloon* but a joint project vaguely on the cards in 1993 has not materialised.

16. *Q*, 1/96.

17. At the time of writing Andrew Hunter, out of the country for an extended period, could unfortunately not be contacted.

18. *Rock'n'Reel*, 95.

19. *Rosemary Lane*, Spring 1996.

20. In the middle of the 12 Bar era, Loren had suggested to Bert that he might like to see Page & Plant at Wembley Arena: 'I was amazed – it was just like a folk club!' says Bert. 'Every song, with an audience made up of people all my age, the whole place was singing along.' Loren had organised backstage passes and was amused to find that Robert Plant seemed even more flattered to meet Bert than the man who had been consistently lauding him to the international press for the previous quarter century. Bert had no complaints: 'It was my first time meeting up with Jimmy and it was really quite nice.' [*Guitar*, 4/96]

21. As note 19.

22. Both albums, including musical contributions from Bert, were duly completed. At the time of writing they had yet to be placed with a record company. Strangely, Bert feels he has 'let them down' by not yet managing to do so. One may reasonably feel that the responsibility for doing so should perhaps lie at other doors.

23. Stuart Bailie, *Vox*, 5/98.

24. 'Lost Singer Found', T. J. McGrath, *Dirty Linen*, April/May 1995.

Select Bibliography

A sizeable quantity of books, journals and other printed ephemera were consulted in the making of this book. Some were even read from cover to cover, in an undulating fusion of fear at possibly missing some crucial detail and old-fashioned procrastination at actually doing some writing myself. While this bibliography is strictly selective for reasons of space, and any sources of direct quotation credited as they appear in endnotes to the main text, the following works were among the most useful:

Vox Pop: Profiles Of The Pop Process, Michael Wale (Harrap, 1972).

The History Of Rock, ed. Michael Heatley (part-work, Orbis Publishing, 1981 – 84).

London's Rock Routes, John Platt, (Fourth Estate, 1985).

Journeyman: An Autobiography, Ewan MacColl, (Sidgwick & Jackson, 1990).

Cod Liver Oil And The Orange Juice: Reminiscences Of A Fat Folk Singer, Hamish Imlach & Ewan McVicar (Mainstream Publishing, 1992).

As Far As The Eye Can Sing, Frankie Armstrong with Jenny Pearson (The Women's Press, 1992).

Guinness Encyclopedia Of Popular Music, ed. Colin Larkin (concise edition, Guinness Publishing, 1993).

In Session Tonight, Ken Garner (BBC Books, 1993).

Alexis Korner: The Biography, Harry Shapiro (Bloomsbury, 1996).

The Democratic Muse: Folk Music Revival In Scotland, Ailie Munro (revised edition, Scottish Cultural Press, 1996).

The Who Concert File, Joe McMichael & 'Irish' Jack Lyons (Omnibus Press, 1997).

Rockin' Croydon, Chris Groom (Wombeat Publishing, 1998).

The Skiffle Craze, Mike Dewe (Planet, 1998).

The Great Rock Discography, Martin C. Strong (revised edition, Canongate Books, 1998).

In addition to the above titles, the *Record Collector Rare Record Price Guide* and the *Guinness Book Of Hit Singles* and *Guinness Book Of Hit Albums* were standard reference tools. In terms of magazines, journals and periodicals, the following were consulted most comprehensively:

Melody Maker 1961 – 72 – the journal of record for British music in this era; *English Dance & Song* 1961 – 67; *Folk Scene* 1964 – 65; *Folk Review* 1977 – 79; *Folk News* 1977 – 79; *Southern Rag* 1983 – 85; *Folk Roots* 1986 – 99; *Rosemary Lane* 1993 – 99.

Numerous other publications were consulted more selectively. Additionally, an insane collection of print interviews and reviews regarding Bert Jansch, his peers and the Pentangle was accumulated in preparation for this book. To detail every item would be impractical, but a list of every previously published Bert Jansch print interview used herein (with the omission of previously published interviews conducted by myself) is possibly of interest. Until recently, Jansch interviews in print were relatively rare and certainly I am unaware of any others from the 1960s. I would welcome copies of any interviews additional to the following:

'Jansch – 'Don't ask what my message is'', uncredited, *Melody Maker*, 28/8/65.
'Really doesn't want a hit . . .', John Emery [*Beat Instrumental*], 11/65.
'Bert Jansch', Robin Denselow & Charles O'Hagen, *Isis* [Oxford University], 2/2/66.
'Jansch digs back into tradition', Karl Dallas, *Melody Maker*, 16/7/66.
'Single for Jansch?', 'K.S.', *Beat Instrumental*, 12/66.
'The many talents of the Pentangle', Karl Dallas, *Melody Maker*, 18/5/68.
'Pentangle – now reaching a much wider audience', uncredited, *Beat Instrumental*, 9/68.
'The Pentangle', Pete Frame, *Zigzag* #7, 11/69.
'Bert could be a giant – but he likes being small!', David Hughes, *Disc*, 18/4/70.
'Bert Jansch / John Renbourn', Eleanor Houldson, *Guitar Player* [USA], 3/71.
'Bert Jansch: part one', Jerry Gilbert, *Sounds*, 9/1/71.
'Bert Jansch: part two', Jerry Gilbert, *Sounds*, 16/1/71.
'Jansch', Rosalind Russell, *Disc*, 24/7/71.
'Band Breakdown: The Pentangle', Karl Dallas, *Melody Maker*, 10/9/72.
'Pentangle dies . . . with a whimper', Karl Dallas, *Melody Maker*, 31/3/73.
'Bert expecting no miracles', Jerry Gilbert, *Sounds*, 21/4/73.
'Jansch: painter in song', Colin Irwin, *Melody Maker*, 29/6/74.
'Rumours of my retirement were rather exaggerated', James Johnson, *NME*, 24/8/74.
'From Edinburgh beatnik to Aberystwyth cowboy', Pete Frame, *Zigzag* #45, 9/74.
'Turnaround for the country bumpkin', Jerry Gilbert, *Sounds*, 19/10/74.
'Turnaround Jansch', Joe Robinson, *Sounds*, 28/6/75.
'Bert Jansch? Not still going is he?', Fred Dellar, *NME*, 18/10/75.
'An everyday story of funky folk', Michael Watts, *Melody Maker*, 17/1/76.
'Lonesome Cowboy Bert', Hugh Fielder, *Sounds*, 8/1/77.
'Jansch reveals: I was true to Elvis . . .', Patrick Humphries, *NME*, 21/5/77.
'Bert Jansch: A Rare Conundrum', *Beat Instrumental*, 8/77.
'Jansch – a charismatic conundrum?', Tony Bacon, *International Musician*, 1/7/77.
'A Raver's Guide To Soho', John Platt, *Comstock Lode*, c.1979.
'Bert Jansch: From Folk To Pentangle And Beyond', Mark Humphrey, *Frets*, 3/80.
'The Bert Jansch Conundrum', Karl Dallas, *Melody Maker*, 10/1/81.
'Jansch and the Pentangle on the point of a comeback', Alistair Clark, *The Scotsman*, 31/8/85.
'Pentangle: A Celebration' [inc. 1980 Jansch interview by Stefan Grossman], *Dirty Linen*, 10/90.
'Bert Jansch', uncredited, *Hokey Pokey*, Spring 1992.
'Bert's Blues', uncredited, *Evening News* [Edinburgh], 20/12/92.
'Gardener's World', Gordon Giltrap, *Guitarist*, 3/95.
'Tangled Up In Blue', Danny Eccleston, *The Guitar Magazine*, 10/95.

'Bert, magnet for the stars', *Evening Standard* [London], c.late 1995.

'Bert Jansch', Robb Johnson, *Rock'n'Reel*, c.late 1995.

'Stage-divers will be ejected', David Cavanagh, Q, 1/96.

'Bert Jansch: the making of his new album', John Higgins, *Rosemary Lane* #9, Spring
.1996.

'Bert Jansch', H. P. Newquist, *Guitar*, 4/96.

'Guitar man's '90s revival', Paul Stewart, *Sunday Telegraph Sun* [Australia], 29/9/96.

'Father of the revolution', Jane Cornwell, *The Sunday Age* [Australia], 29/9/96.

'Who's that man?', Peter Jinks, *Spectrum* [Edinburgh], 9/3/97.

'Bert Jansch', Paul Simmons, *Ptolomaic Terrascope*, 7/97.

'Been on the road so long!', John Higgins, *Rosemary Lane* #12, Summer 1997.

Additional period Jansch quotations were gleaned from interviews on Danish television
in 1967, 1976 and 1983; from interviews on Capital Radio 1982 and BBC Radio 1
1993; and from *Acoustic Routes*, BBC2, 1992. A number of further British television and
BBC radio broadcasts regarding other players in the story – Bill Leader, Al Stewart,
Robin Hall, Jimmie Macgregor, Davy Graham and Peggy Seeger – were also of value.

Acknowledgements

This book would not have been possible without the generous co-operation of a great number of people. Firstly, I wish to thank David Reynolds of Bloomsbury for commissioning the work and for his and Helena Drakakis's encouragements and criticisms of draft chapters – all taken on board. Also, with the departure of David from the company, my appreciation to Matthew Hamilton and his team for seeing the thing through with professionalism and commitment. Esther Jagger edited the final draft with an extraordinary eye for detail and irrelevancy. I was most surprised to find myself agreeing with many of her judgements on the latter, and this book is ten per cent briefer as a result.

Regarding content, I gratefully acknowledge the recollections, and often subsequent time and effort in responding to written queries or in referee-ing draft chapters, freely given by the following:

Kresanna Aigner, Ian Anderson (*Folk Roots*), Ian Anderson (Jethro Tull), Dave Arthur, Steve Ashley, Chris Barber, Steve Benbow, David Blass, Maggie Boyle, Anne Briggs, Martin Carthy, John Challis, Rod Clements, Frank Coia, Gail Colson, Gill Cook, Charlotte Crofton-Sleigh, Judy Cross, Maggie Cruickshank, Donovan, Bruce Dunnet, Pete Frame, Dick Gaughan, Owen Hand, Roy Harper, John Harrison, Dorris Henderson, Mary Hogg (*nee* Jansch), Mick Houghton, Ashley Hutchings, Hamish Imlach, Andy Irvine, Bert Jansch, Heather Jansch, Loren Jansch (*nee* Auerbach), Martin Jenkins, Wizz Jones, Nathan Joseph, Peter Kirtley, Danny Kyle, Bill Leader, Jo Lustig, Bruce May, Jacqui McShee, Dolina MacLennan, Ralph McTell, Christy Moore, Michael O'Dhomnail, Clive Palmer, Len Partridge, Nigel Portman Smith, Duffy Power, Val Power, John Renbourn, Brian Shuel, Al Stewart, Sue Stockwell (formerly Thompson), Steve Tilston, Pete Townshend, Norma Waterson and Robin Williamson.

I have also benefited from correspondence, some very detailed and much included herein as direct quotation, with the following people who were not interviewed on tape: Joe Boyd, Dan Ar Braz, Dave Cartwright, Karl

Dallas, Robin Denselow, Jerry Gilbert, Gordon Giltrap, Davy Graham (via Kay Thomson), Rab Noakes, Stuart Wallace and John Watt. In addition, many of those who *were* interviewed also corresponded with clarifications, corrections and more than enough words of encouragement to keep the worst excesses of self-doubt at bay. Thanks also to David Palmer (whose personal circumstances sadly precluded an interview) and to Dave Pegg, for whom *my* circumstances precluded an interview.

In addition to the cooperation of those who played a direct role in the story, I am grateful to everyone who responded to my requests for reminiscences as published in *Acoustic Guitar*, *Blues & Rhythm*, *Folk Roots*, *Mojo* and *Record Collector* and also to the readers of *Rosemary Lane*. Although it is not possible to list all those who corresponded – all of whom, I hope, I managed to respond to in person – I would like to thank in particular, for photos, memorabilia and 'ordinary fan' recollections: Kieran Bracken, Neil Brown, Dave Burrows, Doug Dalwood, Alan Davidson, Steve DiBartola, Mike Fox, Lars Fromholt, John Gibson, Colin Grafton, Rod Harbinson, Mike Head, Bob Jones, Richard Lewis, Mauro Regis, Chip Reynolds, Bill Stephens and David Suff. Particular thanks to Brian Shuel and to Phil Smee for great generosity with regard to the photo section. It, and I, would have been considerably poorer without them.

There are many people who provided generous support either practical or in terms of encouragement, and often over the protracted period of this book's creation. Very special thanks go to Colin and Anita Davies for putting me up innumerable times in London, with a remarkable generosity which made research trips and consequently, in no small measure, this very book possible. If Anita suspected the whole thing to be a figment of my imagination, I am relieved at last to prove her wrong! Also, for hospitality, grateful thanks to Jules, David and Connie; Kate Casey; John Platt; John and Jo Renbourn; Heather Jansch; Steve and Maggie Tilston; Bert and Loren.

A number of record industry people were most helpful. I would like to thank particularly: Mark Anstey (Pig's Whisker); Roger Armstrong (Ace); John Beecher (Rollercoaster); Joel Bernstein (re: Neil Young); Chris Biller (Ignition Management); Cliff Dane (Wooded Hill); Donal Gallagher (Capo); Brian Hallin (Bert Jansch management); Nicola Joss (Eel Pie); Peter Muir (Market Square); Pat Naylor (Rykodisc); Alan Robinson (Castle); Harriett Simms and Tony Engle (Topic); John Whyton (Virgin). Additionally, for regular interruptions of much merriment, my salutations to Barry Riddington and Malcolm Holmes at HTD – keepers of the flame of prog, guardians of the mothership fusion, riders on the range of rock, toe-dippers in the field of folk, scourge of morris-dancers everywhere, etc, etc.

For regular encouragement, and for years of most agreeable coffee shop philosophising, thanks to Mark McCluney, Mark Shields, Colin Reid and Owen McFadden. My round is it? Thanks also to all my other friends who have been kind enough to voice support or interest in recent months. Any list I might attempt would invariably not be comprehensive: suffice to say, you know who you are and your encouragement has been appreciated. A number of musicians, who are beyond the scope of this book, have also expressed a keen interest in its completion, not least the Bird-Dogs: the legendary Ivan Muirhead, Professor Roy Lynas and Colin 'Hillbilly' Henry. And, you know, I don't believe I mentioned the word 'dobro' once . . .

I am also grateful for the support of the following writers – from phone calls or letters of general encouragement to specific help on their topics of expertise: Dr Mark Archer, Stuart Bailie, Johnny Black, Sean Body, Chris Charlesworth, Tony Clayton-Lea, Nick Coleman, John Crosby, Karl Dallas, Mike Dewe, Peter Doggett, Pete Frame, Jerry Gilbert, Pat Gilbert, Ceasar Glebbeek (*Univibes: the International Jimi Hendrix Magazine*), Raymond Greenoaken (*Be Glad: the I S B Magazine*), Chris Groom, Geoff Harden, David Harrison, Clinton Heylin, Dave Ian Hill, Trevor Hodgett, Patrick Humphries, Ken Hunt, Jim Irvin, Richard Johnson, Neville Judd, Anthony 'The Destroyer' McCann, Ewan McVicar, John Platt, Chris Smith, Mat Snow, Kay Thomson (*Midnight Man: the Davy Graham Fanzine*), Val Wilmer and Ian Woodward. I am especially grateful to Sean Body of Helter Skelter, the specialist music book store and mail order service (4 Denmark Street, London, WC2H 8LL), for his regular 'on call' assistance in answering queries at no cost to myself. I feel duty bound to buy some books now, Sean!

For access to archive print material I am indebted to: the staff of the National Sound Archive at the British Library; the staff of the National Library of Scotland, Edinburgh; Ian Anderson for the Eric Winter archive; and many other individuals credited above. For particularly elusive material, a number of rare magazine dealers were approached. I recommend the service offered by Clive Whichelow at 'Backnumbers', 4 Charnwood Avenue, London, SW19 3EJ.

Somewhat tangentially perhaps, I would like to credit two books that were directly inspirational to both my approach and my confidence in this venture: *The Inklings: C. S. Lewis, J. R. R Tolkien, Charles Williams and their friends* by Humphrey Carpenter (HarperCollins, 1978) and *Alexis Korner: The Biography* by Harry Shapiro (Bloomsbury, 1996). I recommend both as triumphs of biographical writing. On a similar tangent, my gratitude to the educational standards of Sullivan Upper School, Holywood (under headmaster John Young) and the History Department of Queen's University Belfast (under the late Professor Lewis Warren). One often doesn't appreciate the quality of such institutions and individuals at the time. It is with sincerity that I acknowledge the generosity of John Young – a man who penned the immortal words 'He's not going to make it' on my last report – for his promise of spending the cover price of this book to find out if he was wrong.

I would like to honour the enormously generous and unconditional support of my family – my mum and dad and my brother Keith – who have stood by me metaphorically and often financially when a terrible string of dead-end jobs and periods of unemployment after graduating in 1989 led, in 1994, to a desperate decision to try writing professionally. By that stage my luck, my earnings and my sense of purpose could not have got any worse. The road has been one of pretty regular ups and downs ever since but my family and friends have been a constant source of comfort and the whole journey richly rewarding in experience, music and a host of terrific new friends – all in the same gutter gazing at the stars.

I have also been lucky enough to have worked with and to have met a number of really exceptional editors who have not allowed their own pressures of work to cloud their civility or their pursuit of excellence. Those people are an inspiration. I would like to pay tribute here especially to Paddy Woodworth (*The Irish Times*), Nick Coleman (*The Independent*) and Mat Snow and Paul Trynka (*Mojo*). Thanks for giving me a chance.

Finally, thanks for all the reams of cheap photocopying to Joan and all the office staff at Christian Fellowship Church, Strandtown. I'm sure you're wondering what it was all for . . . Also, to Grace'n'Groove coffee shop in Strandtown: the finest coffee in Belfast and my regular venue for morning proof-readings (*'So that's what that guy was doing . . .'*). Also, to Mark Case for a mountain of photo scanning and photo section design and to Matt Quinn and Jan Leman, film directors and fellow travellers in the 'promote Bert' club, for their moral support. My respects to the management of the CSU, Department Of Finance NI, for turning a blind eye to my contractual obligations as a part-time survey interviewer for many months – a weight off my shoulders. Last but absolutely not least, my love and my deepest gratitude to my wife Heather, who first met me in December 1997 and was thrust fairly swiftly thereafter into the rarefied lifestyle of playing partner to a biographer. I'm still not sure her family know quite what it is I do. Now that I've finished this book, I'm not sure that I do any more. Career quandaries aside, it has been in no small measure through Heather's unquestioning support that it has been possible for me to dedicate a year, more or less exclusively, towards the writing this book. And now it's done. What a curious thought that is.

Readers may also like to know that Bert's current work and a great deal of his back catalogue is available from: Castle Communications, A29 Barwell

Business Park, Leatherhead Road, Chessington, Surrey, England, KT9 2NY. www.castlemusic.com An excellent tribute album featuring many of those interviewed for this book, amongst others, is available from: Market Square Records, Market House, Market Square, Winslow, Buckingham-shire, England, MK18 3AF. www.marketsquarerecords.co.uk

Index

A NOTE ON THE AUTHOR

Colin Harper was born in Belfast in 1968 where he
still lives, and has been a music writer since 1994. His
work appears regularly in *Mojo*, The *Independent* and The
Irish Times. He contributed to the BBC2 documentary on
Bert Jansch, *Acoustic Routes* and to the C4 documentary
Dream Weaver and was a member of the panel
of the Belfast Arts Awards.

A NOTE ON THE TYPE

The text of this book is set in Bembo. The original
types for which were cut by Francesco Griffo for the
Venetian printer Aldus Manutius, and were first used in
1495 for Cardinal Bembo's *De Aetna*. Claude Garamond
(1480–1561) used Bembo as a model and so it became
the forerunner of standard European type for the
following two centuries. Its modern form was
designed, following the original, for Monotype
in 1929 and is widely in use today.